MW00639030

DISTURBING THE NEST
Family Change and Decline in Modern Societies

SOC. 6φ1
SP. 92   # 2 of 4

923

922
914

SOCIAL INSTITUTIONS
AND SOCIAL CHANGE

An Aldine de Gruyter Series of Texts and Monographs

EDITED BY

Peter H. Rossi
Michael Useem
James D. Wright

DISTURBING THE NEST
Family Change and Decline in Modern Societies

DAVID POPENOE

ALDINE DE GRUYTER
New York

About the Author

David Popenoe is Professor of Sociology, Rutgers, The State University of New Jersey. A Fulbright scholar, Dr. Popenoe is a specialist in the comparative sociology of communities, housing, and the family. He has authored or edited six books: *Housing and Neighborhoods: Theoretical and Empirical Contributions* (co-ed., 1987); *Private Pleasure, Public Plight: American Metropolitan Community Life in Comparative Perspective* (1985); *The Suburban Environment: Sweden and the United States* (1977); *Neighborhood, City and Metropolis* (co-ed., 1970); *The Urban-Industrial Frontier* (ed., 1969); and *Sociology* (1989), a college textbook now in its 7th edition. He has served on the boards of many national associations and is a former Chairman of the Board of the American Institute of Family Relations, Los Angeles.

Copyright © 1988 Aldine de Gruyter
All rights reserved. No part of this publication may be reproduced or transmitted in any form or by any means, electronic or mechanical, including photocopy, recording, or any information storage and retrieval system, without permission in writing from the publisher.

ALDINE DE GRUYTER
A Division of Walter de Gruyter, Inc.
200 Saw Mill River Road
Hawthorne, New York 10532

Library of Congress Cataloging-in-Publication Data

Popenoe, David, 1932–
   Disturbing the nest.

   (Social institutions and social change)
   Bibliography: p.
   Includes index.
   1. Family—Cross-cultural studies.   2. Family
—Sweden.   I. Title.   II. Series.
HQ518.P67   1988   306.8'5   88-22131
ISBN 0-202-30350-0
ISBN 0-202-30351-9 (pbk.)

Printed in the United States of America
10   9   8   7   6   5   4   3   2   1

Contents

Preface

The subject of this book is the changing family in modern society. Is there any other current social topic so value-laden and vulnerable to the bias of personal experience? Perhaps not; the family, it has been said, is a kind of intellectual Rorschach blot. People project onto it their own attitudes and feelings. A caveat to the reader about "value-free" social science, therefore, seems especially important at the outset.

I consider detached objectivity to be the very highest goal of the sociological enterprise. Without this goal, sociology and the social sciences in general can lay scant claim to public acceptance and support to say nothing of social and intellectual influence. In this book I have sought to be objective to the best of my ability. I have tried to give the reader the empirical evidence, the logic, and the theory by which my main conclusions have been reached; and I have striven to examine issues from a variety of perspectives.

Yet the experience of the social sciences over the last few generations has clearly shown, in my opinion, that except perhaps in the narrowist of studies social scientists can seldom escape entirely from their own personal values. If nothing else, these values strongly shape the selection of subject matter that social scientists analyze. Thus it is a real disservice to the cause of science and truth when social scientists, as too often seems the case, profess a kind of absolute scientific objectivity that goes well beyond the known limits of social science thought as well as the realities of the human condition. Because of this, I am of the school (pioneered, incidentally, by the great Swedish social economist Gunnar Myrdal) that believes social scientists should be much more open and above-board about their personal values, indicating what their basic value assumptions are.

Perhaps in other areas of sociology such a caveat about the role of personal values is less important. But there are few areas in the social sciences so fraught with ideology and subjectivity as family sociology. The personal values of sociologists concerning the family range from open antipathy toward almost everything the family stands for to the opinion that the traditional family can hardly be improved upon. And the family itself is viewed "objectively" within sociology as an institution that ranges from being highly oppressive, concealing dangerous anti-democratic and anti-egalitarian attitudes, to one that is immensely liberating, inculcating the supreme values of human civilization.

It defies logic and human nature to think that the personal values of social scientists do not in any way shape their sociological views. In my experience, indeed, there are few other areas of sociology in which a scholar's personal life history so clearly comes out in his or her work. Historically, most analyses and interpretations of the family have been suffused with the special interests and biases of men. This is true, for example, of much of the writing that bemoans the loss of the traditional family. For men, the traditional family seems to have been a largely unconditional benefit (especially in conjunction with the double standard of sexual behavior), and it would seem that many men are not willing to give it up without a fight. In recent years more family analysts have been female; they too have often written from the point of view of their own gender. To many women the traditional family appears not so much a benefit as a cost, and it is not surprising that "the decline of the traditional family" has come to be viewed in a less negative, and indeed sometimes a totally positive, light.

What is often omitted from both of these gender-driven positions, however, is a consideration of the family from the perspective of the interests of children. As family scholars are no longer children, this is understandable; but it is nonetheless regrettable, for children could be said to be, after all, the main reason for the institution of the family in the first place. When I analyze the family I am realistic enough to know that I can never completely overcome my bias as an adult male. Yet to me the family is primarily a social instrument for child rearing, and I value "strong families" for that reason. I hold to the old ideal of parents living together and sharing responsibility for their children and for each other. If this book has any special, underlying perspective, therefore, it is that I have tried to consider the changing family and its effects, to the extent that I am able, with what I perceive to be the child's viewpoint particularly in mind.

The information on Sweden, a special focus of this book, is based on lengthy stays in that nation in 1984, 1985, 1986, and 1987, plus prior knowledge gained through extensive contacts with Sweden over a period of more than 15 years beginning with a Fulbright year in 1972–1973. During recent visits, intensive, unstructured interviews were conducted with over one hundred persons in many walks of Swedish life, including academics in a number of disciplines, political figures, social workers, journalists, census officials, marriage counselors, lawyers, and leaders of the women's movement. In addition, historical and contemporary literature pertaining to family trends and family policy—both in Swedish and English—was searched, the latest statistical data were gathered, and the most recent social science research was reviewed. As will be seen, there are still some major gaps in our knowledge of the Swedish family (though it should be noted that Sweden has what are probably the best family data in the world), but I have attempted to give the most up-to-date account possible about current Swedish family conditions.

To compare the situation of the family in Sweden with that of other advanced, Western nations, visits were made over the last 4 years and research materials gathered in nine other countries: Australia, Denmark, Great Britain, France, Iceland, the Netherlands, New Zealand, Switzerland, and West Germany. Much comparative material also comes, of course, from the United States. There are three broad types of comparative methodology: case studies, analysis of statistical and archival data, and studies employing standardized (usually survey) methods. In this work, I have conducted only the first two types, although available comparative survey materials have been extensively utilized. Statistical, archival, and survey data are presented throughout, and comparative case studies of three nations selected because of their traditional familism—Switzerland, New Zealand, and the United States—are presented in later chapters. These comparative materials have strongly shaped my conclusions.

In view of the amount of research that went into it, this book is obviously intended as a contribution to the sociology of the family and more generally to knowledge about social change in the modern world. The "modern family" is not just a topic of scientific interest, however, but even more of popular interest. I have tried to write what follows, therefore, in a manner that is as accessible as possible to the general reader.

I want gratefully to acknowledge the support of the American Council of Learned Societies, which awarded me a Fellowship for the academic year 1985–1986 to work on this project; the Commission for Educational Exchange between the United States and Sweden (Fulbright Commission) which awarded me a Fulbright Travel Grant; Rutgers University, which granted me an academic leave and a Rutgers Research Council grant during 1986–1987; the Department of Sociology at the University of Stockholm, which provided me with office space during my stays in Sweden; the Swedish Institute in Stockholm, which helped to arrange many of the Swedish interviews; and my good friends Barbro and Bengt Hellermark, who went out of their way on so many occasions to make my visits to Sweden so rewarding. I also extend heartfelt thanks to all my colleagues and other friends in Sweden, the United States, and many other countries without whom my work would not have been possible. A special word of appreciation is extended to those persons who read portions of the manuscript and provided me with valuable feedback: (for Sweden) Anders Agell, Edmund Dahlström, Åke Daun, David Gaunt, Carl-Gunnar Janson, Mona Mårtensson, Ann-Sofie Ohlander, Stein Ringen and Jan Trost; (for Switzerland) Francois Höpflinger and Ralph Segalman; (for New Zealand) David G. Pearson and Claire Toynbee; (for family history) John R. Gillis; and to Cynthia Halpern, who made editorial suggestions for several of the chapters, Valda Aldzeris, who copy edited the manuscript, and Sheila Johnston, my Aldine de Gruyter editor.

Finally, my deepest thanks are given to my wife Kate, who read major portions of the manuscript and edited them with the skill of a true professional, and contributed an abundance of knowledge and insights.

This book is dedicated to my daughters, Rebecca and Julia, who have taught me much about the value of the family and brought me more joy in life than any person could reasonably have expected or even thought possible to obtain.

David Popenoe

Introduction

This is a book about what has happened, and is happening, to the institution of the family in modern society. It focuses on one highly developed society, Sweden, but in scope transcends that one small nation. For through investigating Sweden I have sought to better understand the impact on the family of those social forces throughout the industrial world that, for want of a better term, are labeled "modernization." What is occurring in Sweden, I shall argue, represents in many ways the most advanced stage of the family trends associated with modernization that are underway in all developed, Western societies.

That Sweden should have the most "advanced" family system will come as no surprise to many people; Sweden has commonly been regarded as the most "modernized" nation in the world.[1] Because it is so general and often used with ideological overtones, the term "modernized" (together with its companions "advanced" and "developed") is ambiguous and widely debated. Despite these problems, scholars keep having to return to it (or one of the synonyms) because, at least at a high level of abstraction, it seems to capture something real—a collection of near universal trends that are "rationalizing the social organization" of the world.[2]

The universal social trends of which the general concept "modernization" is frequently said to consist are themselves less ambiguous and fairly well accepted by scholars. It is with respect to most of these specific trends that Sweden has been found to have the leading or "most advanced" position among those Western, industrial nations that are often compared. This is the case, for example, regarding the trends toward an egalitarian income distribution,[3] centralized planning,[4] secularization,[5] dominance of the culture by science and rationality,[6] and a high level of overall social welfare.[7]

To this diversity of modernizing social trends one more is typically added: a global trend toward the nuclear (conjugal, elementary) family.[8] While the movement toward nuclear familism is a widely recognized trend of modernization in developing nations, in advanced, industrial societies, where the nuclear family has long been dominant, it is useful to think of the

xi

continuation of this trend as extending beyond the nuclear family, at least beyond the "traditional" nuclear family that has been a cultural ideal for the last few generations. Virtually all scholars believe that the family in advanced societies is on a trajectory of social change that leads away from the "bourgeois" form of the past century, for which the cultural ideal is a "legal, lifelong, sexually exclusive marriage between one man and one woman, with children, where the male is the primary provider and ultimate authority."[9]

If the family in advanced societies is moving away from the traditional nuclear form, in what direction does it appear to be headed? In this book, the extension of the global family trend is analyzed in terms of movement toward what can be called a postnuclear family system. But the more important question may be, how should this trend be evaluated? Is the family improving, fading, dying, or just reorganizing? Scholars can be found on all sides of this broad question, with the currently most widely accepted position, perhaps, being the rather noncommittal one that the family is "here to stay."[10]

There is surely little evidence in Sweden or any other nation with which to challenge this position—although the structure of family units is changing, the family does not seem to be "disintegrating" or "dying out." But at the same time there are strong indications, in my judgment, that the family in these societies is in *decline*. By this I mean that the institution of the family is growing weaker; it is losing social power and social functions, losing influence over behavior and opinion, and generally becoming less important in life. In Sweden, I shall argue, the institution of the family has declined further than in any other society.

In addition to being most modernized, there is one other dominating feature of contemporary Swedish society that commands attention. Sweden has long been regarded as the world's quintessential welfare state, a society devoted, to use familiar journalistic language, to the governmental provision of happiness and security from womb to tomb. To this end it has had the Western world's highest tax rate, the greatest portion of the economy devoted to public expenditures, and the largest percentage of employed persons working in public social welfare.[11]

Much to the chagrin of free market enthusiasts, who have tried for years to use Sweden as a whipping boy, Sweden's welfare state has in many important respects been a marked success. For example, that nation has achieved the Western world's most egalitarian income distribution, the lowest infant mortality rate, and the longest life expectancy, the latter two indices constituting perhaps the most widely used measures of social progress.[12] And far from being bankrupted by excessive government expenditures, Sweden, for a period in the 1970's, attained the distinction of being the world's most affluent nation.[13]

Of course, Sweden's degree of success in achieving extensive social welfare without damaging the economy has been the subject of widespread debate, and the Swedish economy today, like that of most other European countries, does not have the strength and momentum it had in the 1960's. In the late 1970's and early 1980's, in fact, much international attention came to be devoted to the so-called crisis of the welfare state, focusing typically on the issue of economic downturn as well as on such social and political problems as excessive bureaucratic centralism.[14] As in most other Western nations, this "crisis" was accompanied in Sweden by a political shift toward conservatism which, although relatively slight, emphasized lower taxes and a more market-oriented economy. How many of the welfare states' current economic problems are due specifically to an overactive government, however, is an unresolved issue highly charged with both ideology and emotion.

In the general debate about the welfare state, its problems and its future, the situation of the family seldom seems to command the attention it deserves. Sociology and anthropology textbooks commonly assert that the family is a society's "most basic" institution. While such an assertion is subject to a variety of interpretations, one prominent meaning is reflected in the widely quoted statement Margaret Mead once gave in testimony at a United States Senate Hearing: "As families go, so goes the nation."[15] By this statement she was implying that changes in the family, a fundamental provider of human welfare and basis of the moral order, inevitably have widespread societal ramifications. Even if exaggerated, the assertion that the family is our most basic institution suggests the importance of inquiring about how the family is faring in an advanced, welfare state like Sweden. For example, how, to what extent, and with what consequences, is the institution of the family affected by welfare state measures and by the ideological climate of a welfare-oriented society?

Not widely known about the modern Swedish welfare state is the fact that its founding in the 1930's was based in large part on the belief that it was necessary for the state to intervene in society in order to improve the situation of the family. Of great concern at that time was the low birth rate, which was felt to pose a threat to the very survival of Swedes as a national population group. Under the banner of a pronatalist population policy, the ruling Social Democrats pioneered welfare measures that, in the words of party leader Alva Myrdal in her 1941 book *Nation and Family,* "aimed to strengthen the family, to alleviate its worst trials and tribulations, and to make possible harmonious living."[16] She saw the institution of the family as being in a state of "crisis," noting that "The family even in its modern structure has its moorings in a preindustrial agrarian society. One after another these moorings have been lost."[17] With the Social Democrats remaining in power continuously until 1976, a period of almost 45 years, Sweden went on to implement governmental "family policies" that are among the most comprehensive (and expensive) in the world.

In view of this major policy goal of family improvement, the actual situation of the Swedish family today presents what could be considered an irony; some have even claimed that the Swedish welfare state policies have had consequences that are the opposite of those originally intended. Comparing contemporary Swedish family patterns with those of other advanced nations, one finds a high family dissolution rate, perhaps the highest in the Western world, and a high percentage of single-parent, female-headed families. Even marriage has fallen increasingly out of favor, with Sweden having the lowest marriage rate and the oldest average age at first marriage, and the largest percentage of households in which unmarried persons of the opposite sex cohabit. In addition, Sweden possesses the highest rate of children born out-of-wedlock; although no longer of legal significance, almost half of all Swedish children are now born to unmarried mothers. Certainly the early pronatalist aspirations of the Swedish government have been spectacularly unsuccessful, as Sweden continues to have one of the world's lowest birth rates and smallest average family sizes.

If they were alive today, the early pioneers of the Swedish welfare state would probably be dismayed at such things as the current rates of family dissolution and single-parent families, which are not only high but have been rising rapidly over the last few decades. They almost certainly would have felt that, once Swedes had achieved world leadership in both affluence and material equality, the kinds of family problems these rates purport to measure would be reduced to minimal proportions. Yet the wealthier and more equal Swedes become, through both economic productivity and governmental edict, the weaker grows the family, at least as measured by indexes such as these.

These changing rates are of deep concern to many people in contemporary society, but it should not necessarily be inferred from them that family life and intimate human relationships in Sweden today are marked by any special emotional insecurity or pattern of child neglect. In terms of most objective "quality of life" criteria, as I will show, Sweden compares very favorably with other advanced nations. One should also not necessarily infer that Sweden is in some way unique, containing societal attributes found nowhere else. Every society in the world has distinctive characteristics, of course, but most of the differences between Sweden and other advanced nations are of degree, not of kind.

It does not take professional training in the social sciences to realize that an enormous number of interacting forces accounts for the situation of the contemporary Swedish family. These forces include demographic and economic change, historical legacy, and national culture, at least as much as specific acts of government, and these are all explored in the following chapters. Nevertheless, one of my conclusions is that, in a paradoxical way, the political actions of the Swedish welfare state designed to strengthen the family have probably contributed to its weakening. This was not necessarily the intention of Sweden's Social Democratic majority; and it certainly was not in the minds of the welfare state's founders. To the degree that Swedish government action has had a negative impact on the family as an institution, I shall argue, it is mainly through the unanticipated and unintended consequences of political measures whose goals were in themselves entirely worthy.

It is not an intent of this book, therefore, to be part of a general attack on the welfare state as it currently exists in Sweden, although there certainly will be those who interpret my conclusions in that light. For what it is worth, politically I am not an unequivocal proponent of everything that the Swedish welfare state has tried to do, but neither am I one of those Americans who, from a right-wing ideological stance, is seeking to find ammunition for political purposes. For those who wish to use my conclusions for negative attacks on Sweden, I can only say (in words attributed to Mark Twain): "Get your facts straight first, then you can distort them as much as you wish."

In my analyses of the family, I have sought always to keep in mind Bronislaw Malinowski's dictum (first stated nearly three quarters of a century ago in his first publication in English, but too seldom heeded in the years since): "the essential features of the individual family . . . depend upon the general structure of a given society and upon the conditions of life therein. A careful and detailed analysis of family life and of different aspects of the family unit in connection with other social phenomena is therefore necessary."[18] What Malinowski did not have available in his studies of preliterate societies, however, was a knowledge of the history of these societies. Fortunately, this knowledge is available for Sweden, and for the history of Western families in general. I have ransacked this knowledge and incorporated many historical themes into the analysis of contemporary conditions. Thus, following a social science tradition that is more European than American, this is perhaps as much a book of history as of sociology.

The book is also strongly comparative in nature. I am a firm believer in Emile Durkheim's well-known admonition that "comparative sociology is not a particular branch of sociology; it is sociology itself, insofar as it ceases to be purely descriptive and aspires to account for facts."[19] Statistical and other data comparing the family situation in many advanced societies are presented throughout the work. And detailed comparisons with the situation in Sweden are given for the United States, and for two other highly developed nations which have relatively traditional family systems: Switzerland and New Zealand. A comparison of the world's nations is the greatest "natural experiment" available to the social sciences, in my view; it is an experiment whose results are too seldom considered, especially by American sociologists.

Using these approaches and perspectives, answers to the following kinds of specific questions about the situation of the Swedish family have been sought: What are the main social, political, and economic forces that have shaped the Swedish family? What, for example, have been the respective roles of the women's movement, the changing economic situation, welfare state programs, and the Swedish "national character?" To what extent can it reasonably be argued that deliberate public policies enacted by the Swedish government actually have had effects on families opposite to those intended? What are the negative social consequences, if any, of the dramatic family changes in Sweden over the last few decades? How relevant is Sweden's current family situation to the experience of other advanced societies? What do current trends in Sweden suggest about the future of the family in advanced societies?

There has been no dearth of hypotheses to account for what is happening to some aspects of the Swedish family in a debate among Swedish intellectuals and policymakers, ranging from the conservative position that the welfare state has sapped individual responsibility to the social democratic position that the welfare state has not been carried far enough, with various feminist, religious, and other groups posing still more alternatives. But this debate has focused almost exclusively on the material condition of the family; about the nonmaterial condition of the family Swedes have been, in public at least, remarkably mute. And so far no outside observer of Swedish society has examined family issues there in historical depth, and in comparison with trends in other nations.

In summary, the central purpose of this book is to increase our knowledge of the condition and future of the modern family. Through a detailed and comprehensive study of one landmark society, it is hoped that some new light will be shed on family trends and conditions in all advanced, Western societies, and on the future of the family as an institution.

---

[1]For example, Richard F. Tomasson (1970), *Sweden: Prototype of Modern Society*.

[2]Wilbert E. Moore (1979), *World Modernization: The Limits of Convergence*.

[3]Stein Ringen (1986), *Difference and Similarity: Two Studies in Comparative Income Distribution;* Francis G. Castles (1978), *The Social Democratic Image of Society*.

[4]Thomas J. Anton (1980), *Administered Politics: Elite Political Culture in Sweden*.

[5]David Martin (1979), *A General Theory of Secularization*.

[6]Tomasson (1970), *Prototype of Modern Society:* Chapter 6; Hans L. Zetterberg (1984), "The Rational Humanitarians," *Daedalus* (Winter): 75–92.

[7]Erik Allardt (1975), *Att Ha, Att Alska, Att Vara: Om Valfärd i Norden*.

[8]William J. Goode (1970), *World Revolution and Family Patterns*.

[9]E. Macklin (1980), "Non-Traditional Family Forms: A Decade of Research," pp. 905–922 in *Journal of Marriage and the Family* 42 (November): 905.

[10]Mary Jo Bane (1976), *Here to Stay: American Families in the Twentieth Century.*

[11]Sweden's taxes as a percentage of gross domestic product (GDP) in 1984 were 50.6%; the next highest nation was Denmark with 47.3%. The United Kingdom had 38.6% and the United States 29% (1983): *The OECD Observer* 136 (September 1985):32. Swedish public expenditures as a percentage of GDP were 62.2 in 1982, compared to 58.3 for the Netherlands (in second place), 44.3 for the United Kingdom, and 36.9 for the United States. *The OECD Observer* 133 (March 1985):21ff. The Swedish percentage of the total labor force in public social-welfare employment (1981) was 26%, followed by Denmark with 23%. The United Kingdom had 13% and the United States had 9%. OECD data reported in Martin Rein and Lee Rainwater, (eds.) (1986), *Public/Private Interplay in Social Protection: A Comparative Study:* 4.

[12]For comparative income data see Peter Hedström and Stein Ringen (1983), "Age and Income in Contemporary Society: A Comparative Study." The nations of the world frequently shift positions in the world rankings in regard to infant mortality and longevity, but Sweden has been in the lead on many occasions. The latest available data for Sweden at the time of writing are an infant mortality rate of 6.8 and a life expectancy of 77 years. Population Reference Bureau (1987), "The 1987 World Population Data Sheet."

[13]"The World's Richest Nation," *The Economist* (April 1974).

[14]For example, OECD (1981), *The Welfare State in Crisis,* and S. N. Eisenstadt and Ora Ahimeir, (eds.) (1985), *The Welfare State and its Aftermath.*

[15]Quoted in Edward F. Zigler et al. (eds.) (1983), *Children, Families and Government:* xi

[16]Quoted from p. 327 of the paperback edition (1968).

[17]*Ibid.:* 4.

[18]From *The Family among the Australian Aborigines: A Sociological Study* (1913), quoted in Sylvia Junko Yanagisako (1979), "Family and Household: The Analysis of Domestic Groups," *Annual Review of Anthropology* 8:161.

[19]Emile Durkheim (1950), *The Rules of Sociological Method:* 138–139.

*Family Change in History
and Theory*

Part

What Is Family Decline?

"Few popular ideas are more widespread than the belief that the importance of the family in human affairs has been weakening, that the family as an institution is under great strain. . . ."[1] So said sociologist Alex Inkeles, echoing a familiar and probably accurate perception. This postulation of a decline in the institution of the family is buttressed by compelling evidence that the family in advanced societies has undergone greater change, and at a faster rate, in the past several decades than in any previous period of similar length in human history, except after some major catastrophes.

A belief in the reality of family decline, however, is by no means widespread among sociologists of the family, the experts who presumably have the facts. Inkeles goes on to state, for example, that "one cannot make a convincing case that in modern society the family has suffered a substantial decline in its human importance relative to the other institutions and relations in which individuals invest their emotions, their loyalites, and their time."[2] Many sociologists have put this no-family-decline view in stronger terms. Glen Elder referred to the idea of family decline as "a fictional image of family change that had managed to survive from the 1920's."[3] In a recent pathbreaking family textbook Randall Collins concludes that "although it lives with strains, nevertheless the family seems to be in better shape than ever."[4] Theodore Caplow, discussing family change in "Middletown, U.S.A.," asserted in a chapter entitled "The Myth of the Declining Family": "Insofar as changes in the institution can be measured, they seem to reflect a strengthening of the institutional form."[5]

Labeling the idea a myth has become one of the most common devices adopted by sociologists who appear to be vigorously engaged in a battle against the idea of family decline. Thus a widely read book on the family decries the fact that "the myth of the decaying American family is often publicly used to bolster arguments for legislative action."[6] A book of marriage and the family readings for undergraduates has sections on "the marriage-breakdown myth" and "the family-breakdown myth."[7]

The sociological thesis that the family is not in decline is of relatively recent origin, and has been put forth with intensity only in the last few decades. Family decline is one of the oldest ideas in the social sciences, having been promulgated in one form or another by many of the prominent sociologists of the past. Contradictions between the views of today's sociologists and those of the past, and between sociological and popular opinion, give rise to some interesting questions that are explored in Chapter 2. What has happened to modify the perspective of sociologists? Has newly uncovered evidence shown the sociologists of the past, as well as the general public, to have been wrong in their views? Have recent family events required a reshaping of sociological opinion?

A central problem in discussing family decline is confusion over the meaning of the idea. Few in the current debate ever take the trouble to define exactly what they mean by either family or decline. It is important, therefore, to begin with an attempt to develop conceptual clarification in this area. I admit to some trepidation at starting a book with sociological definitions, and running the risk of providing more grounds for the common criticism of sociology that "it tells us in bad English things we already know." My fears are overridden, however, by the knowledge that definitions are fundamental in giving clarity and significance to ideas; and by the realization that for a topic such as the family, which is so embedded in our personal experiences, extra efforts must be made to refine meanings if we are to rise above those experiences into the realm of objective analysis.

"Family" and "decline" have multiple meanings, and trying to define "the family" has long posed a difficult task; scholars have never been able to agree on a single definition. My goal, however, is not to provide a scholarly arbitration of definitional problems. It is, rather, to explore the common sociological meanings of "family" by examining the components of definitions, and to put forth the definitions of family and decline that guide the analysis of family change in this book.

Defining the Family

The term "family", simple and straightforward though it may seem, refers to a complex social reality. In the dictionary I use, 15 definitions are listed. Certain meanings of the family are better suited for some purposes than for others, and the definition one selects has serious implications for scholarly analysis. Take, for example, the definition of the family used by The U.S. Bureau of the Census: "two or more persons living together and related by blood, marriage or adoption." This is useful for the collection and aggregation of census data, but it presents problems for the type of analysis of the family presented here. Among other things, it seems to rule out all families in which the adults are "cohabiting outside of marriage." Moreover, it includes two or more adult brothers or sisters living together, a group not normally thought of as a family. Another definition of family, one gaining currency, is "anyone living in a household." By this definition the family manifestly has not declined, for there are more households per capita today than ever before.

As is the case with other complex concepts, no single set of features can define all families at all times in all places. There is one approach that helps in developing a definition of the family suitable for sociological analysis. A prototype set of features that is recognized widely as making up a "true" family is put forth. The more of these features that are taken away, the less likely it is that one is talking about a family. At some point, when enough features are taken away, a unit may no longer be considered a family.

But the point at which something ceases to be a family is a matter of controversy. So, too, is the original prototype. The prototype family most commonly used today is "a married couple who live together with their children." With this prototype, much of the debate about defining the family revolves around the question of whether one still has a family if (to cite some examples) one half of the couple is taken away, the couple is not married, the children are removed, or some members do not live together. Because so many actual families today are not married couples who live together with their children, a number of social scientists no longer consider this prototype to be very useful.

Another prototypical family used in scholarly analyses, one more suitable for our purposes, is as follows: The family is a relatively small domestic group consisting of at least one adult and one person dependent on that adult. Thus the family is defined, first, as a domestic group (a group of people who live together and perform domestic activities), to distinguish it from other groups that may carry out some of the family's traditional functions. Second, the family is a group that includes dependent persons, usually children, to distinguish it from merely an "intimate relationship" between two adults (whether married or not).

The family as a domestic group must also be differentiated (although there is often great overlap) from the broader kinship group that is typically concerned not with domestic activities, but with the structuring of kinship relations. A problem here is that the English term "family" is typically used to refer both to the domestic and to the kin group. In a common definition that combines the ideas of kinship and domestic group, the family is "a group of kin (or people in a kinlike relationship) who live together and function as a cooperative unit."

Note that such terms as "domestic activities" and "function as a coopera-tive unit" refer to what a family does, not what it is. This, too, is a necessary part of a family definition for purposes of scholarly analysis. To look at a family with regard to what it does is to see it as a social institution. In sociological terms, a social institution is a relatively stable cluster of social structures (roles and norms) organized to meet some basic needs of a society. Such a meaning denotes a cultural frame of reference (roles and norms) and emphasizes that lynchpin of functionalism—a society's "basic needs."[8]

Social scientists generally agree that the basic needs the family as an institution is intended to meet (functions or activities of the family) are as follows: the procreation (reproduction) and socialization of children; the provision to its members of care, affection, and companionship; sexual regulation (so that sexual activity in a society is not completely permissive and people are made responsible for the consequences of their sexuality); and economic cooperation (the sharing of economic resources, especially shelter, food, and clothing). Other minor activities could be added, but these are the main social functions performed by families for advanced societies. These functions, then, should consitute another important part of a definition of the family.

Combining these definitional pieces, one comes up with a general, albeit cumbersome, definition of the prototypical family: a relatively small domestic group of kin (or people in a kinlike relationship) consisting of at least one adult and one dependent person, the adult (or adults) being charged by society with carrying out (although not necessarily exclusively) the social functions of procreation and socialization of children; provision of care, affection, and companionship; sexual regulation; and economic cooperation.

A "domestic group" is one in which people typically live together in a household and function as a cooperative unit in the pursuit of domestic activities, particularly by sharing economic resources. The term "socialization" is intended to include the upbringing, economic support, and regulation of the conduct of dependent children. Finally, "kin" refers to people "related" through blood, marriage, adoption, or their equivalents (including informal pledges and vows). This definition signifies the family not just as a type of social group but as a social institution. To speak of the social institution of the family, or more simply the family, is to refer collectively to all such domestic groups in a society and the functions they are intended to perform.

This meaning of family still poses many problems, but I am not going to bore you with a long definition when I have already done so with a shorter one. As a prototype, this definition cannot cover all family situations. There will be those who object to the inclusion of dependents, wishing the term "family" to have a wider application. For academic studies like this one, however, it is important to distinguish mere "intimate relationships between adults," no matter how permanent, from the group that results when children are present. Both psychologically and institutionally the group with children is significantly different.[9] Others may point out that the definition makes no reference to the fact that a family does not dissolve merely because the children grow up and leave home, usually setting up their own families. This life-course shift is typically dealt with by distinguishing between the family of orientation (or origin), and the family of procreation (or marriage).

Still others may object that the definition focuses on a discrete domestic group. They may argue that parents need not be living together (coresiding) to form a family unit. For example, divorce and separation need not mean family dissolution, but merely marital dissolution; the family remains, though geographically split into several households. Furthermore, a family split by divorce may be no different from the family, for example, of a traveling salesperson who is frequently away from home.

In addition, the definition is tied to particular conditions in modern societies; it has aspects that make it less useful for cross-cultural anthropological studies. It focuses on the separate household, for example, which is not appropriate for families in highly extended family systems where households may be large, complex, and comprised of many different kin groupings. Also, the idea that the nuclear family's basic function is to provide its members with affection and companionship is foreign to most nonmodern societies; even in advanced societies it is a relatively recent historical development.

Our definition, however, does not mean by family merely the traditional nuclear family, as do some other definitions. It allows for considerable structural variation and flexibility, with only the basic social functions and the presence in a domestic group of at least one adult and one child (or other dependent) necessarily held constant.

The Meaning of Family Decline

For purposes of social analysis one cannot be very happy with the term "decline." Like "family," it is an imprecise and ambiguous word with multiple meanings. This becomes clear immediately when one poses an antonym to "decline." In my analysis "decline" is used with the common meaning of "getting weaker"; its opposite is "getting stronger." Thus if the family is not declining, it is either getting stronger or remaining unchanged. Others consider the opposite of "decline" to be "advance" or "progress."[10] With this meaning, family decline involves not just weakening but the much more general "regress." This meaning is to be avoided in social scientific analysis, in my judgment, because weakening is a measurable concept while regress (and progress) are to a much larger degree complex value judgments.

As noted above, it has become faddish for sociologists to attack the belief (using the words of one family sociology text) "that the family is 'breaking down,' 'falling apart,' 'declining,' 'disintegrating,' 'disappearing,' 'besieged,' or . . . 'in trouble,'" as if all of these words meant approximately the same thing.[11] Yet the difference between "decline" and "disappear" is enormous. The issue that is the proper focus of attention is one of tendencies, not of extremes. Declining or weakening, or what Victor Fuchs has called "fading,"[12] does not necessarily mean "falling apart" or "disappearing." To be sure, one *result* of something declining or weakening could be eventual breakup or disappearance; but other possibilities are stabilization at the weaker level and eventual reorganization with renewed strength.

Using "decline" to mean "weakening" and defining the family as indicated above, the concept of family decline in this book refers to the weakening of domestic groups in a society—the groups of kin who live together and function as cooperative units in the performance of their functions. This perspective, I believe, is little different from that held by the great majority of people when they discuss family trends. The principal focus is: what is happening to and within the home, why is it happening, and with what effects? Because the family is a social institution, one can also speak of the "deinstitutionalization" of the family, and that rather unpleasant term will be used occasionally as a synonym for family decline.

Family Decline in Advanced Societies: An Overview

How does the concept of family decline apply to contemporary family change? The institution of the family in advanced societies is weakening, as I document in this book, in five main ways.

1. Family groups are becoming internally deinstitutionalized, that is, their individual members are more autonomous and less bound by the group and the domestic group as a whole is less cohesive. In a highly institutionalized group or organization there is a strong coordination of internal relationships and the directing of group activities toward collective goals.[13] Families, I shall argue, are becoming less institutionalized in this sense. Examples of this are the decline of economic interdependence between husband and wife and the weakening of parental authority over children.

2. The family is weakening in carrying out may of its traditional social functions. With a birthrate that is below the replacement level, this is demonstrably true for the function of procreation. It seems true as well, given the amount of premarital and extramarital sexuality, for the control of sexual behavior. I shall maintain, in addition, that the family is weakening in its functions of socializing children and providing care for its members.

3. The family as an institution is losing power to other institutional groups in society. Examples of this are the decline of nepotism in political and economic life, the rise of mandatory public schooling, and conflicts between the family and the state, in which the state increasingly wins.

4. The family is weakening in the sense that individual family groups are decreasing in size and becoming more unstable, with a shorter life span, and people are members of such groups for a smaller percentage of their life course.

5. Finally, family decline is occurring in the sense that familism as a cultural value is weakening in favor of such values as self-fulfillment and egalitarianism.

Each of these dimensions of family decline or family deinstitutionalization, I shall suggest, is clearly expressed through the trend in advanced societies for people to invest a decreasing amount of their time, money, and energy in family life and to turn more and more to other groups and activities.

It is important at the outset to put forth some caveats about what I shall *not* be asserting. I shall not assert that family decline is necessarily "bad." It may well be that many aspects of family decline are "good," for the individual, for society, or for both. To think of family decline only in the negative makes no more sense than to think only negatively about the decline of feudalism, hereditary monarchies, or dictatorships.

Perhaps societies today need the family less than they once did. Perhaps other insitutions are now more capable than the family of performing traditional family functions. The fact that an institution has declined or weakened does not necessarily imply that its traditional functions are no longer being performed or are being performed in an inadequate manner. (Nor does it mean, of course, that *all* individual institutional units are weakening in carrying out their functions.) Rather, it may be that these traditional functions are being performed by other institutions to which, at least in part, they have been transferred (the sociological issue of "functional alternatives"). Thus child care may be provided more adequately today, even though it is conducted less by the family than in previous generations. The questions of transfer and adequacy must remain open in any discussion of institutional decline and be subject to close empirical scrutiny.

I shall also not assert that the general life conditions of individuals living in (or outside) declining family groups are necessarily getting worse. Despite family decline, so many things have improved in life, such as health and economic security, that most people living today in advanced societies may indeed be happier or more satisfied than ever before (at least this is what people tell survey researchers). Children, even if parents could be shown to be increasingly "neglectful," might still be "better off" because of improved schools, day-care centers, therapists, and medical care. Life is a series of tradeoffs, and it could well be that any negative effects of family decline on individuals are more than offset by positive effects. Such issues need to be explored theoretically and empirically, not taken for granted.

Despite these caveats, I take issues with those contemporary sociologists and other social scientists who find little in modern family trends about which to be concerned. Family decline, in my view, is not only real, but also has an impact, especially on children and thereby on future generations, that should be of concern to the citizens of every modern nation. Yet if the moral and social judgments of sociologists can lay claim to any special legitimacy, it can only emanate from a refined knowledge of empirical reality. The main purpose of this book, therefore, is not to make judgments about family decline, but to provide an objective analysis of family change—to present as much solid knowledge as possible about how the institution of the family in modern society is changing, why it is changing, and what the social implications of that change may be.

Notes

[1]Alex Inkeles (1980), "Modernization and Family Patterns: A Test of Convergence Theory," pp. 31-63 in Dwight W. Hoover and John T. A. Koumoulides (eds.), *Conspectus of History I-IV: Family History: 48-49.*

[2]*Ibid.*

[3]Glen H. Elder, Jr. (1978), "Approaches to Social Change and the Family," pp. 1-38 in John Demos and Sarane S. Boocock (eds.), *Turning Points: Historical and Sociological Essays on the Family: 9.*

[4]Randall Collins (1985), *Sociology of Marriage and the Family: 475.*

[5]Theodore Caplow, Howard M. Bahr, Bruce A. Chadwick, Reuben Hill, and Margaret Holmes Williamson (1983), *Middletown Families: 327.*

[6]Mary Jo Bane (1976), *Here to Stay: American Families in the Twentieth Century:* 69.

[7]John F Crosby (1985), *Reply to Myth: Perspectives on Intimacy.*

[8]It might be noted here that using a functionalist definition is not the same as using a functional analysis.

[9]There have long been attempts by sociologists and others to confuse the family and marriage by maintaining that they are essentially the same thing, or to reduce the one to the other. See Christopher Lasch (1977), *Haven in a Heartless World:* Chapter 2 and pp. 137-39. Recently, we can see this confusion in the heading "Family and Intimate Lifestyles" to cover family books in sociology's leading book-review journal *Contemporary Sociology* (the heading was introduced in the 1970s and lasted until March 1984) and in books that discuss under the heading "alternatives to the family" such "alternative life-styles" as homosexuality and remaining single. These, of course, are alternatives not to the family, but to marriage.

[10]For example, Bane (1976), *Here to Stay:* 3.

[11]Arlene S. Skolnick and Jerome H. Skolnick (1986), *Family in Transition:* 2-3.

[12]Victor R. Fuchs (1983), *How We Live.*

[13]Marvin E. Olsen (1968), *The Process of Social Organization:* 82.

Family Decline: The Career of an Idea

A surprising contradiction between public opinion and the views of many prominent sociologists has arisen in recent years. While in the public mind family decline seems to have become an established fact, many sociologists have sought to cast serious doubt on the idea. Moreover, within sociology the views on family decline have changed markedly over the years. The current view of many leading sociologists that the family has not declined was not shared by many nineteenth- and early-twentieth-century founders of the discipline, who thought of family decline the way most Americans do today—as a notable social trend. Indeed, it is fair to say that the popularly held opinion about family decline stems in part from the writings of earlier generations of sociologists.

This dichotomy of opinion, and the marked shift of sociological views, is so intriguing that it is a worthy focus of analysis in its own right, apart from the empirical question of whether or not the family actually has declined. Why has the view of this issue within sociology changed over the years? Does sociology know something about recent family change that is not yet known by the public at large? Answering such questions is the purpose of this chapter, which analyzes the intellectual development of the idea of family decline against the backdrop of Western family change. In exploring how sociological and other social scientific views of family decline have historically evolved, this chapter raises many of the key issues of the chapters that follow.

Nineteenth-Century Sociological Views of the Family

Sociology as we know it today first emerged in Europe in the nineteenth century amid the social dislocations stemming from the French and Industrial revolutions. Focused broadly on social change, nineteenth-century sociology became strongly influenced by an evolutionary perspective and tended to analyze social change, particularly family change, in terms of institutional origins in human prehistory and subsequent stages of evolutionary development. Most of the sociology also tended to have a conservative cast, being preoccupied with the maintenance of social order in the face of the emerging urbanism and industrialism and the cultural trends of individualism, secularism, and egalitarianism.[1] For many early sociologists, a very important component of this concern for social order and control was the reestablishment or maintenance of a strong family.

Family Decline in the Thought of Sociology's French Founders

The persons most widely regarded as the principal founders of sociology in the early nineteenth century were French. They saw the family as being both a fundamental social institution and in a state of serious decline, notably a decline of paternal authority hastened by the French Revolution. In just a few years this revolution had brought profound changes to the family, including the introduction of marriage as a civil contract with divorce permitted under certain circumstances, the placement of strict limitations on paternal power, and the enactment of inheritance laws requiring an equal division of family property among children. These social changes were looked at askance by the French sociological founders, setting the tone for the idea held by some sociologists today that a belief in family decline reflects a devoutly conservative, even reactionary, impulse.

The reputed father of sociology, Auguste Comte (1798–1857), regarded the family, not the individual, as the basic unit of society and saw the family as the prototype of all other human associations. Perceiving society as an organism, he stated; "The collective organism is essentially composed of families which are its true elements."[2] One German historian expressed Comte's view of the family's importance as follows (showing Comte's strong conservative leanings):

> Desires and urges were molded within the family, and it was in the family that man learned that discipline and "sweet obedience" were necessary. It was in the bosom of the family that men were conditioned to submit themselves to the authority of the State.[3]

As an outgrowth of his belief in the importance of the family in society, Comte showed great concern about the "leveling effect" on the family of the new egalitarian impulses of his time and advocated a full restoration of the patriarchal authority taken away by the revolution. The social reformers had gone much too far, he said, when they sought "to carry into the very bosom of the family their anarchic doctrines of leveling."[4] Although Comte was not known for his "family sociology," Robert Nisbet has suggested that Comte provided "the first systematic and theoretical statement of the family as a unity of relationships and statuses."[5]

Comte's lesser known contemporary Fréderic Le Play (1806–1882), a pioneer in the empirical study of societies, was probably the world's first true "family sociologist." While Comte's veneration of science provided "the means of translating the conservative principles into a perspective more acceptable to later generations of social scientists," as Robert Nisbet has put it, Le Play "transformed the moral insights of the conservatives into a set of concrete problems calling for rigorous field investigation."[6] Like Comte, Le Play believed that "society is made up of families, and that the family is the 'moral cell' of society."[7] He regarded the study of the family as the key to the study of society ("tell me the kind of family you have and I will tell you the kind of society you have"[8]), and he thought that social happiness depended on family happiness. With deep conservative conviction, he was of the opinion that "the erosion of paternal authority attributable to the revolutionary inheritance laws was the most important cause of the social instability of his time."[9]

Le Play's family ideal was the European stem family—a partly extended family consisting of parents, their unmarried children, and one married child to whom the father would eventually turn over the family property. Le Play recognized that this family form remained only in isolated rural regions of Europe (including parts of Scandinavia), but believed that it once was more common (a position challenged by recent research) and was swept away by the forces of change.[10] He referred to the European nuclear family of his time as the "unstable" family, because it failed to allow for family continuity, and called it a "frail shrub":

> It establishes itself by the union of two free adults, grows with the birth of the children, shrinks with the successive departure of the members of the new generation, and dissolves finally, without leaving a trace, with the early death of the abandoned parents.[11]

Another prominent contributor to sociology at this time, somewhat less conservative in outlook than Le Play, was the Comte de Tocqueville (1805–1859). Because of his strong feelings against political democracy, Le Play described Tocqueville's landmark *Democracy in America* as "the most dangerous book written in the century."[12] Le Play did not disagree with many of Tocqueville's conclusions about America, but thought that Tocqueville should have taken a strong moral stand against the American egalitarian trends that he so carefully documented. Writing between 1835 and 1840, several decades before Le Play, Tocqueville had found in America an even more "diminished" family than existed in Europe:

> In America, the family, in the Roman and aristocratic signification of the word, does not exist. All that remains of it are a few vestiges in the first years of childhood, when the father exercises, without opposition, that absolute domestic authority which the feebleness of his children renders necessary, and which their interest, as well as his own incontestable superiority, warrants. But as soon as the young American approaches manhood, the ties of filial obedience are relaxed day by day.[13]

Tocqueville saw this decline of paternal authority as a direct result of democracy. He was not sure whether society might be the loser in this decline, but he was "inclined to believe that man individually is a gainer by it."[14] In contrast to Le Play, and in keeping with modern historical research, Tocqueville thought that relationships within the nuclear family became warmer and closer as a result of the decline of paternal authority. He also noted, with a certain degree of approbation, a growing equality between the sexes.

The Evolutionists

Coming into prominence in the latter part of the nineteenth century, anthropological evolutionists, as noted above, devoted a great deal of attention to speculations about family origins and evolutionary paths of family development, typically using primitive peoples still extant as proxies for early humans. They portrayed social evolution as something in which everything moves forward in a stepwise fashion, and each step is an improvement over the former step. Although these early anthropologists all saw the family as changing form radically over the course of history, unlike most sociologists who both preceded and followed them they had very little to say about the issue of family decline in their own time. This was due in part to their belief that the modern family represented the pinnacle of family progress.

The first of the great social evolutionists, the Englishman Sir Henry Maine, viewed historical family change in terms of the social bonds that held families (and societies) together. In *Ancient Law* (1861) he portrayed the family bond as evolving from "status" to "contract." By "contract," a prominent feature of Western law, he meant that social relationships, among other things, were negotiated not between families but between individuals:

> The movement of the progressive societies has been uniform in one respect. Through all its course it has been distinguished by the gradual dissolution of family dependency and the growth of individual obligation in its place. The individual is steadily substituted for the family, as the unit of which civil laws take account.[15]

Although Maine did not emphasize the point, this portrayal was later picked up and used by American family reformers to mean that there had been an excessive growth of individualism at the expense of the family.[16]

Most of the evolutionists in this period who came after Maine viewed the family, in the words of William J. Goode, as having "'progressed' from the primitive sexual promiscuity of a semi-animal horde, through group marriage, matriarchy, and patriarchy in some polygynous form, to culminate in the highest spiritual expression of family, Victorian monogamy."[17] The dominant idea that families had evolved from matriarchies to patriarchies (an idea not seriously challenged until the end of the nineteenth century) was first posed by a Swiss jurist named J. J. Bachofen, whose book called *Mother-Law* was published in 1861, the same year as Sir Henry Maine's.[18]

The person acknowledged as the true father of evolutionary anthropology was the American Lewis Henry Morgan. Writing in 1877, Morgan's basic idea was that widespread promiscuous sexuality in early societies caused an inability to determine paternity, hence early humans lived in female-dominated groups.[19] He saw the family as historically having passed through stages ranging from "savagery" to "civilization" and believed that in modern times the family had achieved "its highest known perfection." As for the future, Morgan speculated that the family "must advance as society advances, change as society changes . . . it is at least supposable that [the family] is capable of still further improvement until the equality of the sexes is attained."[20] (In social ideology, Morgan was somewhat left of center.) Taking a position opposite to that of Le Play, Morgan said of the family that "it is the creature of the social system, and will reflect its culture." Mainly because of this perspective his theories provided the basis for Engels' later writings on family development.

The major social evolutionist of his time was Herbert Spencer (1820–1903), who was generally regarded as Comte's main successor in sociology, although the two held widely divergent political and social views. Spencer is perhaps best known (and discredited) for having promulgated a "social Darwinism." His main, and very important, contribution to sociology, however, was the development of structural-functionalism and the idea that social life evolves from simple to complex (socially differentiated and functionally specialized) forms. The evolution of the family was central to Spencer's thought. Like Maine, he saw the family and marriage evolving through "inevitable processes" away from ascribed social duties and toward voluntary contractual relationships. He believed that monogamy was the "ultimate and final form evolution has brought into flower." Yet Spencer's master scheme of social evolution toward greater complexity did not seem well fitted to the case of the family and kin group; it was generally acknowledged that the family and kin group had evolved over time not from simpler to more complex forms but rather in the reverse order.[21] Thus his treatment of the family has been described as showing him at his weakest.

Unlike most of his French sociological predecessors and contemporaries, but like his fellow evolutionists, Spencer showed little interest in the changing structure and functions of the family in his own time (he, himself, never married).[22] At the same time he felt that all was not well with the Victorian family and saw "imminent dangers of family disintegration," which he linked not to such trends as industrialization and urbanization, as did later theorists, but to excessive state intervention.[23] He tended to be fairly liberal on contemporary family issues, however, believing, for example, in the right of divorce and taking a positive view of the fact that marriage would eventually be bonded by affection and sentiment rather than the imposition of legal and social sanctions.

Marx and Engels

Karl Marx (1818–1883) and his colleague Friedrich Engels portrayed historical family change in a radically different light than did most of their sociological and anthropological contemporaries. The evolutionists saw family change as progressive, Marx and Engels saw it as regressive. Far from being the highest state of perfection, the monogamous, bourgeois family form was perceived by Marx and Engels as essentially an economic unit based on the "private gain" of capitalism and an instrument of class oppression reflecting the class antagonisms of nineteenth-century society. Capitalism, they felt, had made the family a sham. Marx focused in *Capital* not on the new bourgeois family, but on the way in which capitalist industrialization was tearing apart the family life of the working class.[24] He placed greatest emphasis on the introduction of the machine, whose demands for cheap labor caused massive exploitation of women and children, leading to economic misery and child and family neglect.

Relying heavily on the work of Morgan, Engels took an evolutionary perspective and viewed the monogamous, bourgeois family (he was careful to stress that it was characteristic only of the bourgeoisie) as the end result of the introduction early in human history of the right to private property, a step culminating eventually in capitalism. For women, he said, the bourgeois family form was decidedly inferior to "the old communistic household" in prehistoric hunting and food-gathering societies. The early shift from matriarchy to patriarchy, he believed, was "the world historical defeat of the female sex," and he asserted that "the modern individual family is founded on the open or concealed domestic slavery of the wife."[25]

Thus Marx and Engels, from somewhat different perspectives, saw the family in their time as being "in a severe state of dissolution," as one scholar put it.[26] The contemporary nuclear family would not only decline but disappear entirely, according to Marxist thought, with the sweeping away of capitalism and private property. "The bourgeois family will vanish as a matter of course when its complement vanishes."[27] It was essential especially for the liberation of wives, Engles felt, to abolish the monogamous family entirely as an economic unit of society. What family form would take its place, if any, was never made clear, except that "private housekeeping [would be] transformed into a social industry," including the collectivization of child rearing.[28]

The Turn of the Twentieth Century

By the end of the nineteenth century, with the publication of the massive, multivolume *History of Human Marriage* (1894–1901) by Edward A. Westermarck, evolutionary anthropology came to a temporary resting point concerning the debate about the origins and the presumed evolutionary stages of the family.[29] He found no evidence for early promiscuity and matriarchy and concluded that monogamous and patriarchal family patterns were universal. Another influential book, with similar conclusions, was *A History of Matrimonial Institutions* by G.E. Howard.[30] Most anthropologists came to agree that the evolutionary theory of original promiscuity and matriarchy on which Engels' views had been based was without scientific foundation, and evolutionary theories of family change fell into eclipse in the early twentieth century, later to be revived in a very different form in the 1970s.[31] In place of evolutionary approaches, anthropologists in this century developed an ahistorical functional perspective and accelerated the assembly of a vast amount of comparative family and kinship data about still existing primitive peoples around the globe, data that have proved invaluable for the scientific study of family change to this day.[32]

Marxists, interestingly, continued to promulgate the nineteenth-century theories of family evolution long after they had been abandoned by most other scholars. Yet the importance Marx gave to technology as a factor in family change and even the Marxian emphasis on family decline had a more lasting impact on twentieth-century sociology. At the turn of the century, sociologists, like the evolutionists, tended to see the Victorian family as basically "good" but nonetheless under great stress. The stress was not the result of capitalism and private property, as the Marxists would have it, but of industrialization, urbanization, and the unfettered operation of the free market. This is a debate about family change that has continued between Marxists and non-Marxists to the present day.

The Family Sociology of Emile Durkheim

The turn-of-the-century scholar who, probably more than any other person, both gave definition to the discipline of sociology and provided a bridge from evolutionism to current theoretical approaches was Emile Durkheim (1858–1917). Because of Durkheim's seminal role, it is worth considering his views of the family in some detail. He not only provided a balanced and reasoned summary of what was then known about family history and development (Durkheim made no distinction between sociology and anthropology), but also developed perspectives on the family that brilliantly anticipated many of the developments in family sociology that were to come.

Because he never wrote a book on the subject, Durkheim's views on the family are not well known. Yet he started his academic career with a strong interest in the family—his second public-lecture course during his first major academic appointment at Bordeaux was on the sociology of the family—and late in life he planned to make the comparative history of the family the subject of a magnum opus, but the work was never written.[33] His lifelong interest in the family can best be seen in the contributions to his journal *L'Année Sociologique*. Durkheim kept well abreast of the family literature appearing in his day and, under the heading "Domestic Organization," contributed most of the family-literature reviews in this journal; there were in fact more reviews on the family than on any other topic in *L'Année*.

Durkheim saw Comte and Spencer as his intellectual progenitors, but his views of the family bore some resemblance to those of Le Play, although he disdained most of Le Play's ideas and never indicated any intellectual indebtedness to the Le Playist school. In general, he followed the broad comparative and evolutionary approach to the family of his predecessors, including the posing of various stages of family development, but rejected the idea of family origins in promiscuity and matriarchy. With the exception of his evolutionary speculations (many of which have not held up in the light of later evidence but are rather incidental to his views on the contemporary family), Durkheim's analyses of the family were remarkably modern in perspective and have in fact been considered "among the first truly modern studies in this field."[34]

Durkheim viewed family evolution as having moved through six evolutionary stages. They exemplified a "law of contraction" within which the circle of kin-group members had decreased in size and power over the course of time and (anticipating the later functionalist view) so had the tasks or functions assigned to domestic organizations. This contraction of the family was closely associated with changes in family relationships.[35] For the previous few centuries he portrayed a contraction (the last two evolutionary stages) from the paternal family to the conjugal (nuclear) family, with family relationships changing from a largely material or economic basis to a basis in "personal motives" and the main focus of the family becoming the conjugal relationship between husband and wife. All of this, in turn, was associated with the development by individual family members of more "independent spheres of action."

He also suggested that there would be "an ever growing intervention of the state in the internal life of the family."[36] One dimension of state intervention, he thought, would be the further decline of the right of family inheritance, with the transfer of family property through hereditary inheritance eventually disappearing altogether because of state regulation.[37]

In what sense, if any, did this type of family change represent family decline in Durkheim's view? For the modern or contemporary family especially, Durkheim believed, it was important to distinguish between two aspects of a family unit: the conjugal tie between husband and wife and the nuclear tie between parents and children. He viewed these two relationships as being very different in most respects: "One springs from a contract and elective affinity, the other from a natural phenomenon. . . ."[38] The conjugal tie within the family unit, according to Durkheim, had over time become more intimate and stronger. But the nuclear tie, which Durkheim considered to be the main defining characteristic of the family, had declined in solidarity and importance as a source of personal relationships ("Whereas the family loses ground, marriage contrariwise becomes stronger").[39]

> Formerly domestic society was not just a number of individuals united by bonds of mutual affection; but the group itself, in its abstract and impersonal unity. It was the hereditary name, together with all the memories it recalled, the family house, the ancestral field, the traditional situation and reputation, etc. All this is tending to disappear.[40]

Early in his career Durkheim envisioned the family as eventually contracting to an extreme point and possibly being replaced by the occupational or professional group as a principal source of moral solidarity in society. "Only this group [the occupational and professional group]," Durkehim suggested, "is able to perform the economic and moral functions which the family has become increasingly incapable of performing."[41] And, in anticipation of the situation in our own day, he stated: "In the hearts of men, professional duty must take over the place formerly occupied by domestic duty."[42] Yet later in life he seemed to mellow on this point and came to see the continuing importance of the family as a moral force in society. His opinions on this were summarized by Georges Davy:

> It [the family] is not only the framework which socially sustains the individual and constitutes the organized defense of certain of his interests. It is also the moral milieu where his tendencies are disciplined and where his aspirations toward the ideal are born, begin to expand, and continue to be maintained. . . . the family is a center of morality, energy and gentleness, a school of duty, love and work, in a word, a school of life which cannot lose its role.[43]

It is not clear here whether Durkheim is speaking in realistic or ideal terms. In any event, such views gave rise to the notion that Durkheim anticipated the Parsonian position (discussed below) that the family is not necessarily a weakened version of its former self, but has new, more specialized roles and greater functional importance than ever before.[44]

There can be little doubt, however, that Durkheim, unlike Parsons, saw the family as a weakened institution. In his famous analysis of suicide in modern societies, for example, he linked rising suicide rates strongly with family decline, seeing the modern family as having become a small and isolated institution that provides only limited resistance against suicide.[45] Also, despite his early views on the conjugal tie in the modern family, he grew very apprehensive about the quality of that tie in modern families and was especially concerned about the rising divorce rates:

> The truth is that divorce cannot advance without threatening the institution of marriage; and it is the sufferings of the individual, caused by the sickness of a social and fundamental institution, that are coming to be translated in the yearly total of suicides.[46]

In opposing the further liberalization of divorce laws he noted that "The institution of marriage has in itself a moral validity and has a social function, the implications of which go beyond concerns of the individual."[47] Showing his strong moral conservatism, Durkheim also opposed "free sexual union": "Any sexual union not contracted under matrimonial regulation is . . . subversive of duty and of domestic bonds . . . [and] undermines public order."[48]

Weber and Simmel on the Family

The other most influential turn-of-the-century European sociologists were both German: Max Weber (1864–1920) and Georg Simmel (1858–1918). Weber was virtually silent on family questions (although his wife in 1907 wrote an important book on the subject, which was critically reviewed by Durkheim in *L'Année Sociologique*).[49] Simmel, who turned away from the study of social change to develop a more "formal" sociology, also had little to say about the family as an institution. He did, however, analyze the institution of marriage as a "sociological form," mainly from a social psychological or small-group perspective.[50] What general views he held about the family seem to have agreed in major respects with Durkheim's. Simmel saw the family as an institution that had decreased in size and also had lost many of its functions when the nuclear-family form replaced "the traditional three generation household."[51] Anticipating the later argument of functionalists, Simmel saw the stripped-down nuclear family as fitting very well the new individualized and differentiated society.

Relations within the family had become more person and less task oriented, Simmel believed, and he pointed out an "institutional lag" between marriage as an institution and the growing individualistic wishes and aspirations of modern society. It was important nevertheless, in his opinion, to strive to maintain the institutionalization of marriage so as to help prevent the further dissolution of marital relationships. Again anticipating later views, Simmel discussed what sociologists came to portray as the "vulnerability" of the marriage relationship because so much was expected of it. He noted that the marriage relationship in modern society is increasingly the only intimate relationship, hence there is strong pressure to make it carry a larger burden than it is structurally able to do.

Despite the relative disinterest of Weber and Simmel in the family, continental and especially German and French sociology has continued for most of the twentieth century to show a concern for macrosociological family trends. Included are such issues as the transition to the nuclear family, declining familial solidarity, and weakening paternal authority, as well as the relationship between the family and other societal institutions.[52] This emphasis could also be found in American sociology at the turn of the century. But as the twentieth century advanced, American sociological concern with family institutional change was pushed into the background almost to the point of obliteration; history was virtually eliminated from family sociology. In its place, building on the perspective of Simmel as well as the Americans C. Cooley, G. H. Mead, and W. I. Thomas, the main focus of American family sociology became the family as a social group.

The Development of Family Sociology in the United States

The principal late-nineteenth-century American sociologists such as William Graham Sumner, Lester Frank Ward, and Franklin Henry Giddings (each of whom lived and worked into the twentieth century) shared the family evolutionary views of such European scholars as Spencer and Durkheim. Each of them took a rather liberal position on family change, however, and had "a common faith in the adaptability of the family as an institution to new social conditions."[53] This faith in family adaptability was not shared by a growing army of American social reformers, who tended to see the family as a fundamentally conservative institution whose protection was essential to prevent the growth of unbridled individualism and moral decline.[54]

American Family Sociology in the Progressive Era

Sociology became institutionalized in American universities in the first two decades of the twentieth century. Having mainly come out of the ranks of the reformers, many of the new academic sociologists also had a strong reformist bent and seem to have been in general agreement "that the family had entered a period of painful 'transition'."[55] Their views of the family were shaped also by the fact that most of them came from a rural and often strongly Protestant background. One family sociologist recently summarized the sociological attitudes of that time: "We understand both the family and the effects of urban and industrial developments; what we must do is solve the resulting problems and strengthen the family."[56]

The most important empirical analysis of the early twentieth century, which lent some support to the family-decline thesis, was the pioneering study *The Polish Peasant in Europe and America* by W. I. Thomas and Florian Znaniecki. Work on this study was begun in about 1910, but the book was not published until 1918–1920. It showed how the large extended families of Eastern Europe (and their traditional culture in general) tended to become disorganized under the forces of urbanization and industrialization when their members moved to America.[57] Although Thomas and Znaniecki commonly referred to the decadence, decay, or distintegration of the traditional Polish family, they preferred "disorganized" over "declining," defining disorganization as "a decrease of the influence of existing social rules of behavior upon individual members of the group."[58] The main cause of family disorganization as they saw it was the influence of new individualistic values, so that family "we" attitudes were threatened by "I" attitudes. Because of the growing prevalence of "I" attitudes, they concluded, "disorganization of the family as a primary group is an unavoidable consequence of modern civilization."[59] Moreover, they believed that a weakened primary group was a main cause of modern social problems:

> The prevalent general social unrest and demoralization is due to the decay of the primary-group organization, which gave the individual a sense of responsibility and security because he *belonged to something.*[60]

In addition to giving a new twist to the old theme, *The Polish Peasant,* however, also set the tone for the more optimistic view of the family that was to come. First, Thomas and Znaniecki were careful to distinguish social disorganization from personal disorganization, thus leaving open the question of the effects of family change on the individual. Furthermore, in place of continued disorganization they emphasized the issue of family reorganization:

> Reorganization of the family is then possible, but on an entirely new basis—that of a moral, reflective coordination and harmonization of individual attitudes for the pursuit of common purposes.[61]

In particular, they wanted to see the full assimilation of the Poles into American life, and felt that on this issue there could be no turning back.

The Interwar Years

After World War I sociology in the United States burst into flower as an academic discipline, leading several decades later to unchallenged hegemony in the international sociological community. As American sociology during this period became more differentiated as a scientific discipline apart from social work and social reform, the family-decline thesis and the study of historical family change in general was curtailed.[62] In an endeavor to be more "scientific" as well as to eschew the by-then discredited evolutionary views, many sociological scholars purposely refrained from entering the popularized debate about family decline. Also, the focus of family sociology turned away from family change to the comparative study of family organization (and disorganization) and especially to the internal structure of the family "as a unity of interacting personalities." This move was paralleled in anthropology by the turn away from evolution to functionalism.

Spurring on the new family focus within sociology was an emerging intellectual excitement in the social psychology of small groups. With his influential article published in 1925, the Univeristy of Chicago's leading family sociologist Ernest W. Burgess broke completely from the European historical and evolutionary perspective: The family was essentially a process, he argued, which changed with time and whose essential nature was both created and influenced by the individuals within it.[63] This conception not only refocused family sociology, but helped to bulwark the growing belief by sociologists that the family was a strong and flexible institution: the family was made by its members, and not by external social trends.

Studies of the Depression provided empirical support for this new viewpoint. Regarding this period when families might be expected to show marked signs of disintegration, several studies using the Burgess perspective concluded that "the family was an excellent institution for adjustment to a crisis" and that "the family had great abilities to resist social changes."[64]

In contrast to Burgess and the Depression studies, however, a number of other sociological analyses in the 1920s and 1930s supported the family-decline thesis. Sociologists compared what they saw as strong rural families with the much weaker urban counterparts, emphasizing the negative effects of urbanization and industrialization. Using a Durkheimian approach, they maintained that their various measures of "social pathology" and "social disorganization" provided solid empirical evidence for their position.[65] Studies using an anthropological approach to analyze the adaptation of immigrant groups to the United States, along the lines of *The Polish Peasant,* also found strong evidence for the proposition that the transition from the traditional to the nuclear family resulted in personal and family disorganization.[66] In their landmark application of social anthropological techniques to the American small town "Middletown," the Lynds uncovered strong signs over a 30- or 40-year period of growing marital discord, increasing generational conflict, reduced parental authority, and declining dominance of the home.[67] In his famous 1938 article "Urbanism as a Way of Life" Louis Wirth concluded that

> the distinctive features of the urban mode of life have often been described sociologically as consisting of . . . the weakening of bonds of kinship, and the declining social significance of the family . . . these phenomena can be substantially verified through objective indices.[68]

Finally, in what Ernest Burgess touted in its introduction as the most valuable contribution to the literature of the family since *The Polish Peasant,* E. Franklin Frazier's *The Negro Family in the United States* (1939) documented the great damage done to black families in the move to the city; "The City of Destruction" was one of his section titles.[69]

Despite these important studies many leading American family sociologists of the time were, as noted above, both turning away from the analysis of how the larger social environment affects the family and coming to feel that the family was "doing O.K., thank you." In the words of the historian of family sociology, Ronald L. Howard, family sociologists came to see the family, at least that in America, as "a social institution with remarkable powers of adaptation and survival."[70]

At the same time, sociologists were beginning to regard institutional family change not as decline but as the more neutral loss of functions to other institutions. The idea that the family had lost functions over time was by no means unknown to the nineteenth-century European sociologists, such as Spencer and Durkheim,[71] as well as to the earlier generation of American scholars. A very forceful American advocate of the loss-of-functions thesis emerged in the person of William F. Ogburn, whose collaborative work on *Recent Social Trends* in 1933 has come to be regarded as one of the major contributions to social science in its time.

The family chapter of this widely read document began: "The institution of the family has been attacked and defended with unusual vigor in recent years."[72] Ogburn concluded that such institutions as the school, industry, and the state had "grown at the family's expense." He presented a detailed description and analysis of this change ("Laundering has not left the household to the extent that baking has . . . in 1930 . . . two thirds of the farm households used baker's bread only").[73] Yet at the same time, he believed, the "personality functions" of the family had grown in importance and were now the family's most important contribution. "The chief concern over the family nowadays is not how strong it may be as an economic organization but how well it performs services for the personalities of its members."[74] Anticipating a theme that later was to have great prominence within sociology, Ogburn suggested that the family's loss of functions may have made that institution more efficient in managing its remaining "personality" functions, such as affection, companionship, socialization, and character development.[75]

Thus the loss of functions was not seen as a general family decline but more as an adaptation to a changing world.[76] Ernest W. Burgess later put a still more upbeat label to these changes by calling them transitions. He asserted that "the family in historical times has been, and at present is, in transition from an institution to a companionship."[77] To the degree that he was interested in family change, Burgess saw the family as moving from being "institutionalized in formal and authoritarian law" to a companionship form based on "mutual affection, sympathetic understanding, and comradeship."[78] He regarded family disorganization not as social pathology "but rather as a response to a changing society and as incidental to the transition from the institutional to the companionship family."[79] Thus Burgess, together with many other leading sociologists of his day, came to agree much more with the family-progress thesis of the nineteenth-century evolutionists than with the decline viewpoint of Durkheim or Marx. He even accepted a rough unilinear scheme of family evolution.

American Family Sociology: 1945–1965

These revisionist views on family decline became incorporated in the post-World War II period into the influential theories of Talcott Parsons, the leading sociologist of his time. In keeping with the principal thrust of structural-functionalism, Parsons saw the family as a specialized or differentiated unit performing an important function in society, one that contributes to the society's ability to operate smoothly. This approach, as his critics have never failed to point out, often leads to a kind of unwarranted optimism about society. Parsons agreed with the loss-of-functions thesis almost in the extreme ("the family, on the 'macroscopic' levels, [has become] almost completely functionless"),[80] but he was skeptical of the view that it represented family disintegration or breakdown:

> This represents a decline of certain features which traditionally have been associated with the family; but whether it represents a "decline of the family" in a more general sense is another matter; we think not.[81]

Over time, Parsons added, the family had not only lost functions but become isolated from other institutions. He believed, however, that these changes left the family better able to perform those functions that remained, especially the functions of affection and companionship in the marital relationship and the socialization of children: "These developments enhance the significance of the family as a provider of a secure emotional base for its members' participation in society."[82]

Many sociologists today would agree with this appraisal of family change. What they would not agree with, however, and what raised the ire of his most severe critics, was Parsons' implication that the particular family form still dominant in advanced societies in his day—patriarchal, nuclear, with the traditional division between the roles of men and women—was somehow necessary or justified because of the functions the family performed for society. This aspect of Parsons' thought has often made his views on the family a whipping boy of the sociological left.

The family-decline thesis received a small shot in the arm by the post–World War II investigations of and theories about the modernization of underdeveloped nations. The contributions of modernization theory to family change were nowhere better discussed than in William J. Goode's *World Revolution and Family Patterns*. Although not without numerous caveats, Goode's main conclusion was as follows:

> Wherever the economic system expands through industrialization, family patterns change. Extended kinship ties weaken, lineage patterns dissolve, and a trend toward some form of the conjugal system generally begins to appear—that is, the nuclear family becomes a more independent kinship unit.[83]

Moreover, since industrialization was beginning to occur everywhere, he maintained that there existed a worldwide trend toward the nuclear (conjugal) family. Using functionalist terminology, Goode put forth as an important reason for this the better fit of the conjugal family system to an industrial society. To a certain extent the new modernization theories represented a resurgence of evolutionary thinking (and for this they often have been criticized). In contrast to evolutionary thought, however, they focused primarily on social change in the twentieth century.

Despite the contributions of modernization studies, the family-decline thesis and the sutdy of family change in general went into a quiescent period during the 1940s, 1950s, and early 1960s.[84] To a large extent, conclusions about family change in the Third World passed by, on an alternate track, the mainstream world of American family sociology. One reason for this was that whereas most of the previous debates had dealt with European and American family trends, the new students of modernization focused their attention on situations where the "traditional three-generation" family unit was still powerfully embedded in society. There was growing evidence that this situation had not been common in the West. More broadly, the family-decline thesis became buried in a general disinterest in the study of family institutional change.[85] In a review of family sociology in the period 1945–1956 prepared for the International Sociological Association, Reuben Hill pointed to a sharp shift away from "broad-scale" institutional analyses of the family" toward studies concerned with "the internal workings of marriages and families in their home neighborhoods and on the impact of family life on personality development."[86]

In family sociology and introductory sociology textbooks of this era, family change was for the most part very briefly considered and subsumed under the concepts of functional decline or a move from the extended to the nuclear family. When family functional decline was discussed, it was typically given the Parsonian progressive gloss. In one popular introductory sociology textbook in 1954, for example, there was almost no discussion of family change, and the functional-decline thesis was given the following upbeat treatment:

> In complex urban societies many of the earlier functions of the family have been assumed by other more specialized institutions. . . . However, these changes, instead of pointing to the decline of the family institution, are designed to strengthen it as a device for regulating relations between the sexes and ministering more effectively to people's cravings for comradeship and affection.[87]

Ten years later, in another introductory text, the message became still more positive: "Although the family has lost some traditional functions, it has gained others."[88] The functions gained had to do with "emotional support."

Few sociologists of this era spoke any longer of breakdown, disintegration, or decline, stressing instead the stability and continuity of a nuclear family that was undergoing "only moderate change." Indeed, sociologists came to view family-decline theories with scorn. One prominent review of family sociology during the 1945–1955 period began: "In bygone years dour critics were sounding the death knell of the American family and had been virtually extending invitations to the funeral."[89] An important issue was not how the family is changing, but how one can explain the persistence of the nuclear family in every known society.[90] The imprint of the functionalist perspective on this issue should be clear. But the seeming persistence of the nuclear family was also presaged by the recognized worldwide trend toward the nuclear family discovered during modernization studies, as well as by the growing knowledge that all attempts to suppress or supplant the nuclear family had failed, notably in the Soviet Union. Moreover, anthropological findings suggested that the nuclear family was indeed found almost everywhere, even if usually embedded in a kin network.[91]

Whatever the reasons, for sociologists of this period the nuclear family became something equivalent to what the Victorian family was for the evolutionists: the end of the line and the highest state of perfection. Ernest Burgess saw his "companionate" family as "adapted to urbanization and exemplifying the American ideals of democracy, freedom, and self-expression."[92] Family change was looked at in the best possible light. Whereas in the past, Burgess noted, "stability has been the great value exemplified by the family," today that value is "adaptability." "The growing adaptability of the companionship family makes for its stability in the long run."[93] Reuben Hill reached a similar conclusion: "We see the family surviving with a minimum of scars and a maximum of vitality."[94]

As for the future, few sociologists foresaw the dramatic family changes that were about to occur, and some even discounted the possibility that much further family change could ever occur. The common belief seemed to be that things could only improve. As Hill added to his statement above:

> We see great possibilities in the family of tomorrow as an improved small-family organization geared to assure maximum self-expression of family members while maintaining integrity and inner loyalty to the whole.[95]

The Career of Family Decline to 1965: An Interpretation

Insofar as the views of the sociologists presented above are reasonably representative of at least the leading edge of sociology as a whole, one can summarize the career of the idea of family decline within sociology as follows. The French founders clearly preached a family decline due to the loss of the extended kin group and especially the weakening of patriarchy. They were soon followed by the evolutionists, who, in place of family decline, saw the historical arrival of the family at its all-time apogee. The evolutionists, in turn, were followed by turn-of-the-century sociologists who viewed the family as badly battered by the pervasive forces of industrialization and urbanization and in rather serious trouble. As the twentieth century wore on, views within American sociology of the family's decline softened with each passing year until, by the late 1940s and the 1950s, the whole idea had been mostly thrown overboard.

How is one to account for these varying interpretations of the direction and meaning of family change over the past 150 years by leading sociological scholars? Had the family itself changed over that period of time, being stable in some periods and unstable in others? Had the theories of family change within sociology become progressively more refined and accurate with the availability of new scientific evidence? Or was it that the views of sociologists had merely changed for reasons extraneous to actual changes in the family, such as ideology? Although we cannot present here in any detail a "sociology of knowledge" on this topic, certain likely connections can be suggested.

To a large extent, it should be noted at the outset, sociologists over this long period of time probably did not differ very much in their view of the facts. That is, they would all agree that over time there had been a decline of paternal authority; a partial removal of the nuclear family from kin-group embeddedness; a partial loss of functions, at least with regard to economic production (and, over the very long run, politics, religion, etc.); a decrease in size; a rise of individualism; an increase in affective relationships within families, especially between husband and wife; and so on. How they differed was in their interpretation of these facts.

Partly their interpretations differed because of the different time periods they were studying. While the long-run family trend remained the same, short-run family trends could have looked very different depending on the particular vantage point and historical epoch in which the contemporary analysis of the family took place. The strongly conservative family-decline views of sociology's founders were developed out of the European family changes of the eighteenth and early nineteenth century associated with the Industrial and French revolutions. This was a time in which traditional kinship groups and patriarchies manifestly "lost power" to other groups in society and to individuals. These changes were abrupt, far-reaching, and unsettling to many with a conservative persuasion. They also came at a time when social change of all kinds had filled the air, thus giving them still greater impact.

In addition to having the vantage point of all human history, the later-nineteenth-century perspective of the evolutionists, in contrast, came at a time when the Victorian nuclear family had gained some stability and certainly a measure of ascendency. In becoming a closed domestic group with a clear role of "homemaker" for the wife, the affluent middle-class nuclear family not only marginally strengthened its position in society but even gained power over its members, power that previously had been shared with kin and community (this is discussed in Chapter 4). It was this very power of the bourgeois family that Engels saw, of course, in an entirely different light. Marx may have been partly correct in his characterization of the decline of working-class families during this period, but these families were not the focus of the evolutionists, except insofar as such families were seen as progressively evolving toward middle-class status.

By the turn of the twentieth century, in both Europe and America, the bourgeois family was beginning to show signs of weakness at the same time that the plight of the working classes became of greater societal concern. The dislocations stemming from rural-to-urban and international migrations in Western nations had reached a peak, and such family-associated problems as divorce, crime, and suicide were rapidly rising. Especially in America, the term "family decline" referred not only to the negative impact of urban industrialism but more generally to a moral decline focused on the marital instability that accompanied the growth of individual rights and sexual permissiveness. Although perhaps less dramatic than the European family changes a century before, these family changes were accorded special concern because of the growing belief that societies both could and should collectively organize to combat the social ills of the time. The social-service professions were becoming organized. So also were the social sciences, leading to the regular deliverance of new empirical data that anchored people's perceptions in hard reality. To speak of family decline in this period, then, would seem to have been very much in the spirit and conditions of the time.

The weakening of the family-decline idea in American sociology during the interwar years, however, seems more related to changes in sociology than to changes in the family. The family-decline perspective survived for some decades, but mainly in the limited and sanitized form of loss of functions. This was the period of ever-stronger attempts by sociologists to establish their field as a respectable science and an independent discipline.[96] One thing this professionalization required was not using the kind of general and seemingly value-laden terms—such as decline—that had long been used by social reformers. It also required a severance from the historical (and thus social-change-oriented) perspectives of the discipline's founders, a move that was hastened by the new proclivity of sociology for static structural and social psychological approaches.

After World War II, the idea of family decline became all but dead and buried, with even the loss of functions coming under challenge. Unlike the situation in the interwar years, this near demise of the idea of family decline seems directly related to the social and family conditions of the immediate postwar era. The sanguine sociological views of the family that marked the years around the mid-twentieth century surely must be related to the fact that this was a time of remarkable and unexpected familism and family stability. The family had not only weathered but perhaps been strengthened by the Depression, and in seemingly every advanced society the institution of the family and the cultural value of familism had revived in strength. After decades of decline in certain respects, such as lower birthrates and higher divorce rates, the family molded along Victorian lines had had a renaissance, and a new era of nuclear-family domesticity pervaded these lands. Things looked bright in general after the war, and the sociological view of the family was apparently no exception. This period was short-lived, however, for soon the empirical measures of familism started to reverse themselves again, and the career of the idea of family decline entered its most muddled period.

The Past Two Decades

In the United States and to a lessor extent in Europe, family change in the 1965–1985 period suddenly reemerged as a compelling issue, both among sociologists and in general public debate.[97] The history and fate of the family have again become widely discussed and even politically charged questions. Probably the main triggers for this debate were the sudden turnaround in such family trends as divorce and birthrates and the rapidly changing role of women. Starting in the early 1960s, in virtually every advanced, Western nation family changes that had been under way before the World War II not only resumed their force and character, but began to accelerate at breakneck speed. (These decades, of course, were also a time of rapid social change in many other sectors of life.) With hindsight, the rather placid and stable family situation of the early postwar years turns out to have been, in reference to long-run trends, a sociological fluke.

During these two decades popular opinion that the family was in decline became both widespread and solidified. At the same time, evaluations of this decline became polarized into two competing and often warring camps. In the United States, on the one side, was the right-wing "moral majority," whose religiously based opinion, similar to that prevalent at the turn of the century, was that family decline was the equivalent of moral decay and was seriously weakening the very fiber of the nation. On the other side were some left-wing groups, especially radical feminist groups, who regarded family decline as a positive human achievement because it meant the decline of patriarchal tyranny and the continued liberation of the individual.

These two sides at least agreed that the family was declining; many sociologists do not (especially those who are neither very conservative, nor very radical). What have sociologists had to say about the sudden and unpredicted changes in family patterns of the past few decades? Their evaluations have often been ambiguous and confusing. To a large extent sociologists have carried on the family optimism of the late 1940s and the 1950s: don't worry; everything is going to be all right; the family is here to stay. At the same time they have begun to assert, often with a note of alarm, that there has been "tremendous change," "massive change," tending to agree with the position that the rapidity and magnitude of this change is virtually unprecedented. There are also a few sociologists, caught unprepared when rapid family change returned after the somnolent early postwar years, who have found it difficult to abandon the static views of the family that had emerged in sociology throughout the twentieth century; the significance of what is happening to the family has seemingly passed them by.

Perhaps the outstanding characteristic of the sociological evaluation of family change in recent years, however, is the lengths to which it has sometimes gone to discount the idea that the family is declining. Thus at the same time that a large segment of the public has again become very concerned about the old issue of family decline, many sociologists have abandoned all such allegedly negative judgments about family change. Sometimes they have even suggested that, in the final analysis, many of the empirical family changes that had previously been associated with the idea of family decline did not even take place.

This sociological argument has taken interesting twists. For example, a number of sociologists have pointedly disclaimed the extreme positions that the family is disappearing, that it has been fundamentally undermined, that it has been stripped of functions or has no economic functions. But what serious scholar has ever put forth these positions? They seem to have been set up to serve as straw men against which these sociologists could more vigorously express their point of view.

A related argument has been conducted over the definition of the family. Some sociologists suggest that there is no such thing as the family, and since we cannot even define it, how can it be in decline? What we have, they say, are many types of family, and (with more than a hint of moral relativism) there is little way to choose among them. Of course for analytical purposes it is very difficult to define the family, as issue discussed in the preceding chapter. But the problem of definition as applied in this manner does little to advance our understanding of family decline.

Sociologists have become especially fond in recent years, as noted in Chapter 1, of challenging views they dislike as based on myths—usually about the past—and thereby trying to dismiss those views as based on some kind of mistaken knowledge or mental illusion. This is nowhere more evident than with the family.[98] Thus we have an entire book of readings on the American family, intended for undergraduates, that seeks to destroy such myths as "the alleged breakdown (or, as some say, the decay—the decline—the obsolescence) of both the institutions of marriage and the family."[99] This "myth," the author suggests, has

> become a whipping boy for alarmists and oftentimes well-intentioned conserva-
> tive folk who remain tied to an illusive image of the family in the good old days

> . . . most of the thunder about the breakdown of the family results from a naive and nostalgic comparison of today's family with the past.[100]

Most people do tend to have a nostalgic view of the past (a fundamental tenet of the demythologizers). Being nostalgic about the past may be in the same class as being optimistic about the future, and it is quite possibly a natural human propensity. But challenging popular nostalgia about families of the past says little about how the family as an institution has in fact empirically been changing, and whether or not that change could be defined as decline.

The author of a widely read book about the American family takes to task "a child psychologist with considerable experience in government" who testified at a U.S. Senate hearing that family life in America today is "more difficult than it once was." The author cites the psychologist's testimony to assert that "the myth of the decaying American family is often publicly used to bolster arguments for legislative action."[101]

Even the relatively mild loss-of-functions thesis has come under sharp criticism. Most sociologists today probably still agree that there has been a general worldwide movement of family structure from kin embeddedness to the conjugal form (at least in Third World nations, if not the West, as summarized above by Goode). Apparently fewer would now agree with Parsons, Ogburn, and almost all sociologists before them, however, that the family has had much functional loss. In reviewing this issue, the introduction to a recent family reader concluded: "These ideas about the family have lost their credibility."[102]

In *Middletown Families,* the early 1983 book about family life in middle America, Theodore Caplow even purports to have found empirical evidence to prove that functional decline is a myth (he claims that the myth "now seems nearly as indestructible as the American family itself").[103] There has been "no appreciable decline in the Middletown family during the last 50 years," he concludes.[104] Without reference to historical analysis before their time, he blames Ogburn and Burgess for having first promulgated "the myth of the declining family," saying that the data Ogburn presented "were, by modern standards, remarkably inadequate. . . ."[105] Even if Caplow's data are valid, the question remains: just how representative of the families of the United States (to say nothing of other Western societies) are the people of "Middletown" who agreed to answer his questions?

Caplow is one of the few sociologists who indicate why such a myth should, if untrue, remain so pervasive (it was widespread in his "Middletown" sample!). He suggests that people who believe in the myth of family decline can "discover with pleasure that their own families are better than other peoples;" that the myth provides a "consoling explanation" that "offers some comfort for certain frustrations" relating to family change; and that the myth is nationally promulgated "to provide livelihoods for thousands of scholars, journalists, and social workers and tens of thousands of government employees" who make up a "thriving industry" dedicated to studying, writing about or helping families.[106] As an employee of a state university, I read the last statement with a certain detached amusement.

To me, the interesting question is not why people believe in the "myth" of family decline, but why so many sociologists think of family decline as a myth and seek to dismiss the idea with such vigor and seeming certainty. The irony of the vigorous promotion by sociologists today of the antidecline position is that it comes at precisely a time when the family has been changing rapidly, far more rapidly than in those previous historical periods when the idea of family decline was pervasive among members of the social-science community. The demythologizers implicitly recognize this rapid change when they make such statements as "the political uproar [over the family in recent years] followed almost two decades of dramatic changes in family life." They even recognize the problematic aspects of it: "however grim the present moment may appear, there is no point in giving in to the lure of nostalgia."[107]

Reviewing the empirical evidence both for and against the idea of family decline is beyond the purvue of this chapter, but it is useful to look at some of the "new" evidence on which the antidecline argument is partly based. One source of evidence is survey and other data that indicate a general improvement in the social quality of life. There can be no doubt that in very many important areas—material standard of living, health and longevity, equality and the rights of women, literacy, and even psychological awareness—the situation in the past really was inferior to that of the present.[108] It is often pointed out, for example, that because people live longer today, marriages and nuclear-family units can and sometimes do last longer than they once did. These kinds of general social improvements, however, say little about what has happened to the family as an institution.

More penetrating evidence about the issue of family decline has been the growing volume of historical information suggesting that the "traditional three-generation family" was much less prevalent than previously thought. That is, the majority of households in many Western nations, going back many centuries, seem not to have been extended. This important finding, which is discussed in the chapters that follow, has led some sociologists to suggest that the shift from the extended to the nuclear family was insignificant. This is an incorrect interpretation. The fact remains that many more households were three generational in the past than today; moreover, in the past most persons probably lived in three-generational households sometime during their life course. Today this is not the case. Unlike the family itself, the extended-family household has all but disappeared in advanced societies.

The main empirical contribution of sociologists to the notion that family decline is a myth relates to this last point—that extended-family households have all but disappeared. In what is now often called "the rediscovery of kinship," sociologists uncovered in urban-industrial conditions what they believed to be more extended-kinship relationships than had previously been thought to exist.[109] This led to the conclusion that the extended family lives on in the form of a "modified extended family."[110] Yet this conclusion has become a source of confusion. It is not the extended-family household that survives, nor is it kinship as a system of normative control over its members. What has been discovered is that many people in advanced societies still have regular contact with their kin and engage in a certain amount of mutual aid. Although this is a significant finding, it certainly is far from being the important challenge to the idea of kinship decline that it originally sought to be.

Empirical evidence of the type mentioned above adds interest to the debate about family decline, but does not really address the changing family situation as it is seen by the general population. Today's family decline is only in part the continuing decline of the extended family. What most people have in mind when they speak of family decline is the decline or breakdown of the *nuclear* family. Seen in this light, they point to such hard evidence as rising divorce rates, later age of marriage, declining birthrates and smaller family sizes, the increase in child care outside the nuclear family, and the various family-related social pathologies that seem to be (but may not actually be) on the increase, such as child abuse and teenage suicide.

If the sociological view that family decline is a myth flies in the face of the rapidity of family change, and cannot be entirely accounted for by the availability of convincing new empirical evidence, to what other factors might this sociological perspective be attributed? I suggest, with all due respect to my colleagues, that it is partially inspired by ideological shifts. To a much larger degree than their predecessors, sociologists today tend to *favor* many of the family trends taking place, as well as many of the social changes associated with these trends. Such changes include the decline of paternal authority and the rise of female equality and women's liberation, economic egalitarianism, secularism, and sexual permissiveness. In view of this ideological leaning, there is reluctance in using a term such as "decline."

It should be noted that the discipline of sociology today is certainly no longer practiced mostly by Protestants from rural backgrounds, as was true in earlier times. Rather, it consists mainly of secularists with urban and suburban backgrounds. It is no secret either that most sociologists today are politically left-wing on most social questions. Precisely because the family-decline theme has been pushed hardest in recent years by conservative forces who disfavor family trends and disavow the social changes just mentioned, sociologists have sought to do battle with these groups by trying to undercut whatever factual basis the conservatives have relied on (much of which came originally from sociology!) Under these circumstances, to see the institution of the family as in any way declining is to risk selling out to the opposition.

Despite pious claims about objectivity in the social sciences, values are inescapably involved in the interpretation of empirical data. Social-science explanation cannot be invalidated simply because it was influenced by a particular ideology, therefore, but this is not to say that objectivity does not sometimes suffer from ideological blinders. In this case, even though agreeing with most aspects of the ideology that seemingly gives momentum to the antidecline position, I nonetheless think that empirical reality has unwittingly been distorted. The new demythologizers, in my judgment, have not only overthrown a good deal of traditional sociology, but have clouded our understanding of an important social trend that is under way in the world today. As discussed later in this book, the institution of the family in advanced societies seems manifestly to be continuing what I think must be regarded as a long-term historical decline.

Notes

[1] For example, Robert Nisbet (1966), *The Sociological Tradition*.

[2] Quoted in Lewis A. Coser (1977), *Masters of Sociological Thought*: 10.

[3] Heinz Maus (1966), *A Short History of Sociology*: 14.

[4] Quoted in Nisbet (1966), *The Sociological Tradition*: 60.

[5] *Ibid.*

[6] Robert Nisbet (1968), *Tradition and Revolt*: 85.

[7] Catherine Bodard Silver (ed. and trans.) (1982), *Frédéric Le Play on Family, Work and Social Change*: 29. In a lengthy essay on Le Play, Silver makes a convincing argument that Le Play, because of his pioneering use of empirical methods, belongs in the company of Saint Simon, Comte and de Tocqueville as one of the major founders of sociology.

[8] Carle C. Zimmerman (1947), *Family and Civilization*: 119.

[9] Silver (1982), *Le Play*: 32.

[10] *Ibid.*: Chapter 6.

[11] Quoted in *Ibid.*: 80.

[12] *Ibid.*: 35.

[13] Alexis de Tocqueville (1956), *Democracy in America*: 228–229.

[14] *Ibid.*: 231.

[15] Henry Sumner Maine (1888), *Ancient Law*: 163.

[16] Ronald L. Howard (1981), *A Social History of American Family Sociology, 1865-1940*: 12. I am indebted to this work, whose publication was sponsored by the Family Section of the American Sociological Association, for many important references and perspectives in this section. Note that the first American family

textbook was heavily influenced by Maine's views. Writing from a strongly Christian perspective, the authors stated that "the individual has come to be regarded as the crown and the centre of social and legal order. The family, as an institution of prime importance, has passed . . . [it] has ceased to exist as a social unit." Charles Franklin Thwing, and Carrie F.B. Thwing (1913), *The Family: An Historical and Social Study:* 139.

[17]William J. Goode (1970), *World Revolution and Family Patterns:* 3.

[18]J. J. Bachofen (1861), *Das Mutterrecht.*

[19]Lewis H. Morgan (1963), *Ancient Society.*

[20]*Ibid.:* 499.

[21]Stanislav Andreski (1969), "Introduction," pp. ix–xxxvi in Herbert Spencer, *Principles of Sociology:* xvi.

[22]Jay Rumney (1965), *Herbert Spencer's Sociology:* 120ff.

[23]*Ibid.:* 124.

[24]Karl Marx (1936), *Capital:* Chapter XV.

[25]Frederick Engels (1942), *The Origin of the Family, Private Property and the State:* 50, 65.

[26]Philip Abbot (1981), *The Family on Trial:* 77.

[27]From the Communist Manifesto (1848) in Max Eastman (ed.) (1932), *Capital and other Writings by Karl Marx:* 339.

[28]Engels, *Origin:* 67.

[29]Edward A. Westermarck (1894–1901), *History of Human Marriage.*

[30]George E. Howard (1904), *A History of Matrimonial Institutions.*

[31]For a good account of recent neoevolutionary family theory see Pierre L. van den Berghe (1979), *Human Family·Systems: An Evolutionary View.*

[32]Notably the work of George Peter Murdock.

[33]Steven Lukes (1972), *Emile Durkheim: His Life and Work:* 179–80. Durkheim's opening lecture in his family course is "Introduction to the Sociology of the Family," pp. 205–228 in Mark Traugott (ed. and trans.) (1978), *Emile Durkheim on Institutional Analysis.*

[34]Ernest Wallwork (1972), *Durkheim: Morality and Milieu:* 89.

[35]For a general discussion of Durkheim's contribution to family sociology see Louis Th. Van Leeuwen (1981), "Early Family Sociology in Europe," pp. 95–139 in Howard, *Social History.*

[36]George Simpson (1965), "A Durkheim Fragment," pp. 527–536 in *The American Journal of Sociology* 70:5 (March): 530. This is a translation of the final lecture in a course on the family that Durkheim gave at Bordeaux in 1982.

[37]Pp. 49–50 in Joseph Neyer (1960), "Individualism and Socialism in Durkheim"; pp. 32–76 in Kurt H. Wolff (ed.), *Essays on Sociology and Philosophy by Emile Durkheim et al.*

[38]Emile Durkheim (1951), *Suicide: A Study in Sociology:* 185.

[39]Simpson (1965), "Durkheim": 536.

[40]From Durkheim's *Suicide,* quoted in Wallwork (1972), *Durkheim:* 96.

[41]Simpson (1965), "Durkheim": 535.

[42]*Ibid.:* 535–536.

[43]Quoted in Robert N. Bellah (1965), "Durkheim and History," pp. 153–166 in Robert A. Nisbet, (ed.), *Emile Durkheim:* 163. This quotation is a summary of Durkheim's views of the family by Georges Davy in *Sociologues D'Hier et D'Aujourd'hui* (1931).

[44]Bellah (1965), "Durkheim": 163.

[45]Durkheim (1951), *Suicide*. See especially Chapters II-3 and III-3. Durkheim's views on this are aptly summarized by Robert Nisbet: "The modern family . . . is not only too small to absorb the ills of the human spirit, it has been separated by the forces of modern history from centrality in the economic and political processes that govern man's life and attract his allegiances. The family, far from being a haven for man's fears and inadequacies, is itself in need of the kind of reinforcement that can come only from a role in a larger and more relevant form of association. . . ." Nisbet (1966), *The Sociological Tradition*: 155.

[46]This passage is from a review by Durkheim in *L'Année Sociologique* of a French book on divorce published in 1905. In Yash Nandan, (ed.) (1980), *Emile Durkheim: Contributions to L'Année Sociologique*: 431. Durkheim's views on divorce, and on the high correlation between divorce and male suicide, are put forth in "Divorce by Mutual Consent," pp. 240-252 in Mark Traugott (ed. and trans.) (1978), *Emile Durkheim on Institutional Analysis*.

[47]Nandan (1980), *Emile Durkheim*: 284.

[48]Simpson (1965), "Durkheim": 536.

[49]Mme. Weber had strong feminist views for her day. She took the position, for example, that to end the bondage of patriarchy, the marriage tie should be loosened so that it could be broken simply at the wish of those involved. Respectfully, Durkheim challenged this view by noting that in the modern family the home and nuclear family had become culturally much more important than in previous eras and that women's position had thereby improved over where it once was. He pointed out that as women have gained respect, the "moral scope of the wife and mother has increased" and husband and wife have become closer and more constantly in touch. While not denying that women would gain through playing a larger role in civic life, Durkheim was worried about a loss in the substantial gains they had won over time within the home. Nandan (1980), *Emile Durkheim*: 285-289.

[50]Kurt W. Wolff (trans. and ed.) (1950), *The Sociology of Georg Simmel*: 128-132, 326-329.

[51]Van Leeuwen (1981), "Early Family Sociology": 118-121.

[52]*Ibid.*: 129.

[52]Howard (1981), *Social History*: 16.

[53]Howard, *Social History*: 16-26. A good example is the textbook of the Thwings, *The Family* (he was President of Western Reserve University). They thought that the family needed to be somehow "reinstitutionalized" to provide a conservative force against excessive individualism and secularism, and they were very conservative in regard to sexual behavior. On other family issues they took a liberal point of view, however, calling for the full equality of husband and wife within the home and with respect to property rights.

[55]Christopher Lasch (1977), *Haven in a Heartless World*: 28-29. A prominent book on the family of that time by a British woman, Helen Bosanquet, was an exception. She states that "the modern family is in no sense a weakened or degenerate form" (336), but she goes on to discuss what she feels is the sorry state of many families in cities and among the poor. Helen Bosanquet (1915), *The Family*.

[56]Bert N. Adams (1986), *The Family: A Sociological Interpretation*: 8.

[57]William I. Thomas and Florian Znaniecki (1927), *The Polish Peasant in Europe and America*.

[58]Morris Janowitz, ed. (1966), *W. I. Thomas On Social Organization and Social Personality*: 4.

[59]*Ibid.*: 67.

[60]W.I. Thomas and Florian Znaniecki (1958), *The Polish Peasant in Europe and America:* 1826.

[61]Janowitz (1966), *W. I. Thomas:* 69.

[62]The family itself was not an important interest to leading sociologists in this period. The most influential sociology text of the time, for example, had only a few pages on the family per se (and virtually nothing on family change), treating it mainly as one of the "human groups." Robert E. Park and Ernest W. Burgess (1921), *Introduction to the Science of Sociology:* 213–223.

[63]Ernest W. Burgess (1926), "The Family as a Unity of Interacting Personalities," *The Family* 8:3–9. See Howard (1981), *Social History:* 66–68. In the Park and Burgess textbook of 1921 it was suggested (p. 215) that the idea of "the family as a unity of interacting members" was emphasized by Helen Bosanquet in *The Family* (1906). This early work was called "an excellent theoretical study of the family."

[64]Howard (1981), *Social History:* 72.

[65]The classic work is Pitirim Sorokin and Carle C. Zimmerman (1929), *Principles of Rural-Urban Sociology.* See also Carle C. Zimmerman and Merle E. Frampton (1935), *Family and Society.* Both Sorokin and Zimmerman were unusual among sociologists in having a high regard for the work of LePlay.

[66]Howard (1981), *Social History:* 76–78.

[67]Robert S. Lynd and Helen M. Lynd (1929), *Middletown: A Study of Contemporary American Culture,* and (1937), *Middletown in Transition: A Study in Cultural Conflicts.* See Howard (1981), *Social History:* 78–79.

[68]Louis Wirth (1970), "Urbanism as a Way of Life," pp. 54–69 in Robert Gutman and David Popenoe (eds.), *Neighborhood City and Metropolis:* 66. First published in the *American Journal of Sociology* 44 (1938).

[69]E. Franklin Frazier (1966), *The Negro Family in the United States.*

[70]Howard (1981), *Social History:* 85.

[71]Nisbet (1966), *The Sociological Tradition:* 155.

[72]P. 661 in William F. Ogburn and Clark Tibbitts (1933), "The Family and its Functions," Chapter 13 in President's Research Committee on Social Trends, *Recent Social Trends.*

[73]*Ibid.:* 664–665.

[74]*Ibid.:* 661.

[75]Another theme he pointed to, which is very prominent at the current time, concerns the growing number of women in the work force: "Where both husband and wife work outside the home . . . the housework of the married woman who works out is a double burden, since in many cases she does some work at home after business hours." Ogburn and Tibbitts, *ibid.:* 666.

[76]Ogburn was not oblivious to family problems, however. He concluded the chapter by saying that "a major problem of the family is its instability. Divorce is still increasing . . . Increased divorce is due to the weakening of the functions which served to hold the family together . . . the future stability of the family will depend . . . on the strength of the affectional bonds." Ogburn and Tibbitts, *ibid.:* 708.

[77]Ernest W. Burgess and Harvey J. Locke (1945), *The Family: From Institution to Companionship:* vii. One serious problem with this concept is the implication that the family is no longer an "institution."

[78]Robert E. L. Faris (1970), *Chicago Sociology: 1920–1932:* 104.

[79]Burgess and Locke (1945), *The Family:* vii.

[80]Talcott Parsons and Robert F. Bales (1955), *Family. Socialization and Interaction Process:* 16–17.

[81]*Ibid.:* 9.

[82]Talcott Parsons (1971), *The System of Modern Societies:* 100–101.

[83]Goode (1970), *World Revolution:* 6.

[84]Two exceptions to this, although neither made much impact on the field, were Carle C. Zimmerman (1947), *Family and Civilization,* and William F. Ogburn and M. F. Nimkoff (1955), *Technology and the Changing Family.* Zimmerman believed not only that the family was rapidly decaying, but that family decay leads to the decay of society. Ogburn and Nimkoff, in what was really an update of Ogburn's earlier theories, concluded (p. 320) that "The functions of the family have been greatly reduced in number, and the family has suffered a great loss in its influence on society apart from its influences on its own members." Family change remained a more important focus in European family sociology.

[85]An exception was studies of social influences on the young. See Glen H. Elder Jr. (1978), "Approaches to Social Change and the Family," pp. S1–S38 in John Demos and Sarane S. Boocock, (eds.), *Turning Points:* S3.

[86]Reuben Hill (1958), "Sociology of Marriage and Family Behavior, 1945–56," *Current Sociology* 7-1: 6–7. The same finding was made in a concurrent review by Winch covering the same period. He did not even have a section on institutional change because he found only two books on that topic. Robert F. Winch (1957), "Marriage and the Family," pp. 346–390 in Joseph B. Gittler (ed.), *Review of Sociology.*

[87]George A. Lundberg, Clarence Schrag, and Otto N. Larsen (1954), *Sociology:* 546. A partial exception to this perspective was in the popular textbook by Broome and Selznick. "In the present, as in the past, the family is of vital importance, both for the individual and for the social order . . . However, kinship has grown steadily less important in the total fabric of social organization. Although the family is still strong, it has lost many of its old functions, especially in economic life, and fewer obligations and relationships are determined by family membership. Other groups carry the main burden of social organization." This passage did not appear in the family chapter, however, but in an up-front section entitled "Basic Trends in the West—Social Organization." Leonard Broome and Philip Selznick (1958), *Sociology:* 35.

[88]James W. Vander Zanden (1965), *Sociology: A Systematic Approach:* 337.

[89]Winch (1957), *Marriage and the Family:* 346.

[90]For example, Ezra F. Vogel (1968), "The Family and Kinship," pp. 121–130 in Talcott Parsons (ed.), *American Sociology: Perspectives, Problems, Methods.*

[91]The most influential statement was that of Murdock. "The nuclear family is a universal human social grouping. Either as the sole prevailing form of the family or as the basic unit from which more complex familial forms are compounded, it exists as a distinct and strongly functional group in every known society." Although this conclusion has since been widely challenged, Murdock found no exceptions in the 250 cultures that his survey included. George P. Murdock (1949), *Social Structure:* 2.

[92]Ernest W. Burgess (1948), "The Family in a Changing Society," pp. 417–422 in *The American Journal of Sociology* 53-6:417.

[93]*Ibid.:* 420.

[94]Reuben Hill (1947), "The American Family: Problem or Solution," pp. 125–130 in *American Journal of Sociology* 53-2:130.

[95]*Ibid.*

[96]For example, Roscoe C. Hinkle, Jr., and Gisela Hinkle (1954), *The Development of Modern Sociology:* Chapter 2.

[97]One of the first sociological works of this period to take up again the issue of family change was John M. Edwards, (ed.). (1969), *The Family and Change.*

[98]The same demythologizing approach has been used in Sweden. See David Gaunt and Orvar Löfgren (1984), *Myter om Svensken:* 38–45.

[99]John F. Crosby (1985), *Reply to Myth: Perspectives on Intimacy:* 503.

[100]*Ibid.:* 572–573.

[101]May Jo Bane (1976), *Here to Stay: American Families in the Twentieth Century:* 69.

[102]Arlene S. Skolnick and Jerome H. Skolnick (1986), *Family in Transition:* 4. For a strident attack on the loss-of-functions idea in Britain, see the influential book Ronald Fletcher (1973), *The Family and Marriage in Britain.*

[103]Theodore Caplow, Howard M. Bahr, Bruce A. Chadwick, Reuben Hill, and Margaret Holmes Williamson (1983), *Middletown Families:* 326.

[104]*Ibid.:* 327.

[105]*Ibid.:* 324.

[106]*Ibid.:* 327.

[107]Skolnick and Skolnick (1986), *Family in Transition:* 1, 17.

[108]For reviews of the data, see Richard F. Hamilton and James D. Wright (1986), *The State of the Masses,* and Ben J. Wattenburg (1985), *The Good News is the Bad News is Wrong.*

[109]The early evidence from the 1950s, 1960s, and early 1970s is reviewed in Robert F. Winch (1977), *Familial Organization: A Quest for Determinants:* 13–15. For a recent empirical contribution, see Claude S. Fischer (1982a), *To Dwell Among Friends* and Claude S. Fischer (1982b), "The Dispersion of Kinship Ties in Modern Society: Contemporary Data and Historical Speculation," *Journal of Family History* 7-4:353–375.

[110]This term was used by Eugene Litwak (1960), "Occupational Mobility and Extended Family Cohesion," *American Sociological Review* 25:9–21. For a review of the debate over this concept, see Graham Allen (1985), *Family Life:* 9–12.

The Global Family Trend

There does not exist, unfortunately, a well-developed theory of family change within which the issue of family decline could be considered, nor does such a theory seem within the present capabilities of the social sciences. Some high-level generalizations about the directionality of historical family change do fit the available empirical evidence, however. Many of these generalizations have been given the label "the global family trend," that is, the broad trend for family-kinship systems to move from an extended to a nuclear or conjugal form. This trend has been under way in advanced societies for many centuries and is evident in all industrializing societies today. In this chapter the global family trend is introduced in theoretical terms, to be followed in Chapter 4 by a detailed discussion of the original rise in the West of the nuclear family.

The global family trend is relatively recent in world history. It is closely associated with historical developments that fit under such labels as moderniza-tion, industrialization, or urbanization (to name but a few). At the same time, the global trend is a "modern" segment of long-term evolutionary changes in the nature of families and societies. To explore family evolution in detail would take us far afield; the subject is unquestionably speculative, and solid evidence about human origins is (and probably always will be) in extremely short supply. Nevertheless, a few general propositions about the historical evolution of the family have some empirical support, and to place the global family trend in context it is useful to begin with a discussion of them.

Social Evolution and the Family

Family evolution was in the nineteenth century the focus of anthropology, as we discussed in Chapter 2, but the subject was virtually abandoned in the first half of the twentieth century. About the middle of the present century, however, interest in human evolution arose again, and in recent years, particularly with the advent of sociobiology, family evolution has become once more an important focus of intellectual endeavor. At one time, most knowledge of human origins and development had to be inferred from the study of preliterate societies still extant. But with each passing year, the accumulation of archaeological evidence helps to fill in the picture of the history of human beings on earth.[1]

Probably the least controversial proposition about early human origins is that society, as that term is used by sociologists, consisted entirely of family and kinship networks, social networks of people who were related by family ancestry or origin or by marriage or adoption. Originally there were no separate social institutions for such specialized purposes as religion, education, politics, or economics. As anthropologist Robin Fox has put it:

> For the longer period of human development, mankind lived for the most part
> in societies in which kinship-based groups were the constituent units. A man's
> health and security, his very life and even his chance of immortality, were in the
> hands of his kin. A "kinless" man was at best a man without social position: at
> worst, he was a dead man.[2]

Presumably, this situation also held true for women.

Over time separate social institutions developed for activities that were originally performed by these primal, multipurpose family and kin groups. This is the general reason why sociologists often say that in the course of history the family has lost functions and has fewer today than it once did. No longer controlled by family and kinship networks, the political functions of most societies today are in the hands of the state, and religious, educational, and economic functions are controlled by various institutions and organized groupings set up for those purposes. This loss of family functions occurred irregularly and at different stages of history, depending on the function and the state of societal development. For some functions, such as economic production, the loss has been quite recent in many societies and is still incomplete. For others, such as political and religious functions, the historical timing of the changeover came earlier.

Thus societies over time have become socially differentiated into separate institutions with specialized functions, and the family-kin group has evolved from an all-purpose social unit to one of the many specialized social institutions within a larger society.[3] From this perspective it is reasonable to say that through the process of social or functional differentiation the family as an institution has declined in importance over time, if by importance one means social power within societies. The family has lost social power to other institutions; other social institutions have emerged to draw people's time and energies away from family and kin groups.

Although not all scholars are enamored of such a "neoevolutionary" perspective,[4] this evolutionary trend of social differentiation and the family's loss of functions in this sense are widely accepted. Depictions of the trend can have a nineteenth-century "evolutionism" aspect (Herbert Spencer emphasized the trend strongly in his work), but today's interpretations of it differ considerably from those of the past century. Most nineteenth-century evolutionists, for example, regarded this process of social differentiation as a measure of progress. Contemporary social scientists are much more circumspect about making such evaluations; they are reluctant to suggest that increased social differentiation in some way increases the sum total of human happiness.

Moreover, the nineteeth-century evolutionists considered the trend to be a relatively consistent, unilinear development over time. When viewed in the light of presently available empirical data, however, this trend has followed an uneven and circuitous path. Throughout history the importance of family and kinship in societies has waxed and waned, perhaps the most commonly cited example being the family changes that occurred during the rise and fall of the Roman Empire.[5] Some scholars, although they have never received much intellectual support, see a cyclical trend instead of a unilinear or even multilinear trend. They think that societies rather mechanically moved back and forth throughout world history from the pole of family dominance, on the one hand, to the pole of individual dominance, on the other.[6] If such cyclical theories were to be proved valid, one could make some very interesting and powerful predictions about the future! Most scholars today, however, would be more likely to posit an uneven unilinear or multilinear trend. They would also emphasize, unlike many of their predecessors, the possibilities for human control over social events and would suggest further that even a basic trend, such as social differentiation, could in the future turn back on itself.

The Global Trend of Family-Kinship Systems

The knowledge that there has been an evolutionary process of social differentiation does not take us very far in understanding family change in the world today. It merely supports the idea that over time family and kin groups vis-à-vis other institutions within a given society have declined in function and social power. While it is compatible with long-term social differentiation, the global family trend refers less to a decline in family functions than it does to changes in the structure or form of the family. It emphasizes that there has been a marked shift in many of the world's nations from one form of family-kinship system, the extended form, to a very different one, the nuclear form.

The Polar Types of Family-Kinship Systems: Extended and Nuclear

Studies of family form and family change in the world's societies have uncovered an almost bewildering variety of family-kinship stages or, to use a term that is more neutral with respect to evolution, family-kinship types. This diversity of types has provided a fertile field for the often exotic investigations of peripatetic social anthropologists, and the study of kinship within anthropology has become a well-developed, highly technical, and very complex area of knowledge.[7] Learning kinship terminology is almost like learning a new language. Our aim here is not to give a precise description of these types suitable for detailed analysis, but rather to examine them as indicators of family change over time. We can, therefore, condense this great diversity into two polar types of family-kinship systems—a gross simplification from an anthropological point of view, but a useful heuristic device for the analysis of family change.

In theoretical terms, each polar type is at one end of a continuum, and all known family-kinship systems can be placed on this continuum at some point (thus the ends of the continuum in pure form are "ideal" types).[8] At one pole is what can be called an *extended family-kinship system* (this term should not be confused with an extended-family domestic group or household, as discussed below, which is why I have used the hyphenated phrase family-kinship system). A fundamental characteristic of this system is that "adult children continue to be members of, and subject to the authority of, the group in which they were born."[9] At the other end of the continuum is the so-called *nuclear family-kinship system,* characterized by the release of young people, at or before marriage, from the authority of and the duty to contribute to the family group into which they were born.

In the extended family-kinship system, kinship ties (to parents and "relatives") are more important than conjugal ties (the ties that bind the married couple). For this reason, the kinship network in the extended family-kinship system has authority, for example, over new family formations, with most marriages being "arranged," and also over the norms that govern the division of family roles and the socialization of children. The nuclear family-kinship system, in contrast, emphasizes conjugal ties. New family formation is based on a relatively free choice of marriage partners (without parental or kin control), and norms governing the division of marital roles and the socialization of children are determined to a larger extent than in the other system by the conjugal pair.

The Industrial Connection

In association with what is sometimes called the great transformation of the past few centuries, a transformation that included the rise of the state and nationalism, growing individualism, urbanization, industrialization, and economic development, a notable shift has taken place in many of the world's nations from the extended family-kinship system to the nuclear family-kinship system. This shift is what is being termed the global family trend. The association of social elements does not necessarily imply cause, however, and one must be careful not to jump too quickly to conclusions about the causes of this trend. Each type of family-kinship system is associated with certain cultural values, economic systems, and types of society. Yet the precise connections or linkages between family systems and other societal phenomena are extremely complex, still poorly understood, and subject to continuing (and often quite heated) debate among historians and social scientists. Among the thorniest and most unresolved of theoretical questions, for example, is the degree to which certain characteristics of the family-kinship system may be an important cause, rather than merely an effect, of such cultural and social phenomena as individualism and industrialization.[10] At the very least, one should be careful not to conclude that industrialization is *the cause* of family change.

The worldwide movement of family-kinship systems toward the nuclear form has been and continues to be extremely uneven with respect to geography, culture, social class, and time. In every society, the process starts from a different position on the continuum of family types. In this connection it should be kept in mind that the family systems of the West have been more nuclear than those of other major civilizations for 1000 years or more.[11] Also, family systems are moving toward the nuclear form at different rates of speed and not in a strictly unilinear fashion. For example, there is some evidence that kinship ties in Western societies were actually strengthened for a time following the Industrial Revolution. This strengthening of kinship ties also seems to be occurring today in some industrializing Third World nations.[12]

A number of scholars have argued that kinship ties in Western societies have strengthened again, more recently, in the post–World War II period. It is very important, however, to distinguish between three meanings of the term "kinship ties"[13]: (1) the extent to which extended kinship obligations and rights take precedence (have control) over their conjugal and nonkin-ship counterparts; (2) the extent of interdependence among nuclear families within kinship networks; and (3) the number of people encompassed in a person's web of kinship obligations and rights. The latter two dimensions of kinship are especially affected by economic and demographic considerations and have therefore fluctuated widely in time and space. The first dimension, however, which directly concerns cultural norms, is the one most fundamental to our typology, and this dimension clearly shows a gradual but essentially unilinear trend toward less-binding kinship connections. In modern societies, for example, kinship obligations and kinship control have without doubt become comparatively weak, while at the same time the members of these societies may still be in touch with a large number of kin by way of the advanced technologies of transportation and communication.

Another important distinction to be made using this typology has already been mentioned: that between the type of family-kinship system and the type of family as a domestic group or household. Not making such a distinction has been a source of great scholarly confusion over the past few decades. Extended-family domestic groups ("complex" households, consisting of relatives in addition to a married couple and their offspring) are assuredly more common in the extended family-kinship than in the nuclear family-kinship system, but they are found in both. And even within a strongly extended family-kinship system, extended-family households may not be the predominant family type; most households in the world may be, and possibly always have been, essentially nuclear. By the same token, nuclear-family domestic groups (consisting of a married couple and their immature children) are assuredly more common in the nuclear family-kinship than in the extended family-kinship system, but they have never been so common as to totally exclude extended-family groups.

Despite the numerous caveats that must be attached to any discussion of the family-kinship trend associated with industrialization, this trend is, I believe, one of the most securely known in the social sciences (which, in turn, preside over an area of knowledge with very low levels of security). As noted above, the trend is most clearly visible (and most analyzed) today in comparing less- and more-developed countries and in studying Third World development over time; contemporary economic and social development in the Third World to some extent mirrors the historical development in the West. The less-developed countries today are much more kinship oriented than are the advanced industrial societies, which are the most nuclear, and over the long-term nuclear familism grows with economic and social development. With industrialization now virtually worldwide, it is not unreasonable to argue that there is a steady, albeit sometimes faint and uneven, global trend toward worldwide convergence around the nuclear-family system—or what William J. Goode in his seminal book *World Revolution and Family Patterns* calls the "western conjugal family system."[14] By the trend toward the Western conjugal-family system Goode means not only a move in the direction of the nuclear family-kinship system, in our terms, but also a fainter and more uneven, yet unmistakable, move from complex extended or multifamily households to nuclear-family households.

The strength of the global trend toward the nuclear family-kinship system in the Third World today can be appreciated by reviewing some of Goode's propositions concerning what is highly likely *not* to occur with the continued advance of modernization and economic development.[15] We can confidently predict, he states, that over the long run there will be no continuing movement toward greater power in the hands of corporate kin groups such as clans and lineages; no steady increase in the authority of males (who have dominated in virtually all traditional kin networks); no steady growth in the percentage of marriages in which parents have a primary voice in the mate selections of their children; and no rise in the percentage of extended, multigenerational households.

Such predictions, of course, could ultimately prove to be wrong, but there is little empirical indication today that this trend, at least with respect to these dimensions, will change course or turn back on itself in the forseeable future. At the same time, it should be stressed that much of the world is still located quite far along the continuum in the direction of kinship domination, and worldwide social resistances to family nucleation remain very powerful. The leaders of traditional family-kinship systems do not give up their power easily or willingly.

A Note on the Evolution of Family-Kinship Systems

If one looks not just at currently modernizing societies but at the full range of world societies, from tribal to highly developed, a slightly different picture of family change emerges. Taking this range of societies as a rough indication of long-term evolutionary development, there is evidence that some dimensions of the historical evolution of family-kinship systems have been curvilinear and that the recent trend of the family toward the nuclear form has in a sense brought the world full circle. In the words of Pierre van den Berghe, "advanced industrial societies have recreated, through a long evolutionary path, much the same kind of mobile, seminomadic, nuclear, bilateral family, minimally restricted by collateral relatives [and] by extended kin obligations . . . as existed in the simplest, smallest societies."[16]

The curvilinear trend becomes most evident in the fluctuation between extended and nuclear *households* (rather than the extent of kinship control). Nuclear households predominate in the "simpler societies," such as those based on hunting and gathering. These societies are unable to support complex households because of their particular ecologies, technologies, and economies.[17] Only when local economies become more sophisticated, for example, when they are based on settled agriculture (the stage at which most Third World industrializing societies are today), can the large, complex household be supported. Then, at a still later stage of development, the nuclear-family household again becomes predominant as societies move into the industrialized age. In Western nations, the shift from complex "back to" nuclear households, as we shall see in the next chapter, took place well before industrialization in many countries, and in at least one country,

England, comparatively few complex households seem to have existed during its entire period of recorded history.[18]

Despite this curvilinear trend in household composition, shifting from the nuclear to the extended form and back again, it is probably still the case that both in the recent history of family change and in long-run family evolution there has been a more-unilinear decline in the authority of kinship ties. The normative control of the kinship group over its members has tended to continuously weaken over time, and the concomitant social obligations of members to their extended kin network have also declined.[19] Archaeological evidence is much more adequate for making inferences about household size and composition than about the normative dimensions of extended-kinship relations.

Characteristics of the Nuclear Family-Kinship System

Because this book is concerned mainly with the nuclear pole of the continuum of family-kinship systems, it would be well to describe that end of the continuum here in greater detail. Reviewing what has already been discussed, we know, in view of its association with the evolutionary process of social differentiation, that the family unit in the nuclear family-kinship system generally has fewer functions than its extended-family counterpart. In connection with the Industrial Revolution most families lost their economic-production functions and became mainly consuming units; with the rise of mass education they lost part of their education functions; and so on. (In later chapters we discuss the degree to which modern families are still losing functions today.)

A second feature of the nuclear family-kinship system is that kinship ties, especially in terms of authority and control, become attenuated. There are comparatively few obligations and rights that members of extended kin groups can expect others in the group to observe. Kinship obligations and rights have given way to a great importance being placed on the conjugal bond between wife and husband and to a growing significance of nonkinship ties.

Beyond these fundamental dimensions are a host of associated traits that characterize the nuclear system as it has emerged, especially in advanced societies. Traits that directly relate to attenuated kinship ties are the relatively free choice of marriage partners; the establishment of "neolocal" residences separate from the kin groups on each side of the marriage; and the relatively free choice of norms for both the division of labor within the marriage and the socialization of children. As Goode has stated: "The ideology of the conjugal family proclaims the right of the individual to choose his or her own spouse, place to live, and even which kin obligations to accept, as against the acceptance of others' decisions. It asserts the worth of the *individual* as against the inherited elements of wealth or ethnic group."[20]

Not so obviously related to the attenuation of kinship authority is the relative equality of women in the nuclear family-kinship system. While the reasons for women's "liberation" go well beyond the changing nature of family forms, it is important to stress that virtually all extended family-kinship systems have been patriarchal in their authority structure. This means that a weakening of kinship structure involves at the same time a weakening of a patriarchal-authority structure. In the nuclear system, there is less subjugation of women, less sex segregation in the marital division of labor, and more development of bilineal descent—one that emphasizes both the male and the female line.

This weakening of the patriarchal-authority structure, in turn, is related to the family's loss of functions to other institutions in a society. The loss of the family's economic-production function proved especially consequential for female equality because it undercut the patriarchal domination that was associated with such production. Although it remains a topic of controversy among scholars, the loss of the family's production function in the industrialization of Western nations seems at first to have given at least middle-class women new authority in the home (albeit at some cost in regard to other dimensions of their lives), and much later it brought women into the labor market alongside men. The latter development, which has been very marked in the past few decades, is, of course, the one associated with womens' greatest egalitarian gains.

Other traits of the nuclear family-kinship system (these are all considered in detail later in this book) are the choice of marriage partners based on romantic love and the resulting highly affective or emotional quality of the conjugal bond; the relative autonomy of children and youth; low fertility levels and small family size; high geographic mobility; and a high level of divorce and family instability.

Beyond the Nuclear Family

The nuclear family-kinship system was described as a polar ideal type at one end of a continuum, within which the world's family systems can be classified, toward which historically all family systems have been moving. This family-kinship type has provided a theoretically useful "end state" for an understanding of family change around the world, especially in Third World nations. But how useful is it in analyzing family change in the advanced societies? Several advanced societies, after all, have been at or near the nuclear end of the continuum for a century or more. To be sure, in recent years, nuclear family-kinship systems in advanced societies have undergone major internal changes. And kinship networks have continued to wither away, certainly in terms of their normative dimension. In this sense, these societies have been gradually becoming slightly more nuclear over time. But the theoretical utility of thinking of advanced societies as gradually becoming more nuclear is rapidly diminishing. Such societies are reaching the point where they are about as nuclear as they can be, under any definition of the term. Unless one assumes that advanced nations will just sit at a nuclear end state indefinitely, which is an unlikely assumption, it becomes increasingly important to consider the next stages of family development.

What might follow the nuclear stage? There was the view, popular in the 1970s as an outgrowth of the utopian "new consciousness," in the 1960s, that not only traditional forms of kinship will continue to wither away and disintegrate, but also (all to the good, it was claimed) the nuclear family itself, together with the institution of marriage. These will be replaced, it was argued, by communal or collective forms of "family" that are not "founded on our old notions of marriage and kinship ties."[21] Thus it was suggested that a radical social discontinuity would come about. The trend toward individualism would come to an end, and people would choose to live in large, collective households containing "as many as 20 or 30 members, few of whom will be related as kin."[22] These new communal families were expected to bring with them dramatic increases in social stability and personal intimacy, as well as personal freedom and excitement ("friendship will replace kinship"). Needless to say now, this "great social experiment" proved to be one of the great social failures of its time, and few of the communes that were set up during the period have survived. There is virtually no evidence that communal living will become an important alternative to the nuclear family, at least not in America. In Sweden, as we shall see, there are only a few weak tendencies in that direction.

Another viewpoint, derived from the 1960s and 1970s and still alive today, assumes vaguely that the nuclear family-kinship system does not actually predominate in advanced societies after all or, even if it does, that this system is being replaced by a "plural-family system." This viewpoint is based partly on the empirical finding that every society in the world contains a multitude of family (household) types and that strong resistances to the development of the nuclear family-kinship system exist everywhere.[23] In part, this view also constitutes an ideological attack on the nuclear-family model as "a normative ideal," taking the position that many other family forms (such as single-parent families) can be "just as good" as the nuclear family. The plural-family-system perspective has utility in stressing that there is greater household complexity in any society than most glib generalizations suggest; it has less utility in providing a real handle for the understanding of family change.

Based on the acceptance of empirical evidence supporting the validity of the global family trend and positing no radical social discontinuities, a better hypothesis about the future of family development is that advanced societies are moving beyond the nuclear-family end of the continuum, but on a path that represents a logical continuation of the global family trend.[24] It is not clear how far or how fast advanced societies will move along this path, but a new end state can be envisioned; one can call it a postnuclear-family system. A scenario of developments leading to a postnuclear-family system, based on the logical extension of existing trends, can best be described in the following way. The extended kin group will weaken further and eventually become a negligible force in society. The nuclear-family group itself will become curtailed, as people, pursuing the value of individualism, become less and less embedded in it. Instead of being arranged, marriages will move to the opposite extreme and will cease to have any social or legal form at all; more adult sexual and social relationships could come to be random liaisons. Norms of gender roles and socialization would mainly be determined by the two or more parties in a relationship. Finally, but unlikely, societies could become so socially differentiated and specialized, and the nuclear family so weak, that child rearing is taken over by agencies outside the family, such as those controlled by the state.

Thus if the global family trend is logically extended in terms of continued evolutionary social differentiation and additional freedom from traditional cultural ties, one eventually reaches the end of the nuclear family and family-kinship systems as they have been known historically. There seem to be only two fixed points in the postnuclear end state in such a proposed scenario. The adults in any society will presumably continue to relate sexually to one another in some fashion, although it need not be within the confines of anything that resembles the historical family. And, if the society is to survive, some way must be found to bear and raise children. Women will presumably continue to bear the children (although extrauterine childbearing could eventually become possible), but these women, and the biological fathers, need not necessarily raise their offspring themselves.

No society today, of course, is anywhere near this extreme point. Still, since the global family trend is empirically well founded there is considerable intellectual merit in speculating about the extension of this trend into the future. At the very least, it is worth examining empirically the dimensions of family change in advanced societies today to see to what degree these changes may correspond to postnuclear tendencies.

In pursuing these theoretical abstractions here, however, we have gotten well ahead of our analysis; the possibility of a postnuclear trend is examined in Chapter 13. In the next chapter a detailed summary is presented of one piece of the global family trend—the emergence in Western Europe and America over the past few centuries of what Goode has called the "Western conjugal family system" and historians have labeled the "modern nuclear family."

Notes

[1]For example, Bernard Campbell (1985), *Human Evolution.*

[2]Robin Fox (1983), *Kinship and Marriage:* 15.

[3]See Talcott Parsons (1966), *Societies: Evolutionary and Comparative Perspectives;* Gerhard Lenski and Jean Lenski (1987), *Human Societies;* Pierre L. van den Berghe (1979), *Human Family Systems: An Evolutionary View;* and Robert M. Marsh (1967), *Comparative Sociology.*

[4]For example, Robert A. Nisbet (1969), *Social Change and History.* But see also Lenski's answer to Nisbet's antievolutionary views: Gerhard Lenski (1976), "History and Social Change," *American Journal of Sociology.* 82-3:548-564.

[5]For example, Carle C. Zimmerman (1947), *Family and Civilization:* Chapters 14–17.

[6]See Zimmerman, *ibid.,* and Pitirim Sorokin (1937), *Social and Cultural Dynamics.*

[7]For an excellent general introduction to the topic, see Robin Fox (1983), *Kinship and Marriage.* Fox has suggested (p. 10) that at least half of all anthropology literature has been devoted to the study of kinship. For an example of the current technical debates within anthropology, and especially the degree to which kinship is culturally based, see David M. Schneider (1984), *A Critique of the Study of Kinship.* For a review of the related area of "family and household," see Sylvia Junko Yanagisako (1979), "Family and Household: The analysis of domestic groups," pp. 161–205 in *Annual Review of Anthropology.*

[8]For intermediate types, a good typology has been put forth by Bert N. Adams (1986), *The Family: A Sociological Interpretation:* Chapter 5.

[9]C. C. Harris (1983), *The Family and Industrial Society:* 93. I am indebted to Harris for several of the distinctions made in this section.

[10]A fascinating contribution to this debate as it relates to the effect of family forms on political systems is Emmanuel Todd (1985), *The Explanation of Ideology: Family Structures and Social Systems.*

[11]Jack Goody (1983), *The Development of the Family and Marriage in Europe.*

[12]See Bernard C. Rosen (1982), *The Industrial Connection: Achievement and the Family in Developing Societies.* For a review of anthropological findings, see Yanagisako (1979), "Family and Household": 1981–82.

[13]Marsh (1967), *Comparative Sociology:* 72.

[14]William J. Goode (1970), *World Revolution and Family Patterns.* See also Alex Inkeles (1980), "Modernization and Family Patterns: A Test of Convergence Theory," pp. 31–63 in Dwight W. Hoover and John T. A. Koumoulides, (eds.), *Conspectus of History: Family History I–VI.*

[15]These are summarized in William J. Goode (1980), "The Resistance of Family Forces to Industrialization," pp. ix–xviii in John M. Eekelaar and S. N. Katz (eds.), *Marriage and Cohabitation in Contemporary Societies.*

[16]Van den Berghe (1979), *Human Family Systems:* 132.

[17]The main source for this within sociology is the work of Winch. See Robert F. Winch (1977), *Familial Organization: A Quest for Determinants.* Chapter 5 of this book reviews the anthropological literature on the issue.

[18]Alan Macfarlane (1979), *The Origins of English Individualism.*

[19]See Marsh (1967), *Comparative Sociology:* 72–82.

[20]Goode (1970), *World Revolution:* 19.

[21]Robert Thamm (1975), *Beyond Marriage and the Nuclear Family:* 112. This book is a good example of a large genre and one that focuses more than most on family change.

[22]*Ibid.:* 121.

[23]Luis Lenero-Otero (ed.) (1977), *Beyond the Nuclear Family Model.* This is a collection of papers given at the 1974 World Congress of Sociology in Toronto.

[24]My thinking here has profited from the theoretical schemes contained in Chapter 5 of Adams (1986), *The Family.*

The Rise and Fall in the West of the Modern Nuclear Family

The historical emergence of the "modern nuclear family" represents, in the words of Lawrence Stone, "one of the most significant transformations that has ever taken place, not only in the most intimate aspects of human life, but also in the nature of social organization."[1] The modern nuclear family is the family type that came to social and cultural predominance in association with the Industrial Revolution in the nations of the West. It was constituted by the monogamous, relatively patriarchal family, consisting of a married couple living with their children, the man working outside of the home and the woman being a mother and full-time housewife. The marital union tended to be lifelong, and divorce was uncommon. Although life spans were short by today's standards, most people lived in such family households for the greater portion of their lives. The family attempted to achieve and maintain, even if not always successfully, an intimate, protective environment in which the principal goal was to provide nurture and care for its members. Referring both to the historical period in Britain during which, some maintain, it reached its zenith and to the social class with which it is most strongly identified, this family type is sometimes called the Victorian, bourgeois family.

The field of family history has been burgeoning in the past few decades, and there is a wealth of information (but also much scholarly controversy) on which to draw. One point of confusion in reviewing the history of the Western family is that the family type labeled "modern" by family historians is regarded by most people today as the "traditional" family. It is the image people have in mind when they say "the family today isn't what it used to be." The time frame for these popular images seldom goes back very far in history: the period within living memory, perhaps two or three generations, 100 years at most. This coincides with the general time frame of the modern nuclear family, which has been predominant in the West only for most of the past 100 years, if not entirely as a behavioral reality, then certainly as a cultural ideal. At the start of this time period the modern nuclear family was more common in the middle and upper classes, in which it originated (according to most scholars), but by the mid-twentieth century it had become nearly universal in Western nations.

The Preindustrial Western Family

The nuclear or conjugal family-kinship system toward which there is a worldwide trend, as discussed in the preceding chapter, first arose and became dominant in the Western world. Late preindustrial (early modern) societies in western Europe shared many of the basic social and economic characteristics of other parts of the world at that time and of the developing world today. They were in the main rural societies based on subsistance agriculture, with productive activities customarily carried out in and by households rather than at separate work places specialized for that purpose. They had relatively high fertility and mortality rates, leading to a very young age structure (with more than 44% of the population under age 20.)[2] Yet it is now known that the family systems of preindustrial societies in western Europe were unique. Why and when these societies broke away from the rest of the world to lead the trend toward the nuclear family are questions that are currently the subjects of scholarly ferment and debate. Knowledge about the origins of "the Western family" is still in very short supply, and unfortunately, in view of its intrinsic interest, a review of what is known lies well beyond the scope of this book.[3] The main features of this then historically new family form, however, are no longer so much in doubt. They have been reasonably well established by the scholarship of the past few decades.[4]

Recent scholarships has brought about a considerable reshaping of common perceptions of the family in Western history. Many Western scholars, such as the nineteenth-century French sociologist of the family, Le Play, as well as notable early-twentieth-century Americans, gave support to the rather fond look backward of the average person at what is now often called "the classical family of Western nostalgia": a large, rural, self-sufficient, patriarchal, extended household made up of many generations.[5] Associated with a peasant society, this family type was commonly thought to have been predominant right up to the Industrial Revolution, which, in turn, was said to have severely undercut it. (Usually a part of this conception was the belief that the preindustrial extended family was a harmonious and fulfilling group for its members, in contrast to the cold, isolated, and unfulfilling nuclear family that the Industrial Revolution presumably left in its wake.)

Probably the main conclusion to be drawn from recent historical scholarship on the family is that major aspects of this "classical Western family," to the degree that they ever existed, died out in portions of Europe well before the Industrial Revolution and, indeed, that the nuclear family is now seen to be as much a cause as a consequence of industrialization.[6] Thus the peasant family steeped in extended-kinship ties has not been a part of Western culture for centuries, and family conditions in the Third World today bear little resemblance to the situation in Europe in the period before the Industrial Revolution. Alan Macfarlane (not without serious academic challenge) maintains that in England, which seems to have been the leader in the historical advance of the nuclear-family system as well as the pioneer of the Industrial Revolution, a truly peasant society with an extended family system may, in fact, *never* have existed.[7]

Size and Composition

What were the structural characteristics of the Western family system in the few centuries before the Industrial Revolution that made it so different from the rest of the world? There is, to be sure, so much diversity in western Europe that any discussion of "the Western family" must be heavily qualified. Life in England in 1700, for example, was quite different from life in rural Austria or Sweden. Different national histories, geographies, and levels of development make generalization difficult and general conclusions misleading. Nevertheless, in northwest Europe in the seventeenth and eighteenth centuries, certain common and distinctive attributes of the family system have been identified that distinguish this region from eastern and Mediterranean Europe, as well as most of the rest of the world.[8] (Northwest Europe refers here to northern France, the low countries, the German-speaking areas of central Europe, as well as the British Isles and Scandinavia.)

As summarized by the scholar who has played the leading role in developing "the new demographic history," Peter Laslett, the most important of the distinctive family-system attributes that marked northwest Europe were a proportionately large number of nuclear-family households, with very few households consisting of relatives in addition to a married couple and their offspring; a relatively late age for marriage and childbirth, with a significant percentage of the population not marrying at all; only a few years separating the ages of husband and wife; and the presence of servants in a large portion of households.[9] These family and household attributes, he suggests, are highly likely in turn to have been causally associated in complex ways with such social and cultural facts as weak kinship authority, less rigid segregation of the sexes and greater equality for women, and more personal freedom, to say nothing of the rise of Western individualism and of capitalism and industrialization.[10]

Historical demographer J. Hajnal has put forth in some detail a useful conceptualization that contrasts the family- and household-formation process characteristic of the nuclear family system of late preindustrial northwest Europe with its counterpart in such places as China and India, as well as other parts of Europe, which featured a more extended family system.[11] First, in northwest Europe the average age of first marriage for men was over 26 and for women over 23, compared to women less than 21 in most other parts of the world. Because it runs counter to common beliefs about the traditional European family, this comparatively late age of marriage has been called by Lawrence Stone "the most startling and significant finding of the past two decades of [family] demographic history."[12] Apparently, it was true of almost all segments of the population, including the lower classes. Second, newly married couples tended to take charge of their own households, rather than become a part of households in which older couples were in charge, which was the normal pattern in extended family systems. And third, young people before marriage often circulated among households as servants, whereas in extended family systems servants were much less needed because of the presence of relatives.

These three features of the nuclear family system, Hajnal suggests, had far-reaching implications for other aspects of life and social structure. For women, later marriages led to a lower birthrate by pushing back the time of the first conception. It also permitted more young adult females to be in the work force, which in turn gave these women a greater opportunity to create some wealth of their own. This not only meant that they could bring a greater maturity to their marriages, but it also made it more likely that the young married couple could maintain a separate household and be self-sufficient. These characteristics, again, are associated with weaker kinship structure, less gender-role segregation, and greater equality between men and women.

Hajnal and also Peter Laslett stress the great importance of servants in this family system. Servants were an essential component of many preindustrial European households and were not merely (as we think of servants today) "people ministering to the personal comforts of the more prosperous section of the population."[13] They lived as integrated members of the household, usually participated in common meals, and shared in the household's productive tasks. Becoming a servant was merely a premarriage stage of the life cycle for many, leading Peter Laslett to refer to them as "life-cycle servants."[14] There was no notion of inferiority connected with the position, and most servants eventually married and went on to other things.

According to estimates by Hajnal, well over 50% of all adolescents and young adults in some areas, mostly the children of farmers, entered service at some point in their lives. Many but not most were relatives (nephews, nieces, and cousins) of members of the households in which they served, but servants generally worked under short-term contracts and tended to circulate among households.[15] Hajnal notes that "it seems highly probable that the circulation of servants made possible the late age of marriage, for service provided a function for young unmarried adults."[16] Also, he points out, one reason for the servant system to begin with was the need of newly married couples living in separate households apart from their parents, brothers, and sisters, for additional help. In general, the servant system allowed for a rather adjustable labor force, with households being able to expand and contract based on changing work loads.

The Distribution of Nuclear-Family Households

Just how widely distributed were nuclear-family households in preindustrial northwest Europe? This question has generated one of the grand historical debates of the recent decades. Triggered by a group of demographic historians at Cambridge University, led by Peter Laslett, the debate was initiated after careful analyses of community records drawn from a variety of European, but mainly English, villages had found no areas in which more than one quarter of the households contained relatives outside of the conjugal family (not counting servants.)[17] Also, the findings showed that the average size of the Western household had not changed very much over the past few hundred years, remaining at approximately 4.75 in England throughout the seventeenth, eighteenth, and nineteenth centuries (compared to about 2.5 today). It was such findings that caused Laslett to conclude that the classical extended-family household may never have been the predominant form in preindustrial Europe.

Peter Laslett's early generalizations have since been modified as the evidence comes in from a wider range of European nations. Large extended or complex households were more common among the preindustrial rural peasants of central Europe and Scandinavia than they were in England, northern France and the Low Countries. Laslett has summarized the main differences in the histories of family and kinship between England and Central Europe that help to account for these variations. He emphasizes the earlier fading away of the traditional social order in England, and he points out that there was more economic and social individualism in England, even during medieval times, than had been thought.[18] (Outside of the northwest region, in southern Europe and Russia, complex households were even more prevalent.)

Nevertheless, Michael Mitteraurer and Reinhard Sieder in a chapter from their informative book *The European Family,* entitled "The Myth of the Large Pre-Industrial Family," can confidently state:

> In so far as present research allows us to compare European families, it may be said that multi-generational families and others with living-in relations were relatively rare during pre-industrial times in large regions of Western and Central Europe. . . . It cannot be maintained, therefore, that the dominant family form of

pre-industrial times was the large family community in which several generations lived together.[19]

In the Austrian countryside, for example, they found that "three-generational families were almost entirely lacking among the lower classes," although they also noted that households in preindustrial Austria tended to be relatively large because of the large number of servants.[20]

The northwest European family's "exceptionalism" in preindustrial times is typically attributed to unique cultural and geographic factors. Two reasons are commonly put forward to explain the low percentage of complex households. Impartible inheritance practices (usually primogeniture) forced sons who did not inherit anything to leave home. And intense cultivation and strict allocation of village lands made the coresidence of more than two generations very difficult for economic reasons.[21]

There is a more prosaic reason why large, complex households might never have existed in any region of Europe in large numbers: people did not live long enough for such households to develop. The high adult mortality rates alone could account for most of the absence of elderly parents. This fact would also help to explain why, in view of declining death rates, there seems to have been a slight increase in three-generation households with the onset of the Industrial Revolution.[22]

For such basic demographic reasons, in fact, nuclear family households seem to have predominated in strictly numerical terms in many parts the world, even in today's developing countries.[23] Also, studies of the preindustrial household in many parts of the world suggest that household sizes in most areas average around five members, no matter what the family and kinship system. It is worth noting that household size in most preindustrial situations is heavily determined by the need for labor (the household being the primary production unit). Because that need is relatively constant, household size necessarily changes little over time, even though there may well be a constant ebb and flow of different people through the household.[24]

Evidence has been uncovered that many European households might have been extended for at least some portion of their life cycle, especially at the time when surviving parents retired and the eldest son took over the property.[25] And it may well have been the case that, while most households at any single point in time did not contain a third generation, most grandparents who were still alive continued to live with their children. None of these findings, however, has so far seriously challenged the basic conclusion that the Western family system was well along the path toward nucleation before the Industrial Revolution and thus was significantly ahead of other parts of the world with respect to the global family trend.

The Character of the Preindustrial Western Family

Quality of Family Life in Preindustrial Europe

The debate over the size and composition of the preindustrial European household, however, has to some extent masked our knowledge of the profound family changes that actually did take place with the rise of "the modern family" during the late preindustrial period. Even if no great change has occurred in household size and composition over the past three or four centuries, there most assuredly has been a massive change in family functions, in the relations between the family and the community, and probably in the character of family life. Indeed, it is the changes in these areas that Lawrence Stone has called "one of the most significant transformations that has ever taken place," at the same time suggesting that the continuity of family size and composition is "true but trivial."[26]

In the quality of its family life, as we discuss below, the modern nuclear family that rose to importance in the eighteenth century was emotionally intense, relatively egalitarian in authority structure, privatized, child oriented, and individualistic in the sense of stressing individual autonomy and rights. In contrast, the preindustrial family is thought by some scholars to have been relatively emotionless, open and undifferentiated from the society around it, and patriarchal. In the words of Lawrence Stone again, there was a radical shift between the two family types from a quality of "distance, deference, and patriarchy" to what he labels "affective individualism."[27]

Stone's analysis of the changing character of the family in the early modern period has probably been more influential than the work of any other historian, although it has not stood without serious scholarly challenge and focuses only on England and even there mostly on the higher classes. He views the English family before the late sixteenth century as

> an open-ended, low-keyed, unemotional, authoritarian institution . . . it was neither very durable nor emotionally or sexually very demanding. . . . Lacking firm boundaries [it] was open to support, advice, investigation and interference from outside, from neighbors and kin, and internal privacy was nonexistent.[28]

By the eighteenth century the family among the higher classes had evolved to what he calls "the closed domesticated nuclear family" of the modern era, "the first family type in history which was both long-lasting and intimate."[29] Since then, this new family type has diffused downward to the lower classes and has become nearly universal in advanced societies.

How could the family be changing so much internally when its external characteristics, such as size and structure seemed to remain very much the same throughout the Industrial Revolution? Edward Shorter in *The Making of the Modern Family* puts it this way: "The [modern] nuclear family is a state of mind rather than a particular kind of structure or set of household arrangements. . . . What really distinguishes the nuclear family . . . from other patterns of life in Western society is a special sense of solidarity that separates the domestic unit from the surrounding community."[30] Even if one wishes to question the use of the phrase "state of mind" to refer to the complex cultural and social realities involved, Shorter nevertheless has pointed here to something fundamental: that the rise of the modern family is associated with a drastic change in the relationship between families and the communities that contained them.

Almost all historians agree that "in the sixteenth century the notion of the nuclear group as a clearly differentiated unit, with a recognized right to maintain its differentiation through norms of privacy, was absent among almost all sections of the population."[31] As a contemporary sociologist would put it, the family was thoroughly embedded in the community; the social wall surrounding the individual family was extremely porous. The family had little normative structure apart from that of the community, and the community's scrutiny of family members, made easier by the small size of most communities, was a powerful form of social control. As Shorter has stated, with some exaggeration, "such was the tyranny of this community scrutiny that a family's interior life would be mobilized to the all-consuming purpose of preparing a face to meet the faces they would meet in the surrounding community."[32]

As one might suppose, this kind of social situation probably impaired the development of what we now think of as the emotions and sentiments of the modern family. The lack of family privacy extended to personal privacy within the home, which was almost nonexistent. Also, family members often had much stronger social and emotional ties outside the family, especially with peers, than they did with other family members. Stone has even claimed, although the claim has been widely challenged, that preindustrial-family members showed a markedly low level of affection for one another and that within the family "there was a general psychological atmosphere of distance, manipulation and deference."[33] Stone suggests further that this emotional tone of family life was not significantly different from the character of the culture around the family, which was cold, suspicious, violence-prone, and organized mainly in terms of authority, deference, obligation, and self-interest.[34]

These qualitative characteristics of the preindustrial family naturally extended to the function of spouse selection and influenced the character of the marital bond. Marriage partners were selected mainly in terms of economic criteria, with the choice largely controlled by both families and the community, and the marital bond itself was seen much more in economic and reproductive terms than in emotional ones. In the words of Shorter (who, some historians think, portrays too bleak a picture):

> . . . popular marriage in former centuries was usually affectionless, held together by considerations of property and lineage . . . the family's arrangements for carrying on the business of living enshrined this coldness by reducing to an absolute minimum the risk of spontaneous face-to-face exchanges between husband and wife . . . and . . . this emotional isolation was accomplished through the strict demarcation of work assignments and sex roles."[35]

Married women in many preindustrial families had considerable authority, for what it was worth, over their own households and domestic activities. At the same time, they were full partners in the household economy, helping to produce goods for both production and consumption.[36] Yet the evidence suggests Shorter is close to the truth when he states that

> because the woman's spheres were largely removed from contact with the outside market economy, she had little leverage upon her husband. . . . The roles she was obliged to perform in relation to him and the outside world were all inferior, subjugated ones, in which the autonomy she enjoyed within the domestic sphere did her no good.[37]

Stone emphasizes that at least for English families of the higher social classes patriarchy and paternal domination in the domestic sphere actually became stronger in the period from 1500 to 1700. The domination of kinship and lineage (which to some extent held in check the power of individual male family heads) weakened during this time and was gradually replaced by a situation in which power devolved in two directions—toward a more centralized state and toward individual families.[38] He posits a family stage during this period called "the restricted patriarchal nuclear family"—an intermediate stage between what he terms the traditional "open lineage family" and the modern family. It resulted from a decline in loyalty and obligations toward kinship networks and local communities and a rise in obligations toward the more centralized institutions of the state and church.[39]

The Situation of Children

To complete the picture of the preindustrial family, we must look at the situation of children. If the position of women at that time was grim, by the accounts of many scholars that of children was grimmer still. Even more than in regard to adult relationships, however, our knowledge of the character of preindustrial parent–child relations and of childhood is based on evidence that is scant and fragmentary (mostly from Britain and France), and controversy over this question is heated. Some of our knowledge, for example, comes from psychohistorians, whose work was dismissed in one authoritative review of approaches to the history of the Western family with the following statement:

> [This approach] seems . . . to have run into insoluble problems of evidence, and to have involved its practitioners in so much anachronistic judgment and blatant disregard for many of the basic principles of historical scholarship that I have not thought it worth detailed consideration here.[40]

One of the most influential historians of childhood and the man who is even given credit for launching the study of the family in modern historical analysis is the late Philippe Ariès. The general viewpoint expressed in his *Centuries of Childhood: A Social History of Family Life,*[41] first published in French in 1960, is that childhood was not treated as a separate stage of life until the seventeenth and eighteenth centuries. Rather, children past infancy were not clearly distinguished from adults. As soon as they could walk and talk they entered adult society, dressing and working like adults. Childhood was not a time in which children were to be protected, cared for, and taught. For the most part, Ariès believed, before entering the adult world, children were treated with indifference.

Ariès did not view this indifference in a negative light, however, and he hastened to add that it "is not to suggest that children were neglected, forsaken or despised."[42] Indeed, Ariès believed that the traditional child was generally happy, because he or she was free to mix with many classes and ages. The modern "invention of childhood" is seen by him as having deprived children of spontaneity and freedom and subjected them to a tyranny of regulations, moral controls, and punishments by elders. As Stone summarizes Ariès' thesis, "it is a pessimistic one of degeneration from an era of freedom and sociability to an era of oppression and isolation."[43]

Ariès's qualitative assessment of the evolution of childhood has been widely disputed by other scholars, although there is some agreement on the broad structural changes over time that he posited. A more common view is the one expressed in the often-repeated phrase of psychohistorian Lloyd deMause that "the history of childhood is a nightmare from which we have only recently begun to awaken."[44] He continues: "The further back in history one goes, the lower the level of child care, and the more likely children are to be killed, abandoned, beaten, terrorized, and sexually abused." Shorter seems generally to agree with this point of view, stating that "good mothering is an invention of modernization" and referring to traditional child-rearing practices as "the ghastly slaughter of the innocents."[45]

The quality of child rearing at this time, of course, must have varied tremendously among families, just as it does today. And it is not clear to what degree traditional child-rearing practices were based in what we would today regard as psychological misinformation, in economic necessity, or even in malice. A number of scholars have concluded, however, that the bond between parent and child was, like the bond between adults, lacking in affect and emotionality and possibly in love. Shorter, for example, suggests "a traditional lack of maternal love" and a "frozen emotionality."[46] And Stone concludes:

> The cruel truth . . . may be that most parents in history have not been much involved with their children, and have not cared much about them. . . . Most children in history have not been loved or hated, or both, by their parents; they have been neglected or ignored by them.[47]

The effects of these child-rearing attitudes and practices are even more open to speculation. Stone suggests, for example, that there was:

> a "psychic numbing" which created an adult world of emotional cripples, whose primary responses to others were at best a calculating indifference and at worst a mixture of suspicion and hostility, tyranny and submission, alienation and rage.[48]

Revisionist works have recently begun to challenge these theories of the history of childhood that children in the past, compared to the present, were neglected and treated cruelly. One study states that "there is little basis in fact for believing that the parents of Reformation Europe loved their children any less or mistreated them any more than modern parents do."[49] Another finds much more harmony and continuity in child rearing between past and present.[50] At the very least, such works show how little certainty there really is about the quality of family life in times past.

The Rise of the Modern Family: Causes of Change

What could have caused the great transformation from the preindustrial family, seemingly a cauldron of base human passions and motivations no matter what its structure, to the modern family, a "precious emotional fortress"[51] against the outside world, characterized by the dignity of the individual, love and concern for others, and the pursuit of happiness? The attempt to briefly summarize here such a vast area of scholarship is steeped in risk; nevertheless some key points must be made to round out this historical portrait.

First, let us return for a moment to the size and composition of the Western family. It is reasonable to say that with modernization almost everything about the Western household changed, *except* its size and composition. Yet even its size changed by perhaps 25% or more, a not unsubstantial amount, and its composition changed also, despite the continuing absence of family members from three generations. Essentially, during the historical period within which the Industrial Revolution took place the household or domestic unit became one in which only the nuclear-family members resided. Servants gradually secured jobs outside of the domestic unit, and boarders, lodgers, family members reaching adulthood, and the few remaining grandparents were mostly able to set up their own separate households. At the same time, changes in the exigencies of the family as a work unit permitted a wider diversity of household and family types, which generated the rise of "incomplete" families and single-person households.[52] These trends are still prevalent in our own day, and our times have experienced a rapid decrease in household size that is associated with falling birthrates, rising incomes, and a growing diversity of household types.

Also associated with the Industrial Revolution was an increase in nuclear-family households with a more stable composition. The preindustrial household had had a constant turnover of members, the result of high mortality rates, children going into service, and short-run changes in productive work loads. In the household of later historical time, the smaller unit of parents and children, members lived together for a much longer period of time than they had formerly. This new stability of composition presumably provided an important structural basis for the further development of such modern family attitudes and feelings as privacy, intimacy, and companionship.[53]

Loss of Economic Functions

Probably the most important, or at least the most widely analyzed and discussed, societal change that helped to bring about the modern nuclear family was economic: the change in the nature and location of work. Many families in the world today are still what the preindustrial family typically was in Europe: a relatively self-sufficient agricultural production unit in a mostly subsistence economy, in which work life takes place in and around the home and involves the participation of every family member. The most radical (but gradual) change brought about most forcefully by the Industrial Revolution, though preceding it in preindustrial cities and towns and "protoindustrialized" rural situations, was the movement of work outside the home and of one or more family members working for someone else and participating in a wage economy.[54]

Thus the household and family gradually changed over time from a production unit to a unit of consumption. This change had far-reaching ramifications for almost all other aspects of family life. In functional terminology, the most important of these ramifications was that, relieved of the productive function, the family could devote more time and energy to two other main functions or activities: caring for and socializing children and providing adult members with companionship and emotional support. These two functions are regarded by sociologists today as the family's continuing reason for being. Most scholars have concluded that in the modern, nuclear family these functions have been conducted at a far higher level of quality (and equality) than ever before.

Without its productive function and with the separation of work and home, the household became not only somewhat smaller, more stable, and more intimate, but gradually also less patriarchal. As the authors of *The European Family* put it, "The father lost his position as leader of the labour organization and, with it, the strongest institutional support for his authority over the members of the household."[55] The family ceased to be a rigidly hierarchical organization dominated by the male, an organization that originally had been made necessary by the family's incessant fight for survival as an economic unit. Also, persons who had previously been dependents now had the chance to become independent by earning an outside income. The change even reduced the importance of inheritance, which still further undermined the role of the male. These facts are often overlooked by those who stress only that the wife (at least in the middle classes) became removed from the world of work, hence lost a type of power in that respect.

The loss of the family's economic-production function that accompanied industrialization should be seen in the context of the historical evolution of the family discussed in the preceding chapter. Long before the Industrial Revolution the family-kin group had been losing functions to superordinate social structures. Religious functions had moved to organized religious bureaucracies, for example, and judicial-protective functions—to the state. Nor was the function of economic production the only one that the family lost during the Industrial Revolution. Many "impersonal" institutions took over activities that formerly had been mainly the family's responsibility, such as, in the words of Lawrence Stone, "poorhouses for the indigent, alms houses for the old, hospitals for the sick, schools for the children, banks for credit, and insurance companies for protection against catastrophe."[56] Even in our time, there remains a widely discussed loss of one of the family's remaining functions—socialization—to schools and other elements of the larger society. The loss to the family of the economic-production function, however, may have been the most socially consequential loss of all, partly because these consequences were enhanced by many other widespread social changes taking place at the same time.

Cultural Factors

A number of scholars, among them Stone and Shorter, see the main cause of family change not in the economic transitions associated with the Industrial Revolution but in a general transformation of the "collective consciousness" or cultural ethos of society. Although this perspective is not without its scholarly detractors, it is worth discussing in some detail. As a basic premise, this perspective typically stresses that the modern nuclear family predated the Industrial Revolution by many years.

Shorter devotes only 14 pages to the reasons for family change in his widely read 300-page book, *The Making of the Modern Family,* noting that "attempts to explain why such things happened must be very speculative indeed."[57] It is Shorter's thesis that the modern family came about mainly through a "change in sentiments." He suggests that:

> [the rise of] romantic love detached the couple from communal sexual super-
> vision and turned them towards affection, [and the growth of maternal love]
> created a sentimental nest within which the modern family would ensconce it-
> self, and . . . domesticity beyond that sealed off the family as a whole from its
> traditional interaction with the surrounding world.[58]

He defines "domesticity" as "the family's awareness of itself as a precious emotional unit that must be protected with privacy and isolation from outside intrusion."[59]

The rise of these sentiments, in turn, is seen by Shorter as based in the emergence of market capitalism. While he does not overlook the structural changes associated with the emergence of market capitalism, such as wage labor and the separation of work and residence, it is on the ethos of market capitalism that Shorter appears to place the most emphasis. "The sexual and emotional wish to be free came from the capitalist marketplace," he suggests; "the logic of the market place positively demands individualism." "Egoism that was learned in the marketplace became transferred to . . . the whole domain of cultural rules that regulated familial and sexual behavior."[60] In contrast to Stone, Shorter believes that the new sentiments of romance and sexual freedom started first in the working classes, which, he thinks, were most directly affected by the ethos of early capitalism. The growth of maternal love and domesticity, however, he sees as emerging in the middle classes, primarily because of a higher material standard of living that was becoming prevalent in those classes.

Lawrence Stone's venture into noneconomic explanations for the rise of the modern family is far more extensive and has been far more influential than Shorter's. In close agreement with Shorter, he believes that the four key features of the modern family are

> intensified affective bonding of the nuclear core at the expense of neighbours
> and kin; a strong sense of individual autonomy and the right to personal freedom
> in the pursuit of happiness; a weakening of the association of sexual pleasure
> with sin and guilt; and a growing desire for physical privacy.[61]

He views all of these, in contrast to Shorter, as having first become established by 1750 in "key middle and upper sectors of English society," reaching down to the lower classes over time through a process of "stratified diffusion." The dominant change in ethos, in Stone's terms, was the rise of "affective individualism." By individualism Stone means "a growing introspection and interest in the individual personality" and "a demand for personal autonomy."[62]

"What needs explaining is not a change of structure, or of economics, or of social organization," states Stone, "but of sentiment."[63] In his explanation, he does not dismiss the effects of pleasure-seeking economic individualism brought about by market capitalism, but he emphasizes a concurrent transformation of meaning in both religion and politics. Greatly summarizing his argument, Stone regards as essential elements of this transformation the rise of Protestantism, with its stress on the individualistic nature of the relationship between man and God, and the decline of political absolutism, bringing about new concepts of the relationship between people and the state.

Similar noneconomic themes have been put forth in the work of other prominent family historians, such as Trumbach and Flandrin."[64] In his well-known *World Revolution and Family Patterns*, Goode reached conclusions along similar lines—that industrialization and changes in the family are somewhat parallel processes, each having been dependent on prior changes in ideology. The ideologies Goode emphasizes are a belief in economic progress, the worth of the individual, and egalitarianism, especially between the sexes.[65]

The Modern Nuclear Family in Summary

Broadly speaking, the family type that first arose in the West, became dominant there in the middle classes during the nineteenth century, and spread to other classes and regions in the twentieth century had a small, nuclear, and relatively stable demographic structure and was economically oriented toward consumption rather than production and increasingly isolated from the world of work. In character or in the quality of family life, it was emotionally intense, privatized, and child oriented; in authority structure, it became relatively egalitarian; and it placed high value on individualism in the sense of individual rights and autonomy.

This new family type not only became pervasive in Europe during the nineteenth century but prevalent in America as well. In his widely respected work *At Odds*, Carl N. Degler discusses "the modern American family" that emerged first between the American Revolution and about 1830. This new family type, he suggests, had several distinguishing characteristics.

> [First,] the marriage which initiated the modern family was based upon affection and mutual respect between the partners, both at the time of family formation and in the course of its life. The woman in the marriage enjoyed an increasing degree of influence or autonomy within the family.
> [Second,] the attention, energy and resources of parents in the emerging modern family were increasingly centered upon the rearing of their offspring. Children were now perceived as being different from adults and deserving not only of material care but of solicitude and love as well. Childhood was deemed a valuable period in the life of every person and to be sharply distinguished in character and purpose from adulthood. Parenthood thus became a major personal responsibility, perhaps even a burden.[66]

Third, Degler notes that the modern family was somewhat smaller than its predecessors, a factor that, he believes, had particular importance for the changing role of women.

Perhaps the most widely discussed aspect of this new family type has as yet barely been mentioned: the doctrine of the two spheres. This is something to which Degler gives particular importance in relation to the American scene, and it was just as significant in the European context. The doctrine of the two (or separate) spheres refers to the belief that married women should spend their life within the home, creating a domestic "nest" and looking after the well-being of their husbands and children, while married men should devote their time outside the home to earning a living for the family. This belief, made possible by rising affluence and the separation of work and home, had far-reaching implications for gender roles within the family and for the social position and valuation of women in general.

The doctrine of the two spheres went much beyond a mere division of labor within the home. As Degler stresses, married women were also given the assignment to be the moral guardians of their homes, responsible for the ethical and spiritual wholeness or being of family members.[67] These new "angels of the house" were generally perceived as morally superior to their husbands, even though they remained legally and socially inferior to them. In recent feminist scholarship, this moral role has tended to be denigrated as a combination of piety and domesticity, both repressive and limiting, which led women to ever more passive lives removed from the mainstream of human endeavor. But it should also be noted that it represented at the time elevation in the status of women, however modest, and a break from older social patterns in which men were judged superior to women in virtually every aspect of life.

Other characteristics of the modern family flow from this new role given to women. The home of the modern middle-class family became self-consciously privatized and cut off from public scrutiny and public life. At least ideally, it was to be an attractively decorated and furnished place of comfort and repose, a "bastion of intimacy" in which children could be protected and to which men could daily retreat from a turbulent outside world. It was to be a place where people could develop and lead their "real" lives as moral citizens; a place where "civilization" could most fertilely flourish.

In turn, this new privatized home became the center of sociability and social life, the latter having moved away from the streets and public places. Some scholars, such as Ariès, view this as a profound social loss, a decay of sociability. Because more activities were brought into the home, however, others see the change as an enrichment of family and private life. Surely there was something of a tradeoff; as Lawrence Stone has noted, community and privacy are antithetical needs that cannot be simultaneously maximized.

> The highly personalized, inward looking family was achieved in part at the cost of, and perhaps in part because of, a withdrawal from the rich and integrated community life of the past, with its common rituals, festivals, fairs, feast days and traditions of charity and mutual aid.[68]

However it is viewed, the new relationship between family and community provided the family still further opportunities to develop itself as an independent social unit, a place where personal development could occur within the confines of a small "primary" group, apart from the context of the larger community.

To meet these new demands for sociability and social life in a privatized environment, the house of the modern family became a center of material display.[69] In this the middle class was merely emulating what had long been a function of the house for the wealthy. The interior decoration of the new middle-class home was designed not only for the private comfort of its inhabitants, but also to show visitors that the family followed certain canons of taste and culture. A strong pride in one's home developed, and ultimately the house was to become in some segments of society more a place for status display than for personal comfort. All of this, of course, went hand in hand with a rising material standard of living.

The Fall of the Modern Nuclear Family

The allure of the modern nuclear family proved to be widespread, as we have emphasized, and these characteristics of home and family gradually grew to become the predominant ones in every Western nation. At the same time when this family type was spreading from the middle classes throughout all segments of the population, however, several of its major characteristics were already beginning to weaken or decline. The nation in which this decline has been steepest, as we shall see in the chapters that follow, is Sweden. Here it is useful to sketch the general dimensions of this decline and of the conditions in Western societies that precipitated it. The focus of this discussion is the Anglo-American nations.

The modern nuclear family had, by today's standards, a serious social flaw—the situation of women. Women in the new family form may have advanced in overall status, although this is arguable. Some scholars posit a status decline because of the removal of women from the productive work force; in becoming housewives, women lost some control over their working conditions.[70] Others, as noted above, suggest that women had gained in the process a kind of moral superiority and came to be seen as less unequal than before. Women in the modern nuclear family were regarded as having special virtues, in addition to the ability to bear children, that were essential to human progress. In America, in the words of Nancy Cott, "by 1830 'different' had overwhelmed 'inferior' in usage to depict woman's place."[71] It has also been pointed out that men were gradually becoming domesticated and held to a stricter standard of sexual fidelity within the marriage, perhaps adding further to women's status. The secure and sanctified bourgeois home, managed by a woman, became an object to which many men pledged great allegiance, presumably at the expense of their formerly pleasure-seeking, errant ways.

But whatever status women had gained undoubtedly carried with it some personal cost. With the privatization of family life, and through the doctrine of separate spheres, middle-class women became socially isolated within the family and mostly removed from public life, save for the occasional "volunteer" activity. In the early Victorian period women still had virtually no higher education and few legal rights; not much had changed in this regard. What they had definitely lost, however, was being a part of ongoing community life and the world of work. Expressly set aside from work life, the home and family had now become for many women their total community.

When families were large, parents and relatives lived nearby, and servants were plentiful, many dimensions of a rich community life could be duplicated within the privatized home. This "community life" could also be customized to personal taste. Women in such family settings at least did not suffer personal isolation. But as families grew smaller, relatives more distant, and servants more scarce, life within the home became less and less socially rewarding. And as the commute to work became longer, even the husband came to spend less time at home. The apogee of female social isolation and privatization may have been reached in the brief renaissance of modern nuclear familism in the late 1940s and the 1950s, discussed below, when such familism was linked in the Anglo-American nations with a low-density, suburban community pattern.

As the values of individualism, equality, and self-fulfillment gained pre-dominance in Western societies, the socially expected role of women in the bourgeois family became problematic. The rights granted to women to own property, to divorce, and to vote eventually became equivalent to those held by men and created strong pressures for female emancipation from the separate sphere. Furthermore, higher education for women suggested a working life that extended well beyond the confines of the home.

At the same time, the job market was changing.[72] Throughout the nineteenth century there had been a gradual increase in women's participation in the labor force, but of young, single women from the working classes and in low-status jobs, such as domestic and personal services. To most of these working women the homemaking life of the bourgeois woman seemed a significant improvement over their own lives. With the growing bureaucratization of government and industry, however, a wide range of nonmanual jobs for women emerged for the first time in history, giving middle-class women a strong incentive to enter the labor force. First culturally limited to single women before marriage, these jobs gradually grew in number and attracted married, middle-class women. Until well into the twentieth century, most white-collar jobs for women were found in certain heavily female occupations, such as teaching and secretarial work. Eventually, women were to make a push for full equality with males in virtually all occupational categories, a social change that is still in process today and whose final outcome is not yet clear.

In the face of the developments that followed the urbanization and industrialization of societies, then, the situation and role of women in the bourgeois home became untenable for many women. For those who were educated and wanted a larger role in public life, as well as an independent means of economic support, the bourgeois home was as much a prison as a seat of domestic bliss; it was a prison from which the man, but not the woman, was able to escape. The prisonlike quality was accentuated for the ·wife (and children) of a tyrannical husband, whose power and control were mostly unimpeded by local government or the state. For the unmarried, widowed, or divorced woman, a society based strictly in the privatized family home was hardly conducive to much happiness or self-fulfillment.

One of the most problematic aspects of the life of the Victorian middle-class women was in the sexual realm. After a certain degree of sexual liberation in the early modern period, the Victorian era instituted a return to a repression of sexuality almost without historical precedent.[73] Sex became normatively restricted to marriage for both sexes. This represented some advance for women in the decline of the double standard of sexual behavior, but sexuality also became a highly tabooed realm of behavior and discourse, and the moral superiority of women was in part gained through the denial of female sexuality. Good women were thought to be lacking the "carnal motivation" of men; those who showed sexual desire or participated in sexual activities with men outside of marriage were heavily stigmatized. At the same time, many men were never able to live up to the new moral bargain and carried on an active backstage life with prostitutes, a profession that thrived in Victorian times. All of this set the stage for the coming sexual revolution of the twentieth century, in which the double standard at last was dealt a damaging blow in practice as well as in theory.

The Family Renaissance of the 1950s

Many dimensions of family change that are often associated with the fall of the modern nuclear family were first in evidence in the nineteenth century. These include sharp drops in fertility and family size, an increase in divorce, and a shift away from the family in the balance between family (mainly paternal) rights and state power. Other dimensions, such as the movement of married women into the labor force and the growth of sexual permissiveness, became noteworthy in the first half of the twentieth century. Each of these aspects of family change has continued in recent decades, as is discussed in later chapters, and constitutes an indicator of a long-run family trend. The trend involves the demise of the doctrine of separate spheres, a growing instability of marital relationships, and some movement away from the central family focus of child rearing.

After World War II, however, a series of events took place in most Western societies that ran counter to this long-run trend. From the vantage point of today, these countermovements are properly viewed not as a significant modification of the long-run trend, but a temporary aberration. The birthrate rose to its highest point in decades, leading to a larger average family size; the marriage rate reached the highest level on record, with the average age at first marriage achieving a new low. After an initial postwar surge, the rising divorce rate leveled off and began to drop in many nations. And as women in large numbers took on the role of mother-homemaker, the increase of married women in the labor market diminished.[74] This was a time in which home, family, and marriage found high praise in popular opinion, and the traditional housewife-mother was again extolled as the keystone of a successful society.

To pidgeonhole these family events under the heading "the fifties" is not quite accurate, since the family renaissance of this time started in the late 1940s, and even in the early 1940s in Sweden, which remained neutral during the war and was not a combattant. The renaissance also spilled over into the early 1960s. But the 1950s was the decade in which countertrends to the modern nuclear family's decline reached a peak. Family growth immediately following the war was expected, the result of marriages that had been postponed by war and the Depression. What was unexpected was the duration of this effect; the birthrate did not peak in the United States until 1957, for example.

What had happened? One explanation, commonly put forward at the time the events were taking place, was that popular opinion had merely changed. According to this explanation the strong familism of the postwar years was a response to the trials and tribulations of the most extensive war that the world had ever known, which had followed a worldwide economic depression. People had developed from these experiences a strong need and desire to retreat into the sanctity of marriage, home, and family. A more recent explanation, suggested by several scholars, is that postwar familism was linked to the experiences of the Depression-born age cohort that was involved; the strong desire for families was created by some combination of the very low birthrates and economic insecurity during the Depression.[75]

Each of these explanations doubtless has some validity.[76] Yet to me the most plausible explanation for the postwar family resurgence relates not directly to the war, but to the fact that the postwar period was one of unparalleled affluence and upward mobility, at least in the countries that had not been militarily destroyed. This affluence gave the working classes the opportunity at last to achieve the bourgeois family ideal. The bourgeois ideal of the nonworking wife had at the time even more appeal to the working classes than to the middle classes, and the working classes also had a stronger preference for home centeredness and large families. With less education and access only to menial jobs, which they held out of economic necessity, the women of the working classes had long looked with envy at the role of the stay-at-home middle-class wife. They awaited the chance to achieve this role, and the grand goal of their husbands was to have the income to be able to give them that chance.

The postwar economic boom enabled large numbers of working-class families to achieve their middle-class dream. They at last had the economic resources to move in droves to the newly built suburban housing developments, where they could enjoy the life style that middle-class women were coming to reject. This life style included the privatized home, a place for the display of material consumption, and the devotion of the family to child rearing. Thus while the modern nuclear family was coming to be rejected by the old middle class, a new lower middle class had arisen, in which key dimensions of the bourgeois-family ideal achieved their most widespread social dispersion.

Recent Family Change

Beginning in the 1960s, the long-term trend away from the modern nuclear family again came to the fore and with such force that some have looked back on this period as the seedbed of a revolution in family life. Married women, including those with young children, moved into the labor market in record numbers. The divorce rate skyrocketed, the birthrate dropped precipitously, and the age at first marriage climbed. Sexual permissiveness achieved an unprecedented cultural hegemony. In the ensuing decades the doom of the modern nuclear family, in anything like its pure form, became effectively sealed.

In seeking to understand this social development, which apparently was led by the suburban middle class, it is important to recognize that the internal character and community habitat of middle-class suburban families of the 1950s were notably different from those of middle-class families in Victorian times. It is partly in these differences that the explanation for the widespread rejection in the 1960s of aspects of the modern nuclear family is to be found. In sharp contrast to the Victorian housewife, the housewife of the 1950s had full legal and citizenship rights, tended to be educated through the secondary-school level, and often had had labor force experience before marriage. Thus even though her family role bore a structural resemblance to the female role in the Victorian family, her relationship to her husband, position in society, and outlook on life were vastly different. Also, with other options available, her choice of becoming a housewife was more voluntary.

But perhaps the greatest difference between the middle-class home in the 1950s and its counterpart in Victorian times was in social character and ecological setting. Household size in the 1950s was smaller, the husband was away from home much of the time because of the long journey to work, and parents and other relatives often lived at some distance. The presence of servants had become a thing of the past. In terms of the number of people around the home during the day available to help out, this was a severely diminshed family. Child care was still the responsibility of the mother, but now of the lone mother, isolated from all others save for those in similar circumstances. It is true that laborsaving devices performed some of the more onerous tasks around the home, yet studies have shown that the amount of housework performed by the average housewife had not diminished significantly.[77] This is presumably due not only to the decline of help, but to higher standards of homecare; expectations had increased, and housewives were encouraged to reach ever greater levels of cleanliness and material display.

The home of the 1950s, therefore, proved to be an unpleasant environment for many women. Educated women felt trapped in a completely private world, isolated from life, at the same time that their husbands were engaged in an ever-more-salubrious world of work. The privatized home cut off from work may have still been what many women wanted; but they had not counted on a privatized home cut off from life, in which they, and they alone, were left to perform the not-always-stimulating tasks of home and child care.[78]

Also, the economy and job market were changing. There is evidence that the new work behavior of wives and mothers was trigged partly in response to a growing economic squeeze on families.[79] Wage rates for women were rising, thanks in part to the postwar growth of service-sector jobs, making it economically more costly for women to stay at home. In time, with a majority of mothers in the labor market, single-wage-earner families became even more deprived in relative terms.

For these reasons the modern nuclear family, already transformed from its early Victorian prototype, was in the throes of further change. Many dimensions of the modern nuclear family would remain relatively intact, for example, the absence of any economic-production function and the focus on marital affection and companionship. The doctrine of separate spheres, however, would be all but abandoned, patriarchy would be seriously challenged, the marriage bond would weaken, and child rearing would become a less dominant function. With all of these changes the family and home would gradually decline in social power and influence. For reasons to be explored in the chapters that follow, this decline has gone farther in Sweden than anywhere else, yet the phenomenon of family change is widespread, as we shall see, in every advanced society.

Notes

[1]Lawrence Stone (1977), *The Family, Sex and Marriage in England 1500–1800:* 687.

[2]J. Hajnal (1983), "Two Kinds of Pre-industrial Household Formation System," pp. 65–104 in Richard Wall et al. (eds.), *Family Forms in Historic Europe:* 67.

[3]For a fascinating account that emphasizes the importance of early Christianity, see Jack Goody (1983), *The Development of the Family and Marriage in Europe.*

[4]For comprehensive reviews of this material, see Michael Anderson (1980), *Approaches to the History of the Western Family 1500–1914;* Lawrence Stone (1982), "Family History in the 1980s: Past Achievements and Future Trends," pp. 51–87 in Theodore K. Rabb and R.I. Rotberg (eds.), *The New History: the 1980s and Beyond;* and C. C. Harris (1983), *The Family and Industrial Society.*

[5]For the work of Le Play, long mostly unavailable to English-speaking readers, see Catherine B. Silver (ed. and trans.) (1982), *Frederic Le Play on Family, Work and Social Change.*

[6]For an interesting discussion of the nuclear family's contribution to modernization, see Brigitte Berger and Peter L. Berger (1983), *The War over the Family: Capturing the Middle Ground,* especially Chapter 4.

[7]Alan Macfarlane (1979), *The Origins of English Individualism,* and (1986), *Marriage and Love in England: 1300–1840.*

[8]The best discussions of this are Peter Laslett (1977), *Family Life and Illicit Love in Earlier Generations:* Chapter 1, and Hajnal (1983), "Two Kinds."

[9]Laslett (1977), *Family Life:* 13.

[10]In a fascinating but highly speculative recent book, Emmanuel Tood has sought to link traditional family systems around the world even with such political ideologies as Communism, democracy, and fascism. Emmanuel Todd (1985), *The Explanation of Ideology: Family Structures and Social Systems.*

[11]Hajnal (1983), "Two Kinds." See also his earlier (1965), "European Marriage Patterns in Perspective," pp. 101–43 in D. V. Glass and D. E. C. Eversley (eds.), *Population in History.*

[12]Stone (1982), "Family History": 58.

[13]*Ibid.*: 93.

[14]Laslett (1977), *Family Life:* 34.

[15]Hajnal (1983), "Two Kinds": 93.

[16]*Ibid.*: 74.

[17]Peter Laslett (1971), *The World We Have Lost,* and Peter Laslett (ed.) (1974), *Household and Family in Past Time.*

[18]See Foreword (pp. x–xii) to Michael Mitterauer and Reinhard Sieder (1983), *The European Family.*

[19]*Ibid.*: 32, 39.

[20]*Ibid.*: 31.

[21]*Ibid.*: 38.

[22]Michael Anderson, "Household Structure and the Industrial Revolution; Mid-nineteenth-century Preston in Comparative Perspective," pp. 215–235 in Laslett (1974), *Household and Family.*

[23]Laslett (1974), *Household and Family:* 9.

[24]Andrew Cherlin (1983), "Changing Family and Household," pp. 51–66 in *Annual Review of Sociology* (Vol. 9): 52–53.

[25]L. K. Berkner (1972), "The Stem Family and the Development Cycle of the Family Household," *American Historical Review* 77-2:398–418.

[26]Stone (1982), "Family History": 63.

[27]Stone (1977), *Family:* 4.

[28]Quoted in Harris (1983), *Family:* 137.

[29]Stone (1977), *Family:* 679.

[30]Quoted in Anderson (1980), *Approaches:* 45.

[31]*Ibid.*: 42

[32]Edward Shorter (1975), *The Making of the Modern Family:* 48.

[33]Quoted in Harris (1983), *The Family:* 140.

[34]For a "warmer" view of the early modern family, see John R. Gillis (1985), *For Better, For Worse: British Marriages 1600 to the Present,* and Keith Wrightson (1984), *English Society: 1580–1680.* For challenges to Stone's "cold" view of the medieval family, see Barbara A. Hanawalt (1986), *The Ties that Bound: Peasant Families in Medieval England,* and David Herlihy (1985), *Medieval Households.*

[35]Shorter (1975), *Modern Family:* 55

[36]Louise A. Tilly and Joan W. Scott (1978), *Women, Work and Family:* Chapter 3.

[37]Shorter (1975), *Modern Family:* 71.

[38]Stone (1977), *Family:* Chapter 5.

[39]For a view of this period focusing on Germany and Switzerland, see Steven E. Ozment (1983), *When Fathers Ruled: Family Life in Reformation Europe.*

[40]Anderson (1980), *Approaches:* 15.

[41]Philippe Ariès (1962), *Centuries of Childhood: A Social History of Family Life.*

[42]*Ibid.*: 128.

[43]Lawrence Stone (1981), *The Past and the Present:* 221.

[44]Lloyd deMause (ed.) (1974), *The History of Childhood:* 1.

[45]Shorter (1975), *Modern Family:* 168, 204.

[46]*Ibid.:* 203–204.

[47]Stone (1981), *The Past and the Present:* 227–228.

[48]*Ibid.:* 220.

[49]Ozment (1983), *When Fathers Ruled:* 162. See also Wrightson (1984), *English Society:* 104–118.

[50]Linda Pollack (1984), *Forgotten Children: Parent–Child Relations from 1500–1900.*

[51]Shorter (1975), *Modern Family:* 205.

[52]Mitteraurer and Sieder (1983), *The European Family:* 40.

[53]*Ibid.:* 58–59.

[54]The separation of home and work that occurred was by no means a sudden change, for there already was much market-oriented activity in many preindustrial settings. See, for example, Elizabeth H. Pleck (1976), "Two Worlds in One," *Journal of Social History* 10:178–195.

[55]Mitterauer and Sieder (1983), *The European Family:* 87.

[56]Stone (1981), *The Past and the Present:* 222.

[57]Shorter (1975), *Modern Family:* 255.

[58]*Ibid.:* 227–228.

[59]*Ibid.:* 227.

[60]*Ibid.:* 259.

[61]Lawrence Stone (1979), *The Family, Sex and Marriage in England 1500–1800:* 22.

[62]Stone (1977), *Family:* 223.

[63]*Ibid.:* 658.

[64]R. Trumbach (1978), *The Rise of the Egalitarian Family: Aristocratic Kinship and Domestic Relations in Eighteenth Century England;* J.-L. Flandrin (1979), *Families in Former Times.*

[65]William J. Goode (1970), *World Revolution and Family Patterns.*

[66]Carl N. Degler (1980), *At Odds: Women and the Family in America from the Revolution to the Present:* 8–9.

[67]*Ibid.:* 26–28.

[68]Stone (1977), *Family:* 426.

[69]See Jenni Calder (1977), *The Victorian Home,* Clifford E. Clark, Jr. (1986), *The American Family Home, 1800–1960,* and Witold Rybczynski (1986), *Home: A Short History of an Idea.*

[70]Louise A. Tilly and Joan W. Scott (1978), *Women, Work, and Family.*

[71]Nancy F. Cott (1977), *The Bonds of Womanhood:* 197.

[72]See Degler (1980), *At Odds:* Chapters 15–17.

[73]Lawrence Stone (1985), "Sex in the West," *The New Republic,* July 8:25–37

[74]See Andrew J. Cherlin (1981), *Marriage, Divorce, Remarriage.*

[75]Richard A. Easterlin (1980), *Birth and Fortune: The Impact of Numbers on Personal Welfare;* Glen H. Elder, Jr. (1974), *Children of the Great Depression.*

[76]They are discussed in Cherlin (1981), *Marriage.*

[77]Ruth Schwartz Cowan (1983), *More Work for Mother.*

[78]Betty Friedan (1963), *The Feminine Mystique.*

[79]See Valerie Kincade Oppenheimer (1982), *Work and the Family: A Study in Social Demography.*

Part

II

The Case of Sweden

Historical Development of the Family in Sweden

Sweden is clearly part of the northwest European cultural region, and the Swedish family's development did not significantly differ from the pattern we portrayed and discussed in Chapter 4. For reasons similar to those that apply to other nations in the region, the Swedish family went through the same evolution from collective to privatized forms. Several differences in Swedish societal development do stand out, however, which make family history there (and also in many other parts of Scandinavia) distinct from that of the rest of the region, especially from England, France, and the Low Countries. Before the Industrial Revolution Sweden was poorer than England and most of the nations in the European heartland. Compared to many other countries in the northwest region at comparable preindustrial time periods, household and family units in Sweden tended to be more complex and less nucleated. The Industrial Revolution came relatively late to Sweden, but when it came, the nation changed very swiftly. This meant that, in its historical timing, the emergence of the modern family in Sweden was delayed, and once it began, it took place in a comparatively short period of time. This chapter highlights these and other differences and, in addition, provides for a single country detailed family-development information that spells out more concretely the broad European trends discussed earlier.

Industrialization did not begin in earnest in Sweden until the 1870s, nearly a century after it was under way in England. Throughout the nineteenth century Sweden was still largely agricultural. In fact, it was one of the most nonindustrial nations of northwest Europe, and even as late as the turn of the twentieth century it remained one of the poorest countries in the region. Nineteenth-century Swedish poverty is commonly attributed to its geographic isolation, to a lack of natural resources and arable land, and to extreme overpopulation.

Agriculture alone was not always the main foundation of the peasant economy in Sweden, as it was on the Continent, and many parts of Sweden were not basically farm centered. The Swedish peasant is often described

as a jack-of-all-trades, since the growing of crops was typically combined
with the raising of livestock, dairy production, fishing, hunting, forestry, and
handicraft, especially in the northern parts of the country.[1] This complex
local economy provided a certain flexibility of life-style in Sweden that was
not found in many other parts of Europe and it sometimes also generated
a geographic mobility not found elsewhere. In some regions, for example,
it was common to split households into separate residence units used at
different seasons of the year. In these respects, Swedish peasants showed
many similarities to dwellers in the Alpine regions of the Continent.

In keeping with the rest of northwest Europe, there is little evidence
that the very large, extended-family households found throughout Asia and
in eastern and southern Europe, which contained several nuclear families
in addition to other relatives, were present in Sweden to any significant
degree. They were common in eastern and northern Finland (where some
households had 30 or 40 persons) and in scattered Norwegian mountain
areas, but virtually nonexistent in Denmark. The extended families that did
exist in Sweden (mainly in the northern districts) seem to have mostly
died out by the last half of the seventeenth century.[2] These "grand" family
households often consisted of two married brothers living together with
their families and were based in the need to pool labor because of scarce
manpower (conditions typically found in remote areas). They also reflected
the need to keep intact the family's assets.[3]

The average preindustrial Swedish household tended to be relatively large
and complex, however. So-called stem families (usually a son and his family
living together with his elderly parents) were quite common in Sweden before
the eighteenth century.[4] The earliest complete household survey in Sweden
was for a relatively wealthy agricultural parish in the central part of the nation
and dates from 1643.[5] The mean household size there was seven persons,
and a majority of the households did not contain three generations. It is
likely however, that most households did have three generations at some
point in their life cycle. In addition, it is worth noting that almost all of the
households with more than seven persons had one or more servants. The
more complex structure of the preindustrial Swedish family was the basis for
at least one Swedish ethnographer's strong attack on the kind of description
and analysis of European family structure made by Peter Laslett and his
Cambridge colleagues, as discussed in the preceding chapter.[6]

Valid generalizations about preindustrial families in Sweden are difficult
because of marked regional variations in family types. Some variations were
due to differences in local economic conditions. The agricultural areas of the
south, more settled and accessible, resembled Denmark. The settlements in
the deep woods of the north had more in common with those of Finland
and Norway.[7] There were also several distinct types of rural organization.
Throughout most of the preindustrial period, but especially before the nine-

teenth century, Sweden had two main kinds of farm organization: independent peasant farms, either freely held or tenant held, and estates, on which peasants secured a small holding in exchange for labor.[8] The further south the land was in Sweden the more likely it was to be owned by estates, and estates were common also around Stockholm.[9] In general, it is reasonable to say that the strong feudal systems that existed on the Continent were not present in Sweden, where even in the estate areas the majority of Swedish peasants had more control over their resources than did most of their Continental counterparts. Nevertheless, the different types of rural social organization of that time had strong effects on the family systems that developed.

The Preindustrial Swedish Family Before 1750

Following the pioneering Swedish ethnographer Börje Hanssen, it is useful to divide Swedish peasant history into two preindustrial periods.[10] The first period ended in the early to mid-1700s, and the second, sometimes called the classical period of Scandinavian peasant culture, lasted from about 1750 to the last few decades of the nineteenth century. Of course, peasant life throughout both periods was continuously changing, and some damage is done to empirical reality by the use of such a historical dichotomy and by broad generalizations about the family types associated with it. The dichotomy has undoubted utility as a heuristic device, however.

Although information about the earlier preindustrial period is very scarce, scholars have described the presidential condition of most areas of Sweden at that time as small, tightly knit communities organized mainly in terms of large, complex households. These households were not necessarily coterminous with family and kinship networks, and these networks were not as distinct or as important as they came to be in later centuries.[11] As Börje Hanssen put it, "household has precedence over family if we want to understand the pre-industrial world."[12] Up until the end of the 1700s, for example, the meaning of the Swedish word for family included servants living in the household.[13]

It was Hanssen's conclusion that "kin as an exclusive and lasting group does not seem to have existed among the . . . peasants if we go beyond the middle of the 18th century."[14] Much of the reason for this state of affairs rests with the very high death rates of the time, according to Hanssen, which continually broke up biological families and severed ties to relatives. The children of farmers often took employment outside of their households of birth, sometimes at as early an age as 8 to 10 years. Thus normal biological parent-child relations were common only with younger children, of whom nearly 50% would die in any event before the age of 15. It has been also calculated that because of low levels of adult longevity 40 to 50% of all children would have had at least one stepparent had they stayed at home.[15]

Thus the daily behavior of early preindustrial Swedish peasants, in their fight for subsistence, was probably much more oriented to household- and community-based work groups, one could also say gender-based peer groups, than to the conjugal family or to close relatives. And there was an indistinct division between kin and nonkin members of the household. In a southern Sweden estate area of this time, studied by Hanssen, where the mean household size was about seven persons, he found a high percentage of complex households in which, primarily for economic reasons, more than one farm family would make up a cooperating unit. Many of these coresident families, he maintains, were not even related to one another. A common correlate pattern was for two nonrelated families to share a farmstead, but to maintain separate "dining groups." He explains this practice of cooperation as based on the need of peasants to perform their economic functions without hiring outside labor, which in this area they presumably could not afford.[16] Other members of these households were lodgers, "decrepit old people, former holders of the farm, craftsmen or horse soldiers with their wives, and occasionally crippled unmarried women."[17]

Giving an additional blow to the idea of strong kinship ties at this time, Hanssen uncovered little evidence of "pride of patriarchal descent," such as wills and patrilineal inheritance practices. He suggested that "when a farm became vacant through illness or death, it was taken over by somebody who happened to be at hand" and not always a relative.[18] Formal inheritance practices may have been absent, he suggests, both because there was little tangible property to inherit and because land at that time was still plentiful enough for children to simply move on. It should be noted that Swedish inheritance laws never contained rules calling for primogeniture or ultimogeniture (inheritance by the first or last born). Sons were to be awarded double the share of daughters, but all children of the same sex were entitled to equal shares. An enormous variety of inheritance practices actually prevailed throughout Sweden, however, and they did not always conform to the national law.[19]

Firm conclusions about an early nonkinship stage of the Swedish family must await further evidence, and such a stage, if it did exist, probably evolved from the still earlier kinship-oriented societies of Viking times. In any event, with the lowering of the death rate and a rise in material standards of living, kinship and the more typical extended-family household do seem to have been very much in place in most of eighteenth-century Sweden. The area studied by Hanssen may have been exceptional for its time. Swedish historian David Gaunt found that nonstate areas of central Sweden, with their mix of a high percentage of landowners and various nonagricultural economic activities, had both large average households (six or seven persons) and a large number (often one third or more) of extended-family households in the first half of the eighteenth century.[20]

Particularly common in the area studied by Gaunt were stem families, in which a married couple and their children shared the household with members of the older generation, usually the husband's or wife's parents. In the stem-family system an offspring (usually the eldest male) takes control of the parents' farm, but permits the parents to continue living there until their death. As Gaunt notes, "the advantage of this structure is that it guarantees the aged security in their infirmity, and it assures the younger generation a clear right to the property."[21] Even though a majority of all households in the areas he studied were not extended families at any given point in time, Gaunt points out, it is likely that a majority or even as many as two thirds of all households were extended at some point in the family life cycle. For example, he found that fully two out of three elderly persons died while in extended-family households.[22]

The stem family has traditionally been based on a one-heir system of inheritance. While Sweden had no official system of impartible inheritance, Swedish peasants, according to Orvar Löfgren, tended "to leave a bigger share of the farm property to one of the children, in effect, to choose a main heir or heiress to occupy the farm itself".[23] The rest of the children were not disinherited but usually were compensated in other ways, for example, by being given the family's rights to pastures, forest, or fishing waters, which sometimes were more prized than the actual farm. On occasion, one child would buy out the portions of land inherited by the other siblings. Sons tended to inherit rights to land resources, while daughters received much of their inheritance as a dowry, consisting of animals or various material goods.[24] The nature of inheritance practices was greatly affected by such factors as the density of population and the opportunities for economic expansion and for settling new land.

Based on studies in several geographically and socially separate areas of Sweden, David Gaunt has emphasized that different local economic conditions generated quite distinct family structures. In the estate-dominated farming areas of central Sweden, which presumably were more similar to the region in southern Sweden studied by Hanssen, Gaunt found that household sizes were smaller than in other areas, extended families were less predominant (only about one out of five households was extended), and residential life was less stable (persons born outside the parish could amount to over half of the elderly population). He concludes:

> In those areas where geographic mobility was large and where tenant farming was characteristic, the number of complex households is relatively small. In

areas with considerable permanency and self-owning households the complex household can almost be said to be the dominant form."[25]

If this general conclusion is found to be supported by further evidence, the household and family situation in at least certain portions of Sweden can be said to have been substantially different from that in other parts of northwest Europe in the early eighteenth century, as discussed in the preceding chapter. Yet, as we shall see below, this was but one period in the history of the Swedish family, and the era of complex, extended families did not last much beyond it.

Scholarly studies of community life in rural Sweden in the late seventeenth and early eighteenth centuries typically portray a kind of primitive, classless village communism.[26] Such portrayals rang especially true for the few areas that had partible inheritance practices and divided the land among all the children. Farm dwellings were grouped into compact villages, and most farming was on a common-field basis, with "individual holdings consisting of many strips of land, often widely separated. Much of the pasture and wooded land was held in common."[27] Care of animals was often a communal enterprise, and most of the land holdings were too small to be farmed individually. Because of the continual breakup of land at the time of death, the average farmer would have perhaps 30 or 40 separate strips of land, sometimes even 100.[28] Work was therefore mostly a common community endeavor, in which all age groups participated, and the community dictated the times of plowing, planting, and harvesting. In addition, there was much shared ownership. "Several households combined their resources to maintain a common smithy, a water mill, or a bull or shared common natural resource."[29]

This, of course, reproduces the medieval residence-work pattern that was found throughout central Europe during the preindustrial period. In Sweden, however, many elements of this system were still commonly in existence in many regions at the turn of the nineteenth century, long after it had been abandoned in England and in many portions of the Continent.

Rural Family Development After 1750

A swelling population, beginning around 1750, was a factor in gradually forcing the breakup of communal life through the "enclosure" of farms, in which village lands were turned into separate farmsteads of manageable size. This land reorganization at first was voluntary, with permissive legislation passed in 1757. But very little land reorganization took place until the early 1800s, when it was pushed by government decree, and still by 1850 only about half of the land in Sweden had been reorganized.[30] The enclosure movements, together with rapid population increases and improvements in agricultural productivity, generated a growing number of independent farmers, living on plots of land that were geographically apart from the rural communities. At the same time, there was a marked expansion of the rural proletariat made up of landless workers, who, unlike their counterparts in England, were mostly unable to move to towns and cities because of Sweden's then-still-nascent level of industrialization and urban development. The number of such landless "cottagers" in the Swedish countryside quadrupled between 1750 and 1860.[31]

With too large a population for the land to support decently at the then-existing level of agricultural technology, a situation made worse by a series of famines, the turn of the nineteenth century found rural Sweden in relatively dire economic straights compared to much of the rest of northwest Europe. Foreign travelers to Sweden at this time described "the estrangement, poverty and insanitary conditions (not to say filth) in which people . . . lived."[32] Mary Wollstonecraft, who journeyed from England along the west coast of Sweden in the summer of 1795, emphasized the dire poverty in the region:

> The farm houses, in which only poverty resided, were formed of logs scarcely keeping off the cold and drifting snow; out of them the inhabitants seldom peeped, and the sports or prattling of children was neither seen nor heard."[33]

In 1799, Thomas Malthus traveled through Sweden to get a better empirical basis for a new edition of his famous work on population, which had been published the year before. He found in Sweden abundant evidence to confirm his views that population would outrun food supplies and lead to a series of dire "Malthusian checks."

Gradually the quality of the agricultural economy began to improve, however, and with it came additional changes in the social organization of rural life. The landed peasant-farmers took up the specialized production of cash crops, and the growing number of landless peasants became the workers that made production for a cash economy possible. The agricultural economy shifted from a pattern of subsistence to one of market exchange. Most of the new landless workers were the "excess" offspring of farm owners for whom no provision of land could be made. In time, these landless workers also began to start in their cottages such protoindustrial activities as textile weaving, and some became artisans and specialists in such trades as tailoring and carpentry. The products and services, sometimes a sideline to small-scale subsistence farming, were purchased by the landowners with their growing cash wealth.[34]

All of these changes, in turn, hastened the emergence of a more conjugal and kin-oriented family system, because life was increasingly organized around the independent and relatively self-sufficient farmsteads or around the new detached, landless cottages. The farmstead itself became a more closed economic unit, as the traditional communal patterns of agricultural work were made obsolete with the use of wage labor. In stem-family situations, the grandparents increasingly occupied their own separate households on the farm and ate their meals separately. The role of farm wives, too, gradually changed, and their responsibilities centered more and more in the domestic sphere as mistresses of the home.[35] There also arose at this time, partly because of growing wealth, increased kinship consciousness, more visiting among relatives, and the use of more formal inheritance procedures.

Farm households apparently increased somewhat in size during the nineteenth century. According to Louise and David Gaunt, the typical Swedish farm household at this time contained 6 to 12 persons, including 2 or 3 children and 2 or 3 servants.[36] The presence of servants in the Swedish farm household was already quite common by the early 1600s, probably even more common in Sweden than in many other parts of northwest Europe. In the areas of central Sweden examined by David Gaunt, between 29 and 63% of the households had servants at that time, depending on the economy of the area.[37] The number and presence of servants in the household unit did not change substantially during the nineteenth century. But the social source of servants did change. Originally the children from other farm families, the servants increasingly came to be the children of the newly landless rural workers. In both cases, service was usually viewed as a stage in the life cycle, with the young people eventually going on to other occupations.

Also, the status of servants within the household and within the society as a whole began to change, as the newly kin-conscious farm families began more and more to differentiate themselves as a unit apart from the servants who worked for them. In this sense, the farm household gradually became a less egalitarian and more hierarchically organized unit, in which the members were highly dependent on the master and mistress of the farm, who came to possess growing economic authority and power. Gradually, farm families and their servants "no longer mixed freely or shared the same tasks and were no longer united by the same emotional bonds of common identity"; they also ceased sharing the same table at dinner.[38] This segregation of social groups within the household reflected a growing differentiation of social classes within Swedish society as a whole. It was accompanied by a gradual loss of power and privileges among the ruling nobility and a more widespread distribution of political power to the middle classes. Just as in the past local pastors and merchants had tended to be a class apart from the farmers, the farmers emerged as a class apart from the great mass of nonlandowning rural dwellers.

By comparison with farm families, the households of the landless proletariat were smaller and varied greatly in size over the life cycle and even
over the year. In these domestic units, children tended to leave home early
to become servants, thus relieving their families of an economic burden,
and aged parents did not commonly live with their adult children. In addition, few of these households had servants. The fact that men worked mostly
outside of the household resulted in a new division of labor between the
spouses, with women assuming control over all domestic duties. Furthermore, the economic marginality of these households caused husbands to be
away seeking work for long periods of time, thus relinquishing to women
increased responsibility for a wide range of household and family affairs.[39]

Marriage patterns in nineteenth-century Sweden varied considerably, depending on local economic and social conditions. Swedish ethnographer
Orvar Löfgren points out, for example, that in the estate areas of southern
Sweden "parental supervision of premarital contacts was very rigorous" and
many marriages were for all intents and purposes parentally arranged.[40] This
was due in part to the relatively high degree of social stratification in the area
and to the desire of parents to prevent their children from making unsuitable
contacts. In the less wealthy and more egalitarian Dalarna region of central
Sweden, however, premarital contacts were much less controlled, and there
was a relatively free choice of marriage partners. A common tradition in this
area (typical of the northern regions of Sweden) was "night courting" (known
as bundling in Anglo-Saxon countries). Boys could visit girls in their sleeping quarters and establish a stable premarital relationship, leading eventually
to sexual intercourse and then marriage.

Premarital sexual relationships seem to have been fully accepted and quite
common in much of preindustrial Scandinavian society, and not only in
those areas in which "night courting" was practiced. Rather than forming
part of the process of picking a marriage partner, however, as is often the
case in Western societies today, these relationships were initiated only after
a marriage partner had already been picked. Thus premarital sex was an
ordinary part of the engagement process, and "brides did not marry because
they were pregnant, but were pregnant because they were about to get
married."[41]

Nevertheless, Sweden had an illegitimacy rate that is regarded as exceptionally high by west European standards. This rate increased continuously
from the beginning of the 1800s to the 1930s, with a temporary decline in
the 1880s.[42] While the precentage of out-of-wedlock births from 1751 to
1755 was only 2.5%, by the early 1900s it included every seventh child.[43]
At the turn of the twentieth century and still today the illegitimacy rate tends
to increase the farther north in Sweden one goes, with Norrland having one
of the highest illegitimacy rates in Europe. Also, during most but not all his-

torical periods, the illegitimacy rate has been higher in urban than in rural areas, and it has generally been highest among the poorer classes of people.

The acceptance of premarital sex also must have been related, in part, to the rather late ages of marriage in Sweden. Though localities differed, age of marriage generally seems to have conformed to the "European marriage pattern" discussed in Chapter 4: after age 25 for women and almost age 30 for men.[44] These are averages, however. Many peasants and landless workers married earlier. In general, people of higher classes tended to marry at an older age.[45] Age of marriage was also relatively late in the southern estate areas where arranged marriages prevailed. Surveys from the period 1750–1850 in comparable areas of Denmark and Norway show a mean age at first marriage of 28 to 32 years for men and 26 to 28 years for women.[46]

The general history of Sweden in the nineteenth century shows the development of political liberty and equality, but it also shows rampant population growth, which was to alter the character of Sweden late in the century. Between 1800 and 1900 the population of Sweden more than doubled, from 2.3 to 5.1 million, mostly because of improved health and a declining death rate. The additional population swelled the rural proletariat, producing a great increase in tenant farmers, servants, and farm laborers. While farmers increased by 27% between 1800 and 1850, the number of landless rural workers went up by 146%.[47] By 1870, the independent farmers were almost matched in number by the dependent rural proletariat. Because of the late industrial development, in Sweden, unlike England, most of the additional population had to stay in the countryside and in rural occupations. In 1890 the agricultural sector in Sweden still employed more than 60% of the population, and in 1900 almost 80% of the people still lived in the countryside.[48]

Overpopulation, rural poverty, and the lack of industrial development were the main conditions that precipitated "America fever" in nineteenth-century Sweden and caused nearly one fourth of the Swedish population to emigrate to other lands (mostly to the United States). The peak decade of emigration in Sweden was the 1880s, just before that nation's great industrial spurt. Such massive emigration caused much soul-searching in Sweden, but slowed the growth in the population only marginally, especially since nearly one third of the emigrants eventually returned. At the century's end, the growth of the timber and iron industries, improvements in agriculture, and an efficient, government-promoted rail system that opened up much new territory for development led the way for Sweden to quickly become one of the world's richest and most industrialized nations in the twentieth century.

In the rapidly industrializing conditions of the early twentieth century, Swedes tended to look back on peasant life in the decades before the 1870s as a "golden age of peasant culture." This was a time, as they saw it, when rural communities had gained some wealth and stability, yet industrialization, commercialization, and the tentacles of an urban bureaucracy had not yet seriously undermined the rural way of life. Through this golden-age image, in the words of Orvar Löfgren,

> we meet a society dominated by relatively prosperous and proud peasants with a strong local identity and self-esteem . . . in well-integrated village communities where "neighbor is neighbor's brother."[49]

This golden-age image, of course, was partly a myth. Yet it was not entirely removed from social reality. Along with a patriarchy pervading family life and a growing social stratification of rural society, many nineteenth-century rural areas had a very festive and ritualized community life, in which there was a rich effloresence of local arts and crafts. Made economically feasible by support from the growing wealth of farmers, specialists in music, art, and handicrafts flourished.

Partly due to the recentness of this "golden age" and perhaps also because of its special social and artistic qualities, the cultural legacy of nineteenth-century rural Sweden is still deeply embedded in contemporary Swedish life. More than most other Western peoples today, Swedes place a very high value on folk arts, folk music, and the simple life of the countryside. The legacy is further enhanced by the fact that as late as World War II a large segment of the Swedish working class still lived in small places outside of urban areas and often combined wage labor with small-scale farming. Even today an estimated one out of every four Swedes either owns or has access to a summer cottage in the countryside and thus can annually renew contacts, as it were, with the life from which his or her immediate forebears came.

The Rise of the Victorian, Bourgeois Family

During the nineteenth century, the "Victorian, bourgeois" family came to Sweden (just as it did to other parts of Europe; see Chapter 4), but it came later to Sweden than elsewhere and was not in place for as long before the next great change took place. Löfgren sees the period around the turn of the twentieth century as "the classic era of bourgeois culture," a time during which Victorian cultural norms and images seem to have reached their apogee in Sweden, at least insofar as they dominated social norms and intellectual discourse.[50] By this time relatively few Swedes could be said to have been living the life-style of the bourgeois family, certainly not the urban bourgeois family, but nevertheless this life-style had begun to achieve a kind of cultural hegemony, and was understood to be the right way to live.

According to the findings of Orvar Löfgren, Jonas Frykman, and the research group of ethnologists at Lund University, Victorian bourgeois culture, and with it the nuclear-family ideal, started in Sweden among the newly emerging middle classes.[51] In opposition to the "oppressive and petrified structure" of the nobility, the middle classes led the way in emphasizing such cultural values as individualism and self-discipline and developing a new concern for the "home."[52] If that proves to be true, the genesis of the modern nuclear family in Sweden is dissimilar from the one portrayed, for example, by Lawrence Stone, in which the aristocracy is singled out as the originator of this cultural family type.

But the Swedish bourgeois family ideal appears to differ little from what pertained in the rest of Europe. At heart it is based on the idea that the nuclear family and especially one's children are something special, to be given great care and nurturing, and that the home is a private, almost sacred, place where this care and nurturing is to take place. As noted by Orvar Löfgren,

> the family ideal of the rising 19th century bourgeoisie was based upon a new definition of love. Sentiment and love between the married couple and between parents and their children should bind the family together, but the new ideal was also built upon ideas of intimacy and privacy: the sacred and sweetness of home.[53]

By the turn of the twentieth century, continues Löfgren, "the good home had become a key symbol and a powerful metaphor" among the Swedish middle and upper classes."[54]

The character of the bourgeois home was two-faced. On the one hand, this home was a place for the show of social status, where the newly prosperous could display their good fortune and the trajectory of their upward mobility. On the other hand, it was a private place of refuge, a place of intimacy and warmth in the face of a rapidly changing outside world that was becoming ever more rationalized and anonymous. Again in Löfgren's words, the home was

> both a show-case to the world and a shelter against it . . . like a snug and sheltered theater box, from which the family looked at the stage of the busy outside world.[55]

Such a bourgeois home contrasted strongly with the remaining peasant homes of the period. Löfgren quotes a country doctor reporting on his travels in a remote peasant area around the turn of the century:

> For them [the peasants] there is no dividing line between public and private, all is public. Locks are never used in the isolated villages—night or day—and you never knock when entering a house.[56]

The "guardians" of the new bourgeois homes were of course the women of the emerging middle class. Increasingly removed from the outside world of work, these women were given the task of making their home a seat of moral virtue and thus providing a "civilizing force" for the society as a whole. The virtues of home and of the female gender became to some extent inseparable, and the positions of housewife and mother came to be honored roles throughout Swedish society. The domestic role for women was regarded as complementary to that of their husbands, whose task it was in the new division of labor to make all this hominess economically possible by earning a good income. For a husband and father, the worst thing to be was a poor provider; for a wife, the worst thing to be was an inadequate mother and slovenly housekeeper.

The good life for the middle-class family was based in part on the availability of a ready supply of cheap servant labor, the female children of the peasant and working classes. The number of servants a family would have was based on its wealth. As noted earlier in this chapter, the era of equality between family members and servants had long since passed. Servants lived with the family but were not fully of it, and certain normative guidelines regulated the relations between servants and others, even though servants were expected at all times to uphold middle-class values and norms. While service in middle-class households could be drudgery, it also provided an opportunity for working-class girls to learn middle-class ways, and apparently it was so viewed by both employer and employee.[57]

The bourgeois nuclear family apparently first emerged in Sweden's nineteenth-century urban areas. In the rural districts it first appeared in the homes of the new small-town middle class and of the representatives of central authority who resided in local places—church leaders, government officials, and some business people.[58] It then gradually made its presence felt, although not without some modifications, among the growing middle class of farmers.

Börje Hanssen has provided a detailed description of how, in the village he studied, the lives of farm families moved toward the nuclear-family model as they entered the age of commercial agriculture, capitalism, and, later, industrial development.[59] In their social and occupational lives, the farm husbands gradually became entrepreneurs more than farm workers and spent a larger portion of their time in local, formally organized community groups pursuing various commercial as well as social and political ends. At the same time, marking a significant break with the traditional female-gender role in which women could virtually do, and often did, the work of male field hands, farm wives became increasingly removed from the outside world of productive work. Their specialty became home and child care and family consumer activities. The new focus on children was particularly important, and planning and preparation for the children's future life roles were given high priority. For both the husband and wife, relationships with close relatives grew in importance as a way to spend leisure time. This was associated with strong new feelings of kinship identity and solidarity and even a new interest in genealogy.

Many family changes could be seen by means of the physical modifications made to the farm dwellings. These included the addition of a master bedroom for the master and mistress and their small children, reflecting the growing privatization of life. Separate quarters for the servants were built, denoting increased social differentiation. The toilet facilities also became socially differentiated, with separate privies provided for nonfamily members. Owing to the increasing formality of entertaining, a parlor was eventually added for that purpose. The house also came to be decorated not for utilitarian ends, but for social status and for the symbolic display of new bourgeois values and social attachments. Household implements on the walls, for instance, were replaced by pictures of political leaders and works of art of various kinds. Because one hallmark of the true bourgeois home was its separation from the world of work, however, which was not possible on the farm, farm homes could never completely emulate, nor did they necessarily want to, the urban bourgeois practices of architecture and design.

According to Hanssen, not all of these changes were in place in his rural village in southern Sweden before the late nineteenth and even early twentieth centuries. And despite them, strong local-community integration with daily social and economic contacts between neighbors still prevailed until the early twentieth century, albeit in a diluted form, and "much of the old congeniality and companionship survived in the households."[60] It was not until after World War II, he maintains, that cooperation among farmers virtually came to an end and there no longer was much personal dependence on neighbors. Also at this time the last vestiges of the extended-family household were erased, and kinship relations decreased in favor of other kinds of relationships. What was left was the isolated nuclear family, in which "exclusive relations among the family members are intense due to the long period of childrearing, the sharing of leisure time, and due to the fact that meals are taken without any servants." Yet even the nuclear family, he concludes, was beginning to show "tendencies of disintegration."[61]

Industrialization, Urbanization, and Family Change

The natural habitat for the bourgeois family, however, was the nation's growing towns and cities. As part of the Swedish industrial spurt of the late 1800s, an extensive railway network was constructed, in part to open for development previously inaccessible places. This led to an industrial development that was quite decentralized compared to that in other European countries. Hundreds of small towns sprang up around the railway stations, drawing people from the nearby rural districts.[62] To this day, Sweden has remained very much a nation of small and medium-sized towns and cities.

The turn of the twentieth century in Sweden was a time of great residential and social mobility. Together with the few larger cities in Sweden (in 1910 only 13 places had more than 20,000 inhabitants), these new towns gradually became the habitat for a new industrial proletariat. Most of its members had formerly been part of the rural proletariat. The new urban, or semiurban, locales also housed a growing urban middle class, consisting of people in such occupations as industrial management, government administration, small business, commercial trading, and teaching. The new towns were geographically divided into working-class and middle-class districts, with casual workers pushed to the outskirts; typical working-class housing consisted of low-rise, high-density apartments of various kinds.[63] There is some doubt whether, at least initially, the housing and environmental conditions in the new towns were an improvement over those in the countryside. In any event, urban housing remained a major problem in Sweden throughout much of the first half of the twentieth century.

Residential and social mobility, urbanization, and family change all went hand in hand. A study of turn-of-the-century population cohorts showed that those people who migrated the longest distances within Sweden climbed the highest on the ladder of social mobility. Also, there was a strong association between higher social mobility (and status) and both marrying late and having a small family.[64] One consequence of the family changes associated with migration and urbanization at this time was a marked increase in the number of women who remained unmarried throughout their lives. In the eighteenth century only 11 to 13.5% of Swedish women remained unmarried at ages 40 to 49. For women born in the 1850s that figure had climbed to 21%, and it reached its peak of 24% for women born in the 1870s. This peak was due in part to a shortage of men, since the bulk of Swedish overseas emigrants had been male.[65]

Thus at the turn of the twentieth century Sweden had one of the highest rates of unmarried women in Europe, and these rates were highest among the new-town and city dwellers. During most of the twentieth century the rate of unmarried women dropped appreciably, and in 1970 only 8% of all women born in 1920 were still unmarried.[66] In recent years, however, the rate has dramatically risen because of the increase in nonmarital cohabitation.

When it finally came in the last decades of the nineteenth century, the movement toward industrialization and urbanization in Sweden came very quickly indeed. By 1910, 32% of the Swedish people lived off industry, 13% off trade and commerce, and 6% off public service and the professions, while the share of the population residing in urban places had reached 25%. Just as importantly, the agrarian population in absolute numbers in 1910 was of about the same size as it had been in 1860. Thus most of the population increases during the intervening years, according to Swedish sociologist Kurt Samuelsson, "either became engaged in urban occupations or left the country."[67] With these changes came growing prosperity. Samuelsson noted that "A population 50 per cent larger than in the later 1860's enjoyed a standard of living that was at least 100 per cent higher."[68]

This higher standard of living made the ideal of the Victorian, bourgeois family more of a reality for the average Swede. The children of this generation's middle classes grew up with a strong sense of what a "good and proper" family life should be, with its focus on home and children, its emphasis on intimacy and sharing, and its sharp division of gender roles. And many were later to look back with fond memories on all that their mothers had done to create a good home and on the hard work of their fathers as good providers. They remembered with real nostalgia the family get-togethers and regular family rituals, even if the daily reality of family life had been somewhat different.

Much of the urban working class still could not share in this cultural ideal, however. Not the least of the reasons for this was the lack of adequate housing. In many of the very small working-class apartments and homes of the time it was common for all family activities, including sleeping, to take place in the kitchen. It is often said that this was done partly in order to emulate the middle-class practice of having one room completely free and clean for purposes of display and entertaining. Also, economic marginality often forced working-class families to expand their numbers with "lodgers," both kin and nonkin. And many working-class wives were forced into the job market in order to make ends meet.[69]

In common with working-class life-styles in other advanced societies, Swedish working-class families experienced less "togetherness" than did middle-class families. Many more of life's daily activities took place outside the home, and family members tended to be more peer oriented than family oriented. This was especially true in relation to leisure activities. "Men spent their free time with other men outside the home, women formed informal neighborhood groups, and children looked after themselves."[70] This, however, made urban working-class neighborhoods considerably more "communal" in character than were middle-class neighborhoods.[71] The working class also had lower marriage rates and higher rates of illegitimacy.

Spurred on by the contrast between their own good fortunes and the perceived deficiencies of the expanding urban working class, the middle-class leaders of Swedish society in the early twentieth century developed substantial moral fervor for attempting to deal with the emerging problems of an urban and industrial society. As in other Western societies of the time, the path to social improvement was seen to involve not only political and economic, but also "moral" change, that is, "improvements" in the attitudes and behavior of the lower classes. In a sense, the moral fervor of the bourgeoisie that had originally been directed against the Swedish nobility was now turned against the lower classes. Few values stood out more forcefully in this moral tone than the necessity for a strong and secure nuclear-family life, and it was the weakness of the working class in this respect that generated much concern. As Orvar Lörgren notes:

> The virtues of a stable home life were echoed in parliamentary debates, in newspaper articles, and in pamphlets and soon started to spread through channels such as housing and educational reform programs and campaigns for better housekeeping among working class women. By the turn of the century we find the ideal of the happy nuclear family extolled almost everywhere."[72]

Shaped by a national debate over the enormous emigration of Swedes to America, and with the ideals of home, family, and the rural countryside very much in mind, Sweden established in 1904 a public home-ownership program.[73] Through this program, a government fund was set up to provide low-interest loans for the establishment of owner-occupied homes in rural areas. Most of the money was intended for new, independent small holdings in unsettled areas, usually in the Swedish north; thus it was a kind of homestead program. A portion of the funds was to be used to provide worker-built housing in rural areas around cities, however, areas that were destined later to become suburbs. The actual number of people who were resettled through this program was modest, and some critics today view the program as a kind of last and perhaps misguided attempt to stave off the advent of an urban and industrial Sweden.[74] But the program did represent one of Sweden's earliest ventures into national social planning, and it was soon followed by intense national activity in the field of social welfare, leading to new laws governing working conditions and, in 1913, to an old-age pension scheme.

The great turning point in Swedish economic development came around the time of World War I. During and immediately after the war, there was a worldwide demand for the goods that Sweden produced, such as steel, pulp, matches, ball bearings, telephones, and vacuum cleaners. Sweden, having been a relatively unscathed neutral power during the war, suddenly found herself a rich, industrial nation, and this only some 50 years after intense industrialization in that country had begun.[75]

The concern for home and family in Swedish culture lasted until the middle of the twentieth century. Gradually over time the working class did manage to assimilate the main attributes of the middle-class life-style. When in the early 1930s the Social Democrats attained political power, Sweden was well on its way toward becoming a thoroughly bourgeois society, at least in culture, if not in political ideology. It was not that the turn-of-the-century Victorian culture had remained unchanged. Sweden by this time had become dominated by a new world of planners, technicians, and administrators backed by scientists and academics, and science and technology had replaced religion as the supreme legitimizing force for Swedish values. The working class, moreover, did manage to preserve some elements of its own cultural identity, especially through the efforts of the increasingly powerful trade unions. But such Victorian values as rationality and self-discipline had become powerful and pervasive in almost all Swedish social classes and geographic regions.

"Home" remained such a powerful symbol in Swedish life that "it was hardly a coincidence," Löfgren notes, "that the Social Democrats named their vision of a future, more egalitarian society the 'people's home'."[76] And while the goal of the preservation and uplifting of the nuclear family was not a major part of the Social Democratic Party's plans for the development of the welfare state when it first came into power in the 1930s, this was soon to become a prominent theme around which the nation could be rallied for the next moves toward greater equality and economic security, as we shall see in the next chapter.

Notes

[1]Orvar Löfgren (1974), "Family and Household among Scandinavian Peasants: An Exploratory Essay," *Ethnologia Scandinavica* 17–52:18–22.
[2]This is the conclusion of Nils and Inga Friberg (1971), *Sveriges Äldsta Fullständiga Husförhörslängd.* Quoted in David Gaunt (1983b), *Familjeliv i Norden:* 90.
[3]Löfgren (1974), "Family and Household."
[4]For a recent review of the historical demography of Swedish households, see Mona Mårtensson (1985), "Hushållsstruktur i Sverige. Kontinuitet och Förändring."
[5]Friberg in Gaunt (1983b), *Familjeliv i Norden.*
[6]Börje Hanssen (1977/1978), "Notes on Household Composition and Sociocultural Change," *Ethnologia Europaea* 10-1:33–38.
[7]Regional variation has been stressed in the work of the Swedish historian David Gaunt. See his *Familjeliv i Norden* (1983b); "Preindustrial Economy and Population Structure," *Scandinavian Journal of History* 2(1977):183–210; and "Household Typology: Problems, Methods Results" (1978), pp. 69–83 in Sune Åkerman et al. (eds.) (1978), *Chance and Change: Social and Economic Studies in Historical Demography in the Baltic Area.*
[8]Carl Mosk (1983), *Patriarchy and Fertility: Japan and Sweden, 1880–1960:* 67.
[9]Louise Gaunt and David Gaunt (1986), "Le Modèle Scandinave," pp. 471–495 in A. Burguiere et al. (eds.), *Historie de la Famille.*
[10]Börje Hanssen (1979/1980), "Household, Classes, and Integration Processes in a Scandinavia Village over 300 Years," *Ethnologia Europaea* 11-1.

11This is a main theme in the work of the Swedish ethnographer Börje Hanssen. See especially his "Household, Classes" (1979/1980) and a discussion of his work in Orvar Löfgren (1984b), "Family and Household: Images and Realities: Cultural Change in Swedish Society," pp. 446–469 in Robert McC. Netting et al. (eds.), *Households: Comparative and Historical Studies of the Domestic Group.*

12Hanssen (1979/1980), "Household, Classes": 76. See also "The Oikological Approach," pp. 147–158 in Åkerman et al. (1978), *Chance and Change.*

13Gaunt (1983b), *Familjeliv i Norden:* 87.

14Hanssen (1979/1980), "Household, Classes": 79.

15*Ibid.:* 78–79.

16*Ibid.:* 90–93.

17*Ibid.:* 93.

18*Ibid.:* 95.

19Löfgren (1974), *Family and Household:* 34.

20Gaunt (1977), "Preindustrial Economy," and (1983b) *Familjeliv i Norden:* 90–98.

21Gaunt (1977), "Preindustrial Economy": 198. In the eighteenth century the stem-family arrangement was often legally implemented by way of a "retirement contract"—parents legally turned over property to their children at retirement age in return for lifetime care and services from those children. See David Gaunt (1983a), "The Property and Kin Relationships of Retired Farmers in Northern and Central Europe," pp. 249–279 in Richard Wall et al. (eds.), *Family Forms in Historic Europe.*

22Gaunt (1977), "Preindustrial Economy": 201.

23Löfgren (1974), "Family and Household": 38.

24*Ibid.:* 39.

25Gaunt (1977), "Preindustrial Economy": 202.

26See Vilhelm Moberg (1984), "Life in the Villages," pp. 11–20 in Patrik Engellau and Ulf Henning (eds.), *Nordic Views and Values.*

27Dorothy S. Thomas (1941), *Social and Economic Aspects of Swedish Population Movements, 1750–1933:* 49.

28D. Franklin Scott (1977), *Sweden: The Nation's History:* 288–289

29Löfgren (1984b), "Family and Household": 448.

30Scott (1977), *Sweden:* 291.

31*Ibid.:* 292.

32Kurt Samuelsson (1968), *From Great Power to Welfare State:* 133.

33Carol H. Poston (ed.) (1976), *Mary Wollstonecraft Letters:* 42.

34Orvar Löfgren (1978), "The Potato People: Household Economy and Family Patterns among the Rural Proletariat in Nineteenth Century Sweden," pp. 95–106 in Åkerman et al. (1978), *Chance and Change.*

35These changes are discussed under the heading "Mastery Stage," referring to the rise of masters and mistresses, in Hanssen (1979/1980), "Household, Classes": 96ff.

36Gaunt and Gaunt (1986), "Le Modèle Scandinave."

37Gaunt (1977), "Preindustrial Economy": 200.

38Löfgren (1984b), "Family and Household": 456–457.

39Löfgren (1978), "The Potato People": 103–104.

40Löfgren (1974), "Family and Household": 30.

41Jonas Frykman (1975), "Sexual Intercourse and Social Norms: A Study of Illegitimate Births in Sweden," *Ethnologia Scandinavica:* 139.

42*Ibid.:* 111.

43*Ibid.:* 111.

44Gaunt and Gaunt (1986), "Le Modèle Scandinave."

45Sten Carlsson (1978), "Unmarried Women in the Swedish Society of Estates," pp. 220–226 in Åkerman et al. (1978), *Chance and Change.*

[46]Figures cited in Löfgren (1974), "Family and Household": 48 (footnote 22).
[47]Torgny T. Segerstedt (1966), *The Nature of Social Reality*: 161.
[48]Samuelsson (1968), *Great Power*: 166.
[49]Orvar Löfgren (1980), "Historical Perspectives on Scandinavian Peasantries," *Annual Review of Anthropology* 9:205.
[50]Orvar Löfgren (1981), "On the Anatomy of Culture," *Ethnologia Europaea* 12-1:34.
[51]In the discussion that follows I have relied very much on the findings of this research group, whose project is called "Culture and Class: A Study of Social and Cultural Change in Sweden c. 1880-1980." Two major works, in Swedish, have come from this group: Jonas Frykman and Orvar Löfgren (1979), *Den Kultiverade Människan*, published in English (1987) as *Culture Builders*; and Jonas Frykman and O. Löfgren, eds. (1984), *Moderna Tider*. In most of the following I have footnoted material drawn from these sources that has appeared in various English-language articles.
[52]Löfgren (1981), "Anatomy of Culture": 34-35.
[53]Orvar Löfgren (1984a), "The Sweetness of Home: Class, Culture and Family Life in Sweden," *Ethnologia Europaea* 14:45.
[54]*Ibid*.: 45.
[55]*Ibid*.: 47, 49.
[56]Löfgren (1984b), "Family and Household": 459.
[57]*Ibid*.: 462.
[58]Börje Hanssen (1973), "Common Folk and Gentlefolk," *Ethnologia Scandinavica*: 67-100.
[59]Hanssen (1979/1980), "Household, Classes." See also Palle Ove Christiansen (1978), "Peasant Adaptation to Bourgeois Culture," *Ethnologia Scandinavica*: 98-152.
[60]Hanssen (1979/1980), "Household, Classes": 109.
[61]*Ibid*.: 115.
[62]Royal Ministry of Foreign Affairs (1974), *The Biography of a People*: 76.
[63]Samuelsson (1968), *Great Power*: 183.
[64]Bo Kronborg and T. Nilsson (1978), "Social Mobility, Migration, and Family Building in Urban Environments," pp. 227-327 in Åkerman et al. (1978), *Chance and Change*.
[65]Kaare Svalastoga (1954), "The Family in Scandinavia," pp. 374-380 in *Marriage and Family Living* 16-4:374.
[66]Sten Carlsson (1978), "Unmarried Women in the Swedish Society of Estates," pp. 220-226 in Åkerman et al. (1978), *Chance and Change*. Some of the rates listed were originally calculated by the Swedish demographer Gustav Sundbärg (1906).
[67]Samuelsson (1968), *Great Power*: 186.
[68]*Ibid*.: 211.
[69]Löfgren (1984b), "Family and Household": 464-466.
[70]*Ibid*.: 466.
[71]For a good description of community life in a working-class neighborhood of Stockholm early in the century, see Åke Daun (1974), *Förortsliv*.
[72]Löfgren (1984b) "Family and Household": 464.
[73]Waldemar Svensson (1941), "Home Ownership in Sweden," pp. 31-47 in The Royal Swedish Commission, *Social Welfare in Sweden*.
[74]Royal Ministry of Foreign Affairs (1974), *The Biography of a People*: 79-82.
[75]Ingvar Andersson and Jörgen Weibull (1985), *Swedish History in Brief*: 47.
[76]Löfgren (1984a), "The Sweetness of Home": 56.

Chapter	The Family as a Public Issue: The Development of Swedish Family Policy, 1930–1950

The Family as a Public Issue: The Development of Swedish Family Policy, 1930–1950

Chapter

6

The Depression of the 1930s provided the catalyst for a rapid expansion of the Swedish government. This led, as it did in the United States, to extensive state intervention in the society's social and economic affairs. In contrast to the United States, however, Swedish governmental activities during the 1930s laid the foundation for what was to become in the next half century the Western world's most comprehensive welfare state. While economic conditions may not have been quite so severe in Sweden as in many other Western nations, they were severe enough to generate a strong tolerance for increased governmental action. Sweden's export economy was crippled by the Depression, and unemployment was widespread. An additional concern of the time was the rumbling of fascism to the south, which created nationalistic anxieties about keeping Sweden free and democratic.

Thus the stage was set for the emergence into national power in 1932 of the Social Democratic Party, a party that was to rule Sweden almost uninterruptedly for the next 45 years. Allied to the dominant trade-union organization in Sweden, the party had been founded in 1889 and originally propounded a strongly Marxist, revolutionary ideology. Over the years, however, this ideology was greatly toned down by the party's mainstream. From a group of radical visionaries the party developed into a strong political organization dominated by practical-minded labor leaders with the backing of rational planners, social scientists, and technicians.[1] The party's main goal became the furthering of the aims of the working class, but always by way of bourgeois democracy and in cooperation with other political parties. When the Social Democratic Party finally came into political predominance in the 1930s (it had also ruled briefly in the 1920s), it was solidly democratic in spirit and spoke little about the class struggle or even about national ownership of the means of production, although it was very much in favor of active state control of the national economy and a massive redistribution of income through taxation and welfare programs.

Because it did not have a majority in parliament, the Social Democratic Party had to rule by way of extensive coalitions and bargaining throughout much of the 1930s and 1940s. Typically, the coalitions were made with the Agrarian Party. The depression-fighting government measures of the early 1930s consisted of farm supports of various kinds, together with steeply progressive taxation, extensive public-works programs, especially the construction of new housing, and unemployment insurance. But partly to push effectively government activity to a higher, more interventionist and welfare-oriented level, some way had to be found to draw a larger degree of support from the more conservative political camps in Sweden. The issue that provided this possibility was one that had originally been raised by conservatives, one taken up in the end by the Social Democrats only with some reluctance: the population question.

The Population Question

Industrialization and urbanization had brought yet another striking social change to Sweden—a plummeting birthrate and a population that had virtually stopped growing. The nation that Thomas Malthus had once used as a case in point for his theories of overpopulation suddenly found itself with a birthrate that not only had fallen below the level necessary for the replacement of the society, but was the lowest in the world. Throughout the preceding 150 years or more the mortality rate had been dropping steeply, and this was the main reason for Sweden's population increases. But in the 1870s, coinciding with the onset of major industrialization, the fertility rate also began to drop. In the last part of the nineteenth century, the decline in fertility rates was probably due mainly to the drop in the marriage rate. In the twentieth century, when the marriage rate began to climb again, the diminishing birthrate was linked to the use of birth-control measures. Both an increase in the number of childless marriages and a fall in the number of children per marriage occurred.[2] The birthrate reached its lowest point ever in 1934. At that time, each Swedish woman was bearing on the average 1.7 children, which was 60% fewer children than her grandmother had born 50 years before. For adequate replacement of the population, it was necessary for each woman to bear an average of 2.3 children.[3]

This condition provided the backdrop for a fascinating social and political debate within Swedish society, which was to have far-reaching consequences. The debate was triggered by a book published in 1934, entitled *Kris i Befolkningsfrågan* (Crisis in the Population Question), written by the husband-and-wife team of social scientists, Alva and Gunnar Myrdal.[4] Active members of the Social Democratic Party, the Myrdals argued in this book that a declining population would have serious repercussions for Sweden. They noted especially that a nation with an excessively large elderly population would face a heavy economic burden and "that the total cultural atmosphere must tend to become static as the old gain in importance."[5] Too few Swedes were marrying, they said, nor were married Swedes having enough children, and the reasons for these facts seemed to be mainly economic—the economic costs of having large families had become too great. By 1937 the book had sold more than 16,000 copies, which for Sweden at that time was a runaway bestseller.[6]

To remedy the situation, the Myrdals proposed a series of far-reaching government measures that would encourage people to marry and would shore up families economically, especially working-class families, presumably to enable them to have more children without suffering the economic consequences. The measures they outlined made up a virtual catalog of welfare-state programs to help families and the poor, including free health services, free education, subsidized recreation and child care, and housing and rent subsidies.[7] In the ensuing decades, these programs were eventually enacted by the Swedish government, although most had to wait until after World War II.

Before the Myrdals' book appeared, concern about the decline in the Swedish population and about the welfare of families with children had mainly been limited to conservative political circles. As early as the turn of the century, Swedish conservatives had raised serious questions about the consequences of the population decline (at that time mainly due to emigration) in terms of shortages of both labor, particularly in the agricultural sector, and of military manpower. One result of their efforts was a 1910 law that forbade "the spreading of information about contraceptives." By the 1930s "pronatalism" had become a prominent part of the Conservative Party's ideology. The strength of the ideology was based on fundamental anxieties about a loss of national power and identity, a loss that in their view could result either from military weakness or from the need to bring in immigrant labor. The ideology was also based on an overall concern that the traditional family was being pushed aside in the rush toward modernism.[8] The idea of marriage loans, later enacted in Sweden, was first introduced by a breakaway faction of conservatives who favored the German National Socialist ideology, and the idea was consciously borrowed from the Nazis.

Unlike a number of other European nations, Sweden in the early 1930s had virtually no public policies designed to promote fertility by relieving the special economic and other burdens faced by families. Faced with overcoming the economic effects of the Depression, and in keeping with the lack of concern for and even antipathy toward "the family" that characterized most left-wing parties in Europe, the Social Democrats focused their priorities elsewhere. The Conservatives at that time had introduced a bill in parliament that would have changed the tax structure in favor of married couples with children, but the bill did not pass. A later attempt in 1934 to provide economic support to families with children also met with failure.

Pronatalism in Other European Nations

This conservative concern about low fertility was known in many other European nations as well, where it took a variety of political forms.[9] Best known are the attempts of the Nazi Party in Germany not only to turn around their population decline, but to create a pure race of "Aryans." The Nazis forbade the use of birth control and prosecuted abortionists, on the one hand, and tried to eliminate the "genetically unfit" and "racially unpure" through involuntary sterilization, on the other. In addition, they established a system of interest-free marriage loans, financed by taxing the unmarried, for young couples who could satisfy certain criteria of race and character. Their policies stressed that women should stay home and raise children. To say the least, many of these Nazi policies seriously damaged the cause of pronatalism among democratically inclined people in other nations, including Sweden, especially at a later date when it turned out that these policies had formed a springboard for what became wholesale genocide.

French population policies took a different tack, though demonstrating at least an equal concern for maintaining a strong nation. With low birthrates of very long standing, France had been seriously discussing pronatalist measures for a century or more, but with very few concrete public actions to show for it. In the early 1920s the French passed legislation with the objectives of preventing contraception and punishing abortion. On the positive side, the French government had long encouraged private businesses to provide family allowances for their workers, mostly in the form of higher salaries to fathers. With the backing of the Catholic Church, family allowances had first been introduced by private businesses in France in the nineteenth century, mainly for social reasons. But it was not until the 1930s that public monies were made available for that purpose, both as childbearing incentives and for family welfare. A comprehensive family code introduced in 1939 provided family allowances throughout France and also set up a special tax on bachelors and childless couples. Like their German counterparts, some of these French policies were designed to encourage women to stay out of the labor force and to remain full-time mothers. Limited family allowance schemes, together with other pronatalist measures, were also instituted in many other European countries, including Spain, Switzerland, Hungary, Italy, and Belgium.[10]

The Myrdal Proposals

The Myrdal proposals differed substantially from the conservative policies of France and Germany in that they combined in a seemingly contradictory way the goal of pronatalism with a program calling for the promotion of birth control. Estimating that perhaps as many as a half of all births in Sweden were "undesired" due to "faulty contraception technique,"[11] they asked for the repeal of the 1910 law concerning contraception (which had never been strongly enforced), the liberalization of abortion rules, and the widespread dissemination of information about sexual matters. The apparent contradiction between probirth and probirth-control views was reconciled, the Myrdals thought, by the principle that the only pronatalist policy feasible in a democracy was one in which there was voluntary parenthood; an increase in fertility that merely added to the number of "unwanted" children was intolerable. "Children should grow up in normal families. All social experts are agreed that illegitimate births should be prevented to the greatest possible extent. . . . In a democratic society we cannot accept a way of things whereby the poor, ignorant, and inexperienced maintain the stock of the population," stated Gunnar Myrdal.[12] Thus they desired a qualitative as well as quantitative increase in the population, but not a qualitative increase along racial or ethnic lines (although they supported programs, common in many nations of that time, that fostered the eugenic sterilization of the "unfit.")

The Myrdal proposals, unlike most such policies elsewhere, did not ask that women be returned to their traditional domestic at roles home; if anything, the emphasis was on making it easier for working women also to have children. In an early statement on this theme, Alva Myrdal said in her 1941 rewrite of *Kris* that there must be a "defense of the right to earn a living both for women in general and for married women in particular."[13] "What is to be guarded," she noted, "is not so much the 'married woman's right to work' as the 'working woman's right to marry and have children'"[14] She even went so far as to stress that in order to bring more children into the world, "equalization between the two mates in regard to parental discomfort, work and constraint would gradually have to be brought about."[15] These themes, seldom heard at the time, were later to gain great prominence in Swedish society.

To achieve a population turnaround, the women of Sweden were being asked to drastically increase their family sizes. It was one thing for each Swedish woman to have an average of 2.3 children to ensure society's replacement. But not all women marry and not all of those who do are fertile. As careful analyses at the time showed, a majority of all fertile, married couples in Sweden would have to have at least 4 children if reasonable population goals were to be met.[16] At this level of magnitude, what the Myrdals were asking for led to much sneering and mirth among the masses, who began to call large families "Myrdal's families" and invented a new verb, "to myrdal," meaning "to copulate."[17]

But the most radical aspect of the Myrdal proposals, within the Swedish context, was the linking of pronatalist ideas to the necessity for a great deal of state intervention in society to promote economic and social programs, especially for the poor, and to bring about a widespread redistribution of income. "Population policy can be nothing less than a social policy at large," said Alva Myrdal, adding that "influencing the whole structure of modern social life may be the only effective way of controlling the development of the family institution."[18] The Myrdals envisioned a society in which the economic and social structures would be such that most couples would voluntarily choose to have large families. With reference to family changes in the preceding centuries, they stressed that "collectivistic devices must be instituted in the larger national household to substitute for the relative security enjoyed in the family household of old."[19] This meant that "the economic burden of bringing up children must be passed from the individual family to society as a whole, . . . a transfer of income from individuals and families without children to families with children."[20] In answer to the charge of critics that affluence and economic well-being tended in fact to diminish fertility (for most groups in modern society there is an inverse correlation between income and fertility levels), the Myrdals pointed to an investigation of Stockholm families married in 1920–1922 that had found (for possibly the first time anywhere) a positive correlation between income and fertility.[21]

Early Swedish Family Legislation

At first, the Myrdal population proposals were more favorably received by the conservative side than by the Social Democrats. To some extent, after all, the Myrdals were merely embellishing ideas that conservatives had been putting forth, without legislative success, for several years. Yet at the same time, the conservatives were highly suspicious of the long-run implications of the Myrdal proposals, and they viewed them, in part, as "designed to cloak the entrance of socialism through the back door,"[22] and as a "crowbar for social reforms."[23] Following initiatives of the Conservative Party, however, the government set up in 1935 a nonpartisan Royal Commission on Population (with Gunnar Myrdal as a leading member) to examine the issues raised by the Myrdals. The establishment of such special-purpose commissions is a traditional Swedish approach to dealing with political issues, and this commission was a particularly active one, issuing no fewer than 18 reports between 1935 and 1938. Included in these reports were a series of recommendations for extensive social reforms for children, women, and families, recommendations that later were described by one Swedish historian as "motherhood politics."[24] Most of the thinking and specific proposals first put forward in *Kris* found their way into the reports of the commission.

In 1937 and 1938, a number of bills that had been suggested by the Commission on Population were passed by the Swedish parliament. Perhaps the most important provided for the institution of marriage loans, low-interest loans to couples about to be married to assist them in setting up a new household. It was believed that these loans would not only raise the marriage rate, but would also lower the age of marriage, both of which would help to increase fertility. The average annual percentage of marrying couples who made use of these loans between 1938 and 1948 was 17%.[25] Other important measures provided modest maternity allowances and free maternity care at newly established maternal and child-welfare centers for women whose incomes fell below a certain level. Although they flowed from the work of the Commission, these bills were very similar to those that had been introduced earlier by the conservatives and turned down. In giving their support to these measures, the right-wing parties stressed their pronatalist rather than their welfare aspects, defining the population–family problem "as concerning no less than the continued existence of the Swedish people."[26]

Other bills passed at this time provided for the abolition of the anti-contraceptives law of 1910, small income-tax deductions for each child, a guaranteed leave of absence with partial salary for female civil servants during pregnancy and childbearing, and a prohibition against the dismissal of women because of marriage and pregnancy. The Myrdals strongly favored government aid in kind rather than in cash, and programs of this type that were developed (with very modest levels of monetary support) included means-tested vacation trips for housewives and free school lunches for children. This new legislation was in addition to family housing programs that had been passed in 1935, which stemmed from an earlier Committee on Housing. These new programs included rent subsidies for low-income families with more than three children and loans for the construction of new rental housing for such families. In 1938 a fund was added to help large families build their own homes.

Political Motives and Social Impact

Although it represented the initial, pathbreaking steps toward the comprehensive welfare state that was to come, the family-welfare legislation fell far short of the desires of the Myrdals and the recommendations of the Population Commission. One reason more legislation was not passed was that the Social Democratic Party and its labor union constituency were not

particularly accepting of these conservative-generated profamily and pronatalist ideas. The average Swedish worker was little inclined to give up his
hard-earned economic position on behalf of having more children, and he
or she was not especially moved by arguments about the problematic future
of Sweden as a nation. One left-wing newspaper of the time claimed that the
whole pronatalist impulse "was pandering to militarism."[27] And despite the
impeccable liberal credentials of the Myrdals, they apparently were never
fully accepted by the Social Democratic Party because of their pronatalist
ideas, although the party's intellectual wing accorded them some support.[28]

That the Social Democratic Party did in fact come to support pronatalist
policies seems to have been based as much on considerations of short-run
political gain as on anything else. In a frequently quoted speech made at a
party congress in 1936, for example, the Minister for Social Affairs, Gustav
Moller, said:

> I must say that I will not hesitate to frighten no matter how many Conservatives,
> Farmer's Unionists and members of the Liberal Party with the threat that our
> people will otherwise die out, if with this threat I can get them to vote for social
> proposals I put forward. This is my simple view of the population issue and it is
> good enough for me.[29]

There is even some doubt about the degree to which the Myrdals believed
in pronatalism, and it has been charged that they too used the whole issue
as a smokescreen for socialist reforms.[30] In their original work the Myrdals
took some pains to deny that they were using the pronatalist banner merely
to convince a larger segment of the population of the need for extensive
government social programs and a redistribution of income. Yet it is clear
that they believed in radical social reforms, quite apart from the population
issue. Gunnar Myrdal stated that

> the reforms are primarily motivated as investments in the happiness, health and
> productive quality of the rising generation and should from this point of view
> be undertaken even if their quantitative effects upon the population trend were
> slight.[31]

While apparently a stronger believer than his wife in the population issue
per se, Gunnar Myrdal was very clear about the political utility of this issue
in molding both right- and left-wing opinion. When he gave the Godkin
Lectures at Harvard University in 1938 he stated that

> because of the population argument he [the conservative] will find himself, time
> after time, supporting items of social policy which have previously entered his
> mind only as dangerous radical fallacies to be combatted. . . . Its main political
> appeal is to responsibility for the survival of the nation. When this argument is
> incorporated in the radical philosophy it is made much easier for a large number

of people to accept political radicalism. Radicalism cannot thereafter very well be depicted as a destructive force working in denial of national and family values. On the other hand, the population problem also actually strengthens the radicalism in radicalism by calling for a speeding up of the social and economic transformations of society in certain directions.[32]

Alva Myrdal has proclaimed, at least in hindsight, that she was never a committed pronatalist. In a new preface to the 1968 paperback edition of *Nation and Family* she stated:

I should now reduce any semblance I might have to a "pronatalist" approach . . . the message of our work . . . [was] not in reality directing . . . [Swedish] policy to any greater inclination to breed children. The main framework for a positive family policy was, is, and must be that society will shoulder responsibility for the security of the preproductive age group—the children—as well as for the postproductive one, the aged.[33]

Whatever the Myrdals' motivations, the population–family question initiated a very significant breakthrough in Swedish politics. It galvanized Social Democratic ideology around the family, an ideology that resonated well among a surprisingly large segment of the population, and it brought together both right and left political factions in the support of new government social programs.[34] A general consensus developed across the political spectrum that families should be given some compensation for the costs connected with having and raising children. As Gunnar Myrdal put it, the population issue "engineered an entirely new constellation of attitudenal associations."[35] A left-wing ideological position that emerged from this issue, which focused the activities of the Social Democrats for many years to come, was expressed in this 1937 statement by a government official in the social-welfare sector:

It is not much of an exaggeration to claim that the modern [society] surrounds the individual with its care from his cradle to his grave. . . . Socio-political measures which are designed to give to the average citizen greater security and happiness are also beneficial to the coming generation in that they provide for better conditions of care and development for children and youth. They may even contribute to the removal or the weakening of the motives against procreation which today are often nourished by a heightened sense of moral responsibility, combined with worry over an uncertain future. What has just been said applies, of course, in particular to measures which have been taken in late years to protect the family, and which represent aspects of a dynamic social population policy.[36]

Thus the issues of welfare, equality, population growth, and family were all effectively joined. This ideology of state intervention on behalf of family happiness together with the political alliances between right and left that were established in the 1930s around the population and family question were to have profound significance for the further building of the Swedish welfare state.

It is useful to note the kinds of family measures that were *not* passed by the Swedish parliament at this time. The Swedes did not accept the idea of a "bachelors tax," which had been enacted in several other countries. They passed no incentives for women to stay home as housewives. They did not attempt to restrict birth-control measures. And they did not tie family measures to various genetic or character factors, as the Germans did. Moreover, they were not yet ready to institute on a widespread basis what later were to become major government programs geared to the family— child allowances and state support of day-care centers—although modest child allowances had been introduced in 1937 for especially disadvantaged children.

Few additional family-oriented measures were enacted during the last years of the 1930s, because the worsening international situation required increased expenditures for Swedish national defense, leaving few funds for other purposes. By the end of the 1930s, in fact, talk about a population crisis in Sweden had died down substantially. One important reason for this was that, even as the Population Commission was beginning its work in the mid-1930s, fertility in Sweden began to increase again, and the birthrate continued to rise until the outbreak of the war.

As noted above, the Myrdals were disappointed with what they regarded as the government's inactivity in the 1930s. In all, government transfer payments as a percentage of the national income increased from 3% in 1929 to only 5% in 1940.[37] Reviewing the actual policies enacted by the Swedish government following the reports of the Population Commission, Gunnar Myrdal stated that

> these reforms are rather futile compared with the thorough reconstruction of the economic basis for the institution of the family, which in a country like Sweden is necessary if the family is to be rescued from sterility and the population kept from vanishing.[38]

In view of the contradictory messages sent by the makers of Swedish family policies in the 1930s, both pronatalist and probirth-control, the mixture of motivations behind those policies, and the limited amounts of financial support for them, it may not be surprising that their effects in actually promoting higher fertility seem to have been negligible. Although the birthrate did go up in the late 1930s, there is general agreement that this resulted from forces other than government policy. In one careful study of women who had received marriage loans, for example, no increase in fertility was found compared to women without the loans.[39] Studies of the effects of Swedish family policies at this time lend weight to the view that economic incentives may in fact be counterproductive with regard to increasing the birthrate; that, as many liberals in Sweden had maintained, as incomes rise, birthrates will drop. This is not to say, however, that these family policies were unsuccessful in broader, social terms.

The Myrdals, Family Ideology, and Family Decline

Despite their strong leftist political leanings, the Myrdals actually had a relatively conservative view of the family, its role in society, and its path of change. They saw the family as perhaps the main social institution in society, and they oriented the thrust of their policies toward what they regarded as the family's principal function: the socialization of children. Mainly because of its child-rearing functions, the family was something to be protected and enhanced. This put the Myrdals in an ideological camp quite apart from the antifamily tendencies of many radicals in Scandinavia, those who favored a radical change in the structure, if not the outright abolition, of the family.

There were two main streams of antifamilism in Scandinavia, and both were opposed to the same phenomenon: the Victorian bourgeois family as it had emerged in the nineteenth century.[40] One was a literary and intellectual stream of thought that saw the family as standing against personal growth and freedom for the individual. This view was commonly attached to feminism, but interestingly its greatest Swedish advocate was Strindberg, who thought that the family oppressed men more than women.[41] In both the feminist and the Strindbergian versions, however, the traditional family was viewed as an oppressive and even pathological institution. This dark side of the Scandinavian family was highlighted years later in the movies of Ingmar Bergman.

The second antifamily ideology of the time was the Marxist version, which had a limited following within the Swedish Social Democratic Party. Marxists considered the family to be oppressive not so much in psychological terms, but as an embodiment of the bourgeois oppressions of the larger society. The Marxist view was that the family had to be abolished in order to achieve an egalitarian society, and in many versions of Marxism, child rearing was to be taken away from the family and managed by the state. Although one can see some lasting influences from both of these perspectives, neither ideology made a compelling political impact at the time.

Much more pervasive in Sweden, especially during the 1940s, was ideological concern about the family's decline. The 1940s were a decade when, as Orvar Löfgren has noted, there were more books calling for the protection of the home than in any other similar time period.[42] Since sociology and the social sciences were still largely undeveloped as independent disciplines in

Sweden, most of these books were written by government-employed intellectuals. There was much public discussion of a "family crisis" and considerable nostalgic longing for the return of what was felt to be the more stable
and rewarding family life of the Victorian and even the peasant preindustrial eras. In 1941, a government proposal for more and better education in
the art of homemaking in Swedish schools expressed a common theme of
the time when it began: "We need a revival of the family."[43] To some extent, this theme echoed the perspective put forth in the mid-1930s by the
Myrdals, but in the new popular version it was both more nostalgic and more
focused on the declining quality of family life. It was in fact more reminiscent of the conception of family decline that was popular in America at the
turn of the century than the perspective that prevailed during the American
post–World War II years (see Chapter 2); this provides perhaps another indication of just how much later in history the process of modernization had
come to Sweden.

The Myrdals agreed with the conservatives that the family as an institution
was in long-term decline and in something of a state of "crisis." In this regard,
they incorporated into their family perspective Ogburn's-loss-of-functions
argument, a perspective that was at that time popular in the United States.
Alva Myrdal put the argument as follows:

> The population crisis is only the external aspect of what is really a crisis in the
> family as an institution. So deep-rooted and fixed a system of human relations as
> the family has necessarily lacked the plasticity to adapt itself to the fundamental
> and pervasive economic changes of the last century. The family even in its
> modern structure has its moorings in a preindustrial agrarian society. One after
> another these moorings have been lost.[44]

Unlike many conservatives of the time, however, Alva Myrdal did not view
this loss of family functions as a reason for open nostalgia about the past. She
thought that with the necessary help of the state the family should be helped
to adapt to the new order. "Since we cannot, and do not want to, revert to an
agrarian or patriarchal order," she noted, "some collectivistic devices must be
instituted in the larger national household to substitute for the relative security
enjoyed in the family household of old."[45] These "collectivistic devices"
included a much enlarged role for the state in economic support, education,
recreation, and child care. "The task of our generation," she emphasized, "is
to reintegrate the family in the larger society," but not in such a way that
the family is "absorbed through an indiscriminate collectivization of all its
functions into a deindividualized and amorphous communism."[46] Moreover,
Alva Myrdal differed substantially from the conservatives in calling for a
combination of motherhood and remunerative work for married women.
She was even quite prescient in her discussion of the problem of what

was later to be called "women's two roles," and ended her book *Nation and Family* with these words: "The risk is great that society will proceed so slowly in solving these problems of women's existence that new and even more desperate crises may invade the whole field of women, family and population."[47]

It was the Myrdals' family ideology that was to prevail in Sweden over the next few decades. New family ideologies were to come, but they too were to be anticipated by the Myrdals, who ended up shifting considerably away from their original ideological position, as we shall see in the next chapter.

The Embourgeoisment of Swedish Culture and the Family

The Myrdals were the embodiments of a group that had gradually but persistently come into cultural dominance in Sweden following World War I and especially during the 1930s and 1940s: the new middle class. Concurrently with the growth of state intervention, Sweden had become a thoroughly bourgeois society in cultural if not entirely in economic or political terms. The bourgeois ethos that came to prevail was not exactly the cultural style of the old Victorian bourgeoisie that had come into ascendency at the turn of the century. This cultural style, however, did provide the roots for a new middle class composed of engineers, technicians, scientists, intellectuals, social workers, planners, and do-gooders of all shades and sorts. Like the old middle class, the new group that then came to dominate Swedish life was embued with the main canons of the Protestant ethic: hard work and self-discipline, high moral standards in such areas as honesty and trust, cleanliness and neatness, law and order, and the importance of the family. Yet for the new middle class, science and technology had replaced religion as the overarching supreme value. This new class also possessed the characteristic traits of capitalist entrepreneurs: frugality combined with a drive for material acquisition.

In place of the Victorian's feelings of class superiority leading to class protectiveness, the new group leaned toward egalitarianism. It was an egalitarianism that called not for social leveling, but for helping one's brother to make it up the ladder. As a French observer put it, in the Swedish view "true Democracy does not consist in lowering a countess to the level of her chambermaid, but in raising the chambermaid to the rank of the countess."[48]

The rise to dominance of the new middle class in Sweden differed from that of other nations mainly in the speed with which it took place and in its wide impact. Infused with the new intellectual might of science and technology, the new middle class proceeded with all haste and with tremendous success, often under government auspices beginning in the 1930s, to remake the nation in its own image. In the view of some current Swedish intellectuals, this amounted to a class struggle in which the middle class coerced the working class into accepting its style of life.[49] Whether they were used for the coercion of a recalcitrant social class or merely for the pursuasion of a group of people eager to become "modernized," the key concepts that provided the ideological banners for the moral crusade of the new middle class were rationality, efficiency, functionalism, education, and hygiene. In the eyes of the new middle class, of course, these concepts did not stand merely for the cultural style of a particular social class but for the good, the true, and the beautiful—the right—as determined by modern scientific standards.

Already in the 1930s Sweden had become so much a "new bourgeois" bastion that this was a subject of frequent note by foreign visitors. Visiting in the early 1930s, the French writer Serge de Chessin called Sweden "the most bourgeois country one can imagine."[50] In his view, "the Social Democrats rule a bourgeois people." He suggested that a visitor to a Swedish May Day celebration of workers would be prompted to ask: "But where are the proletarians? I see only the bourgeois!"[51] The English travel writer Cicely Hamilton said of Stockholm in the late 1930s:

> The word "middle-class," for some foolish reason, has a contemptuous sound to English ears; but when I say that Stockholm . . . struck me as a middle-class city, the reverse of contempt is intended. I mean that (so far as a stranger may judge) the standard of its people is one of comfortable simplicity rather than display, that there is less of shabby poverty, less of obvious wealth than you will see in other capitals of Europe.[52]

Indeed, the whole reason for the population question having arisen in the first place was the fertility drop that resulted because so many Swedes had become middle class. As Marquis Childs noted in his famous book on Sweden in the 1930s, the Swedish middle class "is determined upon a standard of comfort and leisure incompatible with children and family life."[53]

It was not only in life-style but in many respects in underlying "character" that Swedes had become bourgeois. The American academic Hudson Strode, who spent a great deal of time in Sweden both before and immediately after World War II, stated bluntly what most foreign observers thought:

> Self-control is perhaps the most significant common denominator of the Swedish people. . . .
>
> By nature Swedes are industrious, and everyone works in Sweden. . . .
>
> There is no better housewife in the world than the Swedish, though she is not the Hausfrau type of woman. . . .

> As a people, Swedes are more law-abiding than any I have met in four conti-
> nents. . . .
> A Swede is proud of his reputation for integrity. . . .
> While not a greedy people, Swedes set considerable store on material wealth. . . .
> The Swede is much concerned with making a good appearance. . . .
> A Swede cannot bear not to conform. . . . From birth a Swede is trained in doing
> the right thing, obeying the code, making the proper appearance. . . .
> In Sweden politeness is a science or an art, as you chooose . . . .[54]

All of this is surely somewhat overdrawn, referring as much perhaps to the ideal as to the reality. And of course these attributes were subject to varying personal interpretations. Strode reports on the not untypical comment of one foreigner: "There is everything to admire in Sweden, and so little to love."[55] The middle-class virtues are not everyone's cup of tea. But it is amazing to what extent foreign writers over the years have agreed on these Swedish cultural attributes. Some of the same specific traits had long been found in all classes in Sweden. But it was not until well into the twentieth century that they came to be regarded as characterizing the Swedish people as a whole.

As Orvar Löfgren has noted, "working class life came to be defined by the bourgeoisie not as an *alternative* culture, but rather as a *lack of culture*. Working class life was thus a defective way of life which had to be improved."[56] Beginning about 1930, the canons of culture of the new middle class were promulgated nationwide through an expanding government with an ever-growing network of "agents" and "experts." There was also an extensive system of adult-education programs sponsored by the Swedish consumer cooperatives and other organized social movements, including the trade unions themselves.

It may be considered an irony that this "class cultural warfare," a crusade in which the working class was indoctrinated with middle-class standards, took place under the aegis of a government putatively dominated by the working class. Many of the leaders of the labor movement, however, for the most part were (or had become) middle-class intellectuals. They kept a surprisingly "low profile" compared to middle-class leaders in other industrializing nations, where ostentatious display of middle-class status, Philistinism, and exclusivity tended to be much greater. So the cultural gap between the middle and working classes in Sweden was not so great as elsewhere. Still, it is a tribute to the rapid emergence of class cohesion in Sweden (or, if you wish, to the inherent wisdom of the working class), that this crusade ever was permitted to materialize to the degree that it did.

Of what did the cultural crusade actually consist? One main locale for the "reeducation" of the working class were the homes and everyday lives of working class people.[57] The new middle class eschewed the old bourgeois traits of stern, authoritarian child rearing, with its many rituals of avoidance, including strong taboos against sex and nudity, in favor of a new egalitarianism and the ideals of personal freedom. It also rejected the stuffy, over-furnished, and ostentatious home interiors of the old bourgeosie for a new functionalism, in which homes were to become light, airy, and, most of all, efficient. A central theme of the new life-style, as was pointed out by Jonas Frykman, was "hygiene": mental hygiene, bodily hygiene, sexual hygiene, food hygiene. Hygiene or health of all kinds, and its scientific basis, replaced the older religiously based morality, and it was no accident that the role of religion in Sweden was undercut with extraordinary swiftness by the new doctors of modernity.

Because it was felt that children provided the most efficient target for widespread social change, the importance of the nuclear family was strongly upheld, albeit a family with a diminished patriarchy and with a new, stream-lined role for the mother–housewife. There were probably more full-time housewives in Sweden at the time than ever before, working-class women having been forced out of the labor market and into the home by the De-pression, and middle-class women, unlike their Victorian progenitors, having to make do without servants. The new family was to be an equal partnership between husband and wife, a companionship based on common interests, with the main obligation of the couple being to successfully raise their chil-dren to be full contributors to the new era.

It was not yet envisioned that the wife should become a regular participant in the labor force, a trend that did not get underway until well after midcentury; the role of full-time mother was still regarded as being of supreme importance. Yet it was felt that women could play a much larger role in public life than they had been allowed to heretofore, and much of the concern with "rationalizing the home and housework" was geared to this end. One Swedish enthnographer said of the changing role model for Swedish women during this period:

> As mothers they were expected to give up the old ideal of obedience and rear their children in a democratic spirit. As housewives they were supposed to use their time and energy rationally so that they would have time left to act as professional workers and as citizens with an independent role in society.[58]

It was partly by means of the government's rapidly expanding role in housing construction that the new cultural hegemony was promoted. An ur-banizing population, after all, required a lot of new housing, and in Sweden this task fell largely to the government. A massive research effort was un-dertaken in conjunction with the housing programs, designed to determine the most functional forms of home architecture and interior design for the "rational reorganization of domestic life."[59] One government group, for example, issued a lengthy research report in 1935 on the standardization of kitchens. The report noted at the outset: "A pleasant, practical and hygienic work place for those who handle the daily care of the house is the primary condition for an orderly home."[60] It was felt that home organization could profit greatly from the principles used in modern industry, and by the same token "housewife" became a valued "occupational role." Wherever she turned, the housewife was able to rely, and indeed was expected to rely, on a growing army of government-employed experts in fields ranging from food preparation to child psychology.

Government efforts were also supplemented by such private groups as the Swedish Society of Arts and Crafts (*Svenska Slöjdföreningen*), which engaged heavily in educational programs to improve the taste of the average Swede through good design. As early as the 1920s, for example, educational programs were organized under the slogan "More Beautiful Things for Everyday Use." The general goal of the society was "creating pleasing and comfortable surroundings of good taste for everybody."[61] It was not long before the style "Swedish Modern" became known worldwide, emphasizing color and clarity of line, natural form, and the honest treatment of material.

The rationalization of the home, of course, remained for some time more a middle-class ideal than a widespread working-class reality. Relative to other nations of comparable wealth, the Swedish urban working class was housed at a very low standard until well into the 1960s. Working-class traditions were not easy to dislodge, and workers often resisted change. The strict segregation of gender roles, the diminished privatization of family life in favor of greater neighborhood cohesion, and the lack of participation by both women and men in public life were working-class traits that in some parts of Sweden continue to exist to this day. Moreover, the ideal of "occupation housewife" was made difficult, to say the least, when working-class women were forced into the labor market, as they were during the early stages of industrialization.

Nevertheless, the cultural movement of Swedish society in a relatively short period of time from a religiously based nation of peasants and poor urban workers to a secular nation dominated by an urban middle class was little short of remarkable. The freedom from wars, the relative lack of political or class dissension, the widespread agreement on collective goals, and the late industrialization and rapid ascendency of the nation to a position of wealth, each was an important factor in accounting for this movement. No matter what the reasons, and their analysis would require more space than this book permits, it is fair to say that by midcentury, Sweden had become in many respects the most thoroughly bourgeois nation in the world, with a firmly entrenched pattern of middle-class nuclear familism.

Swedish Family Policy Development in the 1940s

World War II brought yet another opportunity for the expansion of state power in Sweden. Even though, as a neutral nation, Sweden was not directly involved in the fighting, the war necessitated such measures as food rationing and price and rent control, as well as national economic-resource planning. By the war's end, the government had attained substantial control (but not ownership) of business and industry. The war also seems to have had a leveling effect on social attitudes, bringing about a further diminution of class cleavages and class-based political conflicts.[62] Based on an experience of wartime cooperation among people from all walks of life, strong feelings of national identity and solidarity pervaded the land. Unlike most other European nations, Sweden at the end of the war had a relatively intact economy and a high degree of economic self-sufficiency. The Social Democrats attained a parliamentary majority for the first time in the national elections of 1940. Even though a coalition government was maintained during the war, shortly after the war's end a purely Social Democratic government was at last established. Thus the time was ripe for the enactment of a wave of social reforms that had been sitting on the back burner for almost a decade, reforms that represented the true fruits of the activist political debates of the 1930s.

The conservative political agenda of pronatalism had its last gasp in the first half of the 1940s. In the early war years, the Swedish birthrate began to drop again, and, riding on a growing wave of nationalism and defense concerns, the conservatives used the opportunity to rekindle a national debate on the population question. A new Population Commission was set up in 1941, and initially it had a more conservative cast than its 1930s predecessor. Among the proposals considered by the Commission were the establishment of a state agency for handling the population question and of an active state-supported program of pronatalist propaganda. Also, while the earlier Commission had concentrated on the dilemmas of working women, the new Commission emphasized the problems of housewives, seeking ways, for example, to alleviate the drudgery of housework.[63] The concern for housewives and the "need to deal with the practical problems which confront women in the home"[64] led to some modest but innovative policy developments, such as a guaranteed annual vacation for low-income housewives and state-supported home-help services for housewives who were temporarily incapacitated. The latter was provided free to low-income families and was based on their ability to pay for others.

But most of the conservative pronatalist proposals were eventually fought off by leftist political factions. The 1941 Commission's final recommendations dealt with the population question only in a negative way—that population policy should at least try to prevent a decline in the population. In place of the specific goals for population growth proposed by the earlier Commission, the new Commission emphasized the broad goals of social justice and social equality.[65] These were the goals on which Swedish family policy was to be focused in the years ahead, and the population question was all but dropped, not to emerge again until the 1970s.

In the decade after the war, in what has been called "the Great Period of Reform," the Social Democrats pushed through many of the large and expensive government programs that characterize the Swedish welfare state today.[66] With a real burst of political energy and few dissenting voices, there was enacted a sharp rise in old-age pensions, enlargements and reforms in education that prolonged basic education from seven to nine years and introduced a new "comprehensive" school, and the introduction of general health insurance, which became a compulsory national health system in 1956. These new government programs were financed by a much higher, and steeply graduated, scale of income taxation. By 1950 the percentage of the national income devoted to government transfer payments had climbed to 10%, exclusive of the insurance benefits to which the beneficiaries themselves had contributed.[67]

In family policy, the big event of the late 1940s was the introduction of a national family or child allowance program. It had first been introduced in the late 1930s on a limited basis for disadvantaged children, and on a more widespread basis during the war for persons inducted into the armed forces. This was a major proposal of the 1941 Population Commission, one of whose main priorities was to formulate "proposals for transferring, from the individual family to the community, a substantial part of the costs of bringing up children."[68] The political path for this and other far-reaching family proposals formulated by the Commission was cleared when the Commission's head, Tage Erlander, then Minister of Social Affairs, became the postwar Prime Minister of Sweden; this followed the death in 1946 of Per Albin Hansson, who had led the Social Democratic Party since 1925.

Although both the right and left were in favor of support for families with children, they differed considerably on just how this support should be structured. The right wished to transfer money from childless families to families with children, while the left looked at the problem as an opportunity for a broader equalization of income within Swedish society through the redistribution of income from the rich to the poor. The child allowance program of 1948 resulted from a compromise between these two positions.[69] An allowance of money was given to all families with children, without regard to their income level or family size. Thus wealthy families received the same allowance as poor families. At the same time, because it favored the wealthier classes, the right to take a child deduction from income taxes was repealed.

By the early 1950s, child support was being paid to families in an amount that corresponded to almost 30% of the minimum cost of meeting the living needs of each additional child.[70] This program of child allowances, in which Sweden was one of the world's pioneers, is still an instrumental part of the contemporary Swedish welfare state.

A related family-policy debate at that time, one first raised in the 1930s, involved the question of whether families should be helped in cash or in kind. The Myrdals, together with many people of a left-wing political pursuasion, favored the in-kind approach. They argued that this was the best way to ensure that government funds were used as intended. Advocates of the cash approach, however, feared the rise in state bureaucratic power that the in-kind approach might entail and favored cash grants in order to encourage the growth of "responsible family decision making." In the end, both approaches came to mark Swedish family policy. Gradually, the debate was broadened to focus on the issue of collective programs for families provided directly by government versus grants and loans to families that would enable them to purchase the necessary services in the market. This debate is still very much alive in Swedish politics today.

Other family-oriented legislation passed in the late 1940s and early 1950s, most of which was emphasized in the conclusions of the 1941 Population Commission, included a nationwide expansion of the free school-lunch program, a "home-help" service, the requirement that all pharmacies sell contraceptives, and programs of day nurseries. Particularly significant was the right given to women in 1954 to have 3-month's paid maternity leave from their jobs. This was later to evolve into the world famous "parental-leave" program.

By midcentury, government family policy had become a thoroughly ingrained and accepted part of Swedish life. There was general agreement among Swedes that, in the words of a 1953 report on social patterns in the Nordic countries of Europe:

> Society should take upon itself the responsibility for safeguarding and furthering the welfare of the family with respect to a number of vital needs which, save for such intervention, would be met only partially or not at all.[71]

The same report could state that "the whole body of social policy has . . . been pervaded to an increasing extent by family welfare considerations, the needs of the family having come to be accepted as the central issue with priority over all others."[72]

As the Swedish welfare state evolved still further, however, it is reasonable to say that whatever profamily thrust the Social Democrats may originally have made (or been talked into), these goals became overshadowed by two other political goals: income redistribution from the rich to the poor and equality for women, that is, economic equality and gender equality. By the late 1940s, in fact, the political climate in Sweden had already moved appreciably to the left under the successful leadership of the trade unions, and the Social Democratic Party became increasingly less inclined to compromise with the conservatives on such issues as the family. The traditional dominance of egalitarianism in left-wing political thought moved to the fore, and, as we shall see next, a whole new chapter in Swedish life was in the offing.

Notes

[1]Herbert Tingsten (1973), *The Swedish Social Democrats: Their Ideological Development:* 246ff.

[2]Royal Ministry of Foreign Affairs (1974), *The Biography of a People:* 86. For a general discussion of Swedish fertility trends, see Eva Bernhardt (1971), *Trends and Variations in Swedish Fertility: A Cohort Study,* and Erland Hofsten and Hans Lundström (1976), *Swedish Population History.*

[3]D. V. Glass (1970), "Population Policy," pp. 277–293 in M. I. Cole and C. Smith, *Democratic Sweden:* 277, 282.

[4]Alva Myrdal and Gunnar Myrdal (1934), *Kris i Befolkningsfrågan.* This was later rewritten by Alva Myrdal and published in English, together with summaries of the results of various Swedish investigating commissions, as Alva Myrdal (1941), *Nation and Family: The Swedish Experiment in Democratic Family and Population Policy,* with a second, paperback edition published under the same title in 1968.

[5]A. Myrdal (1968), *Nation and Family:* 88.

[6]D. V. Glass (1940), *Population Policies and Movements in Europe:* 317.

[7]For the intellectual roots of the Myrdals' thinking, see Allan C. Carlson (1979), "Sex, Babies, and Families: The Myrdals and the Population Question," and (1983), "The Myrdals, Pro-Natalism, and Swedish Social Democracy," *Continuity,* 6: 71–94.

[8]Gunnar Myrdal thought that fear of immigration to Sweden was particularly strong. Gunnar Myrdal (1962), *Population: A Problem for Democracy:* 86.

[9]The population policies of France and Germany, as well as Sweden, are discussed in C. Alison McIntosh (1983), *Population Policy in Western Europe.*

[10]Glass (1940), *Population Policies.*

[11]G. Myrdal (1962), *Population:* 51.

[12]*Ibid.:* 185, 189.

[13]A. Myrdal (1968), *Nation and Family:* 120.

[14]*Ibid.:* 121.

[15]*Ibid.:* 122.

[16]G. Myrdal (1962), *Population:* 57.

[17]Glass (1970), "Population Policy": 292.

[18]A. Myrdal (1968), *Nation and Family:* 2, 3.

[19]*Ibid.:* 5.

[20]G. Myrdal (1962), *Population:* 201.

[21]A. Myrdal (1968), *Nation and Family:* 63. The study referred to was K. A. Edin and E. P. Hutchinson (1935), *Studies of Differential Fertility.*

22Glass (1970), "Population Policy": 292.
23The "bitter complaint" of a Stockholm economist as reported in G. Myrdal (1962), *Population:* 96.
24Ann-Katrin Hatje (1974), *Befolkningsfrågan och Välfärden:* 239. This is the best single book on the development of Swedish family-welfare policies in the 1930s and 1940s. It has a brief English summary.
25Ann-Sofie Kälvemark (1980), *More Children of Better Quality? Aspects on Swedish Population Policy in the 1930's:* 69.
26*Ibid.:* 55.
27Glass (1970), "Population Policy": 292.
28Based on the opinion of historian A.-S. Kälvemark, as quoted in C. A. McIntosh (1983), *Population Policy:* 75.
29Royal Ministry of Foreign Affairs (1974), *Biography of a People:* 115.
30Carlsson (1979), "Sex, Babies;" (1983), "The Myrdals."
31G. Myrdal (1962), *Population:* 211.
32*Ibid.:* 97, 99.
33A. Myrdal (1968), *Nation and Family:* xviii.
34Hatje (1974), *Befolkningsfrågan:* Chapter 1.
35G. Myrdal (1962), *Population:* 106.
36Otto R. Wangson (1941), "Maternal and Child Welfare," pp. 45–70 in Royal Swedish Commission, *Social Welfare in Sweden:* 45.
37Kurt Samuelsson (1968), *From Great Power to Welfare State:* 245.
38G. Myrdal (1962), *Population:* 78–79.
39Kälvemark (1980), *More Children.*
40Harriet Holter (1962), "Rebellion Against the Family," *Acta Sociologica* 6-3: 185–201.
41Strindberg, however, favored a wide range of women's rights. One of the best of the recent biographies of Strindberg is Olaf Lagercrantz (1984), *August Strindberg.*
42Orvar Löfgren (1984a), "The Sweetness of Home: Class, Culture, and Family Life in Sweden," *Ethnologia Europaea* 14: 59.
43Quoted in *ibid.*
44A. Myrdal (1968), *Nation and Family:* 4.
45*Ibid.:* 5.
46*Ibid.:* 6.
47*Ibid.:* 426.
48Serge de Chessin (1936), *The Key to Sweden:* 71.
49This is the general view of a group of Swedish ethnographers at Lund University. See, for example, Orvar Löfgren (1981), "On the Anatomy of Culture," *Ethnologia Europaea,* 12-1: 26–46; and Orvar Löfgren's forthcoming "Deconstructing Swedishness: Class and Culture in Modern Sweden," in Anthony Jackson (ed.), *Anthropology at Home.*
50De Chessin (1936), *The Key to Sweden:* 75.
51*Ibid.:* 84, 63.
52Cicely Hamilton (1939), *Modern Sweden as Seen by an Englishwoman:* 10.
53Marquis Childs (1947), *Sweden: The Middle Way:* 154.
54Passages from Hudson Strode (1949), *Sweden: Model for the World:* Chapter 8.
55*Ibid.:* 262.
56Löfgren (1981), "Anatomy of Culture": 38.
57Brita Åkerman (ed.) (1985), *Kunskap för Vår Vardag.* For a similar effort in Australia, see Kerreen M. Reiger (1985), *The Disenchantment of the Home: Modernizing the Australian Family 1880–1940.*

58Lissie Åström (1986), *I Kvinnoled:* 200.
59Åkerman (1985), *Kunskap.*
60Quote in Löfgren (1984a), "The Sweetness of Home": 56.
61Strode (1949), *Sweden:* 32.
62Samuelsson (1968), *Great Power:* 248-249.
63Hatje (1974), *Befolkningsfrågan:* 240-241.
64H. Gille (1948), "Recent Developments in Swedish Population Policy. Part 1," pp. 3-70 in *Population Studies* 2: 7.
65*Ibid.:* 8-9.
66Ingvar Andersson and Jörgen Weibull (1985), *Swedish History in Brief:* 60.
67Samuelsson (1968), *Great Power:* 248.
68Gille (1968), "Recent Developments": 7.
69Hatje (1974), *Befolkningsfrågan:* 242.
70George R. Nelson (ed.) (1953), *Freedom and Welfare:* 269.
71*Ibid.:* 235.
72*Ibid.:* 237.

Cultural Transformation: Family and Society in Sweden After the Mid-Twentieth Century

By 1950 Sweden was well on its way to becoming the wealthiest country in the world, a position it was to reach two decades later—around 1970. At midcentury, it had only about one half the per capita national income of the United States, but ranked fifth in the world after the United States, Canada, New Zealand, and Switzerland. Returning to Sweden right after the war, Marquis Childs found that there were "proportionately more telephones, more electrical devices, more bathtubs in Stockholm than in any other European city." And he noted that the rural areas were more electrified than probably anywhere else in the world.[1]

Sweden was not yet commonly thought of in the West as a "socialist" nation. The widespread dissemination of Marquis Child's concept of "the middle way" was a factor in that regard: he saw Sweden as a compromise between socialism and capitalism. The more widely publicized postwar political actions of Britain's Labor Party were considerably more radical than those of the Social Democratic Party in Sweden. Measured by the number of employees, 91% of Swedish industry was owned by private enterprise, 5% by government, and 4% by cooperatives.[2] Sweden had, however, gained an international reputation for extensive social engineering and experimentation by a very activist democratic government.

It is less well-known, then and today, that despite a left-wing reputation in political circles Swedish society at midcentury had come to be dominated by a bourgeois spirit and mentality more pervasively than perhaps any other society in the world. The characteristics and rapid rise to cultural hegemony of the middle class in Sweden were discussed in Chapter 6. It was a new middle class, in which science and technology were the religion and planning, efficiency, functionalism, and hygiene were the mottoes. Even though politics were dominated by the exceptionally strong labor unions, Sweden was in no sense a bastion of proletarian styles and sensibilities. This was noted by virtually all foreign observers of the time. The British historian Stewart Oakley, for example, found in the Sweden of the 1950s "an essentially middle-class society, reminiscent of that of contemporary America, though without such extremes of wealth and poverty."[3] The British writer, Kathleen Knott, somewhat sarcastically entitled her 1961 book on Sweden, *A Clean, Well-Lighted Place.*[4]

In addition to middle-class predominance, Swedish society in the 1950s and early 1960s still had strong elements of the social formality and hierarchy of an earlier era. Foreigners found the average Swede to be exceptionally polite, emotionally self-controlled, and socially reserved. Compared to life in many other Western nations, elaborate rules of social etiquette controlled most social situations. Because of a reluctance to use the familiar form of "you," for example, people in all but the most intimate social situations were typically referred to in the third person by their titles and surnames. As part of a cultural trait sometimes labeled *titelsjuka* (title sickness), the Swedish population also was classified in the telephone books by occupational titles. Like the middle classes everywhere, Swedes also had a strong materialist streak—a drive to possess the latest and best of consumer goods.

A small and geographically isolated nation, Sweden had for a long time engaged in cultural borrowing from other nations. In the eighteenth and early nineteenth centuries French was the second language of most educated Swedes, and French culture was highly influential. When the Swedish royal-family line gave out in 1810, the Swedes went to France and induced a famous Napoleonic marshal to come to Sweden and form a new royal line. The descendents of this French marshal, a Bernadotte, still sit on the Swedish throne today. In the late nineteenth and early twentieth centuries, however, France was replaced by Germany as the foreign culture of choice. This selection was solidified by extensive commercial trade with Germany and Swedish royal intermarriages with the German nobility. During this period, German became the first foreign language that Swedes were taught in school.

World War II put a definite end to the then-already-declining fortunes of Germany in Swedish culture, and English became the main foreign language that all Swedes were taught, starting in primary school. Sweden had already forged strong ties with Britain in the early years of the Industrial Revolution. But just before and following World War II, American culture became highly influential in Sweden through American films, pop music, and, last but not least, American consumer products.

After a severe inflation in the early 1950s, the Swedish economy was exceptionally strong up until the mid-1960s, reaching a high point from 1960 to 1965. Swedes sometimes called this period the "harvest time" (*skördetiden*).[5] It was a time of labor peace, the last major strike having taken place in 1945; of full employment and general economic security; and of relatively low crime rates. It was also a time of continued social progress. In 1950 basic education was extended from seven to a total of nine years, and a compulsory system of national health insurance was introduced in 1956. A 3-week paid vacation for all workers was enacted in 1951 and extended to 4 weeks in 1963. Politically there were relatively few conflicts of note, the major exception being the question of how far the coverage of the Swedish old-age pension system should be extended. After lengthy debate and a national referendum, a comprehensive "supplementary pension program" took effect in 1960.

There was nearly unanimous agreement in the whole society during this period on the desirability of "social engineering," financed by high taxation. In the words of one Swedish historical account, people agreed that "everything (or nearly everything) should be planned, regulated and standardized, investigated, weighed and measured so that we can achieve a good standard in our daily lives."[6] This social engineering, however, was always based on lengthy deliberation, moderation, and compromise. Through these methods, it seemed, the "People's Home" envisaged by the Social Democrats of the 1930s had by the 1960s to a very large extent been achieved.

The very successes of Swedish social engineering, so highly regarded by the Swedes themselves, soon became the target of scorching criticism by foreigners, however. The most critical outsiders were representatives of more capitalistic or individualistic countries, such as the United States and Great Britain, and they found a great deal to complain about. Some noted with alarm the new social problems that were perceived to be emerging, such as crime, suicide, and laziness. The rise of these problems was blamed on a "socialist welfare state" and seen as a kind of social degeneration. The most famous attack on Sweden along these lines was President Eisenhower's comment at the 1960 Republican Convention about a nation that follows "a socialist philosophy and whose rate of suicide has gone up almost unbelievably . . . Lack of ambition is discernible on all sides."[7] Others bemoaned Sweden's loss of religion, finding Swedish society to be crassly materialistic and a "spiritual vacuum"; or an extremely boring and dull manifestation of bourgeois complacency; or a modernistic "chromium nightmare, sterile and empty and faceless." The British magazine *The Freeman* declared Sweden to be a failure for anyone "interested in anything more than beehive security. It is a country without incentive, without hope, and without initiative. . . . Sweden is simply uninspiring."[8] Knocking Sweden, in fact, had become in the 1960s something of a popular sport among foreign journalists.

These foreign criticisms of Sweden were disregarded and even laughed at by all but the most-right-wing Swedes. Indeed, bred by Sweden's comparatively great success among the family of Western nations, a typical attitude of many Swedes was complacency. Foreign observers often characterized Swedes of this time as rather smug and self-satisfied. The Swedes themselves were beginning to loudly trumpet their successes, and there are many Swedes today who look back on the 1950s and early 1960s as Sweden's "golden age." A distinguished Swedish sociologist said in 1967:

> In the history of the West events in one country have sometimes signaled what is to come in other countries many years hence. . . . In looking around the world today for a land of tomorrow attention is immediately drawn to the Nordic countries, particularly to Sweden. . . . [There trends] represent new ways to enact basic cultural values, new arrangements between man and fellowman and between public roles and private pursuits; in short, a new social order.[9]

There were very few hints in the 1950s and early 1960s of the momentous cultural and family changes that were soon to overtake Sweden. Yet beginning in the 1960s Sweden was to enter a period of social and cultural change that was probably more rapid and far-reaching than any change at any other period of similar length in its history. In terms of the scope and rapidity of societal change in such a short period of time, the only international rival among advanced nations was postwar Japan. By the 1980s, as we shall see, bourgeois Sweden had largely been left behind.

The Swedish Family at Midcentury

The bourgeois ethos certainly extended to the family. Although it was a late starter compared to other northwestern European societies, Sweden by midcentury had become largely a nation dominated culturally by small-town and urban middle-class nuclear familism. In an assessment of family patterns in the early 1950s the Danish sociologist Kaare Svalastoga concluded:

> The typical Scandinavian family consists of husband, wife and two children. The husband is the only breadwinner. The distribution of power appears to be patricentral. In-laws do not form part of the household, and there is no maid.[10]

As in the United States and most other Western nations, this "traditional familism" was enhanced by an increase in family formation in Sweden during the 1940s because of higher marriage rates and birthrates. Sweden's neutral position during the war allowed this trend to begin some years earlier in Sweden than in other Western nations; it began while the war was still underway. Svalastoga attributed the baby boom of the war years to "the increased value of home life both as a more efficient consumption unit when food and clothing are scarce, and as a haven of peace for war- and occupation-scarred individuals."[11]

Svalastoga found that nuptuality had increased steadily since the 1920s, with the overwhelming majority of Swedes marrying at some time during their lives. Moreover, they tended to marry only after a relatively long engagement period, with 77% reporting a period of premarital acquaintance equal to or exceeding 2 years; and they married under church auspices, with just 8% having only civil marriages.[12] The percentage of married women who had outside employment in 1950 had more than doubled since 1930, from 6 to 15%, but this still represented a very small minority (although Svalastoga commented perceptively that "the role of the married female is in a stage of transition.")[13] A Swedish Gallup poll found that 90% of the sample considered absolute marital fidelity indispensable to marital happiness.[14] In a comparison between American and Swedish families made by the Swedish sociologist Georg Karlsson with an American colleague, it was shown that the two nations were very similar in their marital behavior.[15]

Nevertheless, in some of its family and sexual ideas Sweden did seem to be a little more "radical" than most non-Scandinavian countries. The foreign press was beginning to ride on the themes of Swedish "free love" and "immorality," focusing especially on the alleged "looseness" of Swedish women. Yet this portrayal, as we discuss later in this chapter, was often wildly overdrawn, and the Swedish "sexual advances" of the time still seem relatively inconsequential compared to the press of traditionalism. It is true that Swedes had long been rather tolerant of premarital intercourse, but this tolerance was extended primarily to "engaged" couples.[16] Sweden had always been famous for high rates of illegitimacy, but this was mainly because couples waited until they had a child before they got married. Sweden had relatively high divorce rates in the first part of the twentieth century, but this trait was shared with such traditionalist countries as Switzerland. There was a history of some nonmarital cohabitation; but statistically it was extremely limited in extent. Finally, Swedes had developed during the 1930s an international reputation for tolerating public nudity, but this seems to be more of a cultural quirk associated with sun worship in an environment where sunlight is scarce than a symptom of any kind of perverse sexuality.

In one other area of family mores Sweden might have been in the lead in the 1950s; it certainly moved into the lead over the next few decades. That area involves the equality or symmetry of power between husband and wife. In a large-scale study of the parents of Stockholm boys in 1956, about 60% of the respondents claimed that they shared equal power with their spouses. Among the remaining respondents, 25% said that the husband had more power and 15% said that the wife had more power (husbands and wives gave very similar answers).[17] This finding would doubtless not have been true of families in rural areas of Sweden, however.

The strong family and sexual traditionalism of the time (at least that is the way it appears from today's vantage point) was aptly expressed in the *Handbook on Sex Instruction in Swedish Schools,* published in 1956. Written by the National Board of Education, the handbook was distributed to all schools in Sweden and provided the basis for nationwide sex education courses. First introduced into secondary schools in the 1930s, national sex education in the primary schools was recommended by the government in 1942 and became a compulsory part of the Swedish educational curriculum in 1956.[18] The booklet takes a very firm, traditional position on sexual morality:

> The teacher must uphold the view that continence during adolescence is the only course the school can recommend with a good conscience. It gives the individual the best prospects for achieving personal happiness later on. . . . Attention should be drawn to the fact that free liaisons for the sake of satisfying instinctual desires can result in children being born without the parents having a home to offer them . . . when sex-life is started too early, it is likely to be detached from its objects—home, family and children. Sex-life should be associated with these from the start, and should accordingly develop with a sense of responsibility and consideration towards the partner and towards society.[19]

The handbook also takes the traditional once-familiar moral position about marriage and the family:

> Marriage occurs at a relatively late age in modern society. Pupils should be made to understand that it is better to establish a home at an early stage, even if under modest circumstances, than to enter without any further scruples into an intimate liaison. The teacher must pay special attention to the loosening of morals involved in the not uncommon tendency to consider it normal and permissible conduct to live according to one's primitive desires within one's social group or circle of acquaintances. This is conducive to self-indulgence and besides reduces the sense of responsibility, thus inviting unpredictable personal and social consequences. There is no place here for advice that is hesitant . . . . It is extremely important that pupils should realize fully that home and family are the groundrock of society, cemented together partly by love between man and woman and parents and children, partly by law. The latter is a support for the former: without it the bonds of marriage would be easier to dissolve, and this would entail great perils, especially for any children by the marriage . . . . Legal marriage has accordingly a moral value which cannot be dispensed with.[20]

The traditional quality of this moral thinking (which is of course a profession of "official" moral norms, not an indication of actual behavior) can be fully appreciated only when it is considered in the light of certain events that took place over the ensuing decades. As we shall see, these traditional moral sentiments were almost completely overturned in the new version of this manual rewritten in the early 1970s and published in 1977. By that time the intellectual climate, led by a vanguard of radical thinkers, had changed into a thoroughgoing moral relativism.

Cultural Transformation: 1960–1985

Political Background and Developments

Despite the strong air of social satisfaction that was found in Sweden in the 1950s and early 1960s, an abundance of social goals remained to be strived for, both new goals and old goals not yet fully achieved. It was in the pursuit of these goals that Sweden was again to be reshaped in the coming decades. Sweden's cities had a severe housing shortage, made worse by a heavy influx of people during and after the war. There were still residual poor in Sweden, people whose lives fell below what was regarded as a reasonable standard of living. There were also goals that grew out of the phenomenon of rising expectations, what Prime Minister Tage Erlander in 1956 called "the discontent of impatient expectations."[21]

The expectation about which Swedes were most impatient, at least the Swedes of the left who dominated the government, was the goal of "true equality." In contrast to the United States, where people by and large seem to be willing to settle for an equality of opportunity, under an increasingly pervasive socialist rhetoric the Swedish political debate began to be dominated by the notion of equality of results. Even a new Swedish word for equality was to come into widespread usage: *jämställdhet,* meaning roughly "equality of condition" (this term was used particularly in the area of gender equality). A quick look around Sweden yielded abundant evidence that the nation was very far indeed from having achieved such a condition. Many legacies of the old class hierarchies still remained. Despite progressive taxation policies, in the strong economy of the 1950s and 1960s the income gap between rich and poor in Sweden had probably widened. Sweden was still, after all, a mostly capitalist nation, where business was conducted on the basis of private profit. The nation had its share of wealthy entrepreneurs; indeed, it was on the success of these entrepreneurs that the achievement of the good life in Sweden very much depended.

It was not just income inequality that concerned the Swedes. Just as important was a growing sense of gender inequality. Even though Sweden may have pioneered many breakthroughs in women's rights and Swedish women may have had "without question the most freedom in the world," as one foreign commentator emphasized in the 1930s,[22] there was a growing belief that Sweden was heavily dominated by men and women were a surpressed minority. On the international scene, among Western nations, Sweden was to pioneer what came to be called the women's liberation movement.

The ideal of equality (*jämlikhet*) had been prominent in the Swedish public mind since at least the social debates of the 1930s. But it had ordinarily been linked with the ideals of "social integration," "solidarity," and "security" under the banner of the People's Home. As Per Albin Hansson first put it in 1928, the good society was a society that functioned like a good home, and "in a good home there prevails equality, thoughtfulness, cooperation, and helpfulness."[23] In a warm and happy family, equality means that people are to receive "equal treatment."[24]

Equal treatment is one thing, but families have never been known for their equality of results. Indeed, they have been the institutional source for some of the most extreme forms of hierarchy and inequality, in which both children and women are treated like chattels and the aged lord it over the young. For breaking down these ancient forms of inequality in society, the metaphor of family and home simply would not do, and it was not long before the political symbol of the People's Home began to be used less and less in Swedish debate. During the 1960s, the idea of a "strong society" became popular.

The 1960s turned into a "left-wing decade"—*vänstervriden* (twisted to the left), as politics in Sweden leaned increasingly toward radical positions. Help in giving the society a more radical and also a more youth-oriented cast of mind than it had ever had before came from a demographic "youth bulge," a result of the wartime baby boom.[25] By the end of the decade, like their cohorts in other Western nations, albeit more mildly, the students in Sweden were rebelling on behalf of left-wing causes. This set the tone if not the substance for Swedish political debate.

In the mid-1960s, support for the Social Democrats, who had been in power continuously since the 1930s, was beginning to grow a bit thin. Charged with having promoted inflation and a questionable housing policy, the Social Democratic Party received one of the lowest popular votes after World War II in the local elections of 1966. In the 1968 elections, however, the party not only recaptured popular support, but achieved the best election result since the war, winning more than 50% of the popular vote. The electorate began to fear that the conservative parties, if they took over national power, would seek to cut back widely favored welfare programs. Also, the Social Democratic Party had been under sharp attack in the 1968 election campaign from the new and vigorous Swedish left, which accused it of being a tool of capitalism and having created a society of gross inequality. This left-wing attack on the Social Democrats may have created a backlash; rather than weakening the party, the attack may actually have helped it to garner the support that led to the smashing 1968 election victory.[26] Whatever the reasons for their electorial success, the Social Democrats interpreted their victory as a popular mandate to move vigorously ahead in the pursuit of egalitarian social policies. Such policies were especially favored by Olof Palme, who became the new Swedish prime minister in 1969, following Tage Erlander.

The 1970s was a decade in which the Swedish "politics of compromise," with broad agreement among the political parties on major social and economic goals, began to fade. New elements of conflict and contentiousness entered the political scene. Pulled in the direction of the New Left, Olof Palme instituted policies that many Swedes came to view as "radical egalitarianism," and the old concerns about the dangers of "socialist leveling" and "collectivism" began to be raised as never before. These issues, together with a weakening economy, finally led in the 1976 elections to the takeover of government power by the so-called bourgeois parties. Bourgeois control was short-lived, however, partly due to a lack of agreement within the right-wing parties. The welfare state was, if anything, further advanced rather than weakened during the 6 years of bourgeois rule.[27]

But the politics and social spirit of Sweden had changed, for the foreseeable future, in a divisive direction. Symptomatic of the change was the return of the Social Democrats in 1982 in an election that was highly ideological in tone. There was rising hostility within Sweden toward the welfare state, and the labor peace that had made Sweden so exceptional among the world's advanced nations began to break down. Much of the change in the political climate was triggered by a continuing downturn in the economic fortunes of Sweden, a decline that the bourgeois parties had been unable to prevent or contain. Between 1974 and 1982, the rate of growth of the Swedish economy was below that of virtually every other member nation of the Organization for Economic Cooperation and Development. Yet the new political disposition also reflected new cultural realities that had gradually overtaken Swedish society. A new middle-class stratum of white-collar workers and technical employees had come to occupy the political center stage, not just as political leaders but as the majority of voters.[28]

Areas of Social and Cultural Change

Despite their seeming bourgeois conformism, there is something about Swedes that makes them not flinch at the necessity for social change. This became apparent during Sweden's late but extremely fast rise to affluence and social security. It became apparent again in relation to the cultural changes of the period from 1960 to 1985. There are two aspects of Swedish society that, in my judgment, are important in accounting for this ready acceptance of rapid change. One is Sweden's leadership, a new middle class of secular social engineers, people who espouse the lessons of the social sciences and believe in far-reaching rational planning (the rise of this group to power was discussed in Chapter 6). The other aspect of Swedish society that makes it open to change is the strong deference that Swedes have to centralized authority, both governmental and intellectual. More than the citizens of most Western societies, Swedes are willing to be led by an elite. There is no streak of cantankerous individualism among Swedes (and they are members of one of the world's most homogeneous societies). All of this adds up to what one American political scientist has described as "an elite culture in which a highly pragmatic intellectual style, oriented toward the discovery of workable solutions to specific problems, structures a consensual approach to policy making."[29]

A modest example of this capacity for change, but one that points up the principle, is the Swedish shift from driving on the left to driving on the right. Mainly for economic reasons and for Sweden's compatibility with its European neighbors, Swedish authorities decreed that Swedes should make this traffic switch. After an educational campaign, a referendum was held, and the Swedes voted against it. Still, the switch was authorized by the government and put into effect about 10 years later. On September 3, 1967, following intensive preparations, all traffic was stopped and nearly every traffic sign and stoplight in the nation was moved. This massive undertaking went off almost without a hitch. As one writer pointed out, "no highly publicised event could have been better calculated to show Sweden at her organizational best."[30] Fortunately, Swedish cars already had left-hand drive, which eased the way considerably. But Swedish pedestrians, too, used to pass each other on the left, and that also was changed. Still today, walking on the sidewalk in Sweden can be a bit of a trial compared to many societies, because the older generation of Swedes has not yet fully adjusted to the new way of doing things.

Few of the cultural changes that have taken place in Sweden are unique to that nation; the only thing that is special about them in Sweden is the length to which they have been carried. A good example is secularization. Every nation in the West has been undergoing a process of secularization for several centuries; it has the status of a master trend, associated with modernization. Yet no other nation has become secularized to the degree that Sweden has.[31] Not so long ago a bastion of Lutheran orthodoxy, Sweden today is possibly the world's most secular society—including the societies in the Soviet block. In contrast to the United States, probably the most religious nation in the West, 52% of the Swedish people said (in 1981) that they believed in God (down from 84% in 1956) compared to 95% of Americans; and only 10% of Swedes believed in Hell compared to 67% of Americans. To the question "Do you find that you get comfort and strength from religion or not?" 27% of Swedes answered yes, versus 79% of Americans. And only 5% of Swedes today are regular church attenders (once a week or more), versus 43% of Americans.[32] Religion and God, moreover, are almost never invoked in Swedish public discourse.

Ironically, there is no separation of church and state in Sweden, although a full separation may be instituted by the early 1990s. Surprising as it may seem to most Americans, the clergy of the state Lutheran church are civil servants, employees of the government, whose salaries are paid by the nation's taxpayers. The clergy have even been given an important secular role, that of gathering and keeping vital statistics on Swedish local areas. Only a few decades ago, this state religion formed an integral part of the education system. The school day started with prayers, students took compulsory classes in the Christian religion, and school graduations took place in the state church. Today, with the exception of those few Swedes in "free churches" and the new immigrant groups, most Swedes think of religion and church attendance as things of the past.

Every Western nation that was formerly a monarchy has modified its form of government as part of the process of modernization. But few have gone so far as Sweden in so short a time. It is not only that the Swedes stripped the King of all remaining formal powers, leaving him only as a symbolic figurehead with ceremonial functions, but they also greatly changed the structure of government. In a major constitutional reform, begun in 1954 with a special government commission and implemented in stages over several years beginning in 1969, Sweden dropped one house of parliament in favor of a single chamber, based on proportional representation and elected every 3 years. One of Sweden's few planning blunders was in setting the number of members of parliament at 350, thus leading to numerous tie votes that required the drawing of lots to resolve issues; the number was later changed to 349. In another striking governmental reform, this time at the local level, the number of local governments in Sweden was reduced in stages over several decades from about 2500 to a mere 278. This reform was undertaken in the belief that larger units of local government would be more efficient in providing services.

In another sudden break with tradition, modern Swedes have discarded much of their earlier social formality. The familiar form of "you" is now used by just about everyone except perhaps when addressing the King and Queen. Rather than wait to be introduced to newcomers, as they once did, Swedes are now much more open and informal. Titles are no longer used to organize the telephone books. And the nation that was once considered "best dressed," at least according to a middle-class standard, has developed an informal, almost working-class style of attire. In many middle-class occupational sectors outside of the business field, for example, ties for men are out of fashion.

Sweden once was considered a highly parochial society. To Continental Europeans its citizens seemed ingrown and unworldly. Few Swedes had ever traveled abroad beyond the neighboring Nordic countries, and it is fair to say that many Swedes went through their whole lives without seeing anyone who was not another Swede. The 1960s saw a quantum leap in Swedish cosmopolitanism. Like other countries in Europe at the time, Sweden found itself with a labor shortage as a result of low birthrates and full-employment policies. To remedy this shortage, women were encouraged to go into the labor market, which we shall discuss shortly. But workers and their families were also imported from abroad in large numbers. Most of the workers at first came from neighboring countries, notably Finland, but soon the net widened to include southern Europe (especially Yugoslavia, Greece, and later Turkey), and it was not long before homogeneous Sweden became a society with a foreign-born group living in its midst that made up nearly 10% of the total population. In the peak years of 1969 and 1970, foreign immigration to Sweden was almost as great as the emigration of Swedes to foreign countries in the peak years of the 1800s.

This influx of foreigners was to change irrevocably the character of Swedish life. Stockholm, for example, was once notorious among visitors for being one of the deadest cities in the world at night. There were few restaurants and virtually no bars, to say nothing of nightclubs, the result partly of strict Swedish controls on liquor sales. But this condition changed dramatically with the influx of foreigners, and today Stockholm is filled with eating and drinking establishments ranging from Greek to Chinese. Throughout Sweden most urban neighborhoods and schools now contain a mixture of ethnic groups. Although the Swedish record on antidiscrimination and assimilation has been enviable (one of the government ministries is devoted to dealing with the problems of immigrants and helping them to integrate into Swedish society), interethnic conflict has also become a fact of current Swedish life.

Swedes were also pulled into the world through the advent of jet-airplane travel. With good disposable incomes and ample vacation time, Swedes have become some of the world's best-traveled citizens. Charter flights galore beckon the Swedish people to see the world, and some areas, such as the Canary Islands, have in commercial terms become virtually Swedish colonies. It is the rare Swede now, at least among urban dwellers, who has not been abroad.

In contrast to most of the areas just mentioned, several other areas of social change have been greatly affected by the ideology of the Social Democrats. That is, if the bourgeois parties had been in power, the change would probably have taken a different form. A good example is housing.

Like other Western nations in the process of industrialization, Sweden during the late nineteenth and twentieth centuries shifted from a nation of independent farmsteads and rural villages to one of towns and cities, as we explored in earlier chapters. Today Sweden is about as urbanized as other Western nations in terms of raw percentages, although Swedish cities and towns are on the average much smaller than cities and towns in

Britain or the United States.[33] The urbanization of the Swedish population was especially rapid after the World War II. In 1940 about 52% of the population lived in urban and suburban places, but by 1970 this figure had climbed to almost its present level of 81%. The outstanding difference in Swedish urbanization, however, is that Sweden, which just a generation ago was a society of detached, privately owned, single-family houses, is today the Western world's most apartment-oriented society.

Since their rise to power in the 1930s, the Social Democrats have favored multifamily over single-family housing.[34] One reason for this is that Sweden had a comparatively serious housing shortage up until the 1970s, and the Social Democrats believed that building multifamily housing was the most efficient way to get the most housing units built in the least possible time. In addition, and in keeping with the general emphasis on central planning in Swedish society, the development of Swedish cities has been heavily shaped by urban planners. The architect-dominated urban planners, in their turn, have favored multifamily housing for Swedish cities in order to prevent the urban sprawl that plagues other societies, with its inefficient transportation networks and central-city decline.

One can also detect a strong ideological element in the Social Democratic preference for multifamily housing. Just as privately owned single-family houses are associated with capitalism, dominated by private property and the free market, multifamily housing seems more attuned to the ideals of an egalitarian democratic socialism. The Social Democrats have largely rejected market approaches to the building of homes in favor of government-subsidized nonprofit housing associations. They have also consistently been leery of private ownership and have promoted instead rental and cooperative forms of housing tenure. The result has been that multifamily housing in Sweden today is characteristic not only of large cities but of small towns, and more Swedes (55%) live in multifamily houses than do the citizens of any other major Western society. This has had significant implications for Swedish family life, which we discuss in later chapters.

Another area of change that became "radicalized" under the political guidance of the Social Democrats is education. Up until the late 1940s the Swedish educational system, even by European standards, was rather traditional and authoritarian. It was also relatively limited in extent. Elementary school was compulsory only for 6 or 7 years in many regions of the country. Only about 10% of elementary-school graduates completed a secondary education (although a much higher percentage spent some years in secondary school), and fewer than 5% of each age cohort went on to higher education.[35] Over the years, the educational system was both "opened up to the masses" and internally democratized. Major ways of accomplishing this included getting rid of most private schools and replacing specialized public secondary schools with single, uniform, "comprehensive" schools. In the new comprehensive schools, the educational tracking of the academically gifted student was mostly done away with, and "practical training" was given equal status with "academic training." Also, because it was considered a symbol of privilege, the *studentexamen* was abolished in 1968. This was the traditional final examination at the *gymnasium* (high school) that entitled the success- ful student to wear a white cap and to continue on to the university. By the late 1970s nearly 90% of all 16 year olds who had completed the compul- sory comprehensive schools were going on to "upper secondary schools," with a sizable percentage continuing on from there to the universities.[36]

Just as dramatic as the widened distribution of education was the chang- ing nature of the educational goals and teaching methods being used in the schools. With egalitarian values uppermost in mind, Swedish education shifted from the use of traditional structured teaching methods that empha- sized high academic standards and strict discipline in the classroom to what in America were called progressive education methods.[37] These methods in- corporated a lack of formal hierarchical structure, a focus on the personal social and emotional adjustment of students, and educational permissiveness in the sense of a wide freedom of choice in curricula. Religion, especially the focus on Christianity, was also displaced from educational institutions, as noted above. At one point, there was even a move to do away with all regular grading in schools although it was not successful.

This new educational climate almost certainly helped to shape the char- acter and world outlook of the young postwar generation of Swedes. It is said today by some that Sweden has become one of the most permissive societies in the world in terms of official tolerance of deviant life-styles (Swe- den's sexual permissiveness is discussed below), and doubtless the progres- sive impetus in education was also instrumental in promoting the new social informality in Swedish life.[38] But in terms of strictly educational effects, the influence of these educational changes has been less clear, and they have been the subject of widespread controversy. The bourgeois side of Swedish society has expressed alarm over what they have seen as a weakening of educational standards and a social leveling, and Swedish educational pol- icy has become a volatile political issue. Statistics have lent some support to these right-wing claims, showing dropping educational-achievement lev- els in some areas. When the bourgeois parties gained political power in the mid-1970s they sought with some success to modify previous Social Demo- cratic educational policies. Since that time there has been, even among the Social Democrats, a backing away from progressive educational approaches in favor of a renewed concern for discipline and high academic standards.

The final areas of "revolutionary" cultural transformation during the post- war period to be discussed are those most directly relevant to the purposes of this book: the role of women, sexual attitudes, and the family. These areas, as we shall see, are also ones whose nature has been considerably influenced by Social Democratic ideology and by government policies.

Equality for Women

Beginning in the 1960s, few other domestic political goals in Sweden were to have the same continuing importance as the goal of equality for women. By then Swedish women had achieved virtually all of the formal rights given by democratic societies, and they often had achieved them earlier than women in other Western societies. These include the rights to equal inheritance (1845); vote in national elections (1921); have an equal legal and economic footing in marriage (1921); attend public secondary schools (1927); not be dismissed from a job because of marriage or pregnancy (1939); gain the priesthood (1958); and get equal pay for equal work (1960). Yet women were still regarded as second-class citizens at home, in school, and at the workplace. Most importantly (as in every other nation), women played major social roles in society that were different from, and were felt to be inferior to, those of men. Men tended to have economically independent occupational roles in the labor force, while most women had the economically dependent role of mother–housewife.

Thus the stage was set for what some have called the major social revolution of the twentieth century in advanced industrial societies. The precise causes of this social revolution are still a matter of scholarly dispute, especially since the change followed so closely upon an era in which "traditional familism" had undergone a revival. Virtually all scholars would agree that the demand for labor in the booming postwar economies was a factor, as were the rising educational levels of women and the widespread availability and use of contraceptives. Other factors included the growth of moral permissiveness in sexual activities, making sex outside of marriage more acceptable; the prolongation of education, leading to later marriages; the smaller size of families and greater longevity, making the role of mother no longer a lifetime occupation for women; and the rising divorce rate, throwing women onto the labor market. These factors were probably all operating, in Sweden as elsewhere, to bring the idea of "full equality" for women to the forefront.

One of the earliest spokespersons for women's liberation in the postwar years was Alva Myrdal, who had maintained her position as one of Sweden's most influential intellectuals. There was much in her writings of the 1930s and early 1940s to suggest what was to come (see Chapter 6), but the issue of women's equality had not yet become a major focus. In 1956, a seminal book was published entitled *Women's Two Roles: Home and Work,* written by Alva Myrdal in collaboration with a British woman, Viola Klein. The book noted the changing conditions of society and emphasized that because of smaller family sizes "an average housewife can be considered to be employed full-time on tasks which are necessary for home-making only during a quarter to one-third of her normal life."[39] Therefore, the authors stressed, most women should have two different roles in life, one at home and the other at work. "Modern mothers who make no plans outside the family for their future will not only play havoc with their own lives but will make nervous wrecks of their overprotected children and their husbands."[40] They advocated such measures as job training and vocational counseling for women, part-time work for the mothers of young children, and more public services to relieve the domestic work load.

Much of their book had a surprisingly traditional cast to it, however, which was to prove anathema to a later generation of feminists. "Nowadays," they said, "not even the most ardent feminist would deny that the claims of children to their mother's time and attention comes first in the order of priorities."[41] Referring to the work of English psychologist John Bowlby, which was widely discussed at the time the book was written, they asserted that

> modern psychology has given support and justification to a belief which at sometimes may have been thought "old fashioned": the view that the future happiness and development of infants is dependent on the loving care of their mothers. . . . We therefore support the view that mothers should, as far as possible, take care of their own children during the first years of their lives.[42]

In general, they leaned toward the position that mothers should stay home until their children are of school age and then go out to work only part-time until the children reach about age 15. Toward the end of the book, they were hedging a bit on this point, however, and, anticipating a big debate to come, they suggested that fathers as well could perhaps do much of the job of parenting then done by mothers. Certainly, as they put it, "making husbands, and fathers, full partners in the affairs of their families . . . seems to us so much to be desired."[43] Indeed, they looked forward to the 6-hour workday in which, with staggered hours, both parents could work full-time and still take proper care of their children. This is a position that in the late 1980s is still widely favored and discussed in Sweden, although it has not yet been implemented.

The "sex-role" debate in Sweden is felt to have really begun in earnest with the publication and wide discussion in 1961 of an essay entitled "The Conditional Emancipation of Women" by the feminist journalist Eva Moberg, daughter of the popular Swedish novelist and social historian, Wilhelm Moberg. At that time the editor of the journal *Herta*, the house organ of the pioneering but middle-of-the-road Swedish feminist group, The Fredrika

Bremer Association, Moberg rejected the idea that the main function of women was child care and homemaking and that everything else should be secondary. She argued that "both men and women have *one* principal role, that of being human beings." Her main thesis was that allowing women to have two roles only liberated them halfway and that the situation of women can not really be improved until men's roles are changed.[44] At first subjected to a torrent of criticism, this position soon became widely accepted. Its importance was, as a Swedish feminist was later to say, that "it was the first time responsibility for the problem was put on the man."[45]

As is very typical of Swedish policy development, the sex-role debate was quickly joined by social scientists, and their expertise and influence were lent to the task of supporting the importance of achieving equality for women. In an influential collection of articles called *Kvinnors Liv och Arbete* (Women's Life and Work), which quickly sold out its first printing, the views of Scandinavian social scientists on the sex-role question were pulled together and the ideological positions of the debate carefully set forth.[46] The lead article not only emphasized the need for married women to get out and work and the "almost insuperable" difficulties put in their path, but, going well beyond the earlier Myrdal and Klein work, also viewed women's traditional family functions as leading to overprotectiveness, "family egoism," "a rejection of much social obligation," and "a relative indifference to social and political problems."[47] The book bemoaned the fact that, as Swedish sociologist Rita Liljeström was later to put it, the mother had come "to be chained to a pedestal of indispensability."[48]

Another article in the collection, by a Swedish psychologist, after concluding that "the fact that the mother is working outside the home and not following the traditional maternal role of full-time housewife is not by itself determinative of the child's development and personality adjustment," put the issue even more strongly:

> As long as the mother's role remains unchanged throughout the course of the child's development, there will be the risk that its later chances for self-realization, as mother or father, in family and professional life will be diminished or lost.[48]

Echoing the Moberg article, the book concluded that "the concept of 'the two roles of women' is . . . untenable. Both men and women have *one* main role, that of a human being. For both sexes, this role would include child care."[50]

This perspective was put forth even more forcefully by Alva Myrdal, who, in a foreword to a 1967 English translation of a revised *Kvinnors Liv*, substantially modified and expanded her earlier positions. "The character of the debate on problems of the family in Scandinavia, and particularly in

Sweden, has taken a new and unusual turn," she noted. "Its scope has been radically enlarged to encompass the two roles of men. . . . it is becoming increasingly recognized . . . that their role in the family must be radically enlarged."[51] Sweden went on to become the first country in the world to frame government policies dealing with gender-role equality that sought to change the social roles of men as well as those of women.[52] Such policies were not at first accepted very readily by Swedish men, and still today in Sweden the constant plea of feminist groups is that men are not doing their share at home.

Alva Myrdal's view of the mother's role also took an abrupt turn. She alluded to "the almost pathological confinement of mothers" and the critical need to "collectivize housework services."[53] In an address on the "new family" in 1964, she stated: "It seems to be about time we accept as a pedagogical objective the conscious preparation of our children to be able to tolerate being 'set aside' to a certain degree."[54]

These attitudinal changes were to lead to what one Swedish historian has called "a total revision of the state's policy toward women."[55] The first policy initiatives were taken by the Social Democratic Party's women's organization when it "forced" the party to form a study group in 1960.[56] As its honorary chairman, the study group had no less a personage than the then Prime Minister Tage Erlander, and the group's report, issued in 1964, became known as the Erlander report. The report's main recommendations were not implemented immediately, partly because of the severe electoral setback the Social Democrats suffered in the 1966 local elections. However, the smashing revival of Social Democratic fortunes in the 1968 national election, in which they had campaigned on a platform of equality, provided the impetus for an attitude of "full speed ahead" on the issue of gender equality.

The main recommendations of the Erlander group were incorporated into the 1969 report of a new policy group entitled the Working Group on Equality, headed by none other than Alva Myrdal.[57] Unanimously accepted by the Social Democratic Party, this report was to be highly influential in establishing the government's legislative program in the early 1970s. More radical than most earlier documents from the Social Democrats, the report did not hesitate to use the word "socialism" and frankly rejected the idea of equality as "the right to compete on equal terms" in favor of an equality of results—"the gradual reduction of the differences in conditions of life."[58] As the gender-role question was still a relatively controversial topic, it was for the most part subsumed under the more general consideration of equality and a concern for the oppressed and the underdog. The report, however, was unequivocal in calling for the immediate termination of all discrimination based on sex and for major attempts to equalize the situations of men and women in the job market.

From the point of view of this book, the most interesting aspect of the report lies in its treatment of the family. It is not in any way to denigrate the worthiness of equality as a social goal to point out that this report, in contrast to those of the 1930s and 1940s, no longer was especially concerned with the stability or health of the family as a social institution. Rather, the whole focus was on the situation of each individual member of the family unit and on ways of "developing his or her talents to the fullest." No longer was the family unit to be "favored" in any way by the government. On the contrary, it was emphasized that "adults should be treated in the same manner by the society whether they live alone or in some form of common living arrangement."[59] While noting that "the family holds a strong position as a social institution, and there is no reason to suppose that its importance in this respect will diminish," the report went on to call for a deregulation of the marriage laws and the provision of "more protection to other forms of cohabitation."[60] In the areas of economics and taxation, the report stated that "the economic independence of marriage partners which is a basic condition for equality should serve as the basis for future legislation."[61]

In a book entitled *Swedish Women—Swedish Men,* published at this time by the Swedish Institute, an organization known for promulgating quasiofficial Swedish viewpoints abroad, the new view of the family was put even more forcefully. Under the heading "The Family Is Not Sacred," the author stated:

> I should like to abolish the family as a means of earning a livelihood, let adults be economically independent of each other and give society a large share of responsibility for its children. . . . In such a society we could very well do without marriage as a legal entity. . . . "Marriage" and "divorce" would be an entirely private affair between individuals, without any interference from society. . . . What I do think is important is that society shall not set a premium on one particular form of cohabitation. . . . In such a society . . . people will always live together in marriage-like conditions. But I hope no one will automatically assume that this relationship should necessarily last for life. Such an assumption only creates problems for all those people who, for one or another reason, afterwards either cannot or do not wish to live in this way.[62]

Clearly this was quite radical stuff, even by Swedish standards. Yet given the political hegemony of the Social Democrats, such a point of view proved to be highly influential in shaping legislation over the next few years. It also represented the kind of thinking, however, that helped to polarize the nation politically during the 1970s and cause a decline in popularity of the Social

Democratic Party, leading to their eventual (although temporary) fall from power in 1976.

New Legislation and Family Policy

One important area of legislative change that resulted from the new egalitarian spirit was taxation. Changes were sought that could achieve the goal of "economic independence of marriage partners" by encouraging women to take jobs or, as the issue was more pointedly put, "to eradicate the principle of the man as a chief wage earner in the family,"[63] or to further "the long-term abrogation of the housewife system."[64] Like most other nations at the time, Sweden had a provision in its tax code permitting a joint tax return for married couples. This was in recognition of the fact that the wife was often dependent on the husband's salary, and it had the effect of lowering the total tax bite for most married couples. With most wives in the work force, the joint tax return made less sense; it worked to the disadvantage of the two-earner family—their taxes would be less if they could be taxed independently at each person's lower income level. Thus joint taxation came to be regarded as a tax advantage for the man, when, as it was put, "his wife remains at home to care for his personal needs." The Tax Reform of 1971 eliminated the joint return in favor of purely individual taxation. (At the same time Swedish tax rates were made much more steeply progressive.) As a consequence of this tax change, the woman who wanted to be "just a housewife" was at a real tax disadvantage compared to her previous situation, because her husband's income was taxed at the full amount rather than being reduced because of her dependency.

It is widely believed in Sweden that the prohibition of joint taxation was a turning point in the gender-equality issue.[65] Together with the rapid growth of public-sector jobs, most of which went to women, individual taxation was instrumental eventually in causing Sweden to have fewer full-time housewives than probably any other Western society. Almost 85% of Swedish women today who have children under the age of 7 are in the labor market (a majority, however, work only part-time). This represents a truly enormous increase over the 27% of such women in the labor market just two decades ago, in 1965.[66] The policy of individual taxation is still a matter of some political controversy within Sweden, and together with several related policies it has been attacked by conservatives as harming the family and reducing women's freedom of choice.

Another important legislative act of the early 1970s that affected the family was a change in the marriage law, permitting immediate divorce if both partners agreed and no minor children were involved. If only one spouse wanted a divorce or if there were children under 16, a divorce had to be preceded by a "think-it-over" period of at least 6 months. The courts no longer were to have any interest in the question of guilt or infidelity when granting marriage dissolutions, deciding alimony payments, or granting custody of the children to one or the other spouse (thus Sweden was one of the early instituters of the so-called no-fault divorce). Custody was to be determined solely on the basis of what is best for the child. Also, the children of unmarried parents were placed in most legal respects on a par with the children of married parents. This law still stands today with little change in these regards.

One of the most important family-policy measures in Sweden had long been the maternity leave. After the establishment in 1954 of paid maternity leave for women, both the length and remuneration of the leave have gradually been increased over the years. In 1974 the "maternity leave" was changed to "parental leave," permitting either parent to take a paid leave from work of up to 7 months after the birth of a child. The relabeling of the leave was accompanied by a massive propaganda campaign to convince fathers actually to make use of this leave, but without the hoped-for success. Today only about a quarter of fathers take the leave at all, and they take only about 5% of the total leave time utilized.[67] There has even been strong sentiment within the camp of the Swedish left to *require* fathers to use part of the leave time (if the couple wishes to make use of the leave program, which almost all do), but so far this sentiment has not prevailed. The Swedish parental-leave system has justly become world famous, both for its beneficence (the maximum permitted paid leave time is now 1 year) and for its attempts to involve men more fully in the process of parenting.[68]

In these and other ways, Swedish family policy over the years has evolved from an endeavor in which the main goal was to promote childbearing families to a bundle of policies expressly designed to change traditional gender roles. As a publication of the Swedish Institute has put it:

> Family policy was seen as a tool that could be used by the government to try to change the traditional division of labor between the sexes. It was now assumed that every adult should answer for his or her own maintenance, and that therefore both men and women must be gainfully employed. The idea of free choice in this matter was more or less abandoned.[69]

An edict issued by a prominent parliamentary committee in 1979 read: "Family policy must take as basic the principle that both parents have the same right and duty to assume breadwinning as well as practical responsibility for home and children."[70]

The principle of gender-role identity expressed in this edict has been strongly upheld in recent years by the Social Democrats. For example, they have successfully fought off attempts, widely favored by several of the nonsocialist parties, to give stay-at-home mothers a "child-care allowance" that would approach in amount the subsidies given to working mothers for public day care. The Social Democrats have argued that such an allowance would help to preserve the traditional housewife system and, moreover, would retard the expansion of day-care centers. Another application of the principle of gender-role identity concerns changes in family legislation in the early 1970s. Earlier legislation had stated that spouses have a duty to support their marriage through paid work or work in the home; for ideological reasons, the phrase "work in the home" was deleted.[71]

Swedish family policy had always been ambivalent in its orientation toward the family, as we saw in the preceding chapter; it has pursued many contradictory goals simultaneously. Thus the developing emphasis on radical gender equality represented not so much an abrupt shift as a gradual evolution of policy thinking. The single goal of women's equality emerged in the 1970s to overshadow all other goals. If the promotion of family life, or childbearing, or strong homes was to mean the preservation of the traditional family and the continued subordination of women, the Swedes went clearly on record as wanting no part of it.[72]

The goal of gender equality, of course, was pursued in many other ways in addition to family policy. It was vigorously pursued in the schools, for example, doing away with the automatic tracking of girls into sewing and cooking classes and boys into woodworking classes by making both subjects obligatory for all. Extensive vocational-education programs were launched nationwide intended for adult women. To get more women into traditional male occupations, special investigations and projects were undertaken.[73] An Advisory Council on Equality between Men and Women, directly responsible to the prime minister, was established in the early 1970s.[74] This later evolved into a high-level administrative division of government with an "Equality Ombudsman," whose job it was to oversee a new law forbidding gender discrimination.

Another legal change, which was symbolically important, was instituted in the early 1980s. If no "official" last name for a child is reported to the local parish office at time of birth (the last name of either parent being permissible), the child automatically assumes the mother's name.

Although it has been very important, gender equality has not been the only value shaping Swedish family policy in recent years. The government has also continuously sought to improve the financial position of families with children. This policy is no longer conducted on pronatalist grounds; few Swedes any longer believe (or care) that people would have more children just because they were provided with financial benefits. The policy has been pursued mainly on egalitarian grounds of fairness. Over time the concept of fairness has shifted from encompassing horizontal transfers from childless to childbearing families (as typified by the granting of child allowances to all families with children), to an emphasis on vertical transfers from rich to poor families.[75] One way this emphasis has been accomplished is by increasing housing subsidies to lower-income families with children.

During the late 1970s and early 1980s, an era in which millions of Swedish crowns were spent on social-science investigations to find out which persons and groups in Sweden were getting a larger and which a smaller slice of the economic pie, families with children turned out to be the "new poor." This was particularly true of single-parent families, of which there had been a sharp increase, and of large families with many children. The finding generated a new interest in family policy in the 1980s, one directed at removing the remaining inequalities faced by these families.

Swedes also have shown in recent years a special interest in the rights of children and in their psychological as well as material well-being. This interest led to the establishment in 1973 of a "children's ombudsman," especially for the purpose of being a friend of children in court. And in 1979 Sweden enacted a law prohibiting parents from subjecting their children to "physical punishment or other humiliating treatment." This law gained Sweden a certain amount of world notoriety when it was interpreted abroad as "Swedes forbid the spanking of children by their parents."

In the early 1980s, a series of exposés by foreign journalists appeared, purporting to show that Swedes were being overzealous in taking children from their parents on account of alleged child abuse. The data seemed to show that Sweden was pursuing this policy far more avidly than any other European nation. The West German magazine *Der Spiegel* even referred to Sweden as a "children's gulag." Swedish officials claimed that there had been a real increase in child abuse, brought about by deteriorating family conditions. Whatever the facts, following a debate on this matter Swedish authorities did back off and reduced the number of children being taken for such reasons from their parents. Both the "antispanking" law and the child-abuse actions in Sweden have been regarded by conservatives, at home and abroad, as further evidence of that nation's antifamily attitudes, in this case undermining the traditional authority that families have held over their own children.

One area in which Swedish family-policy development has lagged behind that of other nations is in the public provision of day-care facilities.[76] It was not until the 1960s that the state began to take an active role in providing subsidies for such facilities, the task up to then having been left to mostly unwilling local governments. Still today the number of children of working parents in public day-care facilities in Sweden is not nearly so great as it is in a number of other advanced societies (Swedes rely more on informal arrangements and on day-care in families licensed by the local governments).

The reason normally given for this state of affairs is that providing public day-care facilities at the high standard deemed acceptable in Sweden is very expensive, and there have always been higher-priority items in the Swedish budget. In the 1960s, for example, one of the highest domestic priorities was housing (especially family housing.) Because more public day care has been an adamant demand of many Swedish women for more than two decades, however, one suspects that the lag may be due at least indirectly to the veto power of male-dominated labor unions and to male-dominated politics in general. Also, it is probably reasonable to attribute this lag to a lingering concern, as expressed in the 1956 work of Myrdal and Klein noted above, that "day-care centers are not good for children," as well as to continued support among the Swedish masses for the traditional family. There still are many people in Sweden today, especially among the working classes, who avoid putting their children in public day-care facilities if other arrangements can be made. And in a 1984 public-opinion poll a majority of Swedes, both women and men, favored policies that would give more financial support to families who did not use public day care.[77]

Yet the political priority being placed on subsidized day care has grown much stronger in recent years, and the Social Democratic government now in power has promised a day-care place for every child by the early 1990s. This follows an earlier expansion of "preschools," a 1975 law having obligated local authorities to provide places for all Swedish 6-year-olds (regular schooling in Sweden begins at age 7).

In hindsight, it is hard to discern an overall plan in the development of Swedish family policy after World War II. This development is probably best viewed as an aspect of what political scientists Hugh Heclo and Henrik Madsen have recently called "adaptive reformism," a process of constant adjusting and innovating to make desirable improvements. They sketch the development of some of the central family legislation as follows:

> If social insurance cannot provide income support for all mothers-to-be who need it, more comprehensive maternity benefits must be made available. If private-sector employment restrictions threaten effective use of these benefits, then new laws must be enacted to guarantee maternity leave with the right to return to work after the baby is born. If a new welfare gap is then discovered to exist after the baby is born but before the return to work, benefits should be extended to the mother's first months with her newborn. If this policy discriminates against couples who would rather have the father stay at home with the baby, then the maternity benefit must be changed to a parent benefit that applies to whichever parent stays at home.[78]

Changing Sexual Attitudes

If Sweden has been in the vanguard on the issue of gender equality, it has also been on the cutting edge in attitudinal changes toward sex. During the 1960s and 1970s, Sweden led the way in instituting the "new morality" in sexual matters, and foreign journalists flocked there to see what might be ahead for their own nations. Sweden developed a worldwide reputation as a center of sex or, as it more commonly was put, of sin. Sin, sex, and Sweden seem to have become for a time nearly synonymous among the prurient minds of the Western world. That sinful reputation was largely undeserved, and it developed into an issue about which Swedes showed a strong sensitivity to the criticisms of outsiders.

Swedish women have long been considered by non-Swedes to be more "forward" and independent than most other women of the world, and there had been for centuries, especially in rural areas, a tradition of sex before marriage among engaged couples. Thus Sweden was already in open violation of the traditional Western moral strictures prohibiting premarital sex, strictures that are still widely promulgated in countries where either Roman Catholic or fundamentalist Protestanism has strong followings. The moral importance of being formally engaged had quietly been dropped in Sweden, but what shocked the world even more was Sweden's disavowal, in keeping with the idea of gender equality, of the "double standard." The attitude became widespread that both men and women have an equal right to sexual experience before marriage.

The new era of sexual freedom showed up in the movies, in which Sweden pioneered in portraying nudity and "daringly frank scenes" on film, and in the open acceptance of pornography. The acceptance of pornography became a kind of litmus test of sexual freedom, and for a time it was displayed openly on the streets of Swedish cities. In 1968, with few objections, Europe's first public exhibition of pornography took place in the southern Swedish town of Lund. One female government official concerned with sex education even proposed the establishment of an institute to make pornography more freely available to those who can benefit from it.[79] Yet Sweden never developed the "fleshpots" that were common in other European cities, and visitors to Stockholm were typically surprised at how staid a city it had remained. (In recent years Sweden has been much more restrictive even about the display of pornography.)

The "new morality" was given the official stamp of approval in a new handbook, prepared by the National Swedish Board of Education, concerning sex education in the schools. Published in 1977 after nearly a decade of strenuous and controversial committee input, the handbook was as different from the one prepared two decades earlier (discussed above) as night is from day. For starters, the title had now become *Instruction Concerning Interpersonal Relations* and the "first goal" of the curriculum concerned "achieving interpersonal relations characterized by responsibility, consideration and care for their fellow beings, and in this way experiencing sexuality as a source of happiness together with another person."[80] A key new moral concept was "intimacy":

> The most important goal of instruction concerning interpersonal relations is to promote the capacity for intimacy. . . . Sexual activities can take place without intimacy, but school instruction concerning interpersonal relations argues that sexuality on a basis of personal intimacy satisfies a profound human need. Experience of such intimacy is one of the essential goals of human existence. . . .[81]

Along the same lines it stated that

> the most fundamental of the values which should characterize instruction concerning sexual and other interpersonal relations [is] that sexual life forming part of a personal relationship has more to offer than an impersonal, casual sexual life. . . .[82]

What a far cry this is from the first government guidelines set forth when limited sex education was initiated in Swedish schools in the 1930s. At that time, the main goals of sex education were love–marriage–children: "Throughout all parts of sex education it must be emphasized that the implied aim of sex life is home life and its success."[83] Gone for the most part from this edition of the handbook were any proscriptions against premarital sexuality; it was often noted that few Swedes any longer actually followed such proscriptions (A 1968 Swedish "Kinsey Report" found that 90% of the adults interviewed had engaged in premarital sex.)[84] Under its "goals" section, the new handbook did make occasional references to the family, for example, "one of the most important tasks of instruction concerning interpersonal relations is to prepare young people for family life." But this statement was buried in the middle of a paragraph that went on to emphasize that the family no longer should be looked at in traditional terms. "Instruction must deal both with two-parent and single-parent families and with the common situation of children having their parents in different places." And "schools must be prepared to explain why divorce is necessary in many cases."[85] In these and many other ways, the handbook stressed the importance of taking a new "pluralistic view" toward sex and family questions.[86]

These changes in attitudes were being reflected in changing sexual behavior (explored more fully in later chapters): Sexuality was becoming disengaged from any necessary association with "marriage and family." Yet Swedes continue to hold fast to the moral principle of sexual fidelity to one's current sexual partner, especially when that partner is a marital or nonmarital spouse. Swedes are tolerant about sexual permissiveness, but they have never advocated sexual promiscuity. Indeed, they may well be less promiscuous than the citizens of many other advanced societies, particularly the United States, in the sense of having only one sexual partner at a time. The 1968 Swedish "Kinsey Report" found that 87% of male and 91% of female respondents regarded "fidelity within marriage as absolutely necessary," and 90% of all married respondents said that they had been faithful to their spouses during the previous 12 months.[87]

The espousal of sexual fidelity may now be changing, however. A survey in the late 1970s found among 18- to 30-year-olds only 69% of men and 77% of women who regarded "fidelity within marriage as absolutely necessary." And the percentage of young Swedes who answered "Yes, love is the only reason for a sexual relationship" dropped between 1967 and 1979 from 47 to 43% for males, and from 73 to 54% for females.[88]

Sweden in the Eighties: The New Social Problems

The great social and cultural changes of the last few decades have left Sweden a vastly different society than it was in the 1950s. The typical Swede of today is part of the first generation to have grown up in an urban place; he or she lives in an apartment, works for the public sector, is surrounded by material plenty, has more leisure time than the citizens of other advanced societies, and has traveled widely abroad. Although the pull of nature and the outdoors is still very strong in Swedish life, and there is a continuing popularity of primitive and remote summerhouses in the still-unspoiled Swedish countryside, most Swedes today say that their favorite leisure-time pursuit is watching television.

In the view of many observers, such as Swedish opinion pollster Hans Zetterberg, a "new breed" of Swede has arisen in place of the stolid, reticent, group-conforming, bourgeois advocate of the Protestant Ethic.[89] The new breed supports individual interests over collective interests, is suspicious of authority, and questions material values in favor of self-actualization. These are increasingly the characteristics of the new generation of Swedish people born and raised in urban areas. Stimulated by the events of the late 1960s, but in fact the result of much broader cultural currents, this new character type is now found in most Western nations.[90] Yet the phenomenon seems especially pronounced in Sweden. In a survey of 11 nations, 87% of Swedish youth, a far higher percentage than in the other nations, gave "to live as I like" as the answer to a question about their life goals. The other possible answers were "to get rich," "to acquire social position," and "to work on behalf of society."[91] Moreover, in Sweden this new character type represents a truly sharp contrast with the traditional national character.

Much of the hierarchy and social formality of earlier times is gone. In terms of a belief system, the new Swede has become thoroughly secular; God is almost never invoked publicly, a minority of Swedes pray, and almost no Swedes attend religious services regularly, as noted earlier in this chapter. The new Swede is still a believer in the values of rationality, moderation, and planned social change, but increasingly he or she finds the centralized bureaucracy rather stultifying and intimidating. There are growing concerns about individual rights, especially the right to protection against invasions of privacy, and a growing desire for some alternative that would humanize the society and bring government closer to the people. There is a fear that "The People's Home" may have become transformed into "Big Brother."[92] Through all this, however, Swedes remain among the most satisfied of the world's peoples. The Scandinavians have typically scored the highest on cross-national comparisons of "happiness" in recent years.[93]

It is impossible to accurately interpret Swedish society today without understanding that, in the recent words of Hugh Heclo and Henrik Madsen, "in no other nation has a reforming party of the political Left held such a grip on the state apparatus and on the public perception of policy choices."[94] The hegemony of the Social Democratic Party in Sweden over so many years is undoubtedly one of the main reasons why Sweden today has the most egalitarian income distribution in the West and also probably the largest amount of legislation and administrative activity devoted to the pursuit of equality.[95] It is also the main reason why Sweden became by the mid-1980s the first Western nation to have a majority of its voters dependent on public funds for their incomes as public employees, as pensioners, or in other tax-supported positions. The Western world's most heavily taxed nation, Sweden also leads in the size of its public sector, with public expenditures at all levels of government (including transfer payments) amounting to about two thirds of the gross national product. This represents a dramatic increase from 1960, when the comparable figure was only about 30%. Almost all employment growth in recent years has been in the public sector, which now employs about one out of every three Swedish workers.

Though far from being a thoroughly radicalized society, Sweden is the most left-wing of Western nations in official ideology if not in popular culture. In the words of Heclo and Madsen:

> The reformist Social Democratic vision of society has imparted a quality to Swedish political life that is at once pragmatic and ideological, adaptable and moralistic . . . [it has] interpreted the national identity as one of an ever-reforming welfare state, a national social community always striving to make itself more of a community . . . [The Social Democratic] mission is the slow, careful eradication of disease and the establishment of a regimen of good health in society. It is always done with the patient's consent, but also with the recognition that some unpleasant medicine and restrictions may need to be accepted because they are good for the people.[96]

They go on to add, perhaps with slight exaggeration, that "the Social Democratic movement and the Swedish national identity have tended to merge into one and the same thing."[97] Along similar lines, Sweden today is sometimes described as a giant "company town."

Because of its highly pragmatic nature, the character of Swedish political radicalism is no longer very predictable, and there are some new social solutions being proposed that would be unacceptable and even unrecognizable to the rational planner who led the working-class reform movements of earlier decades. These solutions typically take the form of radical decentralization and a certain dismantling of government; they seem to project a kind of communitarian socialism. More than anything else, they call for strict limitations on social institutions and the handing of power back to the people. In the fields of social welfare and youth work, for example, there have recently been widely discussed pleas for reducing the power of professionals and seeking to engage people more fully in helping others on a volunteer basis (the role of the community volunteer is today almost completely gone from Swedish life).[98] The idea is to "personalize" society and to bring it back to a "human scale." Such proposals fly in the face of most social trends in Sweden in recent years, however, and their political and social feasibility at this time seems remote. The one trend that works in their favor is the continuing decrease in time spent at paid employment and the concomitant increase in leisure time.

The very rapid and far-reaching social and cultural changes in Sweden from 1960 to 1985 have not been without their problematic social consequences. Once a society where following the letter of the law was one of the supreme commandments, for example, Sweden has witnessed in that period a widespread increase in lawbreaking. According to most international comparisons, the lawbreaking in Sweden may seem miniscule (and it is certainly not violent), but by previous Swedish standards it is immense. The conclusion of one recent review of Swedish criminality was that "in slightly more than 30 years, a very sharp and essentially unbroken increase in reported criminality has occurred."[99] For the Nordic countries as a whole, the number of reported offenses against the penal code trebled on a per-capita basis between 1950 and 1980, and Sweden was in the lead with the highest level of crime.[100] The largest Swedish crime increases were in property damage, fraud, and theft, but crimes of violence such as assault, murder, and rape have also shown significant growth. During the 1970s Sweden had the highest number of reported thefts per 100,000 of the population of the 75 countries included in Interpol's international crime statistics, although this ignominious position was doubtless caused in part by Sweden's efficient police system and accurate record keeping.[101]

Most widely discussed today is what the Swedes classify as "economic crime." Having the world's highest level of taxation, Sweden is now a nation where tax cheating has become quite common. High taxes, for example, have led to a large and growing underground or "black" economy—instead of paying for such personal services as day care, plumbing, or house painting through normal channels—and thus incurring high taxes—people are paying in cash or even in kind within a new barter system. A lawyer will give a painter legal services in return for having his house painted. It has been estimated that virtually all informal day-care arrangements in Sweden today are made "under the table," that is, outside the knowledge of the tax authorities. If they were not, it is argued, such care would be prohibitively expensive. Municipal officials administering overloaded public day-care centers have even been known to advise people to go on the black market for day-care services. In 1987, the underground economy was estimated to make up 20% of Sweden's gross national product.[102] The cultural effects of the underground economy are less quantifiable, but probably are also great, with an increase in cynicism and mistrust, a loss of confidence in the political system, and a decline in feelings of national solidarity.

The growth of lawbreaking extends to other nonviolent areas—the breaking of traffic laws against speeding and running through a red light, business crime, bribery, and embezzlement of and by public employees, and "welfare cheating."[103] Also, especially during the 1970s, there has been an apparent growth in the number of alcoholics (although the per-capita consumption of alcohol has been dropping) and an increase in drug use.[104] The most dramatic postwar development in lawbreaking, however, has been the enormous increase in juvenile delinquency. The leading criminal age group in Sweden (as in most advanced societies) is 15 to 19, which commits more than double the number of reported crimes as the next leading group—that between ages 20 and 24.[105] While the crime rate for cleared serious crimes (those resulting in sanctions more severe than fines) in Sweden increased for all age groups more than four times in the past 30 years, the increase was fivefold for the 18 to 20-year-old group, and sevenfold for the 15 to 17-year-old group.[106] A finding of the landmark Swedish longitudinal study, Project Metropolitan,[107] was that, of some 7000 boys born in Stockholm in 1953, 30% had contact with the police for lawbreaking by the time they reached age 26. The great bulk of juvenile crime is not serious and probably does not inflict great harm on the individual or on society. It does, however, help to weaken further the solidarity and trust that Swedes feel toward one another.

Because almost every advanced nation has seen a sharp rise in juvenile delinquency (and most other crimes), it is unreasonable to put the bulk of the blame for the problem on Sweden's welfare state. But it is equally clear that the kind of juvenile delinquency found in Sweden cannot be attributed to the classic factors of poverty and inequality. The most common general social explanations given for the growth of juvenile delinquency in

Sweden are an increase in "opportunities" for crime, brought about by urban living at a high material level, and a breakdown in the informal mechanisms of social control at the family and neighborhood levels, with a consequent increase in unsupervised peer groups (most juvenile crime is committed in groups). Other explanations that have been given great weight, however, are family conditions such as broken homes and especially the absence of clear standards of upbringing.[108]

These new social problems have been magnified in importance by the fact that beginning in the mid-1970s Sweden, like most other nations in Europe, fell on economic hard times. Certain areas of industry and trade went into a steep decline, leading to rising rates of unemployment. The rate of inflation was rising together with budget deficits, and the economic growth rate had slowed along with a declining balance of payments.[109] This meant that not only was there a decreasing likelihood of additional welfare measures being enacted, or an expansion of existing programs, but also a growing concern about how Sweden would be able to continue paying for the expensive welfare programs that it already had. In addition, the politically powerful new middle class was growing increasingly resistant to any further income redistribution to promote equality of condition.

All of this—the new social problems together with the economic downturn—led to new feelings of insecurity in Swedish society and at times even to an air of crisis. The nation became more politically polarized, and there has been much discussion of the end not only of Social Democratic hegemony but also of the famous "Swedish model" of labor negotiations, which had brought about many decades of relative peace between labor and industry. Most symbolic of this change, perhaps, was the event that took place on October 4, 1983, when some 75,000 businessmen and white-collar workers from all over Sweden arrived in Stockholm and marched through the streets to protest the plans of the newly elected Social Democratic government to institute "Wage Earner Funds." Designed to divert a portion of the profits of Swedish industry into employee-investment funds, partly controlled by the labor unions, these funds came to symbolize the socialist straw that would break the back of the capitalist camel.[110] The funds were later instituted, in a modified form, and in recent years the debate over them has all but died down. But the white-collar protest and antagonism that the fund issue generated have continued to be a central part of Swedish life. Because further income redistribution through taxation has proved to be anathema to much of the new middle class, the funds themselves had represented a kind of sidestep around the redistribution issue in the direction of "economic democracy"—a wider public ownership of the means of production.

Critics have again appeared on the scene to proclaim Sweden's new agonies to the rest of the world. Invoking visions of gloom and doom, one influential group of essays by a West German author in 1982 was entitled "Swedish Autumn" (*Svensk Höst*).[111] Many other critics, both from the right and the left, have written of "the crisis of the welfare state."[112] Focusing on the state of the economy, the left has blamed Sweden for having sold out to capitalism, while the right has maintained that the efficiency of market mechanisms has been impaired. Marquis Childs even came out with a new book entitled *Sweden: The Middle Way on Trial.*[113] The criticism became so rife that Hans Zetterberg was moved to say that "In today's international debate, Sweden is no longer presented as a model to emulate; rather, it is held up . . . as a warning."[114]

Yet by the mid-1980s a stronger economy had returned, and discussions about a crisis had died down.[115] Socially, a mild conservative trend was under way. The number of formal weddings increased; books on etiquette again became popular; young people in schools showed a new sense of purpose; and some Swedes were even returning to the use of the formal "you." Juvenile delinquency rates had leveled off (at least for serious offenses), and drug use was lower.

There were even empirical indications that in some respects life in Sweden had never been better. In the early to mid-1980s great publicity was given to the results of the Level of Living Survey, actually a series of surveys of the Swedish population conducted in 1968, 1974, and 1981 by the Swedish Institute for Social Research at the University of Stockholm. Over the time period of the studies, the survey found improvements in virtually all aspects of Swedish society, especially in the material conditions of life.[116] It also found some equalization in the distribution of income and living conditions among the various social classes, while also stressing that Sweden still has a long way to go before reaching any real equality of condition.

The survey was unable to capture the deep changes that had taken place in Swedish culture, however—the changes in spirit, motivation, and outlook. Also, in concentrating on the material side of welfare, the survey overlooked some very important changes in human relationships in Sweden in the past two decades. In particular, it gave short shrift to the massive changes in the structure and character of the Swedish family. Quietly, and beknown to very few Swedes, the Swedish family had moved farther from the traditional nuclear family of earlier decades than had the family in any other society in the world. The Swedish family also was showing evidence of a marked institutional decline. It is to a detailed analysis of these changes that we turn in the chapters that follow.

Notes

[1]Marquis W. Childs (1947), *Sweden: The Middle Way:* x.
[2]Data from the Stockholm Chamber of Commerce, in Albert H. Rosenthal (1967), *The Social Programs of Sweden:* 159.

3Stewart Oakley (1966), *A Short History of Sweden:* 258.

4Kathleen Knott (1961), *A Clean, Well-Lighted Place.*

5Nordiska Museet (1985), *Modell Sverige:* 51.

6*Ibid.:* 51 (my translation).

7Quoted in David Jenkins (1968), *Sweden: The Progress Machine:* 15.

8*Ibid.:* 12–13.

9Hans L. Zetterberg (1967), "Sweden—A Land of Tomorrow?," pp. 13–21 in Ingemar Wizelius (ed.), *Sweden in the Sixties:* 13–14.

10Kaare Svalastoga (1954), "The Family in Scandinavia," *Marriage and Family Living* 16-4: 375.

11*Ibid.:* 376.

12*Ibid.:* 375.

13*Ibid.:* 376.

14*Ibid.:* 377.

15H. J. Locke and Georg Karlsson (1952), "Marital Adjustment and Prediction in Sweden and the United States," *American Sociological Review* 17: 10–17.

16It was probably in this sense that Mary Wollstonecraft found in Sweden at the turn of the nineteenth century a "total lack of chastity in the lower classes of women." Quoted in Irene Scobbie (1972), *Sweden:* 207.

17G. Jonsson and A-L Kälvesten (1964), *222 Stockholmspojkar.* Cited in Karin Sandqvist's forthcoming "Swedish Family Policy and Attempt to Change Paternal Roles," in M. O'Brien and C. Lewis (eds.), *Problems of Fatherhood:* 6.

18Carl Gustav Boethius (1984), "Swedish Sex Education and Its Results," *Current Sweden* 315 (Swedish Institute).

19Quoted from the English version of National Board of Education in Sweden (1968), *Handbook on Sex Instruction in Swedish Schools:* 12.

20*Ibid.:* 13, 15.

21Quoted in Kurt Samuelsson (1968), *From Great Power to Welfare State:* 251.

22Serge de Chessin (1936), *The Key to Sweden:* 183.

23Quoted in Hugh Heclo and Henrik Madsen (1987), *Policy and Politics in Sweden:* 157.

24The shifting goals of Swedish welfare policy are explored in Kurt Samuelsson (1975), "The Philosophy of Swedish Welfare Policies," pp. 335–353 in Steven Koblik (ed.), *Sweden's Development from Poverty to Affluence, 1750–1970.*

25For an excellent discussion of the political and cultural radicalism of the time, see Lars Gyllensten (1972), "Swedish Radicalism in the 1960's: An Experiment in Political and Cultural Debate," pp. 279–301 in M. Donald Hancock and Gideon Sjoberg (eds.), *Politics in the Post-Welfare State.*

26See Stig Hadenius (1985), *Swedish Politics During the 20th Century.*

27For reasons of economic exigency, the bourgeois government nationalized more industrial companies in its brief reign than the Social Democrats had in 44 years of rule.

28Gösta Esping-Andersen (1985), *Politics Against Markets:* 313.

29Thomas J. Anton (1980), *Administered Politics: Elite Political Culture in Sweden:* ix.

30Paul Britten Austin (1970), *The Swedes: How They Live and Work.*

31David Martin (1979), *A General Theory of Secularization.*

32Data from international surveys done by the Gallup Organization, reported in Oxford Analytica (1986), *America in Perspective:* 121–24. Denmark was almost as secular as Sweden according to these surveys. The percentage of Swedish believers in 1956 is reported in Irene Scobbie (1972), *Sweden.*

33As measured in terms of percentage of population living in urban areas of 50,000 or more, Sweden was only 33% urbanized in 1980, compared to 61% in the United States and 70% in the United Kingdom. *The OECD Observer* 141 (July 1986): 5.

34This issue is explored in my two earlier books that deal with Sweden. David Popenoe (1977), *The Suburban Environment: Sweden and the United States,* and (1985), *Private Pleasure, Public Plight: American Metropolitan Community Life in Comparative Perspective.* See also Heclo and Madsen (1987), *Policy and Politics:* Chapter 5, and Bruce Headey (1978), *Housing Policy in the Developed Economy.*

35Sixten Marklund and Gunnar Bergendal (1979), *Trends in Swedish Educational Policy:* 8.

36For a description of Swedish schools today, see Britta Stenholm (1984), *The Swedish School System.*

37This transformation is explored in Arnold J. Heidenheimer, Hugh Heclo, and Carolyn Teich Adams (1975), *Comparative Public Policy:* Chapter 2.

38Gunnar Heckscher (1984), *The Welfare State and Beyond:* 182–86.

39Alva Myrdal and Viola Klein (1956), *Women's Two Roles: Home and Work:* 12.

40*Ibid.:* 24.

41*Ibid.:* 116.

42*Ibid.:* 125, 128.

43*Ibid.:* 193.

44The best source of this essay "Kvinnans Villkorliga Frigivning" today, albeit in slightly revised form, is the appendix to Eva Moberg (1962), *Kvinnor och Manniskor.* This book also contains various essays and thoughts following the original publication of the essay.

45Quoted from Jenkins (1968), *Sweden:* 193.

46A revised edition of this work in English translation, with a foreward by Alva Myrdal, was published as Edmund Dahlström (ed.) (1967), *The Changing Roles of Men and Women.*

47Edmund Dahlström and Rita Liljeström (1967), "The Family and Married Women at Work," *ibid.:* 19–58.

48Rita Liljestrom (1978a), *Roles in Transition:* 105.

49Per Olav Tiller (1967), "Parental Role Division and the Child's Personality Development," pp. 79–104 in Dahlström (ed.), *Changing Roles:* 103.

50Dahlström (1967), *Changing Roles:* 179.

51*Ibid.:* 9.

52See Hilda Scott (1982), *Sweden's "Right to be Human,"* and Olof Palme (1972), "The Emancipation of Man," *The Journal of Social Issues* 28-2: 237–246.

53Dahlström (1967), *Changing Roles:* 14.

54Quoted in Birgitta Linnér (1967), *Sex and Society in Sweden:* 9.

55Gunnar Qvist (1980), "Policy Towards Women and the Women's Struggle in Sweden," pp. 51–74 in *Scandinavian Journal of History* 5: 68.

56Scott (1982), *Sweden's:* 6.

57In its English translation the report is entitled *Towards Equality: The Alva Myrdal Report to the Swedish Social Democratic Party* (1971).

58*Ibid.:* 13–21.

59*Ibid.:* 82.

60*Ibid.:* 83, 84.

61*Ibid.:* 84.

62Anna-Greta Leijon (1968), *Swedish Women—Swedish Men:* 125.

63Birgitta Wistrand (1981), *Swedish Women on the Move:* 13.

64In a letter from Eva Moberg, quoted in Leijon (1968), *Swedish Women:* 147.

[65]Annika Baude (no date), *Public Policy and Changing Family Patterns in Sweden 1930-1977:* 168.

[66]Swedish Institute (1984), "Child Care Programs in Sweden": 2.

[67]Birgitta Silén (1987), "The Truth about Sexual Equality: A Gap between Words and Deeds," *Inside Sweden* 1-2: 11-13.

[68]See M. E. Lamb and J. A. Levine (1983), "The Swedish Parental Insurance Policy: An Experiment in Social Engineering," pp. 39-51 in M. E. Lamb and A. Sagi, (Eds.), *Fatherhood and Family Policy;* and Sandqvist, "Swedish Family Policy."

[69]Wistrand (1981), *Swedish Women:* 53.

[70]National Committee on Equality between Men and Women (1979), *Step by Step: National Plan of Action for Equality:* 89.

[71]Interview with Anders Agell (October 1985).

[72]See Rita Liljeström (1980), "Integration of Family Policy and Labor Market Policy in Sweden," pp. 388-404 in Ronnie Steinberg Ratner, (ed.), *Equal Employment Policy for Women.*

[73]Liljeström (1978a), *Roles in Transition.*

[74]On the work of this group, see Elisabet Sandberg (1975), *Equality is the Goal.*

[75]Rita Liljeström (1978b), "Sweden," pp. 19-48 in Sheila B. Kamerman and Alfred J. Kahn (eds.), *Family Policy:* 26.

[76]On the development of public day care in Sweden, see Mary Ruggie (1984), *The State and Working Women: A Comparative Study of Britain and Sweden:* Chapter 6.

[77]SIFO (The Swedish Institute for Opinion Research (1984), *Indikator* 1.

[78]Heclo and Madsen (1987), *Policy and Politics:* 6.

[79]Jenkins (1968), *Sweden:* 207.

[80]National Swedish Board of Education (1977), *Instruction Concerning Interpersonal Relations:* 10.

[81]*Ibid.:* 11.

[82]*Ibid.:* 19.

[83]Quoted from "Betankande i Sexualfrågan," SOU: 1936-59, in H. Gille (1948), "Recent Developments in Swedish Population Policy," pp. 3-70 in *Population Studies* 2: 34.

[84] Hans Zetterberg (1969), *Om Sexuallivet i Sverige.*

[85]National Swedish Board of Education (1977), *Instruction:* 12.

[86]Already in 1965, an amendment to the handbook stated: "It is important for the students to realize that laws and norms vary from time to time, from people to people, and that within one and the same country, different groups may have different views on sex relations." Quoted in Linnér (1967), *Sex and Society:* 125.

[87]Zetterberg (1969), *Sexuallivet.*

[88]Statens Ungdomsråd (1981), *Ej till Salu:* 321.

[89]Hans Zetterberg (1984), "The Rational Humanitarians," *Daedalus* (Winter): 75-92; and Hans Zetterberg (1979), "Maturing of the Swedish Welfare State," *Public Opinion* 2-5: 42-47.

[90]In America, it is the new character type discussed in Robert N. Bellah et al. (1985), *Habits of the Heart.* In a recent article the Dutch sociologist Anton Zijderveld sees strong similarities between Sweden and the Netherlands in the growth of this character type and suggests that, although they stem from different social roots, the new character type and the welfare state have a very strong "elective affinity" for one another. Anton C. Zijderveld (1986), "The Ethos of the Welfare State," *International Sociology* 1-4: 443-457. For political dimensions of this new character type, see Ronald Inglehart (1977), *The Silent Revolution: Changing Values and Political Styles among Western Publics.*

91Richard G. Braungart and Margaret M. Braungart (1986), "Youth Problems and Politics in the 1980's: Some Multinational Comparisons," pp. 359–380 in *International Sociology* 1-4: Table 1, p. 363.

92Yet when this issue was raised in a pointed, but extremely exaggerated, form by the journalist Roland Huntford in 1971 it tended to be dismissed by most Swedes as nonsense. Roland Huntford (1972), *The New Totalitarians.*

93Ruut Veenhoven (1984), *Conditions of Happiness:* 142–147.

94Heclo and Madsen (1987), *Policy and Politics:* 9.

95Although with varying emphases, this has now been documented by a great many scholars. See Heclo and Madsen (1987), *Policy and Politics;* Gösta Esping-Andersen (1985), *Politics Against Markets: The Social Democratic Road to Power;* J. Stephens (1979), *The Transition from Capitalism to Socialism;* Francis G. Castles (1978), *The Social Democratic Image of Society;* Walter Korpi (1983), *The Democratic Class Struggle;* Walter Korpi (1978), *The Working Class in Welfare Capitalism;* and Richard Scase (1977), *Social Democracy in Capitalist Society.*

96Heclo and Madsen (1987), *Policy and Politics:* 27.

97*Ibid.:* 44.

98Secretariat for Futures Studies (1984), *Time to Care,* and Benny Henriksson (1983), *Not for Sale: Young People in Society.*

99The National Swedish Council for Crime Prevention (1985), *Crime and Criminal Policy in Sweden 1985:* 19.

100Flemming Balvig (1985), "Crime in Scandinavia: Trends, Explanations, Consequences," pp. 7–17 in Norman Bishop (ed.), *Scandinavian Criminal Policy and Criminology 1980–85.*

101Flemming Balvig (1980), "Theft in Scandinavia, 1970–78," pp. 1–6 in Norman Bishop. *Crime and Crime Control in Scandinavia 1976–80:* 1.

102Steve Lohr (1987), "Now, Tax Revision in Sweden," *New York Times,* May 12: D-9. See also Bo Svensson (1985), "Economic Crime in Sweden," pp. 31–45 in Bishop (1980), *Crime.*

103Brottsförebyggande Rådet (1985), *Brotts-Utveklingen.*

104The Swedish Council for Information on Alcohol and Other Drugs (1983), "On the Alcohol and Drug Situation in Sweden."

105 Jerzy Sarnecki (1981), *Ungdomsbrottslighet.*

106Henrik Tham (1978), "Ungdombrottsligheten Enligt Den Officiella Statistiken," *BRÅ-apropå.*

107 Carl-Gunnar Janson (1982), "Juvenile Delinquency Among Metropolitan Boys," Project Metropolitan Research Report 17. Between ages 15 and 18, 13.3% of these boys became "known to the police," compared to 6.3% for the cohort of boys born in 1925. Carl-Gunnar Janson (1968), "Brott och Sociala Strata," pp. 284–302 in C.-G. Janson (ed.), *Det Differentierade Samhället.*

108Jerzy Sarnecki (1983), "Research into Juvenile Crime in Sweden," *Information Bulletin of the National Swedish Council for Crime Prevention:* 1.

109Organization for Economic Cooperation and Development (1984), *Sweden* (OECD Economic Surveys). This report was rather hopeful about the future of the Swedish economy.

110For a discussion of these funds, see Rudolf Meidner (1978), *Employee Investment Funds,* and Heclo and Madsen (1987), *Policy and Politics:* Chapter 6.

111By Hans Magnus Enzensberger, the series appeared in the Stockholm daily *Dagens Nyheter.* At the same time, Swedes were still being criticized by outsiders in terms of their traditional character traits—too formal, overly efficient, conformist, etc. See Mogens Berendt (1983), *Fallet Sverige.*

112See Per-Martin Meyerson (1982), *The Welfare State in Crisis—The Case of Sweden;* Per-Martin Meyerson (1985), *Eurosclerosis: The Case of Sweden;* Bengt Rydén and Villy Bergström (eds.) (1982), *Sweden: Choices for Economic and Social Policy in the 1980's;* Bertram Silverman (ed.) (1980), "The Crisis of the Swedish Welfare State," *Challenge* (July-August): 36–51; John Fry (ed.) (1979), *Limits of the Welfare State: Critical Views on Post-War Sweden;* Eric Einhorn and John Logue (1980), *Welfare States in Hard Times.*

113Marquis Childs (1980), *Sweden: The Middle Way on Trial.*

114Zetterberg (1984), "Rational Humanitarians": 76.

115A recent study by the Brookings Institution has found the Swedish economy, compared to that of other European nations, to be quite strong, even though it is "a supply-side economist's version of a nightmare." Barry P. Bosworth (1987), "The Swedish Economy: An American Perspective," *Inside Sweden* 1-2: 6–7.

116Robert Erikson and Rune Åberg (eds.) (1984), *Välfärd i Förändring.* An English translation of this work was recently published (1987) under the title *Welfare in Transition: A Survey of Living Conditions in Sweden, 1968–1981.*

Beyond the Nuclear Family: The Changing Family in Sweden Today*

Chapter

8

Over the past quarter of a century, as discussed in Chapter 7, Swedish society has undergone a substantial cultural transformation. A once very formal, integrated, and hierarchical society, guided by the Protestant ethic, has become a "looser" aggregation of people where informality and permissiveness are common and egalitarianism is the dominant cultural motif. In this cultural transformation no other element of Swedish society has changed more rapidly, or in a more dramatic way, than the Swedish family. The purpose of this chapter is to present, with the help of the latest available statistics, an accurate empirical description of what has happened to the family in Sweden over the past few decades in comparison with other advanced societies and to set forth in broad terms what is known about family change in Sweden today.

Contemporary family change in Sweden can be viewed as an extension of the global family trend, under way in all modernizing societies, in which the institution of the family shifts structurally from an extended to a nuclear family-kinship system (see Chapter 3). A fundamental characteristic of the nuclear-family system is the release of young people, at or before marriage, from the authority of and duty to contribute to the family group into which they were born. From this characteristic derive such familiar traits of the nuclear-family system as a relatively free choice of marriage partners, an emphasis on the conjugal bond between the partners, and the independent household of the married couple.

The particular institutional family type that emerged in the Western world over the past few centuries has variously been called the Western conjugal family, the modern nuclear family, or more commonly the traditional nuclear family. In its classical form, this family type is sometimes known as the Victorian, bourgeois family, referring both to the historical period in Britain during which it became predominant and to the social class in which it presumably originated. As a cultural ideal, this family type is a monogamous,

*Portions of this chapter appeared in "Beyond the Nuclear Family," *Journal of Marriage and the Family 49, 1987.*

patriarchal family consisting of a married couple living with their children, the man working outside the home and the women being a full-time mother-housewife. The marital union is lifelong, with divorce very uncommon, and most people are expected to live in such families for most of their lives. Once limited to the nascent middle class, the traditional nuclear family gradually became a nearly universal family type in Western nations, reaching a peak in the years following World War II. After that, in virtually every one of these nations, the traditional nuclear family began to decline.

The Swedish family today, I argue in this chapter, has moved farther from this traditional nuclear family than has the family in any other society. Sweden should not be thought to be in any way exceptional in this respect; the same movement "beyond" the traditional nuclear family is under way in every other advanced society. It is just that the change in Sweden has been both more rapid and more extensive than anywhere else. Answers to the question of why this is the case, to be explored in later chapters, should therefore help us to reach a deeper understanding of the causes of this important social transformation in the modern world.

The most dramatic indicators of Swedish family change today are the marriage rate, which has become the lowest in the industrialized world, and the nonmarital cohabitation rate and rate of family dissolution, both of which are probably the highest in the industrialized world. It is with these three indicators that this chapter begins.

Marriage

Until recent decades the history of nuptiality in Sweden had not shown any remarkable differences from comparable European nations, except for somewhat lower rates of marriage during some time periods. Swedish marriage records go back to 1749, and it is possible to compute the crude marriage rate for every year since then.[1] The percentage of married women in the age group of 20 to 44 years, for example, was 59.4 in 1750 and then dropped (although with many ups and downs) to 52.1 in 1900, which was a low point. During this century the marriage rate rose rapidly, however, passing its earlier high and reaching a peak in the mid-1960s. The percentage of married women in the 20–44 age group in 1970 was 70.4. Before 1900 more men than women married, but in this century the pattern reversed itself with the number of married women outdistancing the number of married men (in 1970 only 61.5% of Swedish men in the age group of 20 to 49 years were married). But the important point is that marriage was never so popular with either sex than it was in the 1950s and early 1960s, and this was as true of Sweden as it was of other countries.

Beginning in the mid-1960s, however, the picture changed with startling rapidity. While the marriage rate in most other advanced nations leveled off or in some cases continued to increase, Sweden's began to drop sharply. During a 7- or 8-year period after 1966, according to calculations made by Swedish family sociologist Jan Trost, the marriage rate decreased by about 40%, a decrease that, he believes, has not occurred "anywhere else or at any other time."[2] The drop was even greater for the younger age groups. For women aged 20–24, the marriage rate (per thousand women) dropped from 194 in 1966 to 91 in 1973, and for women aged 25–29 the comparable drop was from 175 to 96. By 1980 these rates had dropped much further still, to 53 for the 20–24 age group and 78 for the 25–29 age group. An international comparison with Sweden's 1980 marriage rate of 78 for persons in the 25–29 age group shows Denmark with a marriage rate of 99; Japan, 109; France, 117; the United States, 127; and England and Wales, 168.[3] The 1980 Swedish rate was also considerably below the other countries in the age groups of 20 to 24 and 30 to 34. The declining marriage rates in Sweden (as elsewhere) reflect a rising average age of marriage. But in addition, a growing number of Swedes are not marrying at all. By one estimate, based on projecting current trends, 36% of Swedish women born in 1955 will not have married by the time they reach age 50, compared to only 9% of women born in 1940.[4]

A comparison with other Western nations showed that the marriage decline in Sweden started to appear with the cohort born in the early 1930s.[5] In an analysis of the life experience of the cohort born in 1945 in these nations, using marital-status life tables, it was found that Swedes already had the lowest proportion of those "every marrying"—75% for males—compared to 95% in the United States, the nation with the highest rate."[6] Today Sweden has the lowest marriage rate in the industrialized world and at the same time one of the highest mean ages of first marriage—30 for men and 27 for women (1983)—compared to 25.5 for men and 23.3 for women in the United States (1985). The marriage rate in Sweden increased slightly in the mid-1970s and since then has continued to drop, although the total number of marriages has followed a slightly different trend, with some increase in the early 1980s.

Nonmarital Cohabitation

One must not assume, however, that since marriage in Sweden is going out of fashion, people there are no longer living as couples. What has happened is that marriage is gradually being replaced by nonmarital cohabitation, also called consensual unions or "living together in an unmarried state." Although precise data on the amount of nonmarital cohabitation in Sweden today are not available, few Swedish experts would contest the proposition that the rate is the highest in the industrialized world.

Because of the lack of legal registry and a fixed date of inception, data on nonmarital cohabitation are much more difficult to assemble than marriage data. Making comparisons among nations is also fraught with difficulty. For example, Statistiska Centralbyrån—the Swedish Central Statistical Bureau—normally classifies together people who are married and people who are living in a "marriagelike relationship" and divides all households into "persons living alone" and "persons living with others." In contrast, the U.S. Bureau of Census normally divides households into two categories: family and nonfamily households. The latter category includes both those living alone and those living together outside of marriage.

Many careful estimates of the amount of nonmarital cohabitation in Sweden have been made, however. Unmarried couples as a percentage of all couples in Sweden were estimated to be 1% in 1960, 7% in 1970,[7] 13% in 1975, and 21% in 1983.[8] Projecting these data, an educated guess about the situation today is close to 25%. Comparable estimates for other European nations, not easy to come by, are 7% (late-1970) for the Netherlands,[9] 2.5% for Britain, and 13% for France."[10] In this and many other aspects of family life Denmark is only a few steps behind Sweden.[11] For the United States, unmarried couples as a percentage of all couples in 1981 were estimated to be 4%[12] and today are probably slightly above that. Interestingly, the U.S. percentage apparently did not increase during 1984–1985,[13] but then continued its gradual upward climb in 1985–1986.[14] In Sweden, there is no statistical indication of any diminution of this trend.

The data given above for Sweden refer to couples of all ages. If one looks at the younger age groupings the picture changes considerably. In 1980, the percentage of unmarried women aged 20–24 living with someone else was 68% (79% for men), and in the age group 25–29 the percentage was 35% (49% for men).[15] Moreover, it is generally believed that virtually all Swedes now cohabit before marriage (only an estimated 2% of women marrying today have not previously cohabited with their husbands-to-be or with some other man, compared to nearly 50% of women born in the 1930s).[16] The questions one might ask, however, is: Do Swedes still get married after they cohabit and, if so, at what stage of their relationship does the marriage take place?[17]

Living together before marriage is an old custom in Sweden; Swedes have long been permissive about premarital sex in terms of allowing "engaged" couples not to have to wait until the actual marriage takes place, and the marriage commonly occurred around the time the first child was coming due.[18] By one estimate, one third of all marriages in 1963 involved a pregnant bride.[19] But it is only in this sense that nonmarital cohabitation has been a widespread Swedish tradition, and the situation today has changed considerably. Nonmarital cohabitation is now regarded legally and culturally as an accepted alternative rather than a prelude to marriage. This is reflected in the fact that the average length of time couples remain unmarried lengthens each year, with a growing number, as noted above, never marrying at all. According to one recent study, only 20% of young, childless women born in the 1950s married their cohabiting partner within 8 years, compared to 80% of those born at the end of the 1930s.[20]

One of the most striking changes in the cohabitation scene today is that having children is no longer much of an incentive to get married. In other words, the expectation or birth of a child affects only marginally the chances that a couple will marry, and this applies to both first and second children.[21] Indeed, the life course of marriagelike relationships in Sweden is not easy to bring into focus. This is pointed up by a "marital history" that one couple gave to me. They met in 1967, moved in together in 1969, exchanged rings in 1973 (this was around the time their first child was born and was for the purpose of "showing others that they were attached"), and married in 1977. When asked what anniversary they celebrated, they responded: "the day we met."

The rapidly declining influence of childbirth on marriage is brought into relief by the data on the percentage of children born out-of-wedlock. Officially, the concept of children born out-of-wedlock was dropped from all Swedish legislation in the early 1970s (the term "illegitimate" was dropped in 1917), and children of such unions have exactly the same rights as do children of married unions. From Swedish population registration records, however, one can calculate the percentage of all children born in a given year who are born to unmarried mothers.[22] This figure has climbed sharply in recent years, from 10% in 1956 to 22% in 1971 and 32% in 1975.[23] In 1984 the percentage stood at 45%, enabling foreign journalists to state that nearly half of all births in Sweden today are to unmarried parents.[24] The comparable figure for the United States (1983) is 20%.[25] (It should be emphasized that in Sweden, because of the high rate of nonmarital cohabitation, the concept "born to an unmarried parent" usually does not mean "born to a single parent." In fact, the percentage of Swedish children born to a single parent has been dropping in recent years.[26])

The broad social consequences of the decline in marriage and the rise of nonmarital cohabitation clearly are arguable. They are discussed fully later in this book. There is one social consequence of increasing nonmarital cohabitation that must be taken up here, however, because in itself it represents a significant move away from the traditional nuclear form of the family. The consequence is a behavioral one and has been partially verified by empirical research. Although many Swedes see nonmarital cohabitation as only a minor change in social form, Swedish demographers Jan Hoem and Bo Rennermalm have noted that "the distinction between non-marital cohabitation and marriage is still important for individual conduct in Sweden. . . . the universal acceptance of previously unconventional living arrangements has not erased differentials in behavior."[27] They are referring particularly to the higher rate, among unmarried as compared to married couples, of family dissolution.

Family Dissolution

Family dissolution typically tends to be thought of first as the dissolution of marriage, which is reflected in official divorce statistics. The divorce rate has never been a very adequate indicator of family dissolution in a society, to say nothing of the level of marital happiness, but its adequacy has improved slightly in recent decades as the legal bases for divorce in advanced societies have liberalized.[28] Divorce rates have shown a long-term increase in most industrialized nations since around the turn of the century. They reached a high point in many countries immediately after World War II, then declined through the 1950s, only to begin rising again during the 1960s to their current level, which is probably the highest in the modern history of these nations. The Swedish divorce rate was already relatively high after World War II. Since then, beginning in 1963, it has climbed faster than in most other countries, and its current level is generally conceded to be (along with Denmark's) the highest in Europe. By one indicator, the number of divorced persons per 100 married persons, Sweden's rate in 1980 (9.69) fell just below that of the Western world's acknowledged divorce leader, the United States (11.28).[29]

Of the many different rates of divorce that can be calculated, one of the most useful is the proportion of marriages ending in divorce over the life course of a given cohort (rather than ending in the death of one of the partners). For the cohort born in 1945, if we use a projection of rates to the end of its life course, the proportion of marriages (for males) ending in divorce in the United States is 42%, while in Sweden it is 36%.[30] For England and Wales this rate is 27%; Switzerland, 14%; and Belgium, 12%. It is also of interest that the chances of remarriage are considerably less for the Swedish cohort: about 45% of divorces are followed by remarriage, compared to 85% in the United States. This relates to the fact that for the 1945 cohort in Sweden the number of marriages per person marrying (males) is only 1.2 compared to 1.7 in the United States. Also, the mean duration of marriages in Sweden is about 30 years, contrasted with 25 years in the United States. It should be noted, however, that accurate remarriage rates are very difficult to generate. Jan Trost has estimated that about 65% of men and 60% of women in Sweden eventually remarry, and there has been little change over the past 30 years.[31]

The high Swedish divorce rate is surprising because many of the factors traditionally associated with divorce in the United States—brief courtship and early marriage, teen pregnancies, poverty and income instability, interethnic and interfaith unions, and high residential mobility—are mitigated in Sweden. But perhaps the most surprising thing about the high Swedish divorce rate is the amount of nonmarital cohabitation. One could think of many such unions as "trial marriages" in which the step of formal marriage is taken only after the union has matured and the couple desire to signify a certain permanence to the relationship. As Jan Trost put the thesis some years ago, "The decrease in the marriage rate is the result of an increase in trial marriages, and therefore . . . those marriages being formed will be 'happier' and thus the divorce rate, ceterus paribus, will be lower."[32] Trost was one of the first to point out, however, on the basis of information currently available, that this thesis is far from correct. The marriage rate continues to drop, the nonmarital cohabitation rate continues to increase, and the divorce rate remains as high or higher than ever.[33]

Because so many Swedes no longer marry, the use of divorce rates to measure family dissolution in Sweden becomes rather meaningless, especially when making comparisons with nations where the amount of nonmarital cohabitation is relatively low. What is needed is the addition of some measure of the breakup rate of couples living outside of marriage in consensual unions. Yet if it is difficult to get data about the formation of such unions, it is even more difficult to get information about their breakup. There are also numerous problems in comparing the breakup rate of nonmarital cohabitants with that of married couples because, as noted above, marriages in Sweden today represent a kind of final stage of a cohabiting relationship, most marriages having been preceded by nonmarital cohabitation.

To avoid including "casual cohabitation" in the measure of family dissolution, which by definition would be expected to have a much higher breakup rate than do marriages, it is useful to look at the breakup rate of couples, both married and unmarried, who have had a child. This, in fact, has been done for a special sample of 4300 Swedish women, born between 1936 and 1960, who were asked retrospective questions about their life histories. It was found that the dissolution rate of cohabiting couples with one child was, on the average, three times the dissolution rate of comparable married couples.[34] Because of increases in nonmarital cohabitation, and its wider cultural acceptance, one would expect the gap between unmarrieds and marrieds to narrow as time goes on, and this is what has happened. The gap for the 1936–1945 cohort (in which only 15% were unmarried at the time of the first child) was 3.47 to 1, while the gap in the most recent 1951–1960 cohort (57% unmarried) was 2.24 to 1. For cohorts coming of marriageable age today, the difference is doubtless still less. Yet the gap is unlikely to have disappeared (differences of similar magnitude have been found in a number of other, smaller-scale studies) and it seems a well-based conclusion that nonmarital cohabitation, at least at the present time, simply does not have the durability of marital cohabitation.

If the nonmarital-cohabitation dissolution rate is added to Sweden's already high divorce rate (and keeping in mind that nonmarital cohabitation is increasingly replacing marriage), it is reasonable to put forth the following proposition: Sweden may now have the highest rate of family dissolution in the industrialized world. Assuming that this proposition is proved true by further empirical analysis, it is surely a prominent indicator of Sweden's world-leading move away from the traditional nuclear family.

Sometimes it is pointed out, both for the United States and Sweden, that the percentage of "broken" families today is little different from what it was at the turn of the century.[35] Such statements are based on equating the high death rate of spouses in 1900 with the high divorce rate today. One measure that includes both death and divorce as causes of family breakup is the percentage of children at various ages living with both biological parents. For Swedish children aged 17 this percentage in 1900 was very similar to what it was in 1960, a little over 80%. But as the rate of family dissolution increases, the gap is widening. The percentage had dropped to 76% by 1970 and 70% by 1980 (the latest year available).[36] Projections are that it will go much lower in coming years, perhaps as low as 50%. Also, the equating or blending of death and divorce as causes of family dissolution masks what many believe are profound psychological and social differences (especially for children) between the two. This measure does help to put the Swedish family situation in clearer perspective. While the number of "broken homes" may be increasing rapidly, most Swedish children still live in intact families.

Single-Parent Families

Closely related to family dissolution is another feature of contemporary Swedish life that has been widely commented on in the West: the high percentage of single-parent families. In 1980, single-parent families amounted to 18% of all households with children (with another 11% of households with children consisting of stepfamilies).[37] This percentage of single-parent families is very high by European standards, but not quite as high as the 21.5% of all families with children in the United States in 1980 (26% in 1984).[38] Sweden takes the lead, however, if one discounts the United States data for blacks, a group that is extremely small in Sweden. In 1980, 17% of American white families with children had only a single parent, compared to 52% of black families. Both nations have seen a sharp increase in the number of single-parent families in recent years, and in both nations women are heads of households in the overwhelming majority of these families. (It should be noted that the economic and social situation of the single-parent family in Sweden, although worse than that of complete families there, is not characterized by the high level of relative deprivation that is found in the United States.[39])

Household Size

The high rate of family dissolution in Sweden is one factor, but only one of many, that accounts for two other measures in which Sweden now leads the Western world: smallest average household size and highest percentage of single-person households. Because of their high association with family changes, these can be considered to be indirect measures of Sweden's movement away from the nuclear family. The size of the average household in Sweden today is about 2.2 persons. With 1980 data used for comparative purposes, the average Swedish household size then was 2.4, compared to 2.7 in the United States and England, 2.9 in France, and 3.2 in Japan.[40] One of the major reasons for the decline in household size is the increase in the number of single-person households. In 1980, 33% of all households in Sweden contained but one person, compared to only 14% in 1960. The comparable 1980 figure for the United States was 22%. In Sweden another one third of all households consisted of just two persons.

One must be careful in this discussion not to confuse households with persons. While 33% of Swedish households contain a single person, such households account for only 14% of all Swedes. If only persons between the ages of 16 and 74 are considered, about 18%—or nearly one out of every five adult Swedes—lived in single-person households in 1983.[41] These data are for Sweden as a whole. In Swedish urban areas, especially in the inner city, the percentage of persons living alone is far higher. In inner-city Stockholm, for example, 63% of all households consist of single persons.[42]

There is concern in Sweden that these percentages represent an overestimate, because a number of people apparently claim single-person residence when they actually live with someone else (one estimate for Stockholm is 5 to 10% of all persons who claim to be living alone). This is practiced, for example, to lower taxes, secure higher social benefits, and hold on to an apartment just in case a relationship breaks up.[43] In other words, some percentage of single-person apartments stand vacant and unused.

Family changes that have been shown to be closely associated with the decline in household size and the propensity to live alone in the United States are a decline in the marriage rate and later age of marriage, as well as family dissolution.[44] Sweden's leading position in regard to these changes was discussed above. Other family-related changes are a decline in fertility, to be discussed below, and an increase in longevity. Sweden is now the world's "oldest" nation, with 17% of its population aged 65 or over, compared to 12% in the United States.[45] In 1977, 42% of all Swedish women between the ages of 65 and 74 lived alone, as did 75% of widows and widowers between the ages of 16 and 74.[46]

Of course many nonfamily factors are also associated with small household sizes, notably high personal incomes. In an affluent society many people who want to live alone can afford to do so, and demand generates supply. During recent years Sweden has built a large number of small apartments in urban places that are ideally suited for single people. This undoubtedly has helped to increase living alone in all age groups, especially among the young and the middle aged, for whom living alone has been a historical rarity. The fastest growth in living alone today is among the younger age groups.

Women's Roles and Patriarchy

While the data on marriage, nonmarital cohabitation, family dissolution, single-parent families and single-person households strongly indicate that the Swedish family is moving away from the traditional nuclear form, one other area, more highly publicized, easily rivals these areas in importance. It is the changing role of women and the shift of the Swedish family away from both patriarchy and the role of the full-time housewife (see Chapter 7 for its historical development). As in the case of the other areas, a substantial amount of solid empirical data on this topic is available.

In terms of women's rights and equality with men, Sweden today is generally considered to be the most egalitarian society in the Western world. An array of evidence supports this claim, such as comparable-worth data (e.g., the average hourly earnings of Swedish full-time female workers were 90% of those of male workers in 1981, the highest ratio in the Western world) and the percentage of women in the labor force (77% of working-age women in 1983, the highest percentage in the Western world, compared to 62% in the United States).[47] Such evidence has been well analyzed by others.[48] These analysts and most Swedes are quick to point out, one should add, that Sweden is still some distance from the goal of "true equality" commonly agreed upon (and a review of inequality in Nordic countries at the end of the 1970s suggested that Finland might be slightly more egalitarian than Sweden in some respects).[49]

Of special importance for this discussion are those aspects of the trend toward equality for women that relate directly to the changing structure of the family. The most significant piece of evidence in this regard is that Sweden has the highest percentage—at least among Western nations—of mothers of young children (under 7) in the labor force, estimated today to be about 85%.

(This figure includes mothers working part-time and those on parental leave.) This high labor-force participation of Swedish mothers means that Sweden also has the lowest percentage of full-time housewives. Many have called the movement of married women into the labor force the most important change in women's roles and status in recent history.[50] By the same token, it is undoubtedly one of the most significant changes in family structure in our time, representing a major break from the "separate spheres" of the traditional, bourgeois family.

The number of full-time housewives in Sweden may even be smaller than is reflected in the official statistics because, according to some sources, a sizable percentage of those so classified are actually working on the black market, usually taking care of other people's children as well as their own. In addition, the decline of the full-time housewife can be seen through changes in Swedish cultural values. From a normative point of view, being a full-time Swedish housewife today often carries a stigma, especially in urban areas.

Other Dimensions of Nontraditional Familism

With respect to each of the dimensions of family change discussed above—marriage, nonmarital cohabitation, family dissolution, single-parent families, single-person households, and women's roles, Sweden appears, based on available empirical data, to hold the leading position among advanced nations. There are several other possible dimensions of nontraditional familism, however, in which Sweden either does not have the lead position or the comparative position of nations is unknown because of a lack of data. The additional dimensions come to light if one uses the definition of "nontraditional" put forth by one family scholar: "all living patterns other than legal, lifelong, sexually exclusive marriage between one man and one woman, with children, where the male is the primary provider and ultimate authority."[51] We have already discussed the changes in living patterns related to the terms "legal," "lifelong," and "male authority." What remains to be discussed are living patterns other than "a sexually exclusive marriage between one man and one woman, with children." Alternative living patterns in this regard, which can be found in all advanced societies, are voluntary singlehood, homosexual cohabitation, sexual polygamy, voluntary childlessness, and multiadult families. Because so few empirical data concerning these living patterns are available, our assessments must rely heavily on subjective judgment.

Voluntary Singlehood

A lifetime of voluntary singlehood means choosing never to live with another adult in an intimate relationship. As in other societies, almost all

Swedish men and women seem still to want to "pair-bond" or "couple" sometime during their lives. They have not turned against the idea of relatively permanent dyads, despite the instability of these dyads in practice. Although reliable data are unavailable, there appear to be few men or women in Sweden today who are single by choice, for example persons whose dislike of intimacy or whose single-minded pursuit of a career tends to rule out the desirability of having a mate.[52] This is not to say, however, that this picture will not change in the future or that there will be no change over time in the amount of pair-bonding for involuntary reasons, such as sex ratios and "marriage squeezes" that make it harder for people to find a suitable mate.

Homosexuality

The pair-bonding in Sweden appears to be in very large part heterosexual. Because the precise extent of homosexuality in Sweden (and elsewhere) is not known, there is no way to make comparisons between Sweden and other nations in this regard. What fragmentary data are available, as well as my own impressions, suggest that Sweden is a society in which homosexuality is a very minor form of sexual behavior and even less prevalent as a general life-style. In contrast to the United States, no local areas of Swedish cities known to me are inhabited largely by homosexuals. Although homosexual rights have been the focus of legislation and the mass media in recent years, and homosexual-rights groups have become active, the issue of homosexuality in general seems not to be taken up in the Swedish public debate to the same extent as it is in the United States. As one American sexologist, Ira Reiss, noted after a study visit to Sweden in the mid-1970s: "In Sweden, there has been very little open dialogue about homosexuality. It is a topic that seems to arouse a great deal of embarrassment and very little discussion."[53]

Lack of a homosexual dialog, of course, may not be indicative of the extent of Swedish homosexuality. The one reasonably comprehensive survey of Swedish sexuality that has been done in the past few decades focused only on youth in school grades seven through nine (that is, ages 13 through 15) in various Swedish municipalities. In real contrast to the Kinsey report in the United States, which found that early homosexual experiences were common among American boys, this survey found such experiences to be "very rare" among Swedish youth. Of the 81 youth selected for intensive interviewing, only one, a girl, admitted to having had any homosexual contact. Not a single boy admitted to ever feeling homosexual desire, and only one additional girl said that she had once "thought about what homosexual contact would be like."[54] It must be pointed out, however, that in this age group homosexual thoughts are quite threatening; Kinsey's findings, in contrast, were based on asking adults about their early experiences.

Sexual Polygamy

The extent of sexual polygamy, or sexually nonexclusive marriages, in Sweden has been the subject of a number of investigations, so that there is much more solid evidence about this topic. We consider here only the extent of extramarital, not premarital, sexuality (using "marriage" to include all marital-like relationships.) Premarital sex, of course, takes place before a marriage or family is formed and therefore does not directly concern the issue of sexual polygamy as an alternative family form; it may relate indirectly, but such a relationship is beyond the scope of the present discussion.

Evidence from several sources suggests that the extent of extramarital sex in Sweden is relatively low, probably lower than in the United States. This appears to be true even when nonmarital cohabitation is included as a form of "marriage." The Swedish "Kinsey" study conducted in the late 1960s found that about 90% of Swedish adults were "unaccepting" of extramarital sexual relationships, although a higher level of "tolerance" was found.[55] About 25% of the sample felt that "occasional missteps can be expected and should be excused even though not endorsed."[56] With regard to actual behavior, Ira Reiss, based mainly on a comparison of the Swedish sex survey of the 1960s with the American Kinsey data, concluded that "it appears that the Swedish rate of extramarital coitus is lower than the American rate." He estimated the Swedish 5-year rate for people aged 36 to 40 at about 15% and the American rate at about 23%.[57] Sweden has almost certainly grown more permissive in this regard over the past few decades, however, as discussed in the preceding chapter.

The relatively strong Swedish cultural norm proscribing extramarital sexuality was confirmed by the recent study of Swedish youth, noted above, which found Swedish youth to be quite conservative on this and on many other sexual questions (with the exception of premarital coitus). My own impression, along with that of most Swedes I know who are knowledgeable about the matter, is that Swedish adults are on the whole less "promiscuous" than their American counterparts and that the "hedonistic, playboy" mentality is also less well developed in Sweden (at least as long as Swedes are on their native soil, rather than abroad at a vacation resort!). The senior author of the survey of Swedish youth concluded similarly that "recreational sex" does not exist in Sweden to any extent resembling that in the United States.[58] Recreational sex includes such phenomena as "swinging" and "open marriages" that have been widely discussed, and less widely practiced, in the United States. There is good reason to believe that in both nations today such sexual practices are diminishing, in association with a general cultural shift of sexual attitudes in a more conservative direction. In the near future, this shift will likely become more pronounced in view of the new fear of AIDS.

Voluntary Childlessness

Another important dimension of family nontraditionalism is voluntary childlessness—"the deliberate decision of husbands and wives to forgo parenting (procreation and adoption) and the achievement of a lifetime commitment to that decision."[59] Based on a sample survey of women born between 1936 and 1960, almost all Swedish women continue to want to have, and do have, children.[60] Moreover, a two-child norm is very widespread and a family with two children is favored by women in all age groups. The one-child family was favored by only 10%, while 25% preferred a family of three children. These attitudes are reflected in the fact that the fertility rate in Sweden, although low, is higher than in several other European countries (e.g., Denmark and West Germany), and in the past year or two has even increased slightly.[61]

Because the average age of mothers at the birth of their first child is gradually going up, however, and currently is in the high twenties, one might expect that for biological reasons a growing number of Swedish women will be unfulfilled in their desire to have children. It is also not unreasonable to suppose that, apart from the biological capacity for childbirth, the postponement of childbirth will lead to an increase in voluntary childlessness; more women at older ages will simply choose not to have children. Voluntary childlessness may also increase because of the decline in the marriage rate. It was estimated that of ever-married women in the United States in the late 1970s only about 5% would voluntarily remain childless.[62] That rate is probably similar in Sweden; but it may not be as indicative of those who do not formally marry. Nevertheless, with adoption growing more popular in Sweden, there is for the moment little evidence that the desire to have children at some time, and in some way, is decreasing among Swedish women, despite the postponement of childbearing that is under way.

Multiadult Families

The final dimension of nontraditionalism to be considered is what can be called "multiadult families." Single-parent families were discussed earlier in the chapter, but there remains the alternative of families expanding from the traditional two-parent form to include more than two adults in the same household.

The most common type of multiadult household worldwide is the extended-family household, where the married couple is extended by the addition of one or more relatives, usually a parent. Since in terms of modernization and the global family trend the extended-family household is more traditional than the nuclear-family household, extended familism is not a measure of movement away from the traditional nuclear family but rather the opposite. Expectedly, based on household-size data, Sweden probably has a smaller proportion of extended-family households than any other nation.

One widely discussed, albeit seldom practiced, type of nontraditional multiadult family is the so-called group marriage. What is known about group marriages in general is that they have been notoriously unstable and therefore very uncommon.[63] I know of no group marriages in Sweden, although some might well exist, and I think it unlikely that Sweden has a higher percentage of group marriages than do other nations.

Another type of nontraditional "family" with more than two adults is communal living, or living in communes. This is typically not a group marriage, and it is seldom even a multiadult family in the strict sense of the term. It is a group of separate families who live in the same residence unit and share certain activities and facilities. Having reached its high point in many advanced nations in the late 1960s and the 1970s, communal living fell into rapid decline in the late 1970s and early 1980s.

True communes, which involve extensive sharing of functions, seem never to have been as popular in Sweden as in the United States, although I know of no comparative data. Yet the idea of "collective living" has often been held up as an ideal by Swedish women. Alva Myrdal, for example, in the early 1930s called for the building in cities of *kollektivhus,* or collective housing, in which such activities as meal preparation and day care for children are shared by a number of families. The first such domicile was constructed in Stockholm in the mid-1930s, and in the following four decades additional collective housing was built both in Stockholm and other major Swedish cities. All of these early attempts failed for one reason or another, often triggered by the economic collapse of the dining facility.

In the past decade there has been an upsurge of new building for collective housing, and so far—given the changing family forms—these have been relatively successful.[64] The number of Swedes living in such housing is still extremely small, and it remains to be seen how successful the housing currently being built will be in the long run.[65] But it is likely that such housing plays a larger role in Sweden, at least in the public debate, than it does in the United States. Other European nations, however, particularly Denmark, are probably well ahead of Sweden in promoting this new housing form.

Concluding Note

In view of the evidence given above, I think it is a reasonable conclusion that the Swedish family has moved farther from the traditional, bourgeois nuclear form than has the family in any other nation in the world. The case for Sweden's world-leading move away from the traditional nuclear family is based on five main indicators: a low marriage rate, a high rate of nonmarital cohabitation, a high rate of family dissolution, a high percentage of single-person households, and the extensive movement of mothers into the labor force. In regard to each of the family changes that these indicators are measuring, the Swedish family system has few if any peers, and no other society about which we have data (with the possible exception of Denmark) comes close to combining all of these changes into a single family system.

There are many nations, of course, about which we have only limited data. Of these the only possible competitors to Sweden's leading position are some nations of the Eastern European bloc, such as the Soviet Union. But from what we know of these nations they tend, at least in their official moral codes, to have much more traditional views of the family than does Sweden and many other Western nations.

Despite Sweden's advanced position in moving beyond the nuclear family, it should be stressed that strong bastions of the bourgeois family remain, especially in the small towns and the countryside.[66] Much of Swedish social life still revolves around gatherings of relatives (e.g., during holidays and summer vacations). Also, throughout Sweden there continues to be great "pride of home," a trait often associated with strong, bourgeois families. Many Swedes appear to focus love and attention on their homes (and summer cottages) in ways that show little sign of diminishing. Thus it is important to view Swedish family change not in absolute terms, but in comparison with other advanced nations.

It is not only a marked shift toward nontraditional family forms that one finds in Sweden. While there is nothing in the data I have seen to indicate that the Swedish family is in a state of "collapse" or even near it, and the Swedish family is certainly not about to "disappear," the evidence does suggest, in my opinion, that the Swedish family as an institution is in decline. This is the controversial issue to be explored in the next chapter.

Notes

[1]Erland Hofsten (1976), *Swedish Population History.*

[2]Jan Trost (1985), "Marital and Non-marital Cohabitation," pp. 109–119 in John Rogers and Hans Norman (eds.), *The Nordic Family: Perspectives on Family Research:* 109.

[3]United Nations (1982), *U.N. Demographic Yearbook:* Table 26.

[4]Francois Höpflinger (1985), "Changing Marriage Behavior: Some European Comparisons," pp. 41–63 in *Genus* 41-3, 4: Table 2, p. 45.

[5]See Robert Schoen and John Baj (1984), "Cohort Marriage and Divorce in Five Western Countries," pp. 197–229 in Richard F. Tomasson (ed.), *Comparative Social Research,* Vol. 7.

[6]*Ibid.;* and Robert Schoen and William L. Urton (1979), *Marital Status Life Tables for Sweden.* The real rate of marriage of this Swedish cohort may be slightly higher than indicated because the cohort was followed only to age 30, hence the later age of marriage in Sweden was not fully reflected.

[7]Trost (1985), "Marital."

[8]Special tabulation for the author by the National Central Bureau of Statistics.

[9]Geertje E. Wiersma (1983), *Cohabitation, An Alternative to Marriage? A Cross-National Study:* 1.

[10]Rushworth M. Kidder (1985), "Following Europe's Lead," *The Christian Science Monitor,* November 29: 28–29.

[11]Jan Trost (1979), *Unmarried Cohabitation.* On the situation of the Danish family, see Erik Manniche (1985), *The Family in Denmark.*

[12]Graham Spanier (1983), "Married and Unmarried Cohabitation in the United States: 1980," *Journal of Marriage and the Family* 45 (May): 277–288.

[13]John Herbers (1985), "One-Person Homes Show Big U.S. Rise," *The New York Times,* November 28: A32.

[14]*The New York Times,* December 21, 1986: 35.

[15]Anders Agell (1985), *Samboende utan Äktenskap:* 20.

[16]Jan Qvist and Bo Rennermalm (1985), *Att Bilda Familj:* 186.

[17]Jan Trost (1983), "De Familjesociala Gränserna—Vad Kan Vi Få Hushållen att Göra," pp. 20–32 in Åke E. Andersson et al., *Kan Hushållen Lyfta Sverige Ur Krisen?:* 24.

[18]Ira Reiss (1980), "Sexual Customs and Gender Roles in Sweden and America: An Analysis and Interpretation," pp. 191–215 in Helen Z. Lopata (ed.), *Research in the Interweave of Social Roles: Women and Men.*

[19]Jan Trost (1977), "Sweden," pp. 35–52 in Robert Chester, (ed.), *Divorce in Europe:* 50.

[20]Qvist and Rennermalm (1985), *Att Bilda Familj:* 187.

[21]Britta Hoem (1985), "Ett Barn är inte Nog. Vad Har Hänt med Svenska Ettbarnskvinnor Födda 1936 60."

[22]Statistiska Centralbyrån (1985), *Utveklingsarbete med Statistiksystem om Barns och Ungdomars Levnadsförhållanden.*

[23]Agell (1985), *Samboende:* 19.

[24]By 1987 the figure had in fact reached 50%. Åke Nilsson (1987), "Vartannat Barn Föds utom Äktenskapet," *Välfärds Bulletinen* 4: 3–5.

[25]*The New York Times,* September 29, 1985: 65.

[26]Nilsson (1987), "Vartannat Barn."

[27]Jan M. Hoem and Bo Rennermalm (1985), "Modern Family Initiation in Sweden: Experience of Women Born Between 1936 and 1960," *European Journal of Population* 1: 81–112.

[28]Chester (1977), *Divorce in Europe.*

[29]Data from *U.N. Demographic Yearbook;* rate calculated in George Thomas Kurian (1984), *The New Book of World Rankings:* Table 21.

[30]Schoen and Baj (1984), "Cohort Marriage."

[31]László Cseh-Szombathy et al. (eds.) (1985), *The Aftermath of Divorce: Coping with Family Change.*

[32]Trost (1977), "Sweden": 45.

[33]One recent study by American researchers found that Swedish couples who lived together before marriage had nearly an 80% higher divorce rate than those who did not. Reported in *The New York Times,* December 7, 1987: A25.

184 *Beyond the Nuclear Family*

34Hoem (1985), "Ett Barn."

35Robert Erikson (1984), "Uppväxtvillkor under 1900-Talet," pp. 334–349 in Robert Erikson and Rune Åberg (eds.), *Välfärd i Förändring;* and Mary Jo Bane (1976), *Here to Stay: American Families in the Twentieth Century.*

36Statistiska Centralbyrån (1985), *Utveklingsarbete:* 28.

37Socialdepartementet (1983), *Ensamföräldrarna och Deras Barn:* 38.

38*The New York Times,* May 18, 1985: 52.

39Socialdepartementet (1983), *Ensamföräldrarna.*

40United Nations (1982), *U.N. Demographic Yearbook:* Table 41; and E. Hemström (1983), *Utrymmesstandard i Internationell Jämförelse:* 7.

41Special tabulation for author by National Central Bureau of Statistics.

42*Dagens Nyheter,* March 7, 1986: 34.

43Louise Gaunt and David Gaunt (1986), "Le Modèle Scandinave," pp. 471–495 in A. Burguiere et al. (eds.), *Histoire de la Famille* (pp. 15–16. in original English language manuscript).

44Francis E. Kobrin (1976), "The Fall in Household Size and the Rise of the Primary Individual in the U.S.," *Demography* 13-1 (February): 127–138; and Robert T. Michael, Victor R. Fuchs, and Sharon R. Scott (1980), "Changes in the Propensity to Live Alone," *Demography* 17 (February): 39–56.

45Leon F. Bouvier (1984), *Planet Earth 1984–2034: A Demographic Vision.*

46Statistiska Centralbyrån (1982), *Perspektiv på Välfärden 1982:* 46.

47OECD Data. Reported in *The New York Times,* December 21, 1986: E20.

48For example, Carolyn Teich Adams and Kathryn Teich Winston (1980), *Mothers at Work: Public Policies in the United States, Sweden, and China;* Mary Ruggie (1984), *The State and Working Women: A Comparative Study of Britain and Sweden;* Hilda Scott (1982), *Sweden's Right to be Human;* Patricia A. Roos (ed.) (1985), *Gender and Work: A Comparative Analysis of Industrial Societies;* and Birgitta Wistrand (1981), *Swedish Women on the Move.*

49Nordic Council (1984), *Level of Living and Inequality in the Nordic Countries:* 214–218.

50For example, Eugen Lupri (ed.) (1983), *The Changing Position of Women in Family and Society.*

51Eleanor D. Macklin (1980), "Nontraditional Family Forms: A Decade of Research," pp. 905–922 in *Journal of Marriage and the Family* 42-4: 905.

52The percentage of Swedish women living in both marital and nonmarital unions combined is not much below the percentage in other European nations. For women aged 30 to 34 in 1980/1981, for example, that percentage was 81, compared to 85 in France and 88 in Great Britain. Hopflinger (1985) "Changing Marriage Behavior": Table 5, 51.

53Ira L. Reiss (1980), "Sexual Customs and Gender Roles in Sweden and America," pp. 191–220 in Helena Z. Lopata, Nona Glazer, and Judith Wittner (eds.), *Research in the Interweave of Social Roles: Women and Men:* 211.

54Bo Lewin and Gisela Helmius (1983), *Ungdom och Sexualitet:* 219–220.

55Hans L. Zetterberg (1969), *Om Sexuallivet i Sverige.*

56Quoted in Reiss (1980), "Sexual Customs": 207.

57*Ibid.:* 207.

58Interview with Bo Lewin, May 1986. Lewin found that Swedish boys had less permissive views on sexual matters than Swedish girls.

59Macklin (1980), "Nontraditional Family Forms": 908.

60Statistiska Centralbyrån (1984), *Ha Barn—men Hur Många?*

⁶¹The 1987 total fertility rate for selected countries was: West Germany, 1.3; Denmark, 1.4; Italy, 1.4; Switzerland, 1.5; Sweden, 1.7; United Kingdom, 1.8; United States, 1.8; New Zealand, 1.9. Population Reference Bureau (1987), *1987 World Population Data Sheet.*

⁶²J. E. Veevers (1979), "Voluntary Childlessness: A Review of Issues and Evidence," *Marriage and Family Review* 2 (Summer): 1–26.

⁶³L. L. Constantine and J. M. Constantine (1973), *Group Marriage: A Study of Contemporary Multilateral Marriage;* and L. L. Constantine (1978), "Multilateral Relations Revisited: Group Marriage in Extended Perspective," pp. 131–147 in B. I. Murstein, (ed.), *Exploring Intimate Lifestyles.*

⁶⁴Alison Woodward (1987), "Public Housing Communes: A Swedish Response to Post-Material Demands," pp. 215–238 in Willem van Vliet *et al.* (eds.), *Housing and Neighborhoods: Theorectical and Empirical Contributions.*

⁶⁵A survey of youth opinion in the late 1970s showed Swedish youth to be strongly opposed to communal living, believing that it would threaten their individuality. Statens Ungdomsråd (1980), *Än sen då? Röster om Framtiden,* reported in Statens Ungdomsråd (1981), *Ej till Salu:* 317–318.

⁶⁶Annette Rosengren (1985), "Contemporary Swedish Family Life through the Eyes of an Ethnologist," pp. 80–93 in John Rogers and Hans Norman (eds.), *The Nordic Family: Perspectives on Family Research.*

The Swedish Family in Institutional Decline

It is one thing to point out that the family in Sweden is changing its form, as was done in the preceding chapter, and quite another to assert that the Swedish family as an institution is in decline or is weakening. To present evidence and argument that such a decline is in fact taking place is the focus of the discussion that follows. I suggest that in Sweden the family as an institution has declined more, and become weaker, than in any other advanced society. By decline, or "deinstitutionalization," I mean that the family has lost "social power" and generally become less important in social life. In other words, the part played by the family in present-day Swedish society is less significant relative to other institutions than it has been in previous times.

I am aware that a social institution can, in theory, change its structure (e.g., away from the traditional nuclear family) and become a stronger rather than a weaker social institution. This could be said to be the case, for example, in regard to changes in the institution of education over the past few centuries. The argument of this chapter, however, is that family changes, unlike educational changes, have in important ways not signaled a stronger institution. In this respect family changes more closely resemble the changes that have taken place in the institution of religion, which, almost everyone agrees, in advanced societies has gradually weakened and lost social power—the power to influence behavior, opinion, and events.

On the issue of institutional decline of the Swedish family I anticipate no little dissension, certainly from many Swedish intellectuals. Am I not merely making a subjective value judgment? Do I not have a romantic, nostalgic, and idealized image of Swedish families in the past? Can I not see that the Swedish family has improved in a lot of ways? I shall try to convince the reader that the institutional decline of the Swedish family is not a value judgment or an illusion, but a concrete social trend that is supported by the available empirical evidence. Assessing family change inevitably involves many judgments about the meaning of social events, however, and there can

187

of course be differences of interpretation. My discussion is an interpretation of recent family change in Sweden based on the best information available to me.

Much of the controversy surrounding the debate about family decline in advanced societies stems from confusion in the use of terms and concepts (see Chapter 1). Family decline should not be viewed as necessarily negative in its social consequences. It may well be that societies need the family less today than they once did and that other institutions are now more capable at performing tasks once restricted to the family. Thinking of family decline only in the negative makes no more sense than thinking only negatively about the decline of feudalism or rural life; virtually all social change involves benefits as well as costs. Even if family decline is evaluated mainly in the negative, one should not thereby assume that family members are generally "worse off" than they were in some earlier historical time period; the negative consequences of family decline may have been more than offset by improvements in other areas of life. Finally, family decline should not be confused with "family collapse" or "family disappearance." These are possible but certainly not inevitable outcomes of family decline; family decline could as well lead to eventual "family reorganization."

The Declining Institution of Marriage

In most discussions of family decline the weak link in today's families, by almost everyone's reckoning, is the social and emotional bond between the parents. This bond is the basis on which most marriages are constituted in advanced societies. We can begin, then, with what is happening to the institution of marriage in Sweden.

It is important to differentiate the institution of marriage from the institution of the family. At heart, marriage involves a sexual union between two people. But to put the institution of marriage in context, Kingsley Davis has made a useful continuum of sexual unions—from a liaison at one pole through cohabitation, consensual union, and common-law marriage to legal marriage at the other pole.[1] While all of these relationships involve the expectation of sexual relations, as one moves up this continuum other elements are added to the basic sexual union. These elements are common residence (not characteristic of the liaison), a division of labor, the expectation of children, the assumption of permanence, and finally public recognition. Much nonmarital cohabitation in Sweden today has most of these elements, but marriage is the only form of sexual union that has them all. What the institution of marriage stands for, and has always stood for, is the final element added to the continuum—the social (public, formal) approval of a union between a man and a woman for the purpose of engaging in sexual intercourse and the bearing and rearing of offspring.[2]

If marriage is defined in this way, as having a formal (legal) and public nature, there can certainly be no doubt that the institution of marriage is in decline in Swedish society. Moreover, as discussed in Chapter 8, I believe the data indicate that this decline is greater in Sweden than in any other modern society. The specific indicators of such decline include fewer people ever getting married (declining propensity to marry), the postponement of marriage to a later age, a smaller portion of one's life spent in wedlock, a shorter duration of marriage, and a rising preference for competing types of sexual unions. These indicators reflect the outcome of widespread attitudinal changes in Swedish society in which marriage as an institution no longer has the popular support that it receives in other societies. In a cross-national comparative survey of ages 18–24, for example, Swedish youth were conspicuously less in favor of marriage than were youth in the other countries surveyed. Only 28% of Swedish youth were "positive about marriage" (i.e., they answered that one "should be married" or it is "better to be married," rather than "better not to be married" or "don't have to be married") compared to 37% in Switzerland, 42% in France, 48% in the United States, and 73% in Japan.[3]

Swedes seek to explain the recent decline of marriage and the rise of nonmarital cohabitation with a great many reasons, such as freedom from oppressive tradition, freedom from state control, and, more commonly, "what difference does it make; it is our love that counts." A typical response to the question, "why not marry?" is "why marry?"[4] Swedes are also fond of pointing to the fact that living together before marriage is an old custom in Sweden and that in this sense nonmarital cohabitation is rooted in Swedish tradition.

Regardless of the cause of the recognized decline of marriage, what is the relationship of this decline, if any, to the decline of the family? Since nonmarital cohabitation has come to replace marriage in many instances, is the family unit that results weaker? Many young Swedes see little significance of any kind in the move from marital to nonmarital cohabitation. Nonmarital relationships are virtually the same thing as marital relationships, they argue; the only difference is that the former lack a "piece of paper" signifying official (legal and usually religious) approval. The Swedish family sociologist Jan Trost maintains that nonmarital cohabitation has become an institution fully equivalent to that of marriage; "the two social institutions do not 'compete' with each other but they exist along side each other."[5] In other words, both have identical functions.

This also seems to be the view of the Swedish government. It has been government policy since the change in divorce laws of the early 1970s, according to the interpretation of some Swedish experts, to be officially neutral between the two forms of living together.[6] More recently, Sweden has rewritten family law so that married and unmarried couples are relatively equivalent in many legal dimensions of their union. Although unmarried couples do not have rights of inheritance, for example, they do now have rights to some "marital" property in the event of death or breakup. From the perspective of neutrality, therefore, the question of whether one marries or cohabits outside of marriage may seem irrelevant for the family unit and for family functioning. As evidence for this view it could accurately be pointed out that in Sweden there are numerous very stable, loving, successful, and even powerful families in which the adult members are not united by legal marriage; indeed, by all appearances, there are no differences between these families and those in which the adults are married.

Still, it is worth remembering that in all of human history up to the present some form of public marriage has been the basis of the family as a social institution. Putting the issue in even stronger terms, almost all societies heretofore have made the act of getting married one of the most significant ceremonies in their members' lives. It has been a ceremony in which family, religion, and society express their approval of and hopes for, as well as establish the moral and legal rights and duties of, a union between two people who are expected to contribute to the continuance of the society through legitimized procreation.

In Sweden, precisely such a social expression is disappearing. It is reasonable to say that most Swedish young people today are merely drifting away from their families of orientation, usually in stages, and eventually settling with someone else, all seemingly without any form of public or social recognition whatsoever. Gone for the most part are engagement parties, weddings, and even an appropriate time at which one can say "congratulations."[7] Indeed, the situation comes remarkably close to what Engels envisioned would occur once capitalism and bourgeois monogamy were swept away and a new generation based on gender equality had emerged:

> When these people are in the world, they will care precious little what anybody today thinks they ought to do; they will make their own practice and their corresponding public opinion about the practice of each individual—and that will be the end of it.[8]

At the very least, then, the decline of marriage in Sweden signifies a radical departure from cultural practice throughout world history. But, further, it represents a weakening of societal (public) concern for, and involvement with, the pair-bond between two adults.

One fundamental social purpose of the institution of marriage, including its legal dimension, is to ensure the *permanence* of unions between adults. Marriage is society's statement that stability and permanency of sexual unions set up for the purpose of procreation are important social values. The new Swedish attitude toward marriage is, in contrast, an implicit cultural statement that pair-bonding may be significant for the two parties involved, but has little lasting importance for society as a whole; that, in fact, it is none of society's business. The significance of the pair-bond has increasingly been relegated to the purely private worlds of the two individuals. One immediate implication of this attitude is that society holds the couple (as an agent of society) less responsible both for each other and for their offspring. And the traditional cultural message that society regards the permanence of the sexual union as an important social value is missing entirely.[9]

The decline of marriage as an institution has been justified in this age of individualism and individual autonomy by the view that the sexual union between two adults *is* a purely private matter and therefore none of society's business. The decline also represents a further stage in the evolution of personal freedom of choice in selecting sexual partners, an extension of the global family trend (discussed in Chapter 3), in which first the extended kin group and then parents lose authority over the choice of marital partners. Because society still retains some interest in sexual unions, especially when children ensue from the relationship, the complete removal of legal authority over nonmarital unions is far from being the case. But this does not gainsay the fact that in Swedish society today a strong cultural statement is being made—the permanence of pair-bonds no longer has the same social, moral, and religious importance as before.

This cultural statement is reflected in Swedish family policy. As discussed in Chapter 7, Swedish family policy has evolved in such a way that its main goals have become women's equality and the protection of children. The American social analyst Gilbert Y. Steiner has noted that "cohabitation, divorce, and marital questions in general are not part of Swedish family policy."[10] Jan Trost has put the matter more pointedly: "Swede's don't have a family policy *per se*, they instead have individual and household policies."[11]

Family Dissolution

If the institution of marriage is society's statement that it is important for procreational sexual unions to have stability and permanence, perhaps it is no accident that the decline of this institution in Sweden is associated with the growing impermanence of such unions. In Chapter 8 it was noted that, when the high divorce rate is added to the even higher rate of dissolution of nonmarital unions, Sweden now may have the highest "family dissolution" rate among advanced societies. Indeed, quite possibly it is the highest ever known in the Western world. More than any other single factor, this high dissolution rate is seen by many as signifying family decline.

The significance of marital dissolution for the strength of the family as an institution is by no means clear-cut. The rising divorce rate does not necessarily mean that the quality of marriages has become worse; dissolution rates have increased not only because marriages have grown weaker, but because the law now permits weak sexual unions to be dissolved. From this perspective, a rise in the rate of marital dissolution signifies not that families are declining but that they have been weak all along. Often coupled with this perspective is the view that the remarriage of divorced persons in large numbers shows the "continuing vitality" of marriage and the family. There is also the undeniable fact that marital dissolution enables many adults to lead more fulfilling lives.

As the family dissolution rate (both marital and nonmarital) keeps escalating, however, it becomes more difficult to disregard what may be a fundamental family reality of our time. That is, couples dissolve more quickly today because the bonds holding them together have become fewer in number and of a different quality. The American sociologists Ernest Burgess and Harvey Locke stressed the changing reality of these social bonds when they referred at midcentury to a historical family (marriage) transition from "institution to companionship:"

> In the past the important factors unifying the family have been external, formal, and authoritarian, as the law, the mores, public opinion, tradition, the authority of the family head, rigid discipline, and elaborate ritual. At present, in the new emerging form of the companionship family, its unity inheres less and less in community pressures and more and more in such interpersonal relations as the mutual affection, the sympathetic understanding, and the comradeship of its members.[12]

From this perspective, the dissolution rate of pair-bonds is high today precisely because the family has weakened as an institutional reality. The many institutionalized social bonds that once held marriages together, such as connections to the extended family and economic interdependence, have weakened and in some cases disappeared entirely. Moreover, the social stigma against divorce and separation has softened appreciably. Equally significant for pair-bond dissolution (and not emphasized in the quotation above) is the fact that the single most important remaining basis of the pair-bond—the voluntary affection of two people for one another—is not only difficult to institutionalize but is also a notoriously fragile social bond. If marriages and their nonmarital equivalents are based exclusively on the bond of affection and companionship, as most are today, it is little wonder that the dissolution rate is high and climbing.

Most of the arguments contending that family dissolution is not weakening the institution of the family concern the effects on adults. These arguments lose persuasiveness when children are considered. There is little evidence to suggest, for example, that a high marital dissolution rate implies a strengthening of the family unit in regard to what is probably its most important function—the procreation and care of children. Most evidence, indeed, indicates the opposite. The position that there is a close association between stable and lasting marriages and effective child rearing is surely still held by most adults in advanced societies, and it is the position traditionally held in almost all societies.

A basic reason why societies over the course of history have been so concerned about marital stability and permanence, as discussed in the preceding section, concerns not the marriage per se, but the children of the marriage (the assumption being that most marriages lead to children). Recognizing that children lack freedom of choice in marital dissolution, societies have viewed a stable and permanent marriage as part and parcel of a strong family and the latter, in turn, as on the whole "best" for children, and therefore for society.

Certainly not all pair-bond dissolution today involves children. Yet children under 18 are involved in about two thirds of all divorce actions in Sweden (the comparable number for nonmarital cohabitation dissolutions is not known). This figure has remained relatively constant for some years,[13] and is slightly higher than the estimate of 60% in the United States in the mid-1970s.[14] The total number of children of divorce is decreasing somewhat, however, as family size drops.

It is sometimes pointed out that the overall rate of family dissolution today, as measured by the probability that a person will not live through childhood with both biological parents, is similar to the rate at the turn of the 20th century. The difference is that today this rate is based mainly on voluntary dissolutions; then it was based mainly on the premature death of one of the partners. From this perspective, no family decline based on family dissolution alone has actually occurred.

Two issues call this viewpoint into serious question. First, within the past few decades the picture has changed: the overall rate of family dissolution now exceeds the earlier rate. Second, the consequences for children of family dissolution today are quite different from what they once were. Throughout world history the mortality rate has been extremely high and most marriages have been dissolved at a relatively young age. In the event of premature death, however, other family members were usually able to step in and provide instant continuity. With today's "isolated" nuclear family, the social and psychological reality of dissolution is quite different. Children of the modern family are particularly vulnerable in case of dissolution because extended-family members are often no longer available. The children of a dissolved marriage are therefore much more likely to be living with only one adult in the household or in a new nuclear family consisting of mostly unrelated individuals. Also, the psychological consequences of divorce for

children are not the same as the consequences of the death of a parent;
divorce involves far more feelings of guilt, rejection, and animosity.

The Increase of Nonfamily Households

Historically, virtually all household units have been families in some form.
To have lived in a household was at the same time to have been living with a
family. This is no longer the case. Many households do not contain families,
and there has been a steady increase in the portion of time the average person
spends living apart from the family. In view of this trend, social scientists have
come increasingly to distinguish between household and family.

A vivid illustration of the growth of nonfamily households in advanced
societies is the statistic frequently cited by American scholars that only
about 6% of United States households now contain "traditional" families.
This statistic can be misleading. It refers to a family in which both husband
and wife are in their first marriage, the wife does not work, and there are two
or more children. This narrows the definition of "traditional" considerably;
for example, it excludes families where there is only one child, the woman
occasionally works part time, and a widow or widower has remarried.
Moreover, this statistic is sometimes used as if only 6% of all families were
"traditional," whereas in reality the statistic refers to 6% of all households (a
very different thing). Be that as it may, the percentage of households with
"real" families has indeed decreased and is smaller in Sweden than anywhere
else.

The most striking recent change in household composition in Sweden is
the rise in the number of people living alone. They are living apart from family
units however defined, even apart from the daily (or one might more aptly
say nightly) presence of others. The fastest growing groups in the living-alone
category are young people in their late teens and twenties, the elderly, and
the divorced and separated.

In many cases living alone is the result of the voluntary choice of people
who can afford separate housing, and it often reflects a clear preference over
living with others. From one point of view, therefore, living alone can be seen
as a privilege of affluent people and an active expression of individualism
and individual autonomy. Yet when living alone becomes a mass phenomenon, questions must be raised about the changing character and quality of
social relationships, especially when single-person households are considered together with such factors as low fertility and high family-dissolution
rates. In all of world history people throughout their lives have lived in the
close presence of family members. That is, people usually have seen other
family members at least each morning and evening, eaten most meals with

them, and slept nearby. In turn, this generated a common domestic life and shared intimacy that has always marked the human condition, for better and for worse. What happens when this age-old aspect of the human condition is changed?

It is not that Swedish children are brought up in households where no one else is present (although Swedish family size is quite small.) And it is not that Swedes are misanthropes, living their adult lives with no intimates. The evidence suggests that the propensity of adult Swedes to form a dyad with another person, at least for part of their lives, is as strong if not stronger than elsewhere.[15] Nor is it that Swedes necessarily lack intimate social contacts, even if many of these contacts are outside of their immediate households. In 1981 only 6% of adult Swedes stated that they had little or no contact with either friends or relatives outside their own household, and only two tenths of 1% were totally isolated.[16] So perhaps nothing is really amiss with the new life-style; it is merely a full expression of the privacy, individualism, and freedom that have long been among the dominant values in Western civilization.

Nevertheless, it is hard to deny that the rapid growth of living alone also implies that the preference for living with a family throughout one's life has weakened. Moreover, there is a strong likelihood that when people live apart from families during large parts of their lives, family values will weaken.[17] The family mealtime, for example, has always been one of the principal social events of human existence, a time when family values were reinforced. Yet the new household arrangements mean that a large segment of the adult Swedish population ordinarily eats breakfast and probably also dinner alone.

There are many possible consequences of the propensity to live alone that go well beyond family impacts. Especially for young adults, what is the ultimate psychological impact of many years of living alone and not having to adapt on a regular basis to at least one other person? What sort of residential environment results, in terms of its social atmosphere and communal nature, when the majority of residents are unattached? What are the consequences for public social services when so many people have no one immediately available to them for care and sustenance? These questions are discussed in the final chapter.

The Family's Loss of Functions

It is clear that the family has lost functions over the long course of history. The family began as a comprehensive institution that included all the main social functions and evolved into a specialized institution with only a few functions. The main lost functions typically singled out are those of religion, politics, economic production, and education, each of which has largely shifted over time to specialized nonfamily groupings. Industrialized societies, for example, have a wide variety of ways of organizing people apart from the family, including trade unions and professional groups, schools and business organizations, voluntary associations and political parties, and state bureaucracies.

Because it has taken place for the most part over the past few centuries, the shift of functions away from the family most widely discussed is in the areas of economic production and education. The Industrial Revolution led to a rapid decline of the family as an economic-production unit when production was shifted into factories and business organizations.[18] This was closely associated with the rise of formal education, so that children after the age of 6 or 7 spent much of the day for the next decade or more of their lives being educated in schools. Each of these social groupings outside of the family has claimed a growing share of people's time, energy, and money. The family, in turn, has become, in the words of sociologist Pierre L. van den Berghe, "in many respects a diminished family, both in absolute and relative importance, and a streamlined family reduced to its simplest, smallest and most flexible expression."[19]

The question remains whether there has been a continuing loss of family functions in recent years and, if so, whether this has weakened the family as an institution. It is theoretically possible for an institution to lose functions but gain in social power provided that it can perform the remaining, presumably more important, functions with greater efficiency. This does not seem generally to be the case with the family. Let us review the situation in regard to the main functions of the contemporary family typically identified by sociologists: the procreation and socialization of children; the provision to family members of affection and companionship; sexual regulation; and economic cooperation.

Procreation

Procreation clearly remains an important family function in that it has not been taken over by any other institution. Such a nonfamily takeover of procreation, for example, would be the establishment of specialized institutions where it was the main purpose of selected women to bear numerous children—a theoretical possibility, but nowhere put into effect in the modern world. The family remains as the only social institution producing children, which gives the family a signal importance in any society that wishes to survive biologically.

Families in Sweden are producing very few children these days, certainly not enough for Swedish society to replace itself and survive in its present form. As Alva Myrdal once said, Swedish women have been on a "birth strike." Replacement would require every Swedish woman to bear 2.1 children; currently she is bearing only 1.7 children. The population of Sweden will continue to grow over the next few decades, yet the growth will be due not to the biological contributions of Swedish couples but to the immigration of foreigners. In this sense, it can be said that the Swedish family has lost power with respect to the function of procreation. And if a growing number of couples choose not to have children at all, which is likely, this family function could be said to be in still further decline.

As was noted in the preceding chapter, Sweden no longer has the world's lowest birthrate (it did in the 1930s), nor are Swedish women the world's most predisposed to remain childless; so at least it cannot be said that Swedish family decline in these respects is the "most advanced." However, this has not prevented the "population question" from again, for the first time since the 1940s, being seriously considered in the Swedish debate. Beginning in the 1970s, and stimulated not only by low birthrates but by the immigration into Sweden of large numbers of foreigners from southern Europe, Swedes again began to worry about the future of their society and culture in population terms. The debate, which proved to be inconclusive, ranged over such issues as the causes of low fertility, the problems of assimilating immigrants, and the economic burden of supporting the elderly that was being placed on a declining active population.[20] There was concern that government policies designed to increase fertility were of dubious worth in terms of their efficacy and might set back the movement toward full equality for women. By the late 1980s, the debate had died down. One government policy that was enacted granted couples higher child-support payments for each child after the first two. Fertility in Sweden has increased slightly in the past few years, but the reasons for this remain unclear, nor do we know whether it might not be only temporary.

Socialization

There can be no doubt that over the past few centuries the process of socialization has increasingly become the function of nonfamily agencies, beginning historically with the emergence of the school and moving to today's widespread use of nursery schools and day-care centers for young children. Other outside-the-family groups that have gained in importance as socializing agencies are the child's peer group and the mass media. In the process of helping children to "acquire personality and learn the ways of a society," each of these groups has taken some power and influence away from parents and close relatives.

Perhaps the most widely discussed socialization trend in modern societies is the so-called takeover of socialization by the state, a trend that is presumed to have greatly undermined the power of families.[21] One must be particularly careful not to assume that because certain socialization activities have been taken away from the family, and the family has lost power in this respect, the socialization that results is necessarily an inferior one. The main reason that the state took over aspects of socialization to begin with—a process with which most families were in agreement—was the family's unwillingness or instability to do the job (e.g., to provide a rigorous education in technical subjects). By the same token, any improvement in the quality of socialization should not blind us to the fact that through this process the family is, indeed, losing power and authority.

The classic state takeover of the socialization function is in the area of education, and among Western societies the role of the Swedish state in formal education is especially powerful. Virtually all education in Sweden today is public (most private and church-related education has been discontinued) and educational subject matter and curricula for primary and secondary schools are largely planned by centralized state agencies. Educational content therefore varies little from school to school and place to place within Sweden. Sweden does not have the diversity of formal educational experiences that is found, for example, in the United States, a diversity that, insofar as it reflects the values of diverse families, gives the families more power.

At the same time, formal education in Sweden does not begin until a child is 7, one year later than in the United States.[22] Compared to the United States, this gives the Swedish family one extra year of relatively exclusive leverage in the process of socialization. There has been great pressure to change this policy in recent years, mainly because of the growing lack of home caretakers for the child and a shortage of places in preschool programs. But so far the policy has held.[23]

Partially offsetting this Swedish "family advantage," however, is the fact that Swedish children spend more of their early lives in out-of-home day care than do children in the United States. In many ways public day care has become a necessity in Sweden, as there are few women who are still full-time mothers; indeed, Sweden probably has fewer full-time mothers today than any other Western society. Public child-care programs are very extensive in Sweden; yet among European nations Sweden has dragged its feet on the provision of public day care, and has fewer day-care places than, for example, Denmark and France. The difference is made up by women staying home part-time and by private arrangements. But there is currently a major push in Sweden to close the gap and provide public day-care spaces for all who want them. (Swedish public child-care programs are fully discussed below.)

The intervention of the Swedish state in the socialization process goes well beyond formal education and day care. In recent years there has been much discussion of what is felt by some to be excessive *direct* intervention by the state in the affairs of the family, specifically in what has been traditionally the right of parents to raise their children as they see fit. This is often referred to by critics as the "policing" of families. For example, based on the judgment of an agent of the state, a social-welfare officer, by law a child may be taken away from the parents for "state care." From one perspective this intervention shows that the growing emphasis on individual rights in modern societies has not overlooked the situation of children and their needs for protection by the state in cases of mistreatment. Critics charge, however, that the Swedish state has been overzealous in removing children from the custody of their parents based on insufficient evidence of child abuse, thus undermining the traditional parental prerogatives. One West German magazine in the early 1980s, labeling Sweden a "children's gulag," purported to have found that Sweden was taking away from their parents far more children for such reasons than any other European nation.[24]

Sweden has long been in the forefront in protecting children's rights. It was the first nation in the world to appoint a national "children's ombudsman," an official with no legal powers, but charged with protecting children's rights through investigation, recommendation, and information. And Sweden made international headlines when the *Riksdag* in 1979 passed, by a vote of 259 to 6, a law stating that "the child should not be subjected to physical punishment or other humiliating treatment." Arousing much international comment, the headlines read: "Sweden passes law that forbids the spanking of children." Regardless of the social and moral merit of such measures, there can be little doubt that they have the effect of removing some of the traditional authority from families and placing it in the hands of the state.

On a more day-to-day basis, the weakening of family authority occurs through the actions of social workers, psychologists, physicians, educators, and other human-service professionals with whom families come into contact in their communities. It is unavoidable that such professional experts, whose intended purpose is to help families function better, also to a degree take over from parents some authority in the socialization process. One even hears today from Swedish professionals themselves that parents are relinquishing too much responsibility to outside experts. Given the strength and importance of the public sector in Sweden, it is likely that the authority of professionals there has become greater than in almost any other society.

The declining function of parents in the socialization process is by no means simply the result of a state takeover of authority, however. Swedish mothers are simply not at home today as much as they used to be, mainly because they have moved into the labor force. As Sten Johansson, Director of Sweden's National Central Bureau of Statistics, has pointed out, among Swedish adults today nearly 75% said that they grew up in a home where their mother was a housewife during the entire period they were growing up.[25] For the present generation of Swedish children that figure is only about 10%, and for the child born today it has probably dropped below 5%. For children aged 0–6 in 1982, only 44% had at least one parent or guardian at home all the time to look after them, a decrease from 56% only 7 years earlier in 1975. And only 32% of schoolchildren aged 7–10 had a parent at home, while 15% returned from school to an empty home (without adults present) and had no other form of afternoon care.[26] Estimates today indicate that the latter figure, which is twice the estimated percentage in the United States, has climbed to about 20%.[27]

We know very little about the changing quality of the "contact time" between parents and children. Such decreases in contact time are offset, to some extent, by the fact that parents today have fewer children than they once did and therefore presumably can spend more time with each child individually. Yet children could also be said to have "fewer parents." The proportion of Swedes who spent the whole of their childhood and adolescence with both biological parents was about 84% at the turn of the century.[28] Today that percentage has dropped to 70%, and for children now being born it is probably below 60% (very similar to the percentage in the United States.)[29] More often today, the absent parent (usually the father) is still alive, but he clearly is not able to provide the kind of day-to-day parenting of the at-home father. Some Swedes look hopefully to the growth of stepfamilies as a remedy for this situation, but the long-run stability and effectiveness of this new family form is a matter of some doubt.

In addition to a decrease in parent–child contact time, Swedish young people today are less economically dependent on their parents than was the case in the past and than probably is the case in all other advanced societies. This is because much more of the costs of economic upbringing in Sweden is borne by the public sector. The state or local municipalities provide free medical and dental care, abundant and relatively low-cost public transportation, free school meals, and virtually free education through the university level. In America, for example, children to a large extent must depend on their parents' incomes for these items.

Whatever economic dependence Swedish young people still have on their parents largely ceases on other than a voluntary basis between ages 16 and 18. Within that age period, the Swedish young person qualifies for such government benefits as unemployment insurance, social welfare, and government-sponsored employment. The Swedish policy is that "each non-handicapped adult is responsible for his or her own economic well being."[30] One important effect of this policy for the Swedish young adult is that the government provides great assistance in the area of employment. Youth unemployment has become a major problem in every advanced society.[31] To combat the problem, the Swedish government virtually guarantees some kind of at least part-time job for every young adult who wants one. Subsidies are granted to private industry to hire youth, government "relief work" is provided, and, if nothing else is available, municipalities are required to hire unemployed youth for special "youth teams." For short periods of time, various kinds of unemployment insurance are also available.[32] Thus Swedish parents are effectively relieved of any further financial responsibility for their children at what is a very young age by international standards.

It is noteworthy that the tendency in advanced societies today is for young people to prolong their stay in the parental home and, especially for those in school, to prolong their financial dependency on parents. In 1984, 54% of Americans between the ages of 18 and 24 were still living at home, an increase from 47% in 1970.[33] The trend may not be as pronounced in Sweden. Although precisely comparable data for Sweden are not available, Swedish youth seem to live on with their parents slightly less than in the United States. In the age category 18–19, 85% of boys and 66% of girls are still living in their parental home, but in the age category 20–24, only 45% of boys and 20% of girls are living at home.[34] Doubtless many more Swedish young adults would leave their parents' homes if suitable housing were available.

Both decreasing contact time and, especially, diminishing economic dependence tend to reduce the authority and control that parents have over their children, relinquishing some of it to nonfamily agents of socialization. This authority and control are also weakened indirectly by Swedish child-rearing conditions and attitudes. One such condition, ironically, is the high quality of Swedish urban environments. Swedish urban areas are relatively benign environments in terms of human safety; the chances of assaults, muggings, rapes, and robberies are small. These areas are also well supplied with excellent and low-cost public transportation. Taken on its own the high quality of urban environments in Sweden, like youth employment, must be regarded as a major social achievement. Yet in regard to its effect on the authority and control of families, it has certain unintended and undesired social consequences.

In their urban style of life, Swedish youth seem more free of parental supervision than their American counterparts. Two environmental attributes help to account for this. First, because of a relatively safe urban environment Swedish parents do not have the same safety concerns, especially for their daughters, that American parents do. There is less concern, for example, with knowing exactly where one's child is at a given time. Second, because of excellent public transportation Swedish youth have much more freedom of movement around the urban area than do American youth; they are able at much younger ages to "go downtown" and relatively freely roam the metropolitan area. Unlike their American counterparts, who very much depend for transportation on the automobile owned by their parents, Swedish youth have in effect their own means of transport that will take them almost anywhere they wish to go.[35] Thus the tug-of-war that typifies many American parent–child interactions over questions of personal safety and transportation is not so common in Sweden.

This relative safety and freedom of movement in Sweden means that Swedish parents are able to be more permissive with their adolescent children than are American parents.[36] Such permissiveness is further extended by the cultural trends of the past two decades in which, as discussed in Chapter 7, Sweden as a whole has shifted from an authoritarian society in many respects to one of the world's most socially permissive nations.[37] Although permissiveness is regarded by some as a significant human advance in the process of socialization, in which children are enabled to think and to learn to do things for themselves at younger ages, permissiveness can also involve a certain relinquishment of authority and control by parents over their children. To take a simple example, parents who are necessarily more worried and concerned about where their children are at all times and what they are doing, may in the process spend more time interacting with their children, disciplining them, and at the same time perhaps inculcating in them adult values.

Parental permissiveness with respect to freedom of movement does not necessarily mean parental neglect, but it does generally mean that children will be socialized to a larger degree by peers (with whom they spend much of their out-of-home time) and by other outside-the-family agencies of socialization. The norms and values of these nonfamily groupings need not always conflict with those of the parents. There is some evidence, in fact, that such conflict, although not strong in either culture, occurs less in Scandinavia than in the United States.[38] There is also evidence suggesting that Swedish young people are more satisfied with their home lives, and have less conflict with their parents, than youth in other advanced societies.[39]

Swedish Public Child-Care Programs

Whether a result or a cause of the decline of the family's socialization function (certainly some of each), the public child-care policies and programs of Sweden are almost universally regarded by experts as enviable. Conservatives may fault Sweden's attempt to push mothers out of the home and onto the work force, but, given the fact that almost all mothers now hold outside jobs, the public measures taken in Sweden to care for children are well in advance of such programs in most other countries.[40] And if, as some hold, the tension between work and family is one of the great current social problems, the Swedes have come much farther than most nations in at least the search for remedies. Sweden has in fact become so "advanced" in its public child-care programs that they are worth examining in some detail.[41]

For the individual couple planning a family, public child-care programs in Sweden could be said to start with guaranteed pregnancy leaves for mothers, at 90% of salary (all such monetary payments are heavily subsidized by the government), for a maximum of 50 days during the last 2 months of pregnancy. During this period both parents of first children usually attend childbirth education classes, also with the help of paid leaves from their jobs (most first-time fathers attend at least part of the sessions). This prepares fathers so that, at the birth of a child, almost all fathers are present and able to play supportive roles. Following childbirth, fathers have a guaranteed leave from their jobs of up to 2 weeks at almost full salary, and most fathers take this leave for at least a week. Also offered nationwide following childbirth are free parent-education courses, attended by 75% of the mothers of first children but very few of the fathers.

The Swedish parent (either mother or father; adoptive as well as birth parent) is guaranteed 9 months of "parental leave" at nearly full pay (90% of salary), another 3 months at minimum pay, and the option of an additional 6 months at no pay (part of this leave time may be taken before childbirth or in later years up until the child reaches age 4). This leave is intended for both fathers and mothers to share. In practice, however, virtually all mothers take the leave for an average of 7 to 9 months; but only about 22% of the fathers participate in the program, and those who do participate use only 5% of the aggregate leave days taken, almost always in the last few months.[42] One major reason for the preponderance of women is that almost all babies in Sweden are breast-fed; in the later months, of course, cultural and economic reasons become predominant.

By the end of the first year after the child is born, 8 out of 10 gainfully employed women have resumed their jobs, most on a part-time basis. Parents of children under 8 years of age (12 years of age in some communities) must be given (if they so request) 2 hours off from work per day without pay; in other words, they can work a 6-hour workday at a proportionately diminished income. This is the reason Sweden has not only the highest percentage of mothers in the labor force, but also the highest percentage of women who work only part-time.[43] Available to working parents are various day-care facilities for the child, to be discussed below. Until the child is 12 years old, one or the other parent (many fathers participate) can take up to 60 days of leave per year per child at nearly full salary to care for sick children; a portion of this leave may be used to assist children with adjustment problems in day-care programs or schools. The average amount of this leave actually used is 4 to 5 days per year.

Children begin formal education in Sweden at age 7, as noted earlier. For children 6 years of age who are not in a subsidized day-care program, municipalities are required to provide at least 3 hours per day in a preschool program. Most parents make use of this program for their children.

Public day care in Sweden is allocated on the basis of need, with user costs determined by ability to pay. The day-care programs are run by the separate municipalities, but regulated and heavily subsidized by the state. Although an early advocate of public day care, Sweden has been a latecomer among European nations in the mass development of public day-care facilities. But in 1985 the Swedish *Riksdag* adopted guidelines aimed at providing a place in public day care by 1991 for all children over the age of 18 months whose parents want one.

Children as young as 6 months of age are permitted in Swedish day-care programs, but because of the very successful parental-leave program, the percentage of very young children in public day care in Sweden is not high and has even dropped in recent years. For all children in the age group 0–6 in 1982, 38% had a place in the public child-care system (58% of the children of gainfully employed parents), 41% had a parent at home, and the remainder were cared for through other arrangements, such as paid private care. Children cared for by the public system attend one of two types of program: public day-care centers (*daghem;* 23%) and family day care (*familjedaghem;* 15%). Open from about 6:00 AM to 7:00 PM, public day-care centers have as a rule 4 to 5 children per adult (with a lower ratio for infant groups). Family day-care consists of mothers licensed by the municipality to care for children (maximum of four, including their own) in their own homes.

There are also public care programs for children of school age during their afterschool hours (*fritidshem*); in 1982, 17% of children between the ages of 7 and 12 participated in such programs. For teenage children youth centers as well as organized recreational programs are available in many Swedish urban districts.

In addition to parental leaves and day-care programs, Swedish parents are provided with a variety of direct economic assistance. One form is child-support payments (*barnbidrag*), amounting in 1987 to about $925 (5820 Swedish crowns) per year per child, with half an extra allowance for the third and a double allowance for the fourth child and subsequent children. These payments are not means tested and are therefore the same for families at all income levels. Economic assistance to families that is subject to a means test includes housing subsidies (*bostadsbidrag*), currently received by a majority of Swedish families and some 40% of all Swedish households, and social-welfare payments for families whose incomes fall below a certain level.[44] In 1984, about 95,000 Swedish families were receiving some direct social-welfare funds, representing close to 10% of all families with children. In marked contrast to the United States, Sweden also provides families with free medical and dental care, as noted above, and virtually free education through the university level.

The Decline in Family Care Giving

The child-care benefits and services just discussed, together with other public-welfare programs in Sweden, amount to what is only an unattainable dream in the minds of human-service professionals in most other nations, and few Swedes would willingly give up a single one of them. Because of these programs, people in Sweden are no longer very dependent on their families for many forms of socialization and care. This is a plus from an egalitarian point of view: families have always varied greatly in their ability to provide such care, which resulted in far-reaching inequities in care and resources. At the same time Swedes have become much more dependent on the state. In place of the term "welfare state" to signify this new condition of dependency some prefer the label "client society," a society in which citizens are for the most part clients of a large group of public employees who take care of them throughout their lives.[45]

In the words of one influential Swedish report, "care today has to a great extent become paid work," and one should add—the paid work of professionals employed by the government. Public expenditure for care more than sextupled (in fixed prices) between 1960 and 1980.[46] In the latter half of the 1970s the care sector accounted for 90% of the growth in the labor force, the increment consisting almost entirely of women working part-time, and care in Sweden today takes up more than one sixth of the total work force.[47] To a larger extent than in probably any other society, unpaid female care for relatives in the home in Sweden has been converted into paid professional care.

Most care is an extremely labor-intensive as well as time-intensive activity. Unlike industrial production, it cannot be automated. With rapidly rising labor costs there has been a dramatic increase in the cost of care per unit of time. Along these lines there is much discussion today about a "crisis in care giving," referring both to rising costs and to declining quality. On the cost side, as one Swedish report put it, "politicians are afraid to jeopardize their electoral following by demanding full payment for a service that they dare not reduce."[48]

Many Swedes are beginning to realize that such extensive public-care programs have not only very high economic costs, but also some hidden costs of a noneconomic kind. While family care may have been inadequate and poorly given in many cases, at least it was given by persons intimate with and usually biologically or socially related to the care receiver. Care given by government employees—day-care workers, teachers, doctors and nurses, psychologists, social workers, home helpers—may be more efficient, professional, and expert, but it can also be rather depersonalized and lacking in the "human touch," as well as subject to a high turnover of personnel.

Moreover, state care is highly specialized, raising the question of who is to look out for the "whole person."

There are many forms of highly personalized day-to-day care that the state by its very nature simply cannot provide, even if through some hidden source of enormous wealth it were able to afford them. Intimate forms of human care are best provided by persons very close to the client, and the persons willing to provide such care have in almost all instances historically been family members. The danger is that in shedding very many care-giving functions, the family becomes so weakened as an institutional unit that it is unable to provide adequately the intimate care that only it can provide.[49] The Swedish government is well aware of this problem and has tried to rectify it to the degree possible through the rational planning, for example, of child-care programs. Thus working parents are enabled to be with their infants full-time during the first year after birth, attend to their children when they are sick, and even help to see that the children are well adjusted at the day-care centers. But the underlying fear of family decline remains—that as more and more care-giving functions are stripped away, the family will lose its ability, or its will, to "take care of its own."

This dimension of family decline is undoubtedly a concern in all advanced welfare societies. The amount of informal care giving that marks a successful society is enormous, and there is no way that state employees can take over all of it. In Sweden, it has been estimated (very roughly), that nearly twice as many person-hours each year are spent on informal care as on public care.[50] Even the most prosperous welfare states must depend on the continued willingness of informal care givers to ensure that too many matters of personal care are not dumped on the state. To make matters worse in Sweden, not only have families lost many of their former care-giving functions, but so also have most voluntary associations. Paid care under private auspices has also become very rare in Sweden.

All of these concerns with both the cost and the quality of care in the welfare state have led to calls for a return, if not to family care, at least to a stronger Swedish voluntary sector, in fact, somewhat along American lines. There is a belief among some intellectuals that shorter working hours will give people time for more volunteer work. Volunteer work, in turn, is expected to lead to a new "sense of community" in Sweden, something that many Swedes feel is being undercut by social trends and the bureaucratic state.[51] That such a development flies in the face of the current movement toward professionalization of the social services, however, calls the belief in future volunteerism into serious question. Also, it is likely that volunteerism and familism go together, the one being an extension of the unpaid and informal care giving that marks the other. The expansion of volunteerism in Sweden at this time, therefore, appears dubious.

Child care has been the fastest-growing subsector of the Swedish care industry in recent years. The issue of a "welfare crisis," however, has been raised not so much in regard to the socialization of children, but to the other end of the life course—care for the elderly. In keeping with all other advanced societies, Swedish public programs for the elderly are even more beneficent and generous than are those for children; the state has taken over many of the care functions formerly provided by the family.

Most knowledgeable observers would agree that the function of giving care to the elderly has been removed from the family in Sweden more than anywhere else and that in this shift of functions the state has played a major role. For example, 90% of Swedish health-care expenditures are public, versus about 75% in most other advanced societies and 40% in the United States.[52] Virtually all elderly in Sweden are housed independently from their children. In 1980 only about 5% of Swedish unmarried or unattached elderly lived with their children, compared to over 15% in the United States and more than two thirds in Japan.[53] This situation has changed swiftly in recent years. Between 1954 and 1976, the percentage of Swedish elderly, both married and unmarried, who lived with their children dropped from 28 to 9%.[54]

The elderly in Sweden are also largely economically independent of their families. Representing less a major shift in legislative intent than a changing of the law to reflect current reality, a Swedish law requiring children to economically maintain their poor parents was repealed in 1979. One comparative study found that only 19% of old people are assisted economically by their children and grandchildren in Denmark, a nation very similar to Sweden in this respect, versus 59% in England and 69% in the United States. By the same token, grandparents provide less economic assistance to their children and grandchildren: 28% in Denmark versus 44% in England and 60% in the United States.[55] It is also clear that the elderly, and the extended kin group in general, play a much weaker role in influencing the culture and behavior of the nuclear child-rearing families than used to be the case; the authority and control that they once had in this regard have mostly disappeared.[56]

Few in Sweden begrudge these social developments; indeed, most people are delighted with them. The elderly in Sweden for the most part wish to lead independent lives, and the young people are pleased not to have the serious responsibility of care for their elderly parents, to say nothing of not having "meddling" parents in their lives. Nevertheless, these developments are a further indication that the Swedish family (and in the case of the elderly the extended kin group) is a social institution whose power and influence are rapidly growing weaker with time.

Even though it has decreased as a proportion of the total care provided, informal care for the elderly has not deteriorated very much in recent years, according to available data.[57] Contacts between adults and their elderly parents have not significantly diminished, for example, because the advanced technologies of transportation and communication help to promote contact over long distances. Such data do not speak very clearly to the quality of informal care, however; about this we know little.

One important, though seldom mentioned, dimension of family decline in care giving is due to the decreasing size of families. As adults grow older, they tend to rely more than before on brothers and sisters and other close relatives for emotional support and sense of continuity. Yet the pool of relatives each person will have available for such purposes is rapidly shrinking with each successive cohort. The majority of Swedes over the age of 70 grew up in families of six or more.[58] Today such families are almost nonexistent, and many Swedes will be reaching retirement with no brothers or sisters at all. It is reasonable to suppose that this might create an intimate-care crisis sometime in the future.

Internal Deinstitutionalization

A group or organization is strongly institutionalized when there is a high degree of coordination of internal relationships and group activities are directed toward collective goals. The term "deinstitutionalization" thus connotes tendencies working in the opposite direction, tendencies that attenuate the group's collective nature. Within the modern Swedish family, I argue, individual members are becoming more autonomous, less bound to the group, and the domestic unit as a whole is becoming less cohesive. Family members are tending to think less in terms of the success of the family unit than of their own successes. That this tendency is in keeping with the pursuit of individualism and egalitarianism, goals that themselves are highly valued, should not blind us to the fact that it also means a declining family.

The decline of marriage, high rates of marital dissolution, and the diminution or partial loss of the procreation, socialization, and care-giving activities discussed above, all result in the deinstitutionalization of the family not only in its loss of power in society but also in its internal weakening as a social unit. A more direct impact on the family's internal strength and cohesion stems from the diminution of the family's other main functions: economic cooperation, sexual regulation, and affection and companionship.

Economic Cooperation

Throughout history the family has been primarily an economic unit, held together through the mechanism of economic cooperation. Most Swedish families today continue to be economic units and to practice economic cooperation, but they are consuming rather than producing units; the members pool their incomes and other resources and collectively make decisions about what to buy. Such collective decision making, of course, has not been very egalitarian; the person who earned the most money, almost always the male head of household, usually had the larger say, especially over "big-ticket" items. At best, he would be making decisions in the best interests of his family (and his wife would often have strong advisory power.) There is also the tradition, however, associated with the working class, of the man coming home from work and turning his paycheck over to his wife.

Such collective economic decision making within the family has probably become more egalitarian in recent years, but another important shift has been the growth of individualistic decision making; he keeps and spends his money, and she keeps and spends hers, with limited sharing for food, housing, and furnishings. Tax laws have been revised in keeping with this tendency, and recently the use of "prenuptial agreements" has been growing; these contractual agreements sometimes abrogate entirely the principle of family economic cooperation.

Family economic cooperation is further weakened through the loss of the economic dependence of family members on each other, brought about largely by governmental assumption of economic responsibilities, as discussed earlier. Rather than drawing on a pool of family resources, the Swedish family today turns over to the state a large portion of those resources, and its members then become economically dependent on the state rather than the family. Not all of these resources are redistributed from rich to poor families; a large portion could be said to be redistributed by the state back to the same family at different stages of the life cycle. Thus people receive few economic benefits during their young, nonchildbearing years, and many benefits at such life stages as childbirth and old age. All the same, the individual family members are increasingly dependent on the state and less on each other. Indeed, there is a national Swedish edict that all adults are responsible for their own economic well-being; that is, there is no necessity for any adult to economically support another adult, no matter what their relationship may be.

The decline of the institution of marriage has had an effect on the family as a unit of economic cooperation similar to that of state transfer payments. Scandinavia is apparently the only part of the world where, following a legal marriage, all of the income and property of both spouses, and not just the part earned during the marriage, falls under joint ownership. (This provision was sometimes abrogated by a prenuptial agreement.) Until recently, however, when the law was modified, none of the income and property was automatically considered to be jointly owned for the growing number of persons who lived together outside of legal marriage. Recently written into Swedish family legislation is the provision that a portion of all property purchased during a nonmarital relationship will attain the legal status of joint ownership, but the difference between marital and nonmarital relationships in regard to income and property considerations is still great. The decline of marriages, therefore, signals another dimension of the trend away from family-owned toward individual-owned property.

Sexual Regulation

If family economic cooperation is diminishing in importance, what about the function of sexual regulation? One of the main social functions of the family as an institution has always been the regulation of sexual activities in a way that presumably assists in maintaining the stability of the family unit, especially for child-rearing purposes. The family, of course, has never been particularly successful at this, and the Seventh Commandment proscribing adultery probably always has been one of the most widely transgressed, especially by men. There is no reason to think, moreover, that sexual morality in this sense is laxer today than at many other times in human history, although urban living and extensive travel offer more sexual opportunities for the average person. For reasons that are not entirely clear, strict controls over sexual behavior seem to have ebbed and flowed over the course of history, just as they vary greatly among cultures in our own time.[59]

As was noted in earlier chapters, there is no indication that Sweden, despite its weakened family system, holds any particular position of world leadership in extramarital relationships. The weakening of the sexual-regulation function (premarital sexual behavior aside) shows up in Sweden not so much in high rates of adultery, but of serial monogamy. Especially if nonmarital cohabitation is included, the rate of serial monogamy in Sweden is surely one of the highest in the world. Some argue that serial monogamy is a measure of family strength, not weakness: "look how much people still value the family; when one unit breaks up they quickly form another." But this is like arguing that high residential mobility is an indicator of community cohesion: since people are moving to other communities, they apparently continue to favor community life. In fact, community cohesion is highest in those communities where people have lived the longest. (This comparison between the family and the community is not pulled out of thin air; George Peter Murdock once concluded that the nuclear family and the community are the only social groups that are genuinely universal, occurring in every known human society.)[60]

Affection and Companionship

There are almost no hard data about the provision of affection and companionship in existing families, much less about changes over time. Many sociologists in recent decades (see Chapter 2) have come to think that this family function has actually grown stronger over time. Precisely because the other functions have weakened, they argue, more time and effort can be given to the emotional side of family life. I am personally persuaded by recent historical evidence that over recent centuries this family function did indeed gain strength. With the rise of the modern nuclear family the quality of family life changed; adult family members came to devote more time and energy to the emotional care and nurturing of each other and of their children.

On balance, the function of providing affection and companionship may be even continuing to grow stronger today within those families that endure. Partners are picked almost exclusively with that single function in mind (within such constraints as social class and ethnicity), and it is reasonable to suppose that the level of psychological knowledge and awareness has increased in recent years. Yet when making an overall evaluation of the situation, the high breakup rate of marriages and marriagelike unions must at least give one pause. The fact is that probably a majority of all marriages and unions, considered together, do not endure over the life course.

One must also weigh the argument that families are doing surprisingly well today in the face of the tremendous burdens placed upon them. The family is almost the only remaining social institution within which affection and companionship are provided. Gone for the most part in Sweden, for example, is the provision of affection and companionship through such alternative and historically important community elements as neighbors and coreligionists. But whether or not the family's "special burden" is causing that institution to rise to the occasion or merely assisting in its collapse remains an open question.

In such societies as Sweden, the main alternatives to the family as sources of affection and companionship are informal, often same-sex, friendship groups. Perhaps more than anywhere else, in Sweden today informal friendship groups for adults are institutionally anchored in the workplace. There is a probable statistical association in modern societies between the importance of work-based friendship groups for adults and the prevalence of youthful peer groups earlier in life. An international cross-national survey of youth found Sweden at the top in terms of the percentage who had close friends and those who listed "with friends" in answer to the question, "how do you spend your free days?"[61]

It is possible for both families and informal friendship groups to gain in strength and importance as sources of affection and companionship; people thus could end up with the best of two worlds. But some substitution effect is likely; families are declining in Sweden at about the same rate at which informal friendship groups are gaining. Thus friendship groups, according to this conception, could be said to be replacing families as a source of affection and companionship for many.

What does such a shift from families to informal friendship groups mean? One outstanding difference between families and friendship groups is that the latter tend to be homogeneous in age. The shift in the provision of affection and companionship from family groups to friendship groups, therefore, typically involves a growing segregation of people by age. In Sweden and other modern societies more social interaction is concentrated among age peers, whether children, teenagers, or adults. There is also a fundamental difference in the qualitative character of kin ties and informal-friendship relations. Nonkin relationships typically lack the special sense of obligations and responsibilities found in kinship ties and, being voluntary, are more difficult to maintain. The significance of these aspects of family decline is discussed in the concluding chapter.

The Decline of Familism as a Cultural Value

Every institution is not only a bundle of social structures but also a set of cultural values that attest to the worth of the institution. The importance of an institution in society, therefore, can be examined by considering the hierarchical positioning of such values. If religion is the paramount institution, for example, religious values reign supreme in the hierarchy of the society's cultural ideals. Similarly, in the many societies where family remains a preeminent institution, family values rank very high in the cultural hierarchy. Sweden is not one of those societies.[62] The value called "familism" is relatively weak in Sweden and appears to be in decline. Familism can be defined as the belief in a strong sense of family identification and loyalty, mutual assistance among family members, and a concern for the perpetuation of the family unit. It emphasizes the subordination of the interests and personality of individual family members to the interests and welfare of the family group.[63]

How to analyze cultural values and their trends is one of the great problems of the social sciences. Unlike demography or economics, for example, cultural values have few standard indicators. Social-survey results are especially suspect; people are notorious for rationalizing their behavior, saying one thing and doing another, and telling surveyors what they want to hear (how many admit to prejudice and bigotry, for example?) To discern the values of a society, one must rely on indirect indicators and even then one must make many inferences. Probably the best indicators of the values of a society, therefore, are public documents, public pronouncements, and legislation; in these areas people are to some extent put on the line.

The development of Swedish family policies since the 1930s was explored in Chapters 6 and 7. It was noted that over time the value of preserving the family unit has become less and less important, having given way to the values of social equality and individual rights. Little of recent Swedish legislation concerning the family, whether divorce, taxation, or welfare benefits, expresses the value of familism. This legislation is not designed to promote a strong sense of family identification and loyalty, mutual assistance among family members, and concern for the perpetuation of the family unit. Rather than focusing on the family unit, Swedish family legislation tends almost exclusively to focus on the individual family member.

It is instructive to compare the political platforms of Swedish political parties with those of other nations in regard to family values. One would never find in the political pronouncements of the ruling Social Democratic Party, for example, the following language, which appeared in a report of the Democratic (Party) Policy Commission in the United States: "Democrats want strong families that are self-sufficient and independent. . . . Democrats favor pro-family policies that will . . . help keep families together."[64] Current Swedish Social Democratic family policies are couched almost entirely in the language of redistributing financial aid and services (such as day care) to families with children. They seldom speak to the value of familism per se.

Unlike most other societies, Sweden today has virtually no public spokespersons for familism, no organized political forces on the national scene calling for the strengthening of the family as an institution. One exception is the very small Christian Democratic Party, which in 1985 managed to get one member elected to parliament through a political arrangement made with the much larger Center (formerly Agrarian) Party. In many of its political positions the Christian Party seems quite close to the Democratic Party in the United States, yet in many Swedish circles of opinion it is derided as hopelessly reactionary and is the butt of political jokes. Also, its lasting power within Swedish politics appears limited.

Swedes do not necessarily place a low importance on familism. Rather, the importance of familism as a value has been displaced by other values in the cultural hierarchy. There is a common belief that Norway has remained more familistic than Sweden, and one can see this expressed in political priorities. In selecting eight national goals for its long-term development program in 1975, for example, the Norwegian government placed "strengthening the family and the local community" in third place, following "security and good living conditions" and "greater solidarity and equality" and ahead of "employment for everyone" and "better working environment."[65] Although I know of no comparable priority listing in Sweden, it is hard to imagine that Swedes would rank the family so high and place it ahead of employment.

Deinstitutionalization as Disinvestment

The bottom line of family deinstitutionalization—the trend for familism as a cultural value to weaken, for the family to lose functions, and for family units to become smaller, more unstable with a shorter life span, and less cohesive—is that people are less willing to invest time, money, and energy in family life. An adult starting a family today must be wary. Since the chances of the family remaining intact until one spouse's death are perhaps only 50-50, is it not rational to hold back commitment? Rationality dictates that it is the individual, not the family unit, in whom the main investments of time, money, and effort probably should be made.[66] This can become a self-fulfilling prophecy. The less its members invest in the family, the weaker the institution becomes; and the weaker the institution becomes, the less one is willing to invest in it. Thus deinstitutionalization of the family breeds disinvestment in the family, and vice versa. For those who are interested in the enhancement of family life, the question of how to break this vicious circle is one of the serious social concerns of our time.

Notes

[1]Kingsley Davis (1985), "The Meaning and Significance of Marriage in Contemporary Society," pp. 1–21 in Kingsley Davis (ed.), *Contemporary Marriage.*
[2]*Ibid.*
[3]Prime Ministers Office (Japan) (1984), "Outline of the Results of the Third International Survey of Youth Attitudes."
[4]Bo Lewin (1979), *Om Ogift Samboende i Sverige,* and Jan Trost (1979), *Unmarried Cohabitation.*
[5]Jan Trost (1985), "Marital and Non-marital Cohabitation," pp. 109–119 in John Rogers and Hans Norman (eds.), *The Nordic Family: Perspectives on Family Research:* 111.
[6]Anders Agell (1980), "Cohabitation without Marriage in Swedish Law," pp. 245–257 in John M. Eekelaar and S. N. Katz (eds.), *Marriage and Cohabitation in Contemporary Societies: Areas of Legal, Social and Ethical Change;* Anders Agell (1981), "The Swedish Legislation on Marriage and Cohabitation: A Journey without a Destination," *The American Journal of Comparative Law* 29-2 (Spring): 285–314. The Swedish Minister of Justice made the following statement to the Family Law Reform Committee that drafted the family law reform of 1973: "In my opinion a new law ought to be neutral as far as possible in relation to different forms of cohabitation

and different ethical beliefs." Birgitta Alexandersson (1973), "The 1973 Family Law Reform," *Current Sweden* 8: 2.

[7]Louis Gaunt and David Gaunt (1986), "Le Modéle Scandinave," pp. 471–495 in Andre Burguiere et al. (eds.), *Histoire de la Famille.*

[8]Frederick Engels (1942), *The Origin of the Family, Private Property and the State:* 73.

[9]In discussions leading to revisions of the Swedish marriage law in the early 1970s, there was strong sentiment for doing away with language that said "husbands and wives are obliged to give fidelity and support to each other and work for the best of the family." Such language remained, however, after social workers argued that it might prove helpful in family therapy. Interview with Jan Trost, May 1986.

[10]Gilbert Y. Steiner (1981), *The Futility of Family Policy:* 192.

[11]Interview, May 1986. He added that "more than in most other countries, Swedish family legislation has followed marital reality and not tried to set standards."

[12]Ernest W. Burgess and Harvey J. Locke (1945), *The Family From Institution to Companionship:* vii.

[13]Socialdepartementet (1983), *Barn Kostar . . .:* 38.

[14]United States Bureau of the Census (1979), "Divorce, Child Custody, and Child Support," *Current Population Reports,* No. 65: 23.

[15]Jan Trost estimated, in private conversation, that about 90% of adults in both the United States and Sweden will form a dyad sometime during their lives.

[16]Christina Axelsson (1984), "Familj och social Förankring," pp. 267–284 in Robert Erikson and Rune Åberg, (eds.), *Välfärd i Förändring:* 276.

[17]One recent American study found that living alone at an early age by women caused an erosion of traditional family orientations. Linda J. Waite, F. K. Goldscheider and Christina Witsberger (1986), "Nonfamily Living and the Erosion of Traditional Family Orientations Among Young Adults."

[18]This is not to say that the production function has disappeared from the family altogether. A recent emphasis in social history is that many production activities remain, such as the provision of transportation; it is just that many of these activities, like transportation, are different from the ones before the advent of the factory system. [See Ruth Schwartz Cowan (1983), *More Work for Mother.*] Despite this intellectual refinement, it is difficult to deny the long-run decline of the family production function.

[19]Pierre L. van den Berghe (1979), *Human Family Systems: An Evolutionary View:* 172.

[20]See *Barn* (1983).

[21]Jacques Donzelot (1979), *The Policing of Families;* Robert M. Moroney (1986), *Shared Responsibility: Families and Social Policy;* James S. Coleman and Torsten Husén (1985), *Becoming Adult in a Changing Society;* Christopher Lasch (1977), *Haven in a Heartless World;* Philippe Meyer (1983), *The Child and the State: The Intervention of the State in Family Life.*

[22]According to a publication of the "semiofficial" Swedish Institute, this is due to "Sweden's great geographical distances and severe climate, which in earlier times made it difficult to bring together very young children for group activities." Swedish Institute (1984), "Child Care Programs in Sweden": 1. A more persuasive reason, however, one that is still held today by many educators, is the belief that a child is not mature enough until age 7 to be away from home and in a peer group setting for long periods of the day.

[23]In the United States, educators frequently express concern that children are starting school at too young an age and advise moving more in the Swedish direction.

See Sue Mittenthal (1986), "Starting Kindergarten a Bit Older and Wiser," *The New York Times,* November 21: C1.

24One source reported the following comparative data concerning the number of children taken from their parents in 1981: Sweden, 22,000; West Germany, 1900; Denmark, 710; Finland, 552; Norway, 163. Magnus Ivarsson (1983), *Sverige 1984:* 29.

25Sten Johansson (1980), *Barnens Välfärd:* 8.

26Swedish Institute (1984), "Child Care Programs in Sweden": 2. This report rather optimistically refers to what both nations colloquially call "latchkey" children (*nykel barn*) as children who "manage by themselves." A new term heard in Sweden in recent years is *pose barn* (bag children). These are children who are not given a key and are not allowed in the house after school ("they might break something"). Instead, a bag of food is left for them outside the door.

27In the United States, as reported in *The New York Times* (February 6, 1987: A19), the Census Bureau found that 7.2% of youngsters have no adult supervision after school (data from December 1984). Data on such a topic, of course, are subject to an extremely wide margin of error.

28Robert Erikson (1984), "Uppväxtvillkor under 1900-talet," in Erikson and Åberg (1984), *Välfärd:* 336.

29Calculations made by Swedish National Central Bureau of Statistics.

30Rita Ann Reimer (1986), "Work and Family Life in Sweden," *Social Change in Sweden:* 1.

31See Coleman and Husén (1985), *Becoming Adult,* and Kenneth Roberts (1985), "Youth in the 1980's: A New Way of Life," *International Social Science Journal* 37-4: 427–440.

32Such policies have given Sweden a relatively low youth-unemployment rate: Estimates for 1987: 6% in Sweden, 12% in the United States, 21% in the United Kingdom, and 26% in France. *The OECD Observer* 144 (1987): 13.

33Reported in *The New York Times,* November 4, 1985: B11.

34Swedish Institute (1986), "Facts and Figures about Youth in Sweden," *Fact Sheets on Sweden.*

35See David Popenoe (1983), "Urban Scale and the Quality of Community Life: A Swedish Community Comparison," *Sociological Inquiry* 53-4: 404–418.

36"Permissiveness" as used here should be distinguished from both "authoritarian" and "democratic" approaches to child rearing. Very generally speaking, in the author-itarian approach parents alone set the rules, while in the democratic approach the rules are set jointly by parents and children. Both approaches require a great deal of parent–child contact. In the permissive approach rules are set by the child alone, and contact and control are minimal. There is some evidence that, compared to Scandi-navian families, American families have traditionally tended to be more authoritarian with their teenagers and at the same time more permissive with young children (of course, not in the literal sense that young children are allowed to "set the rules"). In Scandinavia, the reverse is more the case. This is sometimes cited as a reason for the fact that Scandinavian teenagers seem better behaved and have lower rates of delinquency than their American counterparts: The Scandinavians have more "struc-ture" at a young age, and are therefore able to be more independently responsible as teenagers. See the comparison between Denmark and the United States in Denise B. Kandel and Gerald S. Lesser (1972), *Youth in Two Worlds.*

37In interviews with two generations of Swedish young people in the 1960s and the 1980s, the latter group was found to be more active and independent and with much less fear of grownups and of being punished. Inga Sylvander and Maj Ördman

(1985), *Jag är Rädd för att bli Börtglomd och Ensam*. Interview with Maj Ördman, May 1986.

[38]Kandel and Lesser (1972), *Youth in Two Worlds*, and James S. Coleman (1961), *The Adolescent Society*.

[39]Swedish youth ranked highest in an 11-nation survey in "satisfaction with life at home" and lowest in terms of "having had any real clashes with father and/or mother in the last two or three years." Richard G. Braungart and Margaret M. Braungart (1986), "Youth Problems and Politics in the 1980's: Some Multinational Comparisons," *International Sociology* 1-4: 359–380. The favorable situation of Swedish youth could be due to the freedom they have via permissiveness. It could also be due to a high level of psychological awareness on the part of Swedish parents, for example, when disciplining their children they tend to "reason" with them rather than use harsh physical punishment such as spanking. Even if the data are valid, all such explanations are highly speculative.

[40]Sheila B. Kamerman and Alfred J. Kahn (1981), *Child Care, Family Benefits, and Working Parents*.

[41]See Ingemar Lindberg and Lena Nordenmark (1980), *Familjepolitik för Små Barn*, and Åke Elmer (1983), *Svensk Socialpolitik*. Unless otherwise indicated, the information in this section is from these sources, updated by the latest available data from various Swedish government agencies.

[42]Birgitta Silén (1987), "The Truth about Sexual Equality," *Inside Sweden*, 1-2: 13.

[43]Many Swedes see such part-time work as being disadvantageous for women's move toward full equality. High on the political agenda of Swedish Social Democratic women's groups, therefore, is not only the continuing encouragement of greater home participation by fathers but also the goal of a 6-hour workday for *all* workers.

[44]Even though a majority of Swedish households are in multifamily buildings, because of housing subsidies about three quarters of Swedish families with children live in single-family dwellings. This is despite the fact that Swedish families with children are disadvantaged economically compared to families without children and nonfamily households. On the economic situation of families with children in Sweden, see Johan Fritzell (1985), *Barnfamiljernas Levnadsnivå*.

[45]Coleman and Husén (1985), *Becoming Adult*: 62.

[46]Mårten Lagergren et al. (1984), *Time to Care*: 153. The Swedish language version is *Tid för Omsorg* (1982).

[47]*Ibid.*: 44.

[48]*Ibid.*: 3.

[49]This theme is explored in Kari Waerness (1978), "The Invisible Welfare State: Women's Work at Home," *Acta Sociologica* 21 (Supplement): 193–207; and Elina Haavio-Mannila (1983), "Caregiving in the Welfare State," *Acta Sociologica* 26-1: 61–82.

[50]Lagergren (1984), *Time to Care*: 72.

[51]*Ibid.*

[52]*Ibid.*: 56.

[53]Gerdt Sundström (1983), *Caring for the Aged in Welfare Society*: 26.

[54]*Ibid.*: 19.

[55]Reported in Gerdt Sundström (1980), *Omsorg oss Emellan*: 64.

[56]For parallel developments in the United States, see Andrew J. Cherlin and Frank F. Furstenberg, Jr. (1986), *The New American Grandparent*.

[57]Sundström (1980), *Omsorg*.

[58]Erikson (1984), *Välfärd*: 335.

[59]See Lawrence Stone (1985), "Sex in the West," *The New Republic,* July 8: 25–37.
[60]George Peter Murdock (1949), *Social Structure:* 79–80.
[61]Prime Minister's Office (1984), "Outline of the Results of the Third International Survey of Youth Attitudes."
[62]See D. E. Weston (1983), "Secularization and Social Theory: Swedish Experience in the Context of an International Theoretical Debate," *Acta Sociologica.* 26-3/4: 329–336.
[63]George A. Theodorson and Achilles G. Theodorson (1969), *Modern Dictionary of Sociology:* 146.
[64]Reported in *The New York Times,* September 21, 1986: 28.
[65]Quoted in Joel S. Torstenson, Michael F. Metcalf, and Tor Fr. Rasmussen (1985), *Urbanization and Community Building in Modern Norway:* 104.
[66]This has been the thesis of a number of "economically oriented" family analysts in recent years, for example: Gary S. Becker (1981), *A Treatise on the Family,* and Victor R. Fuchs (1983), *How We Live.* See also William J. Goode (1984), "Individual Investments in Family Relationships over the Coming Decades," *The Tocqueville Review* 6-1: 51–83.

Swedish Family Decline:
A Search for Explanations

Why has the family become weaker, more deinstitutionalized, in Sweden than in any other advanced society? What can Sweden tell us about the causes of family decline in the modern world? An attempt to answer these questions is the concern of this chapter. Drawing on the historical and contemporary materials presented earlier, I suggest an explanation of Swedish family decline in terms of a set of social and cultural dimensions that characterize Swedish society today. The explanation has been organized in four main categories: structural (socioeconomic trends that accompany modernization and are found in all advanced societies), ideological (belief systems that are linked to, and maintain, various political, social, and class interests), political (actions of the Swedish government), and cultural (values that govern the behavior, psychology, and character of Swedes). Using these categories, it will be shown in what way Sweden differs from other advanced societies and how these differences relate to family decline.

My perspective is that modern family decline is largely a product of the broad structural trends found in all industrialized societies. What makes these structural trends more "advanced" in Sweden than elsewhere is the presence of two other societal dimensions: ideologies that have shown comparative strength in Sweden and actions of the Swedish welfare state. The two dimensions are closely related—government actions are largely responses to widely held ideological beliefs. The advanced family decline in Sweden should not be viewed as necessarily an *intended* product of ideological and political desires, however. It is best considered to be the undesired and unintended consequence, in part, of government actions aimed at achieving other social goals.

Family decline is a very broad concept, and each of its many aspects may be the result of very different social forces. It is therefore unwieldy to deal with family decline per se. To me, the most central and compelling aspect of family decline in advanced societies is the high breakup rate of parents and, unless otherwise specified, this is the main phenomenon on which I will focus. Why should Sweden, arguably the Western world's most benign society, have the highest rate of parental breakup?

It is important to bear in mind that the causes of parental or marital dissolution, looked at on an international scale, are very numerous indeed. As anyone knows who has read one of the numerous reviews of research on the causes of divorce, a great many factors enter into the equation. In the United States, for example, key factors commonly cited as being most closely associated with divorce are brief courtships and early marriages, teenage pregnancies, poverty and income instability, interethnic and interfaith unions, and high residential mobility.[1] None of these factors can account for the high breakup rate in Sweden because they are relatively uncommon in Swedish society. In Sweden, one must look instead for causes of divorce that are associated with marriages and first births relatively late in life, with affluence and economic security, and with ethnic and religious homogeneity.

The intention of this chapter is not to uncover precise causes, however; such a goal, even if it were realistic for sociology, which is arguable, is better left for more narrowly conceived and quantitative studies than this one. The task here is to provide a broad interpretation of the social and cultural climate in Sweden within which the specific factors suspected of being associated with family decline are likely to be embedded.

Structural Trends

Economic Security

Let us first look at those social trends, associated with the modernization of societies, that have been widely used to explain the family's weakening as an institution in every advanced society. They are economic development and the rise of mass affluence, bureaucratization, egalitarianism, secularization, and the growth of science and rationality. I believe that the economic trends must be accorded primary importance. In addition to human reproduction, the family's main function historically has been economic production. For most of human history the family has been a cooperative work unit in which success was measured in terms of the sheer survival of family members. Not to have been part of a family meant not to survive. Obviously, this provided a powerful bond with which family members could be wielded into a cohesive group.

Today, as we saw in the preceding chapter, the family in Sweden is at almost the opposite extreme. Not only is it not a cooperative work unit, but it has virtually no production functions and has lost many consumption functions as well. The economic bond holding the contemporary Swedish family together is a minimal one; indeed, in economic terms, many adult family members would be better off going it alone. One Swedish study showed that, under certain circumstances and considering a mix of taxation and government benefits, living expenses were lower if a couple divorced than if they remained together.[2] Even children suffer relatively little economically when their parents separate. The parent who moves away from the family unit is required to continue economic support, and if he or she is unable or unwilling to do so, the state steps in and either forces the recalcitrant person to give economic support or, if that is not possible, provides the support from public funds.

Without regard to the quality of social interaction, it is a reasonable proposition that families are most cohesive when they are forced to be so, and there seems no better force than economic necessity.[3] By the same token, it is a reasonable proposition that economic security, contrary to common belief, helps to generate family breakup. This is why the divorce rate goes down during economic depressions and up when good times return.[4] It is why the divorce rate went up, in a famous social experiment in the United States, among those families that were given a guaranteed minimum income.[5] It is a main reason why the divorce rate in virtually all advanced societies (now also including Japan) has climbed during their period of greatest economic growth and affluence. And it is almost certainly among the most important reasons why Sweden, the world's most economically secure society and one of the most affluent in terms of material standard of living, should have a weak family system with a high rate of parental breakup.

The economic situation of Swedish families may be envied on most counts. Not only is the family living in material prosperity, but each individual family member is economically secure in his or her own right. The latter is a result both of the advanced stage of women's liberation in Sweden, where women have economic security through participation in the work force, and of the economic rights of each family member, which are guaranteed by the State. Yet what is for the economic good of each family member may not at the same time be best for the family unit as a whole.[6]

It also appears to be largely economic reasons that account in advanced societies for the "birth strike" of women, as Alva Myrdal once called it. Not only do women have other things to do, namely some of the same things that men have always done, but children, once a tremendous economic asset to a family, have now become an economic liability.[7] Even with government subsidies, children today are expensive to raise because of the high standard of living, and every unit of money devoted to a child must be subtracted from what the parents otherwise could spend on themselves. That parents in affluent societies have any children at all, therefore, rests on noneconomic factors.

These economic realities are undoubtedly a large part of the explanation of Swedish family decline. But they are of course only one part. A major and interrelated role is played by another structural trend under way in every advanced society—the changing gender roles of women and men.

Changing Gender Roles

In what one scholar has called the "subtle revolution" and others have called the major social revolution of this century, women in every advanced society have moved increasingly from the role of full-time housewife to at least part-time worker in the labor force.[8] Many single and widowed women for centuries back have worked outside the home or, as servants, at least outside their own home. But following the Industrial Revolution this was generally not true for married women (especially women with children) who, if they could afford to do so, stayed out of the labor market. Furthermore, society was organized to encourage them to do so. The so-called family wage is one example: men were paid on a higher wage scale because they presumably were the sole wage earners in their families. Now this has all changed, perhaps more so in Sweden than anywhere else.

I agree with sociologist Andrew Cherlin that the evidence about changing gender roles, although partly circumstantial, "is stronger and more suggestive than that linking any other recent trend with the rise in divorce."[9] Yet disentangling the effects of changing gender roles on marital breakup from all other factors is no mean task. We can only suggest here the effects for which the evidence appears relatively strong. Some evidence for the effect on marital breakup of the family's general economic security was cited above. Putting the matter in terms of the family's general economic security can be misleading, however, for within the family the husband has almost always been much more secure than the wife. With the growing economic security of advanced societies it has been the wife's economic position that has changed the most. Formerly dependent and economically insecure, she has gained considerable economic independence in recent years.

At the psychological and behavioral levels, women with newfound economic security no longer need to be bossed around by a husband on whom they were once economically dependent. Women in bad marriages no longer need to stick it out because of economic necessity. A women can tell a man who wants to marry her that she does not need a breadwinner, if that is all he wishes to be. She can handle that end for herself; what she wants is a friend, an intimate companion, and someone who will equally share with her the domestic work load of a family. Naturally, all of these changes (many of them quite sudden) have modified the role definitions of men and women found in the traditional nuclear family and have upset the role relations between husband and wife.

In the guaranteed-minimum-income experiment in the United States, cited above, the main reason for increased marital breakup was the abandonment of the marriage by women who had newfound economic independence. A recent study of married couples in the United States concluded that "a wife's employment increases marital instability, especially if her job entails working more than 40 hours per week," one reason for this being that "the wife's income may be lowering the threshold of satisfaction at which divorce is considered."[10] Another study of married couples in the United States found that marital breakup was highest if the wife placed high importance on her own self-sufficiency, and concluded that "it may seem unconscionably cynical to say that wives stay in marriages because they cannot support themselves outside them, but our data show there is some validity to this."[11] There has by now been an abundance of such studies relating income to divorce, and nearly all have reached the same general conclusion. It has typically been found that the probability of divorce goes up the higher the wife's income and the closer that income is to her husband's.[12] Although I am not aware of similar studies in Sweden, it is unlikely that the results there would be any different.

Divorce and marital separation are seldom the result of the actions of just one partner, however. The fact that in advanced societies women tend to file for divorce more often than men (in Sweden about 70% of divorce actions are initiated by women[13]) does not mean that women are necessarily more eager than men to end the marriage. With working wives and state-supported economic security for family members, men can more easily walk away from their families with the knowledge that those left behind will not face undue economic hardship. There is even some plausibility, at least in the United States, to the view that the modern divorce revolution was started by men. As part of the new era of sexual permissiveness, it is argued, men began to abandon the breadwinner role to take up the playboy role, thus throwing women into the job market. Then, as the chances of marital breakup increased, women leaned toward still greater economic self-sufficiency both as an economic necessity and for their own sense of well-being.[14]

The question of who or what may have "started" the modern divorce revolution will never be satisfactorily resolved. In any event, it is greatly overshadowed by the fact that women in every advanced society, mostly since the early 1960s, flocked to the labor market in large numbers. So far there has been no turning back, and the indications are that, on any kind of mass scale, there will not be in the near future. Some evidence suggests that in the United States the work behavior of wives was triggered largely in response to a general economic squeeze on families rather than on ideology or to male abandonment.[15] An economic factor of importance was the rising wage rate for women, making it more costly for women to stay at home, which in turn was generated by post–World War II growth of service-sector jobs. Now that it has become widespread, the two–wage-earner family persists for another economic reason: single–wage-earner families feel (and are) relatively deprived. These economic reasons appear to hold for Sweden as well.

Yet as the educational level of women rises, which, in many respects, is now the same as that for men, it seems likely that this factor alone would lead to a growing similarity between the patterns of labor-force participation of men and women. Other factors of importance are the decline in birthrates and rising longevity, each of which gives women a longer period of life outside of the childbearing years and thus provides more opportunity for full-time participation in the labor force.

Of course the effect of changing gender roles on marital instability must not be viewed solely in economic terms. The modern marital relationship is at heart a bond of emotional affection and support between two people. In a survey 2000 Swedish adults were asked what they considered most important for a happy marriage; the most common answer was "to be able to talk to each other about feelings," followed by "to enjoy the same kind of life."[16] The immediate cause of divorce is a weakening of this emotional bond for some reason, and the changing economic situation of families is but one of those reasons.

The theoretically possible reasons why this emotional bond should be weakening now more than in earlier years, and in Sweden more than elsewhere, are innumerable. There is even the not unfounded position that the bond has *not* weakened in recent years, but that marriages in an earlier era were held together by other elements (and that surviving marriages today are more tightly bonded emotionally than ever before.) The problem is that such qualitative changes cannot be measured. What we do know for sure is that marriages today are based fundamentally on an emotional bond between two people and that, if marriages are breaking up at an increasing rate, *something* must be happening to affect the resilience of that emotional bond.

Many knowledgeable observers regard as central in this respect the fact that we live in an age of gender-role transitions. Unlike their parents, men and women who marry today do not have the relatively firm traditional gender roles of husband and wife to follow. The noted Swedish author and psychologist Barbro Lennéer-Axelson has suggested that a key word of the younger generation in Sweden today is "ambivalence"; there are simply too many choices to be made, and it no longer is clear who should do and be responsible for what.[17] This means that marital roles today are subject to a kind of negotiation on the part of each partner, and, as with all negotiations, the chance of successful resolution is by no means assured over the long run.

There has not been nearly so much research on marital breakup in Sweden as in the United States, but the Swedish data that are available lend strong support to the psychological importance of changing gender roles. Among the predominating problems for which residents of Stockholm sought marriage counseling in 1980, "conflicts related to sex roles" ranked second, after the much more general "disturbed emotional engagement."[18] In one study of Swedish divorce, the two most common reasons for divorce were poor sexual adaptation and "problems related to work inside and outside the home."[19] In a study of Danish divorces, the most frequently given reason for divorce by both husband and wife was that they "had developed in different directions."[20] The issue of "finding oneself" seems particularly important in Swedish marital breakup, especially for women. In the words of two of Sweden's best-known marriage therapists, "a man divorces when he has found someone else; a women divorces when she has found herself."[21]

The concept "changing gender roles" refers to far more than the roles that wife and husband play within a marriage. It signifies widespread changes in the way each gender sees itself in all of life, including ideas of masculinity and femininity, the trajectory of the life course, and power in public life. It is in no way to diminish the overall value of these changes to point out that their negative impact on the strength of the marital bond has probably been great. Whether or not this impact will lessen as new gender roles become stabilized remains to be seen.

Ideological Beliefs

The structural trends of economic security and gender roles discussed above are compelling explanations for family decline in modern societies, at least in its dimension of marital dissolution. We still need to know why the decline has been so steep in Sweden. What else is there about Swedish society that affects family decline either directly or indirectly by way of fostering one of these structural trends? We turn first to the importance of various ideologies in Swedish life.

The term "ideology" is ambiguous, even (or especially) in the social sciences. Karl Marx used it to mean a set of beliefs that supports and maintains a particular social-class position. Others, including myself, use it more generally to mean a set of beliefs that reflects a particular social point of view, whether class based or not. I discuss here certain ideologies that are commonly identified in advanced societies and are held by a large number of people. The ideologies of this type that are relatively strong in Sweden are secularism, feminism, the therapeutic ideology, and radical socialism. Each of these in its own way, I argue, has shaped the cultural climate of Sweden in a manner that has adversely affected the family as an institution.

Secularism

The first and most important "ideology" to be considered may not be a "true" ideology at all; secularism represents the absence of a particular ideology as much as being an ideology itself. Secularism is the end result of secularization, the trend in which religious institutions become less powerful and religious beliefs less easily accepted. Following David Martin, "religious" can be defined as "an acceptance of a level of reality beyond the observable world known to science, to which are ascribed meanings and purposes completing and transcending those of the purely human realm."[22] Sweden is often regarded as the most secular society in the world (see data in Chapter 7).

One importance of secularism for family decline in Sweden is that organized religion has traditionally been, at least in the past few centuries in the West, a great supporter of the family as an institution. This can be seen clearly today in the United States, where the traditional family has the support of the Roman Catholic, fundamentalist Protestant, and Orthodox Jewish religions. These religious bodies continually preach the sanctity of family life, discourage divorce, and attempt to make marriage under religious auspices one of life's most important ceremonies and celebrations.

The Lutheran State Church in Sweden and even more the so-called free churches (all other Swedish religious bodies) are some of the few organized social groupings there that continue to speak out on behalf of familism. But their active membership is small, and their influence is weak. In keeping with the high level of secularism, Swedes simply do not give the same credence to the statements and beliefs of religious leaders that people do, for example, in the United States. On moral and social questions, Swedes are much more inclined to give legitimacy to the views of social scientists and government experts (and to the findings of governmental investigatory commissions). Thus one of the traditional spokespersons for familism has, in Sweden, been all but silenced.

The antifamily effects of secularism show up especially in the declining Swedish marriage rate. In the opinion of many Swedes, the decline of religion is closely linked to the decline of formal marriage. There is no other major institution on the Swedish scene that, like religion, speaks out on behalf of the institution of marriage. Even for those marriages that still take place the religious aspect is diminishing; not only are fewer Swedes getting married today than in earlier decades, but of those who marry only about two thirds do so in a church, a decline from 92% in 1965.[23]

Because even those Swedes who get married tend not to be "believers," one presumes that in Sweden the effect of personal religious beliefs on commitment to the marital (or nonmarital) bond is also relatively weak. Such a relationship has been found in other nations: religiously inclined people tend to have more lasting marriages with a lower divorce rate.[24] The reasons for this are complex, but surely one would expect that a marriage involving a commitment made before and sanctified by God as a lifetime union would endure longer than one that did not have such supernatural attributes. In Sweden, any religious impulse as a part of the marriage commitment seems mostly gone.

Feminism

In their emergence from under the umbrella of patriarchy that has dominated societies throughout most of world history, Scandinavian women in certain respects seem to have been for many centuries in advance of women in the rest of the world. This has been attributed by historians to a variety of special circumstances, especially the fact that the hand of organized religion over life was not as strong in Scandinavia as elsewhere and that because of the nature of the economies men tended to be away from home alot, relinquishing some power to women by default.[25] Whatever the historical explanations, there can be no doubt that Swedish society and relative female equality have been synonymous, at least in the minds of foreign observers, for a very long time. As Swedish women will quickly tell you, however, Sweden is still far from the goal of female equality.

Lasting until well into this century, the leitmotiv of the women's movements in Sweden was not only political and legal equality for women, but also to some degree the social sanctity and integrity of the family. The family, after all, was the social world in which most women dwelled for most of their lives. For Ellen Key, for example, the most famous Swedish feminist writer at the turn of the century, "motherhood" was the highest ideal that women could achieve. She criticized those aspects of the women's movement in her time that focused solely on gaining for women the same occupational standing that men had, and she did not favor the facilitation of paid work for women outside the home. She also rejected public child care, partly on the grounds that "the State lacks nurturing qualities."[26] Instead, Key wanted to elevate the occupation of motherhood into a profession that would be recognized as an important public activity and would be suitably rewarded (as well as controlled) by society. Rather than taking women out of the home, she wanted to elevate the position of women within the home through social action. She envisioned a sort of matriarchy where motherhood would have the highest standing:

> Motherly qualities must be made socially important and the values they represent, emotion and love, must be brought to bear on social legislation and structure. If motherliness becomes a socially important value this would raise women's status and contribute to a more satisfying life for everyone.[27]

This attitude was not to prevail for very long among spokespersons for women in Sweden, as discussed in earlier chapters. Some Swedish writers today even wish to deny Key the label "feminist," preferring to think of her as merely a "socialist and social reformer."[28] The goal of achieving gender equality by elevating the status of women's maternal role was soon displaced by the goal of gender equalization, the equal sharing of all roles by men and women, especially outside the home in the occupational sector and in public life. This called for a thoroughgoing attack on the traditional patriarchal family. The particular values of home and family, which "women's culture" had long stood for, were thus pushed aside for what has been called competitive gender equality.[29] Competitive gender equality, or gender-role sameness, tended to be favored especially by middle-class women who led the feminist movement and often competed directly with men in the labor market.

The unusual thing about Sweden was not how ardently the goal of gender equalization was preached by feminists there, but how fully accepted this goal became by the ruling Social Democratic Party. As discussed in Chapter 7, in 1968 it was one of the main planks of the party's political platform, and, although no nation has yet come close to achieving gender equalization, it is fair to say that no other government in the West has pushed for this goal with more vigor and more success.[30] Sweden today has the Western world's highest percentage of married women in the labor market and probably the lowest percentage of full-time housewives.

It is only fair to point out, however, that most Swedish feminists have never been as single-mindedly devoted to the issue of equal rights for women in the labor force as their counterparts, for example, in the United States. On the contrary, the goal of Swedish feminists—at least as expressed in political policies—has largely been one of seeking ways to enable women to better combine work with home life. Policies to which many feminists have objected in the United States have long been a staple of Swedish life, such as pregnancy leaves. The feeling in the United States has been that such leaves reinforce the notion that women should be treated differentially and unequally. In Sweden, perhaps with more realism, the belief is that since children are born to women and not to men, a certain amount of differential treatment of women is called for. In other words, the ideal of "gender sameness" has never been quite so strong in Sweden as in the United States. While much of the female liberation movement in the United States was tied up in fighting to get an Equal Rights Amendment to the Constitution (it was apparently defeated essentially by women who continued to want differential treatment), the Swedish feminists were fighting for social benefits such as the parental-leave program that has given Sweden the world's most beneficent government-support policy for parents.[31]

Another indication that the Swedish women's movement has accepted women's dual roles is the importance of part-time work in Sweden. It is not that Swedish women favor part-time work in the abstract; on the contrary, many see it as detrimental to the advancement of women in the occupational sector (and the labor unions view it as detrimental to the development of trade unionism.) But they also consider it necessary under the present circumstances of women in modern societies, where most women do indeed have two roles. As a consequence, while Sweden has the highest percentage of mothers in the labor force, virtually all Swedish mothers are home for a period of some months following the birth of their children, thanks to the Swedish parental-leave program, and then most return to work only part-time until their children are older.

If the Swedish women's movement has been more "motherhood oriented" than the American in recognizing women's two roles, it has at the same time been more successful in reshaping its nation's culture along feminist lines. While the situation in the United States is rapidly changing in this direction, the ideal of a mother working outside the home has today all but unanimously been accepted by Swedes, and Sweden, more than any other Western nation, has become economically and socially geared to this reality. Indeed, Sweden has largely moved onto what might be regarded as the next phase of the women's liberation movement: changing the roles of men. To this end there have been nationwide propaganda campaigns to encourage men instead of women to take parental leave and insistent (but at this stage probably economically unrealistic) efforts on the part of Social Democratic women to bring about a 6-hour workday for both men and women, thus effectively doing away with part-time work.[32] The ultimate aim of such measures, of course, is gender equalization for both men and women, not only on the job but in the home. But in pursuit of that goal (and it is a long way from being achieved), the Swedes have become the envy of two-role women everywhere in the provision of parental leave, flexible working hours, and affordable day care.

From another perspective, several of these policy developments show that as a psychological, economic, and cultural reality gender-role equalization has progressed further in Sweden than it has in most other countries. It may be precisely this reality that has strained the Swedish marital relationship. A special "problem" for the Swedish marriage may be women's high expectations of gender equality, seemingly much higher than the average found in the United States. When these expectations come up against harsh reality—in this case the intransigence of men to change—the psychological difficulties in the relationship can escalate. Even though Swedish husbands probably do more around the home and in child care than most men elsewhere, they are a very long way indeed from the ideal of sharing 50% of the domestic work load. A recent study showed that the percentage of housework done by Swedish men doubled between 1974 and 1981, but was still only 22% for 19- to 34-year-old men without children, the category of men who made the greatest home contribution. The percentage dropped sharply when children were involved and differed very little between the homes of full-time housewives and those of women who worked part-time in the labor force.[33]

Another indication of the extent of gender-role equalization in Sweden can be found in the consequences of divorce. Women everywhere used to be the most-afflicted party in a marital breakup. Much of traditional divorce law, in fact, has been predicated on protecting the situation of the woman from an errant man. In Sweden today, however, the tide seems to have turned, and there is a growing belief among Swedish marriage counselors that men as much or even more than women (children aside) come out the loser in many marital breakups. The women no longer needs the man for economic support and, as noted above, is the one who typically initiates the breakup; she may also be the one who is most often dissatisfied with the marriage. But the man is thought to have the most to lose from a breakup—the domestic service of his wife, contact with children, and emotional support. There is a probably well-founded belief that after a breakup men find it more difficult to make friends and to set up a new home for themselves because of their lack of domestic skills. Also, there is some evidence that Swedish men fare worse than women in terms of physical and mental health.[34] This male "disadvantage" after a breakup is counterbalanced, however, by the fact that most women still end up with the care of children and men are more likely to find a new partner.

If many of the factors linking gender-role change with divorce in the United States also hold true for Sweden, and there is no reason to think that they do not, it is not hard to see why the Swedish marital-breakup rate is so high. The new economic and social self-sufficiency of women is often called the "independence effect," and nowhere is the independence effect more evident than in Sweden.

The Therapeutic Ideology

Sweden is probably the Western world's most caring society. It also comes closest to being what might be called a social-service worker's utopia. Much of the kind of care that was once provided only by the family has been rationalized—assumed by state employees who are specially trained professionals and can provide the care in an efficient manner and at a higher standard of quality. Discussed above was the way in which the welfare state may inadvertently have helped to generate marital breakup through the humanitarian policy of providing personal economic security. The focus of this section is on another inadvertent consequence of the welfare state. In connection with its pervasive care-giving role, the welfare state has fostered an ideology, or cultural attitude, that seems also to have indirectly contributed to marital breakup and family decline. This ideology has been called the therapeutic ideology or therapeutic attitude.[35]

The therapeutic ideology is a belief system that is promulgated especially by psychological therapists, social-welfare workers, social engineers, and social scientists as they pursue their various tasks of meeting (or, in the case of social scientists, analyzing) "human needs." In the words of Robert Bellah *et al.* in *Habits of the Heart*, a book that recently examined the therapeutic ideology in the United States, it is an ideology that

> proffers a normative order of life, with character ideals, images of the good life, and methods of attaining it. Yet it is an understanding of life generally hostile to older ideas of moral order. Its center is the autonomous individual, presumed able to choose the roles he will play and the commitments he will make, not on the basis of higher truths but according to the criterion of life-effectiveness as the individual judges it. . . . It enables the individual to think of commitments—from marriage and work to political and religious involvement—as enhancements of the sense of individual well-being rather than as moral imperatives.[36]

This ideology, then, emphasizes the importance of self-fulfillment, one expression of the supreme value placed in advanced societies on individual development and individual rights, and eschews traditional "moralistic" beliefs in human obligations and imperatives.

The term "therapeutic" arises from the fact that this ideology is supposedly characteristics of the therapeutic relationship between professional therapist and troubled client (a relationship sometimes said, with slight exaggeration, to be replacing the family in modern societies as a source of intimacy, psychic comfort, and the enhancement of self-worth). Yet the therapeutic ideology extends well beyond the therapist's couch into the society as a whole. It is not that everyone in Sweden and other advanced societies is in therapy or that therapists as individuals have that much influence in life. The therapeutic relationship is merely the prototype for an emerging form of human relationship in modern societies, and it is the prototype because it often expresses an ideology that many have come to believe.

For its moral justification, the therapeutic ideology draws on many different currents of contemporary philosophy and visions of the social order. Although one would expect to find the ideology more fully expressed in a secular welfare state than in any other form of society, its origins lie well beyond the confines of the welfare state and are part of the modernization of Western culture as a whole, especially in the decline of religion. As Philip Rieff has said in *The Triumph of the Therapeutic,* an early statement on this topic, "that a sense of well-being has become the end, rather than a by-product of striving after some superior communal end, announces a fundamental change of focus in the entire cast of our culture."[37]

While the therapeutic ideology derives its name from the therapeutic relationship, the modern therapeutic relationship in practice is a multifaceted process that expresses many different belief systems. To associate this one ideology with the process of therapy is therefore to do the latter a disservice. Nevertheless, this ideology has been commonly connected with many forms of therapy, and its meaning can be clarified by examining the ways in which it has been expressed through therapy.

The typical focus of the therapeutic relationship is the treatment of the self, rather than any larger social entity, such as a network or group. The goal is that each person, or self, should be (become through therapy) happy, secure, independent, and ultimately self-fulfilled or self-actualized. A common therapeutic answer to the question, why the client is not happy, secure, and self-fulfilled, is that in some way the group or society is at fault. Networks and groups in which the self is imbedded are seen as imposing external social obligations and commitments that interfere with self-fulfillment. This answer of "social blame" stems in part from the decades of social-science analysis whose overriding message has been that society's main interest is "social control" and that "you are what your environment makes you." This message of environmental or social determinism has been particularly strong in Sweden, where it has been largely accepted by the welfare state as a reason for changing society.

The message of social determinism often comes out to mean "you are a victim of unfortunate circumstances and therefore must try to either change or withdraw from the situation in which you find yourself." Using the therapeutic ideology, a therapist typically would not be inclined to put much "blame" on the client for his or her condition. To put it in crude but familiar language, this would be to "lay an unnecessary guilt trip" on the client; also, such a message is clearly not what the client is paying the therapist to hear. From a therapeutic point of view, on both counts, "blaming the victim" would be an unsatisfactory and fruitless position to take.

In such a therapeutic approach the marriage or family, as a principal group external to the individual, is typically viewed as making excessive demands on the self. The basis of modern marriage is a voluntary emotional relationship between two people. Looked at in individualistic terms, the purpose of the relationship is to provide each partner with psychic gratification and personal fulfillment. When strains arise in such a relationship, the outside therapist often tells the partners to try to achieve an open, fuller, and most honest level of communication. Such communication, after all, is what the marriage is all about. "In its pure form," according to Bellah et al., "the therapeutic attitude denies all forms of obligation and commitment in relationships, replacing them only with the ideal of full, open, honest communication." Thus, "the only requirement for the therapeutically liberated lover is to share his feelings fully with his partner."[38] If such attempts at deeper communication fail, the partners can easily feel (or be told) that they have the wrong mate—the wrong life circumstance. Under the logic of the therapeutic ideology it is then time to move on, to find self-fulfillment in some different environmental setting.

Again, this little description greatly simplifies and distorts the modern therapeutic relationship; the relationship between therapist and client is actually far more subtle and complex, and there are numerous exceptions to the therapeutic goal of open communication. The kernel of truth in the description becomes clear, however, when we look at the kinds of message that the therapist is *not* likely to give to the client with a marriage problem: "You made a commitment when you linked up with this person; now you must keep that commitment"; "You have a moral obligation to remain with this partner for the sake of your children." Certainly, in the days when advice came from one's parents, the clergy, the village elders, or meddlesome neighbors, such personal moral admonitions *were* the order of the day. Today these messages are in short supply, not only because the value of self-fulfillment has been raised to great prominence but because, in the nature of the new role relationships that people in modern societies hold, such moral admonitions are not appropriately given.

The therapeutic ideology is a one-sided ideology of individual fulfillment and social blame. Of course, who is to deny the importance of self-fulfillment and who is to say that an unfair social environment does not play an enormous role in shaping human lives? Yet the ideology is one-sided in that little is said about such values as personal obligation, moral responsibility, and self-sacrifice. It is not that these values in practice are totally absent in modern societies, only that the therapeutic ideology greatly deemphasizes them. There is always the danger, therefore, that societies dominated by this ideology can drift into excessive narcissism and self-indulgence and that the public interest can be compromised by rampant individualism. This danger has been aptly summarized by several American social scientists:

> When, finally, individual happiness becomes the criterion by which all things are measured, when the ability to withstand, strength of character, position in a community, the good of the group, exemplary and responsible adult behavior, and/or the welfare of one's children are all subjugated to individual happiness and "self-realization," then social arrangements weaken.[39]

There is no evidence that Sweden has become any more narcissistic or self-indulgent than any other Western society. In fact, little is written or heard in Sweden about the therapeutic ideology. Sweden even seems "retarded" in the development of psychotherapy; Freudianism came to Sweden rather late, and my guess is that there are many fewer psychotherapists per capita in Sweden than in the United States. It is no accident that the therapeutic ideology has received its most trenchant analysis with reference to the United States. It is there that the therapeutic ideology has come to dominate a large segment of the upper middle class, the nation's main cultural style setters.

But the prevalence of this ideology in Sweden is one additional factor that may help to account for the seeming casualness with which Swedes have come to view the marital bond and the act of marital dissolution. While the therapeutic ideology is certainly more visible in the United States, I believe that it is culturally more pervasive in Sweden than anywhere else. Because of the high degree of secularization, the widespread influence of the social sciences, the highly egalitarian-oriented political philosophy, and the extensive rationalization of human services, the ideology is not simply the intellectual plaything of the upper middle class but an important component, at least in a moderate form, of Swedish culture as a whole. Like the feminist ideology, noted above, the therapeutic ideology may not be so forcefully expressed in Sweden as elsewhere, but at the same time it seems to be more influential in the day-to-day lives of Swedes. Sweden may not have many therapists, but some version of the therapeutic ideology is regularly promulgated by the legion of government service workers in their daily activities and by the leading intellectuals in cultural debate.

The dissolution of marital and marriagelike relationships in Sweden is seldom discussed in moral terms, but is seen as some kind of psychological mismatch. This is in keeping with the tenets of the therapeutic ideology and the fact that these relationships have largely become defined as geared to psychic gratification and personal fulfillment. With the notions of personal commitment and social obligation so weakened by the therapeutic ideology, Swedes find difficulty in justifying the permanence of marital bonds on any basis other than personal preference. Few in Sweden are telling parents today, much less childless couples, to "stick it out, it is your social and moral duty." Yet such a moral message was a central part of the cultural matrix surrounding the Swedish family as recently as a generation ago. One obvious effect of the abandonment of this cultural message is that divorce in Sweden today carries much less of a "social stigma" than it once did.

Socialism

A final ideology to be considered, with implications for family decline, is socialism. The importance of socialist thought in Sweden has not been so great as many outsiders, especially Americans, believe. Nevertheless, Sweden is probably the most left-wing society in the West, and socialist views of the family have had enough prominence there to make them worthy of brief discussion.

At this stage of history it is impossible to delineate an "official" socialist or Marxist view of the family. Indeed, the official view of the family in most socialist Eastern European nations today is much closer to that of right-wing America than to anything found in Sweden. So in discussing socialist views of the family I am dealing mainly with certain views of Western Europeans of Marxist or neo-Marxist pursuasion. Within this group, I focus on what can be labeled a radical-socialist view of the family, which opposes not only the traditional patriarchal family, but family of any kind as a strong, independent institution, as well as familism as a cultural value. This is typically the view, for example, of those who call themselves Marxist feminists.

While not many Swedes actually hold the radical-socialist position on the family, it has had some influence in the Swedish family debate. Some of the impact of radical-socialist thought has come from the ruling Swedish Social Democratic Party. The Social Democrats began as a moderately revolutionary Marxist group, but early in this century came to favor democratic capitalism with a strong redistributional bent. Since 1968 they have pushed hard for egalitarian goals, but under an essentially capitalist banner (see Chapters 6 and 7). For much of the past few decades, however, the Social Democratic Party in Sweden has been able to govern (because it did not have a parliamentary majority) only with the help of that nation's small Communist Party; thus the Communist Party has been in a position to exert some political influence. Of greater importance in shaping Swedish culture and politics, however, has probably been the general influence of Marxist-leaning intel lectuals in the universities and the media.

The radical-socialist perspective on the family as an institution fully accepts the goal of gender equalization rather than gender "equality in difference." It vehemently opposes patriarchy, and any attempt to get women "back into the home." It speaks of the "tyranny of motherhood," something thrust on women to their great disadvantage not by biology but by society (women must give birth to children but they do not necessarily have to raise them).[40] Along these lines the Communist Party in Sweden is strongly opposed to paying women to be mothers-homemakers and calls for the eradication of family day-care centers (almost invariably run by women) in favor of public day-care and leisure-time centers for all children up to age 12. The services of these centers, according to the Communists, should be provided completely free of charge to the user and financed by higher taxes.[41]

Radical socialists regard the negative impact of the family as extending considerably beyond the oppression of women, however. In their view, the family has been the bulwark of capitalism and thus is one of the main instruments of class oppression in societies and one of the great perpetuators of social inequality. The family is seen as basically a class institution, one that gives each of us our class position. Through socialization, and through family inheritance (held to be one of the paramount sources of economic inequality), the inequalities of class position are passed on to children.

Even more than being a mere instrument of capitalist inequality, the family, say some radical socialists, infects capitalist culture as a whole; it promulgates all of those values for which capitalism is most despised. Insofar as each family "looks out for its own," for example, it "embodies the principles of selfishness, exclusion, and pursuit of private interest and contravenes those of altruism, community and pursuit of the public good."[42] In its emphasis on family self-help, self-support, and self-sufficiency, the family works against the ideal of collective responsibility. In seeking to be an enclosed and self-contained bastion of privacy, the family engages in wholesale assaults on the human rights of its members (especially women and children). In societies based on familism the family claims a monopoly on intimacy, radical socialists argue, and public life is governed by the assumption that all people will live in families. Yet in such societies the family "sucks the juice out of everything around it, leaving other institutions stunted and distorted."[43] "Caring, sharing and loving would be much more widespread if the family did not claim them for its own."[44]

Thus the achievement of socialism requires, from this perspective, the displacement of the family as "the sole and privileged provider of moral and material support [and the spreading] of these good things more widely through the community."[45] In one sense this means expanding whatever good there is in family life to encompass the community at large and at the same time doing away with what is "bad" in the family. To destroy capitalism, and all it stands for, one must therefore largely destroy the family, or at least the family as it has existed throughout history. To reach the radical-socialist ideal it is necessary to: eliminate marriage ("which provides the major legal support for the current family form"); prohibit the inheritance of family wealth by children; resist the attractions of private, domestic life (it detracts from public life); reduce the pressures (especially economic) that compel people to live in families; and develop alternatives to the family (such as communes) that can provide psychic security and material support.

Again, I am not suggesting that such vehemently antifamily views are actually held by many Swedes; Scandinavians have never been noted for extremism. These views are in fact seldom stated in Sweden in this extreme form, and it is difficult to say precisely how much influence they have had in the Swedish cultural debate. But it is likely that this antifamily ideological position is entertained more seriously in Sweden than in many other Western societies. The average Swede would probably find more truth in this ideology than the average American, for example, or the average Swiss, to whom these views are alien. And in a nation like Japan, perhaps the most familistic of all advanced societies, these views might be simply inexplicable.

It is of interest to note that the radical-socialist position on the family was widely promulgated in the first few years after the Russian Revolution, but today in Russia and the Eastern European countries the family as an institution has officially regained much of its lost importance.[46] Beginning in the 1930s, the family came to be seen in the Soviet Union not as antithethical to socialist development, but as an institution whose stability and well-being are extremely important for both individuals and society.[47] In the early 1960s, two American family-relations experts found in the Soviet Union what they regarded as almost optimum conditions for family life, certainly conditions superior to those found in the West.[48] If anything, the Soviet Union today is more traditional than Sweden on the gender-role question, and the kinds of moralistic statements about the importance of the family made by Soviet representatives are seldom heard in Sweden; they are even reminiscent of the pronouncements of America's New Right.[49] Ideology about the family must be distinguished from family behavior, however; there is some evidence that the actual decline of the family in recent years may even be greater in the Soviet Union than in Sweden.[50]

For the present analysis, the importance of the radical-socialist ideology about the family is that it directly opposes the ideology of familism. As discussed in the preceding chapter, familism has few outspoken advocates in Sweden today. The extent to which a radical-socialist impulse has helped to suppress familistic thought is unclear. But the underlying assumptions of the radical-socialist view, at least, are congruent with the decline of marriage as an institution in Sweden and perhaps also with the seeming lack of concern among Swedes over the high marital-dissolution rate.

The Logic of the Welfare State

We are now in a position to discuss more directly answers to the question that may be uppermost in the minds of many readers of this book, especially American readers. What is the role of the Swedish welfare state in fostering family decline? The Swedish welfare state has pushed more successfully than most nations, as noted above, for economic security and changing gender roles and has been more strongly influenced by secular, feminist, therapeutic, and socialist ideologies. There is one additional dimension: the underlying "logic" of the welfare state as an institution in its own right and its conflict with the family as an institution. By the welfare state's logic I mean the fundamental purposes and processes of the egalitarian and welfare-oriented bureaucracy of which the welfare state consists. In what way does the inherent character of the welfare state, by its very existence, help to undermine family values or familism—the belief in a strong sense of family identification and loyalty, mutual assistance among family members, and a concern for the perpetuation of the family unit?

We have noted that because of the rationalization of economic support and care-giving activities, the Swedish welfare state has probably made Sweden the world's most caring society, at least insofar as government activity in welfare is the prime consideration. One sees in Sweden today a truly massive expansion of welfare services of all kinds compared to what existed in earlier times. Furthermore, whereas the care given previously by families was subject to the vicissitudes of birth—some people were given superb care and others were given none at all—the care provided by the Swedish welfare state is made available to all on the basis of need, a system that seems eminently more fair. What state care may lack in terms of the "personal touch" is partly counterbalanced by the professionalism and inherent social justice that are provided by a state-controlled welfare system. For anyone who knows the degree of suffering found, for example, in the American underclass, to say nothing of the people of Third World nations, the Swedish system seems like an unmixed political blessing from on high.

There are few unmixed political blessings in this world, however. As is well known, every political course of action has social costs as well as social benefits, negative consequences as well as social gains. Political wisdom leads to striking the best balance among competing and often contradictory factors. What we today call the welfare state, often using Sweden as the prototype, has long been the subject of such a political cost-benefit analysis by critical observers. For many Americans, the conclusion of such an analysis is that the welfare state is seriously found wanting. These Americans focus on what is believed to be its high fiscal cost, its curtailment of personal freedom, and its interference with the market economy. In balance, they lean politically toward the so-called free-market society, despite the inherent inegalitarianism of the market in the delivery of social welfare.

That I do not fully share this political assessment of the Swedish welfare state has little relevance for the discussion here, except that I hope it puts in better perspective my highlighting of the often adverse impact of the welfare state on the institution of the family. Though in some ways it may look like a battle between the welfare state and the family, with the welfare state usually winning, I am not at all certain that in many respects, even if the family is the loser, Swedes in general do not come out the winner. I am at this point only suggesting ways in which the very existence of the welfare state compromises the institution of the family, and not making any kind of political, much less moral, judgment of the outcome.

It is difficult to pin down precisely what is meant by the term "welfare state." Historically, social welfare was first provided by families and house-holds, later assisted by the distribution of goods and services through markets, and finally helped by actions of the state. In every advanced society today these three units—family, market, and state—have a continuing importance, and it is the particular mix of the three that varies.[51] In every advanced society the state has accepted the goals of social welfare and increasingly taken on welfare activities, but we give the label "welfare state" only to those societies in which the state has a relatively large welfare role. The pursuit of social welfare in such a society has fallen heavily under the aegis of a large-scale, public bureaucracy run by professionals and supported by taxes.

What is called the logic of welfare states, then, is the logic (underlying purposes and processes) of state-welfare bureauracies with egalitarian goals.[52] The point to be emphasized here is that, like most other large institutions, welfare-state bureaucracies once established assume a life of their own. Irrespective of the goals for which they may originally have been set up, institutions over time tend to become self-protective and very concerned with their own preservation and growth. As part of their own inner logic, they develop a distinctive philosophy and set of goals often apart from the goals for whose achievement they were established.

When an institution's underlying logic carries it too far in a self-protective direction, the result may be not that institution's preservation and growth but its impairment. This has been a common occurrence historically as industries have become overbureaucratized, organized religions overcentralized, and national empires overextended, leading to impairment and in somes cases demise. So it may be with welfare states. The Swedish welfare state began with the goal of helping families to function better (see Chapter 6), in recognition of the fact that society very much depends on the family for a major portion of the total output of human care, but that the family had grown weaker and the social environment in which families existed was changing. The very acceleration of welfare-state power weakened the family still further, however, thus placing an even greater welfare burden on the state and hastening a "welfare-state crisis." The same phenomenon can be expressed in terms of "cultural contradictions," contradictory elements in an institution's culture. The effect of welfare states on the family may thus be viewed as a "cultural contradiction": while assisting families in pursuit of the goal of social welfare, actions of the welfare state unwittingly helped to undermine the achievement of that very goal.

The term "cultural contradiction" was given prominence by Daniel Bell, who described the cultural contradictions of capitalism.[53] Bell's thesis, a persuasive one, is that capitalism depends on people who work hard and have a strong will to achieve, save and invest their money, and honestly uphold their contracts. Yet at the same time capitalism requires avid consumers, and this is the message incessantly pushed by capitalist advertising—not hard work but pleasurable consumption. This message may have led to higher levels of consumption, but it also has promoted a populace oriented toward personal/pleasure, self-expression, and spontaneity. The new consumer orientation, in turn, has undermined the drive to work, save, and produce on which the continuing success of capitalism depends.

This line of reasoning has been extended to the way in which capitalism has undermined the family. By no means does the welfare state stand alone in modern society as an antifamily agency. One of the first to see the possible damage that capitalism by its very success could do to the family was Joseph Schumpeter. Schumpeter was impressed at the way in which the ethos of the traditional nuclear family was closely allied to the growth of capitalism; adults who would work hard and save for the future of their children made the ideal capitalist entrepreneurs. Yet eventually material success and the growth of hedonism would dent these values, and individuals making rational calculations of their own personal gains would come to ignore the nonmonetary values of family life.[54] This would eventually lead, according to Schumpeter, not only to the decline of the family but the decline of capitalism as well.

A variation of this perspective sees family decline as helping capitalism. As the American social welfare expert Neil Gilbert has pointed out:

> The decline of traditional family life is accompanied by increases in both market demands for goods and services and the labor force necessary to produce for these markets. . . . Single-parent families and detached individuals multiply the demands for shelter, household goods, and an array of out-of-home services including laundry, meals, day care and entertainment.[55]

Thus capitalism may not only cause family decline, but also benefit from it.

Our interest here, however, is on the family impact not of capitalism but of the welfare state. We discuss it in terms of effects on the family of the welfare state's pursuit of three broad social goals: the delivery of professional-quality care, economic equality, and social efficiency. One social goal that welfare states do not consciously seek to achieve is a weakened family. Whatever has happened to the family as a result of welfare-state activities, therefore, seems largely an undesired and unintended consequence of these activities and not an intended outcome. The general disposition of the welfare state with regard to the family has been aptly described by Neil Gilbert as "a confused mix of humanitarian sentiments and the egalitarian aspirations of collectivism."[56]

Professional Care

Perhaps the main goal of the welfare state is the delivery of professional-quality care and security to those in need, and much of its bureaucracy is set up with this in mind. The care that most families have been able to provide has been notoriously poor; if its quality had been high, there would have been no need for the welfare state in the first place. This situation has required the provision of care by trained professionals who are not family

members, which in turn has led to the state's takeover of many care-giving
activities formerly provided by the family (as well as to the addition of care
that the family is simply not able to provide at the requisite level of quality.)[57]

Yet the welfare state can never provide all the needed care in a society;
if for no other reason, then because such public care would simply be too
expensive. The welfare state, therefore, strongly relies on continuing care
giving by family members, especially the personalized informal care that
cannot adequately be given by professionals. The welfare state depends
heavily on families that take care of their own, do not make unnecessary
demands on the public purse, and recognize their duties as well as their
rights and responsibilities.

Unfortunately, once the welfare state is fully established it becomes all
too easy for family members to believe that most care is best provided, and
should be provided, by government professionals: they are trained to give it,
they know best, and "that's what we are paying our taxes for." People, after all,
have much to do in life besides giving care to others. From one perspective,
families in the welfare state are penalized when they provide their own
care because they forgo the benefits of public care, and they are rewarded
with public care when they stop providing their own care. Neil Gilbert has
called this the "helping-hand dilemma."[58] At worst, this dilemma can lead to
"welfare dependency" and skyrocketing welfare costs, a problem associated
with the underclass in a nation like the United States but potentially a more
widespread problem in a welfare state.[59] In the words of the Danish welfare
official Bent Rold Andersen:

> The rationally founded welfare state has a built-in contradiction: if it is to fulfill
> its intended function, its citizens must refrain from exploiting to the fullest its
> services and provisions—that is, they must behave *irrationally*, motivated by
> informal social controls, which, however, tend to disappear as the welfare system
> grows.[60]

It is not clear to what extent the Swedish family has thus been weakened
as a care-giving institution; the fragmentary empirical data that are available
were presented in the preceding chapter.[61] In evaluating the data one should
bear in mind that much of the care supposedly "taken" from the family has
in reality been gratefully given up by the family, such as education, medical
care, and the care of the elderly. Education and medical care are activities
for which families clearly do not possess the necessary expertise. Also, when
judging the effects of the welfare state on the family as an institution it is
important to remember that individual family members are not necessarily
worse off as a result of state-welfare programs; most are undoubtedly better
off, especially in those families that provided welfare inadequately to begin
with. In addition, Sweden has enacted many programs that actually support,
rather than replace, the family, programs such as temporary professional

home help, parental leave, and child support payments. But it is likely that, in its undermining of family care giving, the logic of the welfare state has been more insistent in Sweden than in most other societies of the West. This may simply be due to the Swedish welfare state's magnitude.

One area in which indirect evidence for family undermining is strong is the voluntary sector of Swedish society. There remain in Sweden today few voluntary associations devoted to care giving, their functions having been taken over almost entirely by the public sector. Volunteerism and popular welfare movements in Sweden, extending well back into the past century, seem on the verge of being all but snuffed out. Volunteerism at the local level in care giving has always been an extension of family care giving, and Western societies with a strong voluntary sector have had at the same time relatively strong families. It therefore seems reasonable to conclude that the drying up of volunteerism is associated among other things with a decline of family care. The decline of volunteerism, of course, is caused not only by the rise of the welfare state but also by the massive movement of women into the labor force.

A popular theory has asserted that because so many difficult, time-consuming, and expensive care-giving activities formerly provided by families are now provided by the state, there has been an actual improvement in those informal care-giving activities that only the family can provide. Family members, according to this theory, have more time and energy for the informal, personalized care that only they are able to give (and persons who might have been active in voluntary associations can give more time to their own families). In view of what has been happening to the family in Sweden, however, the validity of this theory must be called into question. Many Swedish and other Scandinavian experts on welfare are coming to believe that it may not be so true as once was thought.[62] A main reason is that in order to pay the high taxes necessary for state care, yet still have money left over for their own consumption needs, family members (especially, of course, women) move increasingly into the labor market; this then leaves them with less time to provide informal care. Moreover, high taxes increase the incentive for each family to seek to get all the care that it can, at least its "fair share," from the public sector.

Economic Equality

Another unintended consequence of the welfare state on familism stems from the pursuit of economic equality. The care traditionally provided by families is not only unprofessional, but also inegalitarian in its distribution. One need not be a socialist to see that the family has always been an obstacle to the achievement of economic equality; more affluent families have tended to perpetuate, by favoring their own, the gross inequalities of material wealth that have marked (and still mark) human existence.

In the absence of strong states, families historically have had tremendous and sometimes absolute political power. Every egalitarian-oriented state has sought to minimize the political power of wealthier families, as well as their power over the distribution of economic rewards. This has been done by hiring people on the basis of merit rather than family connection, by progressive income taxation, and by the provision of goods and services outside of the market economy. Sweden has moved in this direction probably farther than any other government in the West. Yet there are still many relatively rich families in Sweden, and Swedish children can still inherit wealth from their parents (although inheritance taxes are very steep, which has led some wealthy Swedes to leave the country.)

In pursuing the goal of economic equality, however, welfare states do not think mainly in terms of family equalization; they tend to think in terms of the equalization of income among individuals. This point of view stems from the nature of bureaucracies, which find it most efficient to treat the individual as the prime benefit unit. After all, families are endlessly fluctuating entities, whereas individuals are not; furthermore, not everyone lives with or even is part of a family anymore. In Sweden it is not families but individuals that have a national identification number, a number that is absolutely basic in the scheme of bureaucratic efficiency and control.

In pursuit of the goal of equality, therefore, the implicit "pact" in the welfare state between the individual and the bureaucracy can cause the family unit to be overlooked. As was discussed earlier in this chapter, there is good reason to believe that the provision of economic security to individual family members, rather than to the family unit, has helped to create an "independence effect" that can accelerate marital dissolution. A clear instance of shifting from a family orientation to an individual orientation in social policy was Sweden's decision in the early 1970s to disallow the taxation of joint family incomes in favor of the separate taxation of the income of each partner. This tax change was in pursuit of an egalitarian goal: the advancement of women in the job market and the liberation of women from the traditional situation of economic dependence on their husbands. Other welfare-state policies, also bypassing the family unit, have been directed toward the elderly, youth, and even children.

Even the value of equality, when accentuated to the degree found in a welfare state, may conflict with other values that necessarily govern the lives of members of strong families. Unlike gender inequality, the inequality that exists between parents and children is intrinsic to the nature of families. Every family with children consists of a social hierarchy sharply divided between adults and children; within the family unit, there is no social equality in the societal sense. Compared to children, adults have a grossly unequal position with regard to power, prestige, wealth, knowledge, and skills. The family, in the words of one Marxist scholar, "remains based on notions of gender, age and authority that are by definition unequal."[63] This has presented a problem for egalitarians; it is easy for them to view the family as a kind of undemocratic tyranny, which sets a bad example for the society as a whole.

The conflict of values between the family and the egalitarian state extends even further than the issue of hierarchy. The ideal of bureaucratic egalitarianism is to "treat everyone the same way." The goal of the family, however, is to treat its members as different from those outside the family. Favoritism is a fundamental family value; strong families tend to favor their members at all costs. It is said that a good family is a place where members can get "unconditional acceptance" and that successful children need from their families "unwarranted love." Robert Frost once said that "home is the place where, when you have to go there, they have to take you in." These all speak to a kind of inegalitarian favoritism on the part of the family that appears unseemly in a highly accomplished, egalitarian welfare state. One suspects that in such a society the family value of favoritism becomes somewhat less compelling and even a little suspect.

For Sweden, as political scientists Hugh Heclo and Henrik Madsen have pointed out, a familiar refrain in child rearing is "You are no better than anyone else."[64] The origin of the values expressed by this simple refrain may lie well back in Swedish history, but it nevertheless illustrates the kind of group-oriented egalitarianism that is favored by a welfare state; one might call it a "social leveling."[65] It runs counter to the value of favoritism that strong families tend to promote. In societies where familism is stronger, the counterpart to the Swedish refrain is more likely to be "You are as good as anyone else."[66] This is directed more at raising than at leveling the individual and expresses the value of family loyalty and solidarity.

A final issue to be considered under the goal of social equality is what Neil Gilbert has called the "egalitarian dilemma."[67] The primacy of egalitarian considerations hampers a government's ability to speak for and promote those family values and arrangements that are socially preferable. As one Swedish informant told me, "you can't any longer speak in Sweden about nuclear families being 'good' because there are now many single parents, and you don't want to make them feel bad." In other words, the government cannot show political favoritism toward the stable, nuclear family, because this would be to treat invidiously and even stigmatize families of a different composition. The government cannot reward families that stay together, because this would be regarded as unfair to families that break up. Thus on behalf of equality, the welfare state becomes moot on a range of traditional moral issues.

Social Efficiency

Alongside egalitarianism, in a strong welfare state the goal of social efficiency becomes a paramount consideration. Why should all societal matters not be dealt with in the most efficient manner possible? After all, the taxpayers' hard-earned money is involved. Efficiency considerations in both the public and the private sectors, as we know from experience, typically lead to certain definite social changes. Smaller units are increased in size so as to achieve the necessary economies of scale. Generalized units become more specialized, with their tasks more limited and focused. And decentralized power and authority become centralized.

Such efficiency inclinations tend to cast the family in a relatively disadvantageous light and can lead to policies that inadvertently may help to undermine it. The family is a small, relatively unspecialized, general-purpose group. Such characteristics, from an efficiency point of view, create some waste or misdirection of human and material resources. We have seen that the family is in many ways an inefficient deliverer of care, for example, and from this standpoint it is regarded by the welfare bureaucracy as something to be modified and supplemented.

Yet it is not just that families fail to provide for their members' special needs; the inefficiency of the family can be seen to extend to its normal, day-to-day activities. Take the family activity of cooking. Does it make any sense from an efficiency point of view for a single street to contain multiple households, each of which at dinnertime has one or more persons preparing a meal for just a few others? It would be more efficient to combine the cooking activities of these households, since not much more time is needed to cook for a dozen than to cook for one. Think of the social time that could be saved. Such a vision has led utopians for centuries to put forth the common mess hall as a substitute for the private kitchen. This vision has not been seriously taken up by the Swedish welfare state, but it is frequently raised in contemporary Sweden and vividly illustrates the efficiency mode of thinking about the family.

Other aspects of the family, when viewed from an efficiency perspective, have generated a greater demand for change. One example is child rearing or socialization. First, most parents are inadequately trained for such an important activity, and some are not trained at all. In fact, some are totally inappropriate for the task. Morever, does it make sense for one or two parents to devote so much time to just one or two children, when much time could be saved, as in meal preparation, by consolidating the activity with others? Enter the logic of the welfare state. The logic of the efficient state dictates that children be raised collectively by persons who are especially trained for that purpose. This approach was followed in the early years of the Israeli kibbutzim and is still to some extent practiced in many today. The day-care centers promoted by the Swedish state are a pale substitute for such collective child rearing, but in terms of efficiency they are a step in that direction.

Collective child rearing is not the only device proffered by the state to improve social efficiency in socialization. Generations ago public schools were introduced to provide children with information and knowledge that most parents were unable to provide in the family. Attendance at such schools has long been compulsory. A more recent innovation of the state has been the mass provision of experts to advise families about child rearing, such as pediatricians and psychologists who had long been retained privately by affluent families.

None of these welfare state activities could be said to have seriously undermined the family in its socialization function. More likely, the efficient provision of education, day care, and expert advice by agencies outside the family has in many ways improved the overall quality of child rearing. Yet it is important to realize that such services are in keeping with the welfare state's goal of social efficiency and based on the belief, whether true or not, that the family as an institution is inadequate for the task. With such a perspective there is always the danger that "assistance to" the family will become "replacement of" the family; this shift has already taken place to a large extent in education and is beginning to occur in child care.[68] This danger brings, in turn, the fear expressed by some Swedes that the state, for reasons of efficiency and equality, will gradually claim a monopoly over child rearing and professional advice giving, just as the Swedish state today largely has a monopoly over formal education. Perhaps the Swedish government's current prohibition of public subsidies to private day-care centers could be regarded as a tendency in this direction.

Even the state's well-intentioned goal of improving the efficiency of the city can, indirectly and over the long run, weaken the family. Sweden's cities are probably the world's best planned from a technical standpoint: public facilities are located where they should be, transportation runs smoothly, there is abundant open space, and the people are well housed.[69] Without meaning to detract from this grand achievement, it must be noted that the one main flaw in Swedish physical planning is that it probably has had some negative impact on people's informal social networks.

As an extension of the care family members give to one another, the care given by informal networks of relatives, friends, and neighbors is an extremely important alternative to state care in most societies. In every modern society such informal care has declined as social networks have diminished in importance and in size; again, however, Sweden may be the

Western world's leader in this decline.[70] A comparison of crime in Sweden and Switzerland concluded that Swedish neighborhood social control was relatively weak.[71] Another study comparing mothers of young children in the United States and Sweden concluded (based on a small sample) that

> Swedish mothers are further removed geographically from their network contacts than are mothers in the U.S. and . . . U.S. mothers are much more involved with extended kin, and they interact more with their neighbors, especially around practical matters like borrowing and building repairs.[72]

Comparative studies of this social phenomenon are few, but the general impression of most foreign observers, as noted in the preceding chapter, is that urban neighboring and local "community attachment" are particularly weak in Sweden.

Among the many reasons for the decline of localized social networks in modern societies is the way in which urban areas are physically laid out. Based on considerations of overall urban efficiency, the centralized urban planning of welfare states has not been immune from negative impacts on the intimate concerns of urban dwellers. The classic example in Sweden was the planning and building in the 1960s and early 1970s of extensive high-rise housing in Swedish cities and towns. Intended to end the housing shortage quickly and with the least expense, which it did, this housing has since proved relatively undesirable when examined from the fine-grain perspective of the daily lives of urban dwellers. People living there feel relatively lonely and isolated, and Swedes have come to shun high rises if at all possible, leaving them for recent foreign immigrants.[73] Here again, then, is a situation in which the efficiency goal of the welfare state can lead to unanticipated and undesired consequences.

The final example of a way in which the welfare state's efficiency concerns can help to undermine the family is in the arena of political decision making. The input of most families on political decision making is necessarily at the local level. The family is not the kind of institution that can collectively organize itself very successfully as a special interest group on a national scale. Typically, those nations that are the most decentralized politically give families the most political power. Mainly because of its pursuit of equality and efficiency, the welfare state is necessarily a centralized political system. Whatever the overall political assessment may be, such centralization generally works to the detriment of the family as an institution. In contemporary Sweden local governments are heavily involved in the delivery of welfare services, but decision making largely takes place at the national level, hence effectively outside the control of families.[74]

National Character

There remains one final component whose discussion completes this
search for explanations of Swedish family decline. National character—the
psychological characteristics of a nationality group—is something that receives almost as much attention from the average person as it receives inat-
tention from social scientists. Many who travel to foreign lands become instant experts on national character. Yet it is a treacherous concept to analyze
objectively, and most sociologists and psychologists have not considered it
a viable subject for study. Some contend that there is no such a thing as national character, only national stereotypes—oversimplified, hackneyed, and
usually inaccurate opinions held uncritically by outsiders.[75]

The nagging question remains, however: might there not be something
special about their national character that has led Swedes to have such a
"relaxed" family situation? After all, Swedes and Swedishness have long had
a particular image abroad, part of which involves some seemingly unique
psychological and social attributes. There is the morose and depressed
Swede of Ingmar Bergman movies, the bizarre behavior of Greta Garbo in
her maturity, the "casual life-style" of Ingrid Bergman well in advance of
what was to become an international trend, the "dumb Swede" of American
immigrant fame, and more recently the reticence and reserve of the legion
of Swedish tennis players. Is there some common denominator in all of this,
some psychological peculiarity that could affect Swedish family behavior?

The difficulties of analyzing national character cannot be overestimated.
National character is almost impossible to measure. Even if it could be
measured, there would be tremendous dispersion around the mean, that
is, dozens or hundreds of exceptions to any given character trait. Within
every society psychological character varies considerably not only among
individuals, but by such social categories as age, gender, class, and region.
The concept of national character is particularly difficult to pin down in a
heterogeneous society like the United States, where the dispersion is great
simply due to the diverse makeup of the population. It is easier in a nation like
Japan, where a homogeneous population has lived virtually untouched for
centuries. Sweden is more like Japan, and in fact Swedish national character
has been regarded as in some respects similar to that of Japan (although the
family situation in the two countries is vastly different).[76]

In recent years, the serious study of Swedish national character has
been taken up by some Swedes and some foreigners living permanently
in Sweden.[77] I discuss here only those aspects of Swedish national character
on which some agreement has arisen among these scholars and which at the
same time seem possibly related to the Swedish marital relationship and the
situation of the family in Sweden.[78] The character traits on which I focus are

the desire or need for independence and personal privacy, the psychological tendency toward social reserve and an avoidance of conflict, and a frame of mind that can be called social rationality. Each of these traits, of course, must be seen not from an absolute but from a comparative, cross-national perspective; that is, Swedes seem to have these traits to a stronger degree than do people in most other advanced societies.

Independence

The Swedish desire for independence and personal privacy is perhaps best summarized by the famous statement attributed to Greta Garbo, "I want to be alone." This was more than a mere statement. After becoming one of the most famous women in the world, she completely dropped from public view and has remained virtually invisible to the public for decades.

A broad-based instance of the desire for independence and privacy is the Swedes' love of summer cottages in remote areas. A surprisingly large number of Swedes find their way each summer to the deep boondocks, where they live in primitive cabins away from everyone else except perhaps a few close family members. They have little intention of making the cabins less primitive or more accessible; the whole point of the cabin is to get away from civilization and other people, away from the duties and obligations of social life, to be alone with nature. Those who do not have such a cabin (and many who do) may be found in a lonely boat somewhere out on one of the numerous lakes or archipelagos that adorn the Swedish countryside. Communing alone with nature in this fashion is a national Swedish cultural ideal.[79] The Swedish ethnographer Åke Daun has pointed out that much of Swedish poetry is an expression of this need for independence through nature.

Beginning in early childhood, Swedish children are taught independence from parental supervision and encouraged to be on their own, being given perhaps more such independence at an earlier age than the young of any other society. As they grow older, Swedes do not want to be unnecessarily indebted to or dependent on one another and like to "settle up accounts" as fast as possible. The sense of independence is particularly strong among young adults. In what Americans find quite strange, for example, few Swedish university students ever desire to have or are given roommates in their dormitories. They prefer to live alone, and often cannot understand how American students can move in with "a stranger."

There is a sharper separation in Sweden than in the United States between people's public and private lives. Knowing someone well in a public capacity, such as a fellow worker, in no way entitles one to relate to that person privately, unless expressly invited to extend the relationship. Many American visitors are surprised at this; they get to know Swedes well on the job, for example, but are never invited into their homes. In general, the private lives of Swedes are protected from the social intrusion of others more than in the United States. Teachers and counselors in the schools are reluctant to inquire about a child's family situation, even though that information may be of great educational importance, for fear of invading the right to privacy. Spontaneous visiting among neighbors, at least in metropolitan areas, is not as common as in the United States. It is more difficult to find out, and one does not ask, about the private lives of government officials. When running for office, the family situation of public officials is not exposed to public view the way it is in the United States.

It is important to realize that this kind of independence and privacy in interpersonal relationships is not the same thing as the kind of individualism that leads people to want to be independent from *society*. One seldom finds in Sweden the person who rejects society and social contact in order to be "his own man," classic examples being the American frontiersman or cowboy and today's loners and "mountain men." Sweden is also not the locale for idiosyncratic individualists who have such a strong independent streak that they are iconoclastic and oppose social conventions. Nor can many libertarians or anarchists be found in Sweden, people who wish that the government would not only leave them alone but quietly fade away.

Far from being individualistic in any of these senses, Swedes are highly socialized beings living in what many foreigners find to be a notably conformist society; in this sense they are somewhat like the Japanese. Sweden is a society with strong guidance and direction from the top, and the Swedish trait of independence must be viewed within the conformity-oriented framework of norms, authority systems, and social control that make up such a society. Indeed, one theory holds that independence is a reaction to a highly conformist society; because they must live in such a society in their public lives, Swedes have a deeper need for independence in their private lives. From another perspective, it could be said that it is precisely because Swedish society is so close-knit and well integrated that Swedes psychologically are able to have a great deal of independence and privacy in their private lives. Although living apart from others, they are still fully encompassed by a stable set of social structures. Americans, in contrast, live in a society that is less well integrated, hence have greater need to "cling to others" and are outwardly more sociable in their private lives. As two political scientists recently put it, with some exaggeration, "just as American individualism creates a land of the gregarious, so Swedish communitarianism creates a land of the truly solitary."[80]

Does this need for independence not have some relationship to the high propensity of Swedes to divorce and to live alone? To my knowledge the issue has never been the subject of investigation, but it seems likely that there might be a relationship, especially when combined with the next trait to be considered, social reserve. A strong need for independence in one's private life might limit the propensity of Swedish marital and marriagelike relationships to persevere, especially when affection and companionship are the only bases of these relationships. After all, if Swedes find it difficult to have a roommate in college, why should they not also find it difficult to have a roommate for life?

Social Reserve

Going well back into history, virtually every foreign observer has commented about the social reserve found among Swedes. It is important to keep in mind that this national character trait applies especially to Swedish men. Swedish women, by contrast, seem less reserved, more outgoing in some respects, and even more assertive than the women in many other societies. The term "social reserve" is used here broadly to mean self-restrained, not socially outgoing or self-assertive, not spontaneous, seldom loud or boisterous (except when drunk), and reluctant to express emotions in public. Related concepts, although more negative in tone, are passive, shy, and emotionally aloof. Swedish men and women are less demonstrative in their emotional expression in public, and probably also in private, than are people, for example, in Latin cultures. They do not touch, hug, kiss, or hold hands as much; they do not even change their facial expressions as much, and they keep their voices low.

It may be this social reserve that makes Swedes seem reluctant to interact with strangers. There are few "cocktail parties" in Sweden; it is difficult for Swedes to be in a social setting where one is forced to put oneself forward and continually interact with strangers. Many foreigners have pointed out that Swedes are very reserved as neighbors in urban settings, much more than the neighbors in urban settings from which the foreigners have come. Swedes in urban settings seem rather reluctant even to neighbor with one another, compared for example, to Americans. In public gatherings, such as an evening meeting of parents in a school, Swedes also show great social reserve toward those they do not know. Scandinavians tell an old joke about what happens when Swedes, Norwegians, and Danes are stranded together on a desert island: the Danes form a cooperative, the Norwegians start a fight, and the Swedes wait to be introduced!

In public life, the trait of social reserve may be associated with what appears to outsiders to be an aversion to social conflict. Like Japan, Sweden is somewhat a "shame society" where the good opinion of others is so important that Swedes are unwilling to take many social risks. In private conversation Swedes tend to avoid bringing up sensitive issues and seek to move as quickly as possible to areas of consensus. Swedish students are reluctant to ask questions in class, especially tough questions that challenge the professor. Swedes are reluctant to take unpopular stands in public, and Swedish political debate is about as mild, with voices seldom raised, as anywhere in the world; Swedes are dissatisfied with a political decision if, after lengthy consideration, strong areas of disagreement still prevail. Thus there seems to exist in Sweden a pervasive aversion to contentiousness and a constant striving for agreement.

How this trait might be reflected in Swedish marriages is of course highly speculative. Perhaps Swedish women do not get enough "show of feeling" from Swedish men. That at least is a common complaint of Swedish women who have marital difficulties. This, however, is a common complaint of married women the world over. Still, in Sweden male social reserve may have special prominence as a problem not only because Swedish males are notably more reserved than males elsewhere, but also because many of the "environmental" problems faced by married couples in other nations are minimized in Sweden and the marriage relationship is based on affect alone.

It is also easy to speculate about how the associated psychological pattern of conflict avoidance could become a threat to the marital relationship. The most logical assumption might be that conflict-avoidance behavior would improve marital relationships. Yet every close marital and parental relationship has some interpersonal conflict, and marriage counselors are continually telling their clients that conflict must be dealt with, not avoided. On this basis, it is likely that successful marriages involve a certain amount of "fighting" between the partners so that conflict is faced up to and in the end worked out. To achieve a successful marriage, the worst thing may be to let the normal conflicts of marital life lie hidden, festering, unresolved, and avoided, in the belief that to overlook conflict is to make it go away.

Of course the best way to avoid interpersonal conflict entirely is to live alone. Could this be a reason for Sweden's special propensity for single-person households?

Social Rationality

With a few notable exceptions, Swedes have never been known as idealistic philosophers, theorists, poets, or romantics. Among the peoples of the advanced societies, they rank as perhaps the most practical and down-to-earth. The question they ask is the pragmatic one—does it work? It has often been said that the quintessential Swede is an engineer, one who takes the world as he or she finds it and tries to make it a little better. As we have seen in earlier chapters, this engineering bent has been applied in Sweden not only to the physical world but also to the social world. In the 1930s Marquis Childs said that the Swedes "are the ultimate pragmatists, interested only in the workability of the social order."[81] Following the lead of the social sciences, Swedes have a strong sense that they can engineer society to a state of high perfection. Thus contemporary Sweden, probably more than any other world society, has become a large-scale social experiment in which planners and social engineers play a very influential role.

With this kind of mind-set, no existing social arrangement in Sweden is sacrosanct; each is looked at with an eye toward its social functioning. Is a given arrangement a useful means to achieve desired social ends? If not, it should be subject to human intervention with the aim of improvement. In Sweden this approach has been used (see Chapter 7), for example, on the national constitution, which was rewritten; local government jurisdictions, which have been massively changed; cities, which have been extensively replanned; and schools, which have been radically modified.

The Swedish family is another social arrangement that has been subjected to this pragmatic perspective. Like all other social arrangements in Sweden, the family has little of the aura found in other cultures of a moral imperative, a permanent fixture, or an inviolate tradition. It is viewed in very functional terms. If the family oppresses women, change it. If it breaks down as a provider of affection and companionship, try something new. If in its new form the family is inadequate for rearing children, develop a new system of public child care. The family exists only as a practical arrangement for meeting human needs. It should be closely examined from all rational points of view; there may be better alternatives.

Although Swedes are not without a strong sense of history, they would be unlikely to stay with an institution just for the sake of tradition or a feeling of sentimentality. To the contrary, Swedes desire things to be new, different, improved. Thus Swedes have largely rejected traditional religion and become the world's most secular society. And they have rejected traditional marriage to become the world's most "cohabiting" society. Marriage is not valued because it represents a tie to the past. Indeed, marriage has been rejected in part precisely because it is, like religion, closely associated with traditional society, a symbol of the past that Swedes desire to leave behind. In Swedish eyes, not marrying is just acting rationally.

Conclusions

If each of these psychological traits—independence, social reserve, and social rationality—not only partly defines Swedish national character but also shapes family behavior, the reader may no longer be in doubt about why in Sweden the marriage rate is so low, the dissolution rate so high, the single-person household so extensive, and the family so lacking in the kind of honored cultural place that it has in other cultures. The reader may also say—aha! the Swedes really are different from everybody else, an exotic people in the far north who are more an interesting curiosity than an example for the rest of us. Now that we know about them, we can forget about them.

This a conclusion, however, to which one should not quickly jump. By definition national character as a whole is a cultural dimension unique to each nationality group. But the psychological traits that have been discussed as possibly related to the situation of the Swedish family happen also to be increasingly characteristic of large segments of the more affluent social classes in every advanced society. They are the traits that in other societies help to define the cultural style of the middle classes as distinct from the working classes. To become middle class is to value one's privacy and independence more, to give up gregariousness and spontaneity in favor of social reserve, and to jettison a great deal of tradition and sentimentality in the pursuit of a higher level of social rationality. These Swedish national character traits more closely match those of American yuppies, for example, than they do those of the American working classes; they are more characteristic of an American college town than of an American industrial town. To the extent that Western cultures as a whole have gradually been changing to reflect more of these middle-class traits, and I believe that is precisely what has been happening, Sweden should again be viewed not as an exception but a pacesetter.

By the same token, virtually every one of the factors that have been discussed earlier in this chapter as contributing to Swedish family decline can be seen in other advanced societies as a significant social trend. The trends toward economic security, new definitions of gender roles, secularization, feminism, the therapeutic ideology, some aspects of socialism, the centralized welfare bureaucracy—each is almost a defining characteristic of what it means to be an advanced, modernized, postindustrial society. Sweden may be in the lead with respect to most of these trends, but I do not believe that it is in other ways especially exceptional.

This is not to say that everything happening in Sweden today is going to happen sooner or later in every other country. The culture of each nation has indigenous peculiarities based on its unique history and circumstances, and Swedish culture is no exception. Sweden and the United States, for example, are substantially different nations in a wide range of sociological respects ranging from scale to cultural heterogeneity. The so-called convergence theory of modernization—whereby all nations will eventually become similar to one another in major respects—can be accepted only in broad outline; pronounced cultural differences will continue to exist, and some may even be accentuated, for as far into the future as we can see. Still, the new technologies of transportation and communication and the ever-expanding network of interregional and international trade do seem to be narrowing many cultural gaps between regional subcultures in the United States and among the nations of Europe, especially among metropolitan dwellers. In the process, these technologies and trading systems appear to be bringing many common cultural configurations to all industrial nations.

Finally, it is important to note that some of these social trends in advanced, industrialized societies may turn around in the future; some, such as the trend toward socialism, have already made a turn within the past decade. Yet these changes of direction are visible in Sweden just as they are everywhere else. Sweden, too, has been party to the conservative political and social winds of recent years, with a new political interest in privatization and decentralization and a new social interest in discipline in the schools and the rules of social etiquette.

However one looks at the issue, then, the social and cultural factors that have created family decline in Sweden seem not to be unique to that nation but to be aspects of international trends that are shaping all advanced societies.

Notes

[1]See, for example, Gay C. Kitson, Karen Benson Babri, and Mary Joan Roach (1985), "Who Divorces and Why?," *Journal of Family Issues* 6-3: 255–293; and Stan L. Albrecht, Howard M. Bahr, and Kristen L. Goodman (1983), *Divorce and Remarriage*.

[2]Anders Wicksell (1981), "Lönar det sig at Skiljas?"

[3]It is important to emphasize that this relationship is posited for the late stages of industrialization. There is evidence that at the early stages of industrialization the family, especially the quality of interaction among family members, may be strengthened by economic changes. See Bernard C. Rosen (1982), *The Industrial Connection: Achievement and the Family in Developing Societies*.

[4]Elder's study of children born during the Depression found that those who came from the most economically deprived families placed the highest value in their own adult years on family life and familism. Glen H. Elder, Jr. (1974), *Children of the Great Depression*.

[5]Lyle P. Groeneveld, Nancy Brandon Tuma, and Michael T. Hannan (1980), "The Effects of Negative Income Tax Programs on Marital Dissolution," *Journal of Human Resources* 15: 654–674.

[6]For an economic theory of marital dynamics, see Gary S. Becker (1981), *A Treatise on the Family*: Chapter 10.

[7]See John C. Caldwell (1982), *Theory of Fertility Decline,* and Becker (1981), *A Treatise on the Family*.

[8]R. E. Smith (1979), *The Subtle Revolution: Women at Work*.

[9]Andrew J. Cherlin (1981), *Marriage, Divorce, and Remarriage:* 55.

[10]Alan Booth et al. (1984), "Women, Outside Employment, and Marital Instability," pp. 567–583 in *American Journal of Sociology* 90-3: 581–582.

[11]Philip Blumstein and Pepper Schwartz (1983), *American Couples:* 309–310.

[12]See, for example, Andrew Cherlin (1979), "Work Life and Marital Dissolution," pp. 151–166 in George Levinger and Oliver C. Moles (eds.), *Divorce and Separation.*

[13]Jan Trost and Örjan Hultåker (1982), *Swedish Divorces: Methods and Responses.*

[14]Barbara Ehrenreich (1984), *The Hearts of Men.*

[15]See, for example, Valerie Kincade Oppenheimer (1982), *Work and the Family: A Study in Social Demography.*

[16]1982 survey by Swedish Institute for Opinion Research, "Det Lyckliga Äktenskapet," reported in Barbro Lennéer-Axelson (1984), "Why Are Families Breaking Down? Opportunities and Risks for Whom."

[17]Interview by author, May 1986.

[18]From Stockholm Familjerådgivningsstatistik (1981), reported in Lennéer-Axelson (1984), "Breaking Down."

[19]Reported in Lennéer-Axelson (1984), "Breaking Down": 2.

[20]Inger Koch-Nielsen (1985), *Divorces:* 18–22. This was an investigation of about 1000 families of people who divorced in 1980.

[21]Gunnar and Bente Öberg, quoted in Barbro Lennéer-Axelson (1985), "Skilsmässopappor och Styvpappor," pp. 59–88 in Philip Hwang, (ed.), *Faderskap:* 63.

[22]David Martin (1978), *A General Theory of Secularization:* 12.

[23]Data from Religionssociologiska Institutionen, Stockholm (1985). The percentage of all children baptized has not decreased quite so rapidly, however, and stands today at about 75%.

[24]See the literature review in Kitson et al. (1985), "Who Divorces and Why?" In the western United States, Stan L. Albrecht *et al.* (1983), *Divorce and Remarriage,* found a particularly strong relationship between divorce and two religious factors: not having had a church wedding and a low level of participation in religious activities.

[25]See Ira L. Reiss (1980), "Sexual Customs and Gender Roles in Sweden and America," pp. 191–220 in Helena Z. Lopata *et al.,* eds., *Research in the Interweave of Social Roles: Women and Men.*

[26]Torborg Lundell (1984), "Ellen Key and Swedish Feminist Views on Motherhood," pp. 351–369 in *Scandinavian Studies* 56-4: 353.

[27]Summary of Key's thinking quoted in *ibid.:* 353.

[28]*Ibid.:* 355.

[29]Edmund Dahlström and Rita Liljeström (1982), *Working Class Women and Human Reproduction:* 23.

[30]Mary Ruggie (1984), *The State and Working Women;* Jennie Farley, (ed.)(1985), *Women Workers in 15 Countries;* Patricia A. Roos (ed.) (1985), *Gender and Work: A Comparative Analysis of Industrial Societies;* Ronnie Steinberg Ratner (ed.) (1980), *Equal Employment Policy for Women;* Carolyn Teich Adams and Kathryn Teich Winston (1980), *Mothers at Work;* Eugen Lupri (ed.) (1983), *The Changing Position of Women in Family and Society;* Liba Paukert (1984), *The Employment and Unemployment of Women in OECD Countries;* Hilda Scott (1982), *Sweden's Right to be Human.*

[31]The difference between feminist goals in the United States and Sweden is discussed in Sylvia Ann Hewlett (1986), *A Lesser Life: The Myth of Women's Liberation in America:* 164–167.

[32]In 1983 the Swedish government officially set up a "work group" to explore the changing male role and make public-policy suggestions. See Arbetsmarknadsdepartementet (no date), *Mannen i Förändring,* and Lars Jalmert (1984), *Den Svenske Mannen.* Jalmert was a member of the work group.

33Johan Fritzell (1985), *Barnfamiljernas Levnadsnivå.*
34S. Nyström (1980), *The Use of Somatic Hospital Care Among Divorced.*
35What is called the therapeutic attitude is a prominent focus of Robert N. Bellah et al. (1985), *Habits of the Heart.* In my discussion, I am indebted to the analysis of the therapeutic attitude presented in this book, especially Chapter 4.
36*Ibid.:* 47.
37Philip Rieff (1966), *The Triumph of the Therapeutic:* 261.
38Bellah et al. (1985), *Habits of the Heart:* 101.
39Joseph Veroff, Elizabeth Douvan, and Richard A. Kulka (1981), *The Inner American: A Self-Portrait from 1957 to 1976:* 140–141, quoted in Bellah et al., *Habits of the Heart:* 316.
40For a clear statement of Marxist feminist principles, see Michele Barrett and M. McIntosh (1982), *The Anti-Social Family.*
41Staffan Herrström (1986), "Swedish Family Policy," *Current Sweden* 348: 13.
42Barrett and McIntosh (1982), *The Anti-Social Family:* 47.
43*Ibid.:* 78.
44*Ibid.:* 80.
45*Ibid.:* 133.
46On family ideology immediately following the Russian Revolution, see H. Kent Geiger (1968), *The Family in Soviet Russia.*
47For Soviet and Eastern European sources, see Edmund Dahlström (1986), "Theories and Ideologies of Family Functions, Gender Relations and Human Reproduction."
48David Mace and Vera Mace (1963), *The Soviet Family.*
49See Gail Warshofsky Lapidus (1982), *Women, Work, and Family in the Soviet Union;* and Julian Kozyrev (1969), "The Family and Family Relations," pp. 65–72 in G. V. Osipov (ed.), *Town Country and People.*
50Vladimir Shlapentokh (1984), *Love, Marriage and Friendship in the Soviet Union: Ideals and Practices.*
51See Martin Rein and Lee Rainwater (eds.) (1986), *Public/Private Interplay in Social Protection: A Comparative Study.*
52For Sweden, this perspective is explored in Jerzy Sarnecki (1985), *Byråkratins Innersta Väsen.*
53Daniel Bell (1976), *The Cultural Contradictions of Capitalism.*
54Joseph A. Schumpeter (1976), *Capitalism, Socialism and Democracy:* Chapter 14.
55Neil Gilbert (1983), *Capitalism and the Welfare State: Dilemmas of Social Benevolence:* 95.
56*Ibid.:* 91.
57The coercive aspects of this have been stressed (for France) by Jacques Donzelot (1979), *The Policing of Families,* and Philippe Meyer (1977), *The Child and the State;* (for the United States) by Christopher Lasch (1977), *Haven in a Heartless World.*
58Gilbert (1983), *Capitalism:* 96.
59For two contrasting perspectives on welfare dependency in America, see Charles Murray (1984), *Losing Ground,* and Daniel Patrick Moynahan (1986), *Family and Nation.*
60Bent Rold Andersen (1984), "Rationality and Irrationality of the Nordic Welfare State," pp. 109–139 in *Daedalus* 113-1: 129.
61For the United States this issue is explored, with a similarly ambiguous conclusion, in Robert M. Moroney (1986), *Shared Responsibility: Families and Social Policy.*

62See, for example, Andersen (1984), "Rationality"; Gunnar Heckscher (1984), *The Welfare State and Beyond;* Swedish Secretariat for Futures Studies (1984), *Time to Care.*

63Diana Gittins (1985), *The Family in Question:* 159.

64Hugh Heclo and Henrik Madsen (1987), *Policy and Politics in Sweden:* 22.

65The traditional elements of this belief are expressed in a "law" or moral code presumably characteristic of Swedish small towns of the past. See Aksel Sandemose (1984), "The Law of Jante," pp. 28–30 in Patrick Engellau and Ulf Henning (eds.), *Nordic Views and Values.*

66Heclo and Madsen (1987), *Policy and Politics:* 22.

67Gilbert (1983), *Capitalism:* 101.

68For the United States, this theme is explored in Moroney (1986), *Shared Responsibility.*

69See David Popenoe (1977), *The Suburban Environment: Sweden and the United States,* and David Popenoe (1985), *Private Pleasure, Public Plight: American Metropolitan Community Life in Comparative Perspective.*

70On the decline of local networks in Sweden, see Åke Daun (1974), *Förortsliv,* and Åke Daun (1976), *Strategi för Gemenskap.*

71Marshall B. Clinard (1978), *Cities with Little Crime: The Case of Switzerland.*

72Moncrieff Cochran et al. (1984), *The Social Support Networks of Mothers with Young Children: A Cross-National Comparison:* 130.

73There is an abundant literature in Swedish on this. See, for example, Daun (1974), *Förortsliv;* Hans Gordon and Peter Molin (1972), "Man Bara Anpassar Sig Helt Enkelt"; Sören Olsson (1979), *Förorten;* Arne Modig (1985), *Grannrelationer i Förort.*

74See Marvin E. Olsen (1982), *Participatory Pluralism: Political Participation and Influence in the United States and Sweden.*

75On the objections of social scientists to the concept of national character, see Dean Peabody (1985), *National Characteristics:* Chapter 1.

76Åke Daun (1986), "The Japanese of the North—The Swedes of Asia?," *Ethnologia Scandinavica:* 5–17. On the family's role in Japanese welfare, see Naomi Maruo (1986), "The Development of the Welfare Mix in Japan," pp. 64–79 in Richard Rose and Rei Shiratori (eds.), *The Welfare State East and West;* and Rei Shiratori (1985), "The Experience of the Welfare State in Japan and its Problems," pp. 200–223 in S. N. Eisenstadt and Ora Ahimeir, (eds.), *The Welfare State and its Aftermath.*

77Daun (1986), "The Japanese"; Åke Daun (1984), "Swedishness as an Obstacle in Cross-Cultural Interaction," *Ethnologia Europaea* 14: 95–109; Jean Phillips-Martinsson (1981), *Swedes as Others See Them;* Ulf Hannerz (1983), "Den Svenska Kulturen"; Paul Britten Austin (1968), *On Being Swedish.* On Norwegian national character, see Christen T. Jonassen (1983), *Value Systems and Personality in Western Civilization: Norwegians in Europe and America.*

78Many of the ideas put forth in the following pages were developed through personal discussions with Åke Daun, and I hereby express my indebtedness to him.

79See especially Austin (1968), *On Being Swedish:* 95ff.

80Heclo and Madsen (1987), *Policy and Politics:* 22.

81Marquis Childs (1947), *Sweden: The Middle Way:* 144.

Part III

The Family in Other Advanced Societies

Outposts of the Traditional Family: Switzerland and New Zealand

At the end of World War II, five nations reigned as the world's most affluent in gross national product (GNP). Sweden ranked fifth, behind first-ranked United States followed by Canada, New Zealand, and Switzerland. In the preceding six chapters we discussed societal developments in Sweden that bear on family change. Our attention now turns to two of the other advanced societies in this privileged category of wealthy states: Switzerland and New Zealand. Each presents a different face of the relationship between affluence and modernization and the institution of the family.

In the mid-1970s Sweden passed the others to emerge briefly as the world's wealthiest nation, only to be surpassed later in the decade by Switzerland. New Zealand, meanwhile, slipped considerably behind in the sweepstakes. In 1987, with a per-capita GNP of $16,380, Switzerland rivaled the United States ($16,400) as the world wealthiest nation (excluding several mineral-rich Third World states). Sweden, with a per-capita GNP of $11,890, had fallen behind newcomers Norway ($13,890) and Luxembourg ($13,380). And New Zealand had fallen far behind, with a per-capita GNP less than half that of Switzerland and the United States: $7310.[1] While Switzerland and New Zealand have diverged in their economic fortunes, however, in another respect they share a striking resemblance. Compared to Sweden and most other advanced societies, in both nations the bourgeois family has remained relatively strong, and familism is an important cultural value. Why this should be so is a subject of this chapter.

It is not the intention to present here a detailed discussion of the family in these nations, much less a comprehensive analysis of each society. The goal is to review briefly the history and contemporary cultural climate of each society, and to compare them with Sweden in order to place the family situation in Sweden in better perspective. In this process, in addition, some light may be thrown on the broad forces in advanced societies that are shaping the family and on the direction of family change in these societies.

Switzerland

Switzerland resembles Sweden not only as a very rich nation, but also as a small urban, industrialized society of about the same size (Switzerland has 6.4 million, Sweden—8.3 million) with a similar economy. Both nations maintain their independence outside the European Economic Community (EEC), yet rely heavily on foreign trade. To maintain high economic growth, both have had to depend strongly since World War II on the importation of foreign workers. Both are noted for their lack of labor-management conflicts, stemming from similar national labor-management agreements drawn up in the late 1930s.

These labor-management agreements reflect the political style of each nation, which very much favors compromise and consensus and deliberately seeks to avoid open political conflict.[2] Moreover, partly because of their official policy of neutrality, Switzerland and Sweden are among the few European countries whose economies were not heavily distorted or destroyed by direct involvement in World Wars I and II. As part of this neutrality policy, both maintain strong national defenses with high expenditures on military equipment and universal military training for all males.[3]

Switzerland and Sweden both show a strong sense of national solidarity that is due, in part, to their relative isolation from the European conflicts of the past few centuries. This isolation has given each a social structure that has been mostly undisturbed by the often momentous events taking place in the world around them. Shaped by this strong base of national solidarity, together with their unique international positions, both nations are noted for their international moral and social leadership. This takes the form in Switzerland of a strong reputation for honesty, efficiency, and rectitude, together with such international efforts as the Red Cross, while Sweden is renowned as a caring society that has provided leadership in the United Nations and promoted egalitarian policies throughout the Third World.[4]

Even their historic family forms are quite similar, at least if the comparison is between the Alpine dwellers and the equally isolated rural people of the Swedish north. Both were protected from most of the social adversities of the European feudal systems and, at the same time, led highly variegated and mostly self-sufficient lives, scraping out a living under difficult conditions. Each of these groups, in turn, is considered to have been the source of many of each society's cultural virtues.

Swiss Family Traditionalism

Beyond these features, however, few societies in Europe differ more from one another. One difference, first and foremost for our purposes, is in the family. While the Swedish family is farthest removed from the bourgeois form, the Swiss family is the most traditional, certainly among those societies that in any way compare with Switzerland in the level of economic development and affluence. Swiss family traditionalism is seen most clearly in the family roles that are played by Swiss women and men. In Switzerland the housewife still holds an honored position, and it is the working mother who is looked down upon, whereas the opposite tends to be true in Sweden. More than in most other northern European countries, Swiss women leave work after their children are born and do not resume employment until well after the children begin school, and then often only part-time. It is said that one of the sacrosanct motherly duties still prevalent in Switzerland is the home-cooked lunch, something long since departed from the Swedish scene, and Swiss school hours in many districts are still organized around this traditional nicety.

The differences between the Swiss and Swedish conceptions of the mother's role are highlighted in a comparison of books on early child care in the two nations, part of a series written in the early 1970s that followed a common format. In the Swiss book one reads that

> the family is seen as the only appropriate setting for the upbringing of small children. There is strong traditional and ideological backing for this view.[5] It is firmly maintained that the child belongs to his mother . . . [and] the mother belongs to the child.[6] Very seldom does one hear requests for the kind of nursery which would allow mothers from all socioeconomic milieus, but especially mothers with professional education, to accept a modest occupational activity outside the home.[7]

In sharp contrast, the Swedish book quotes the head of the national Department of Childhood and Youth Affairs in Sweden as follows: "Society must assume a greater responsibility for the supervision and upbringing of the children."[8] And an authoritative Swedish handbook on preschool methodology is quoted along similar lines: "We can no longer leave children in their limited home environment. . . . It is no longer enough to let parents alone supply the security and love that children need."[9]

The traditional role of women is strongly reflected in the labor-force-participation rate of Swiss females, which is one of the lowest in northern Europe. It stood (1983) at 49%, compared to 77% in Sweden, 63% in the United States, and 57% even in Japan, which is the industrialized society regarded as having the most traditional family structure.[10] Also in contrast to Sweden, marriage in Switzerland is still a dominant institution, and the movement toward nonmarital cohabitation has not gained a very strong foothold. Female nonmarital cohabitation was estimated in 1985 for the 20-29 age group as only about 10% (compared to about 40% in Sweden)[11]; in a number of Swiss cantons cohabitation outside of marriage is still prohibited by law, although the law is not enforced. Most of those who do cohabit marry as soon as they have children, especially since many local Swiss ordinances make unmarried parenting a violation of the civil code.[12] The illegitimacy rate for Switzerland in 1984 was only 5.7 (per 100 live births),[13] compared to Sweden's 45%. It has been estimated that the number of unmarried Swiss couples with children amounts to only 2% of all families with children.[14]

The amount of family dissolution is also considerably smaller in Switzerland than in Sweden. The projected proportion of marriages expected to end in divorce for the cohort of Swiss males born in 1945 is 14%, compared to 36% for Swedish males.[15] And in the number of single-parent families as a percentage of all families with children, Switzerland with 12%[16] falls significantly below Sweden (18%) and the United States (21.5%).

In civil and legal rights, Switzerland has also lagged well behind comparable nations.[17] Perhaps the most striking example is that Swiss women were only granted the right to vote in national elections in 1971, more than half a century after Swedish women; in some Swiss cantons and local communities the granting of this right was delayed still further, and in two cantons the right to vote has yet to be granted. Switzerland was the last major Western democracy to grant women this right. Furthermore, until the Swiss voters narrowly approved a new marriage and family law in 1985, the Swiss husband had clear legal advantages in marriage and divorce. As legal head of the family he could "prevent his wife from working, choose the couple's place of residence, and manage the savings his wife had before the marriage as well as her inheritance."[18] Also, a wife was prevented from opening a bank account without her husband's approval and in case of marital breakup was entitled to only one third of the family wealth.[19]

Explanations for Swiss Family Traditionalism

In view of the many other similarities between the two societies, how is one to account for the striking contrast between the Swiss and Swedish positions on women's roles and on marriage? It is true that women historically were more liberated at an earlier time in the Scandinavian countries than elsewhere in Europe, and the reasons for this are not well understood. One theory is that, historically, Scandinavian men were often away from home for long periods of time because of the exigencies of their fishing, hunting, and forestry economies, giving women by default more power in the home and local community. Whatever the reasons, Scandinavian women were granted civil rights long before those of many other countries, and they long have been regarded as more independent and equal in their dealings with men.

Yet there are three characteristics of Swiss society, making it significantly different from Sweden, that in the modern era appear to have reinforced whatever gender and family traditionalism already existed: religion, a conservative sociopolitical ideology, and a decentralized political structure. Religion is still quite firmly entrenched in Switzerland, whereas Sweden is probably the world's most secular society. Roman Catholicism, long a bulwark of traditional familism, has in recent years (because of higher Catholic birthrates and the influx of foreign immigrants) grown to have a larger allegience among Swiss people than any other religious denomination.[20] Moreover, in both Protestant and Roman Catholic areas the local community is a considerably stronger reality in Switzerland than in Sweden, and one strong element in the local community is the traditional parish church. The role of organized religion is probably not so strong in Switzerland as it is in the United States, but it is strong enough to be influential in the debate "to preserve and protect the family as the moral foundation of society." Organized religion has been particularly outspoken in maintaining the sanctity of marriage and in preserving traditional gender roles, usually under the guise of upholding the sanctity of the family and a high standard in the parenting of children.

Religion is by no means the only force supporting the traditional family in Switzerland, however. A particular constellation of sociopolitical ideologies and structures must also be given much of the credit. Switzerland is noteworthy for being a bastion of market capitalism and the bourgeoisie, with their values of liberty and self-sufficiency as well as material acquisition. In Sweden, on the other hand, the proletarian-based ideology of egalitarianism has long been the dominant political and cultural theme. The twentieth-century proletarian revolution that in many nations of western Europe led to the welfare state under the banner of Social Democracy has largely passed Switzerland by.[21] Today Switzerland politically and socially is probably the most conservative of the western European nations, while Sweden is the most left wing. The difference may stem, in part, from the historical fact that Sweden was long one of the poorest countries of Europe, an isolated nation of mostly poor farmers, while Switzerland, centrally located on major trading routes, became at an earlier date relatively wealthy through commerce. Also, because of the long dominance by rural home industry and small firms, Switzerland never had as much social-class differentiation as Sweden and most other European nations.

Swiss national culture is dominated by the middle-class ethos of the small shopkeeper, the banker, and the businessman, emphasizing hard work, entrepreneurial skill, material progress, and family self-sufficiency. This is precisely the social class in which the modern nuclear family reached its apogee. The husband can put his energy into paid work because of the wife's single-minded activities at home; the husband provides financially, and the wifes gives support socially and emotionally. That Switzerland has become perhaps the world's most successful society economically has certainly done little to restrict the continued preservation of this bourgeois culture. A pervasive attitude, one reflected in the positions of the major political parties, is that the traditional ways seem to work, so let us not change them, at least not too fast. Thus the centrist Swiss political party, the Radical-Democratic Party, has had a plank in its political platform that states: "The party demands: protection of the family as the foundation of society and state; support for all efforts aimed at the cultural and moral protection of the family."[22] The more right-wing parties in Switzerland have even stronger statements in support of the family. Such pronouncements are quite foreign to the political culture of Sweden, even to its Conservative Party, where the focus is much more on equality and individual rights.

One additional characteristic of Swiss society helps to explain why personal liberty and autonomy, "modern" values that have become so prominent in many western societies, have in general not supplanted "traditional family values" the way they have in Sweden. If Sweden is western Europe's most governmentally centralized society, which by all indications it is, Switzerland is at the same time the most decentralized. Swiss political decentralization stems from the historical need to weld into a single nation a diversity of language and religious groupings, a unification made even more problematic by the rugged nature of the Swiss geography.[23] The Swiss constitution grants most political power to the separate cantons, and the Swiss federal government is a rather loose body that sees its purpose as performing only those functions that the cantons cannot perform for themselves. In this respect, Switzerland is considerably less centralized than even the United States. One implication of this governmental decentralization is that the elaborate, centralized bureaucratic structure of educated technicians and administrators who carry out national policy in Sweden is for the most part missing in Switzerland.

Not only is there an aversion to political centralization in Switzerland, however, but also a belief that the public sector in general should be kept as limited as possible. This is in keeping with the dictates of that nation's laissez-faire capitalist ideology. The Swiss constitution contains a so-called principle of subsidiarity—the community should only do what the family on its own initiative is unable to do, the canton should only do what the community is unable to do, and so on up the hierarchy. The miserly Swiss view toward the public sector shows up in comparative taxation data. Total taxes as a percentage of GNP in Switzerland were 32% in 1983, just ahead of that other bastion of laissez-faire, the United States (29%). Sweden, in contrast, was taxed at 50%, the highest of the 24-member nations of the Organization for Economic Cooperation and Development (OECD).[24] Mainly because of the low tax take, Switzerland's take-home pay as a percentage of gross earnings (including family benefits) was 88%, second highest among OECD nations to Japan's 90% and well ahead of Sweden's 73%.[25]

It should be pointed out, however, that to compensate for a weaker public sector (hence less-well-financed public-welfare programs) the Swiss have a high rate of savings (the net national savings as percentage of GNP was 18%, compared to only 6% in Sweden and 4% in the United States.)[26] Switzerland is also reputed to be the country in which people spend the largest percentage of their incomes on private insurance, including health and disability insurance.

One important implication of not having a large, centralized, and well-financed public sector, with a sizable administrative bureaucracy, is that centrally initiated and directed social change is much less likely to occur. The kinds of national social change that the Swedes have pushed through in a rather conflict-free manner—such as various elements of their family policy—would in Switzerland for the most part have to be initiated and carried out by the separate cantons. Federal initiatives that are attempted can be, and often have been, blocked by the veto power of one or another of the cantons. Even when it strongly supports such policies, the Swiss federal government seldom has the political clout to move things past such vetos. Moreover, most important national political issues in Switzerland are put to a popular vote through referenda. As one author put it, "the Swiss cannot imagine that people should not have a say on virtually everything."[27] As is well known in the United States, this may be the most democratic way of doing things, but it also tends to be quite conservative in its political outcomes. Thus Switzerland not only has a relatively traditional family structure, but, like the United States, also tends to lag behind other European nations in government family policy (e.g., in the area of maternity benefits and parental leave at the birth of a child).

Another little discussed implication of having a relatively small public sector concerns rates of female employment. The great influx of women into the labor market in postwar Sweden has largely been in the public sector (60% of employed Swedish women work in the public sector, versus 25% of men). Having only limited public-sector employment, the Swiss economy has therefore been much less accepting of women workers. Related to this, Switzerland has chosen to bring in nearly twice the percentage of foreign workers as has Sweden, so that foreigners now make up about 30% of the Swiss labor force and 15% of the population. In part this appears to have been a deliberate policy to avoid moving Swiss women into the labor market in order to preserve the role of housewife.

The policy of relying on (mostly male) foreign workers was affected by the fact that a higher percentage of the Swiss labor shortages were in the private, industrial sector, and these jobs were judged to be more suitable for male workers. One reason for the male favoritism is that private industry has a greater reluctance than the public sector to permit part-time work, which women prefer much more than do men because of their need to coordinate paid work with family-care activities. In this connection it should be noted that Sweden not only has the highest female-employment rate but also the highest percentage of women working part-time (45% of employed women in Sweden work part-time, versus 5% of men). Even in Sweden, industries are by and large negative toward part-time work; both the high rate of female employment in Sweden and its largely part-time character, therefore, are heavily indebted to the large number of public-sector jobs.

In summary, Switzerland has a market-oriented economy, with a bourgeois culture, and a still relatively intact network of local communities that wield a significant degree of political power and social control. Under such conditions social change tends to be slow and traditionalism finds a ready acceptance. Thus the day-to-day cultural pressures on the family, and on the role of women, are far different in Switzerland than in the Swedish welfare state, and the political mechanisms for changing the situation are in short· supply.

Movement Away from the Bourgeois Family

The Swiss family, however, is traditional in some respects, but modern in others. Switzerland has by no means been able to avoid or resist all of the demographic and family trends that are prevalent in advanced societies. For example, Switzerland had the highest divorce rate in Europe from 1900 to World War I.[28] This was probably related to the fact that Switzerland was one of the first nations, in 1912, to develop a relatively liberal divorce law (today, however, Switzerland has not yet moved to the "no-fault" divorce, as have many other nations). The crude divorce rate today, although much lower than Sweden's, doubled in the two decades after 1963.[29] As in other advanced countries, even children do not seem to be a significant deterrant to divorce in Switzerland: Minor children were involved in 51% of divorce actions in 1951, and this percentage rose to 60% in 1968–1970.[30]

There are other indications that traditional familism in Switzerland is not as strong as the lag in gender-role change would lead one to expect. Age of first marriage for Swiss women is higher than that of other nations of Europe outside of Scandinavia. In 1983/1984 it averaged 25.3, compared to 24.4 in Germany and 23.6 in England and Wales. The Scandinavian countries are still higher, however, with Sweden averaging 27.3.[31] Most noteworthy of all is that the Swiss birthrate in recent years has become one of the lowest in the world. Recently estimated total fertility rates indicate that 1.5 children are born per Swiss women during her lifetime, which is even below Sweden's 1.7 (the United States rate is 1.8).[32] If the more traditional Swiss family is supposed to be geared toward the production of children, this statistic suggests that it is less than successful, certainly no more successful than its Swedish counterpart.

Finally, as in Sweden, the extended family household has almost completely disappeared in Switzerland.[33] This fact, together with the demographic trends just discussed, helps to explain why the average Swiss household size of 2.6 persons[34] is not much different from the Swedish household of 2.4 persons (1980 data). Moreover, the percentage of single-person households in Switzerland, 30% (1980),[35] rivals the pacesetting Swedish figure of 33%.

In addition, the situation of women and the family in Switzerland today is changing very rapidly. In 1981 the Swiss ratified an Equal Rights Amendment to their constitution that is expected to have far-reaching effects in bringing equality to women. One such effect, already mentioned, was the 1985 law that gave women equal rights in marriage and divorce. There will doubtless be many other repercussions in employment, housing, pensions, and throughout Swiss life. Thus it may only be a question of time before the situation of the Swiss family comes close to the situation in other European nations at a comparable level of development, including Sweden.

Concluding Remarks

Switzerland has not yet had the inclination to follow the lead of Sweden and many other European nations in extending much public-sector support to families with children. In this respect Switzerland closely resembles the United States. A 1978 legislative proposal, entitled "For the active protection of motherhood," called for maternity benefits, maternity leave, and a parental leave with job protection for at least 9 months. It was heavily defeated.[36] Similar proposals, under the title "Save the Family," were made again in the 1980s by a special commission of the Department of the Interior, but so far have come to nothing.

This central-government inaction does not mean that the Swiss have a "welfare crisis," however. The Swiss have developed their own system of social welfare, which places great weight on individual responsibility and local initiative.[37] Helped surely by affluence, very low unemployment, a relatively egalitarian income distribution, and the traditional Swiss virtues of thrift and personal responsibility, this system has so far functioned at a very high level of efficiency. It is a system that many Americans view with real envy. Whether it can stand up to all of the corrosive forces of modernism remains to be seen.

I have met many women in Sweden who look upon Switzerland with some disfavor, although it is a country they are by no means loath to visit. Switzerland is regarded by many Europeans with a mixture of envy and concern that it is socially backward, at least with respect to the situation of women. To this outside observer, the modern trends of equality and women's liberation seem so strong that Switzerland will eventually have to pull into line, and traditional familism there would seem to have only a short life ahead. But perhaps the Swiss really do have something that will stand the test of time. The popular demand for social change in Switzerland seems currently to be weaker than in almost any other land on earth.

New Zealand

Like Switzerland, New Zealand bears many similarities to Sweden. Both New Zealand and Sweden are small (New Zealand's 1988 population was 3.3 million), homogeneous, peaceful democracies that have the reputation of being among the world's leading welfare states. Even more perhaps than in Sweden, the New Zealand government is highly centralized and at the same time strongly devoted to egalitarian goals. Indeed, New Zealand was one of the real welfare-state pioneers and developed national welfare programs when Sweden was still a European backwater in social policy.

In a burst of political activity in the 1890s, a Liberal government in New Zealand significantly increased the power of the state. It introduced a graduated tax on land and urban income, the world's most progressive labor code that regulated working hours, wages, and factory conditions, and the world's first compulsory system of labor arbitration. Late in that decade New Zealand became the third nation in the world (following Prussia and Denmark) to establish a system of state old-age pensions for the poor. These measures were widely interpreted abroad as socialistic, and at the turn of the century—when Sweden was still under the political grip of traditional bourgeois capitalism—New Zealand had the reputation of being the most radical state in the world.[38]

New Zealand was a pioneer in women's rights. In 1893 it became the first nation in the world to give women the right to vote (only the state of Wyoming in the United States had acted earlier). Female emancipation was the result in part of a vigorous women's movement, which also saw the passage around this time of progressive divorce legislation that removed the overt discrimination against women contained in the earlier divorce law. Other late-nineteenth-century legislation extended women's rights to property ownership, to education, and to employment in the professions.

As in Sweden, however, the main thrust of New Zealand's welfare-state developments came in the 1930s. A moderate and pragmatic Labor government, not unlike Sweden's at the time, enacted a range of welfare programs that had a pronatalist intent and would by the end of the 1930s make New Zealand arguably "the most advanced and comprehensive welfare state in the World."[39] New Zealand first established a small family-allowance system in 1926, well before Sweden's post–World War II policies. Subject to a means test, the allowance was given for each child after the second. The family allowance was extended to all families and all children in 1946.

Both New Zealand and Sweden emerged from World War II with Labor governments and a strong track record of governmental activism. At this time they shared not only a similar high standard of living, but also a comparable family situation. Both nations were essentially wealthy, bourgeois, welfare-oriented societies in which women played traditional roles. In 1951, for example, the percentage of married New Zealand women in the work force was 10%,[40] similar to Sweden's 16% and well behind the United States figure of 24%.

New Zealand's Family Traditionalism

Despite these many similarities, New Zealand today is far removed from Sweden and rivals Switzerland as an advanced society with a relatively traditional family system. Statistics, in fact, suggest that contemporary New Zealand has an even more traditional family system than Switzerland. New Zealand's female labor-force participation rate is one of the lowest among advanced societies. In 1980, it was 46% compared to 49% in Switzerland, 63% in the United States, and 77% in Sweden.[41] Over 40% of New Zealand's adult women in 1981 listed their occupation as "household duties, unpaid," and 84% of mothers with a child under 1 year of age were not in the labor force.[42] New Zealand was also quite traditional in its large household size (3.1 vs. Sweden's 2.2), low divorce rate (1.9 divorces per 1000 persons vs. 1.6 for Switzerland and 2.4 for Sweden), and high marriage rate (7.2 marriages per 1000 persons vs. 5.1 for Switzerland and 4.5 for Sweden.[43] The percentage of single-parent families of all families with children was 11% in New Zealand, similar to Switzerland and well below Sweden and the United States.[44] Cohabitation outside marriage, though a growing phenomenon in New Zealand, in 1981 was estimated to be true of only about 5% of couples.[45]

Thus New Zealand remains, perhaps more than any other society at its level of modernization, a bastion of the relatively stable, bourgeois nuclear family. Most women with very young children remain out of the labor force, and the development of public day-care facilities in New Zealand is still in its infancy. There still exists, in the words of two New Zealand sociologists, "a marked traditional acceptance of the idea that women should be mothers first and fulfill other roles second."[46]

This family traditionalism manifests itself in New Zealand's urban style of life. In terms of percentage of the population living in urban areas with a population of 50,000 or more, New Zealand with 58% ranks well ahead of Sweden (33%) and Switzerland (51%) and is close to the United States (61%).[47] This makes New Zealand one of the most urbanized nations in the world, belying its reputation as an agricultural nation (agricultural products are New Zealand's principal foreign export). Yet it is not its urban but suburban nature that reveals New Zealand's fundamental cultural character. Contemporary New Zealand could be described as the world's ultimate suburban society, in which working and middle-class couples with children live in small, single-family, detached, and owner-occupied houses built at low urban densities on the edge of cities and towns. As one New Zealand social scientist has put it, "housing in suburbia is a central motif in the post-war social pattern."[48] In the words of another, the present suburban living pattern is "encouraged by a welter of legislation, finance arrangements and planning rules which make it virtually impossible for the ordinary person to live in any other way."[49]

Despite New Zealand's lagging economic fortunes, its suburban areas to-day appear relatively prosperous. The suburban houses, typically wooden bungalows with corrugated metal roofs painted in pastel shades, are situated on their own small lots that often contain, in keeping with the equable climate, well-tended gardens. Most transportation is by private automobile. Thus the appearance of urban New Zealand, and the culture, are reminiscent of the American Levittowns of the 1950s more than of anything found in Sweden, Switzerland, or even the mother country of Great Britain. Certain British traditions remain, however. Milk is still home delivered, secondary-school children wear uniforms, and suburban shopping districts have an unmistakable British look rather than the commercial and gaudy mien common in the United States.

Explanations for New Zealand's Family Traditionalism

When compared to most of the welfare states of Europe, how could New Zealand, a welfare state that was a pioneer in giving rights to women, remain so traditional in its family structure? Let us begin our search for explanations by looking at New Zealand's history, which strikingly differs from both Sweden and Switzerland and bears many similarities to the United States.

New Zealand is a settler's society, a society settled by people from other cultures, in this case those of the United Kingdom. Extensive settlement did not get under way until the nineteenth century, making New Zealand one of the newest of the advanced nations.[50] Both Australia and New Zealand are said to have been settled by the respectable poor who left Britain in search of economic opportunity (in Australia, this followed the original settlement by British convicts). Because the passage to New Zealand entailed a substantial added cost, the economic level of New Zealand settlers is believed to have been higher than that of those who remained in Australia. The culture that developed in New Zealand was thus that of the stable working and lower-middle-classes of Great Britain, but without the strong class distinctions or the cultural and economic hegemony of the upper classes found in Britain. In relative terms New Zealand was an egalitarian society from the very beginning, and this theme still reigns supreme as the nation's cultural motif.[51]

With few class cleavages and without the heavy guiding hand of the upper classes, it was natural for New Zealanders to turn to a strong government for help in economic and social development. In the words of New Zealand's economic historian G. R. Hawke:

> Central government was always accessible, and the colonial instinct was to use its powers and institutions wherever they were likely to be useful, irrespective of European ideas of propriety. European observers thought that New Zealanders practised socialism without doctrines, but they thought in European terms. New Zealanders simply found new roles for government in a pioneering society.[52]

This helps to explain why New Zealand became a welfare-state pioneer. Strong government was seen as a natural ally of the people at an early stage, and, given New Zealand's diminutive size and high degree of urban concentration, central government did not mean distant government.

At the same time, the frontier conditions led to a strong emphasis on individualism, self-sufficiency, and hard work. Yet the great cultural homogeneity, by generating an inherent social compatibility among the residents, helps to explain why New Zealand's individualism was not "rugged," but was tempered by strong local community ties and a rich community life (this was less true in neighboring Australia, whose the individualism has taken on more American connotations). A strong religious strain fills out this cultural picture; one visitor to New Zealand in 1904 observed that "no tradition remained so strong as the religious one."[53] (Although it has weakened, this strain remains in place to this day, and New Zealand, like the United States, is still largely a churchgoing nation). By the turn of the century New Zealand was a nationally cohesive society focused on family farms and strong rural communities that were "inward looking, self-reliant and church centered."[54] This was a setting in which women could, and did, play a significant role.

The family situation of New Zealand in its formative years was therefore much like that of the prosperous and culturally homogeneous farming areas in the Midwest of the nineteenth-century United States. The nuclear family was a very important social unit in the overall scheme of life. In the early years of New Zealand's settlement the nuclear family gained in importance because the extended family had for the most part been left behind in the mother country. Ideological currents that challenged the importance of the family, such as Marxism and radical strains of feminism, found an infertile soil in New Zealand. There were few of the downtrodden masses on which Marxist thought could feed, and the "functional roles" given to women in such a new society as New Zealand typically enhanced female social status, as Toqueville pointed out in regard to the United States. The status of women was no doubt further enhanced because women were in short supply in New Zealand's early years. After decades of harsh frontier life, those women who had the opportunity gladly accepted the privatized comforts of the bourgeois domestic life that became the ideal around the turn of the twentieth century. New Zealand's feminist movements of the time stressed motherhood and domesticity and called for special training to enable women to better fulfill their "natural" maternal roles.[55]

Despite its very different historical foundations, the turn-of-the-century family-based culture of New Zealand was not very different from the culture of Sweden at that time. Yet the Swedish family system radically changed with the continued modernization of the society while the New Zealand system has tended to cling to tradition. What caused this divergence?

An important factor, in my opinion, is that the move from rural to urban life has not been quite so jarring in New Zealand as it was in Sweden. In Sweden, urbanization has typically meant moving from small houses in intact local communities to the relatively anomic setting of urban apartments. Not only was there a radical shift in house type (and job) but also in social environment and life-style. In comparison, the shift in New Zealand from rural small towns to low-density suburban areas seems to cover a very modest cultural distance. The suburban areas still maintain a tie to the land and, to a relatively large extent, sustain a rich local-community life.[56] Referring to the maintenance of small-town values in urban life, one New Zealand observer commented that "main street runs pretty well the whole length of New Zealand."[57] Commuting by car adds a distinct new cultural element to the scene, but the scale of urban life in New Zealand (with the possible exception of Auckland) is not great and suburban commuting has not become the pervading fact of life, as for example, in many United States suburban areas.

For the bourgeois nuclear family, this extensive, low-density suburban-ization seems to provide a supportive urban climate. It is as close to the environmental conditions of the small rural town as can be achieved in an urban setting. The house and yard provide a strong focal point for family activities, and the familistic life-style is bulwarked by intensive neighboring and a rich associational life in the local community. Even in Sweden's residential environments that resemble New Zealand's (or American) suburban conditions, the bourgeois nuclear family remains a predominant social fact.

Why did New Zealand, unlike Sweden, take the low-density suburban path of metropolitan growth? The answer lies partly in contrasting political developments in the two nations (which in turn reflect deeper social and cultural dissimilarities). With different politics, the New Zealand urban pattern would probably not have evolved in the same way. In the 1930s the Labor government embarked on a policy, similar to that adopted in Sweden, of promoting state rental housing. If that policy had been allowed to continue, it is likely that New Zealand's urban areas today would look much more like Sweden's. Even though the typical state rental house at that time was a detached low-rise bungalow (Sweden briefly toyed with the idea of such housing), New Zealand's public-housing densities would probably soon have drifted higher.

We can only speculate about what might have happened, however, because the Labor public-housing-policy momentum ended soon after World War II. The conservative National Party that came into power in 1950 quickly redirected national housing policy toward the private construction of owner-occupied dwellings. As one commentator has observed, "home ownership lay at the heart of the prevailing ethos, reflecting aspirations for security, independence, and respectability." During the 1950s the proportion of owner-occupied housing increased from 61 to 69%.[58]

After 1950, the National Party ruled in New Zealand for most of the next 35 years (Labor returned briefly between 1972 and 1975). This meant that, compared to Sweden and many other European nations, the New Zealand welfare state began to lose its momentum in the postwar years and became a "welfare-state laggard."[59] Welfare-state activism was further curtailed by New Zealand's serious economic decline, hastened when Great Britain joined the European Economic Community, causing New Zealand to lose favored trading status for its agricultural products. The New Zealand welfare state would thus have found it difficult to expand with Sweden's generosity, even if the political climate had been different, and in several indicators of state-welfare prowess New Zealand is closer today to Switzerland and the United States than to most northern European nations. In total taxes as a percentage of Gross Domestic Product (GDP), New Zealand with 32% is the same as Switzerland, only slightly ahead of the United States (29%), and well behind Sweden (50%).[60] In total social expenditures as a percentage of GDP, New Zealand with 20% is about even with the United States (21%) and higher than Switzerland (15%), but well below Sweden (34%).[61]

This societal matrix of economic decline and diminished state welfare must be accorded significance in helping to preserve the familistic suburban life-style. The lack of welfare assistance has placed a greater burden of economic responsibility on families than is the case in Sweden, and the lower taxes have, in turn, given these families proportionately more take-home pay. At the same time, economic decline has forced New Zealand families into the kind of struggle for economic survival that characterized the Depression and that, as we now know, militates against family breakup. The absence of employment opportunities has hit women especially hard, probably reinforcing traditional gender roles and reducing the independence effect as a cause of family dissolution.[62]

The persistence of New Zealand family traditionalism is not only a by-product of economic trends and government economic policies, however. In sharp contrast to that of Sweden, the government policy of New Zealand until very recently outspokenly favored the bourgeois family, emphasizing the importance of marriage and full-time motherhood.[63] Rather than fund such programs as maternity leaves and public day care, for example, which would have brought more women into the labor force, cash allowances to all families with children were increased. Such political priorities may be evaluated from many different perspectives, but their effect on the preservation of the bourgeois nuclear family is probably significant.

Movement Away from the Bourgeois Family

Perhaps just because of its geographical isolation, most modernizing social trends seem to reach New Zealand later than other places at comparable levels of development. Thus New Zealand ranks relatively low among OECD nations in such "pathologies of modernization" as high rates of property crime and suicide. It is likely that New Zealand is fundamentally no different from other advanced nations, however, and that these trends will probably eventually reach it. This holds true for family trends as well as others.

The signs of family change in New Zealand are already distinct. In virtually every statistical measure of the contemporary family trend in Western societies, such as falling fertility rates, decreasing family size, higher rates of marital dissolution, and more married women in the work force, New Zealand is currently shifting in the direction of Sweden.[64] The total fertility rate in New Zealand at 1.9, for example, is close to that of Sweden and below replacement level. It is very likely that the percentage of women in the labor force will sharply increase if and when economic conditions in New Zealand improve. In regard to at least one measure, the percentage of illegitimate births, New Zealand is already well in advance of Switzerland. An estimated 25% of all New Zealand births in 1984 took place outside of marriage, compared to 6% in Switzerland (and 45% in Sweden).[65] There is also some indication that nonmarital cohabitation in New Zealand is on the increase.[66] Finally, following a change in the divorce law in 1980, the crude divorce rate skyrocketed to one of the highest in the world.

As in Switzerland, New Zealand's pace of social change seems somnolent in comparison to Sweden's. Yet, also like Switzerland, New Zealand gives evidence of being not a society apart, but a society behind.

Notes

[1]Population Reference Bureau, (1987), "World Population Data Sheet."

[2]See Carol L. Schmid (1981), *Conflict and Consensus in Switzerland.*

[3]For an entertaining account of the importance of universal military training in Swiss life, see John McPhee (1983), *La Place de la Concorde Suisse.*

[4]For a general discussion of Swiss society, See James Murray Luck (ed.) (1978), *Modern Switzerland.*

[5]Kurt K. Lüscher, Verena Ritter, and Peter Gross (1973), *Early Child Care in Switzerland:* 23.

[6]*Ibid.:* 7.

[7]*Ibid.:* 34.

[8]Ragnar Berfenstam, and Inger William-Olsson (1973), *Early Child Care in Sweden:* 17.

[9]*Ibid.:* 18.

[10]Organization for Economic Cooperation and Development (1986), *OECD Observer 139:* 15.

[11]Francois Höpflinger (1987), *Wandel der Familienbildung in Westeuropa:* Table 4, p. 83.

[12]Ralph Segalman (1986), *The Swiss Way of Welfare: Lessons for the Western World:* 151.

[13]Höpflinger (1987), *Wandel:* Table 23, p. 190.

[14]Kurt Lüscher (1983), "Die Schweizer Familien der achtziger Jahr," *Neue Zurcher Zeitung,* October 10: 18–19. Cited in Segalman (1986), *The Swiss Way of Welfare:* 151.

[15]See Robert Schoen, and John Baj (1984), "Cohort Marriage and Divorce in Five Western Countries," pp. 197–229 in Richard F. Tomasson (ed.), *Comparative Social Research,* Vol. 7.

[16]Lüscher "Schweizer Familien." Cited in Segalman (1986), *The Swiss Way of Welfare:* 151.

[17]See Ilda Simona (1985), "Switzerland," pp. 147–53 in Jennie Farley (ed.), *Women Workers in Fifteen Countries.*

[18]*The New York Times,* September 23, 1985.

[19]For a discussion of the legal situation of women before this new legislation, see Margrit Baumann, and M. Näf-Hoffmann (1978), "The Status of Women in Society and in Law," pp. 361–380 in Luck (ed.), *Modern Switzerland.*

[20]Kümmerly and Frey (1986), *Switzerland:* 28.

[21]For example, in 1981 Switzerland ranked last among the western European nations in total social expenditures as a percentage of GDP. The figures are Switzerland: 15%, Sweden: 33.5%, United States: 21%. OECD (1984), *OECD Observer 126* (January): 5.

[22]Armin Gretler and Pierre-Emeric Mandl (1973), *Values, Trends and Alternatives in Swiss Society: A Prospective Analysis:* 86.

[23]See Jonathan Steinberg (1976), *Why Switzerland?*

[24]OECD (1985), *OECD Observer 136:* 32.

[25]OECD (1986), *OECD Observer 139:* 22.

[26]*Ibid.:* 17.

[27]Steinberg (1976), *Why Switzerland?:* 190.

[28]Robert Chester (ed.) (1977), *Divorce in Europe:* 301.

29United Nations (1982), *U.N. Demographic Yearbook:* Table 33.

30Jean Kellerhals et al. (1977), "Switzerland," in Chester (1977), *Divorce in Europe:* 209.

31Höpflinger (1987), *Wandel:* Table 6, p. 61.

32Population Reference Bureau (1987), "World Population Data Sheet." By other estimates, the Swiss and Swedish birthrates are about the same. See Höpflinger (1987), *Wandel:* Table 18, p. 164.

33d'Olivier Blanc (1985), "Les Ménages en Suisse," *Population* 40–4,5: 657–674.

34*Ibid.*

35James Murray Luck (1985), *History of Switzerland:* 828.

36*Ibid.:* 724.

37 See Segalman (1986), *The Swiss Way of Welfare;* Ralph Segalman (1986), "Welfare and Dependency in Switzerland," *The Public Interest* 82: 106–121; and Walter Rüegg (1985), "Social Rights or Social Responsibilities? The Case of Switzerland," pp. 182–199 in S. N. Eisenstadt and Ora Ahimeir (eds.) (1985), *The Welfare State and its Aftermath.*

38See Keith Sinclair (1984), *A History of New Zealand.*

39Francis G. Castles (1985), *The Working Class and Welfare:* 26.

40David G. Pearson and David C. Thorns (1983), *Eclipse of Equality:* 176.

41OECD (1986), *OECD Observer* 139: 15.

42Social Monitoring Group (1985), *From Birth to Death:* 83, 87.

431980 data from: United Nations (1982), *U. N. Demographic Yearbook.* The relatively low divorce rate is due in part to the fact that "no-fault" divorce did not come to New Zealand until 1980; since then divorces can be granted to marriages that have dissolved irrevocably after a married couple has lived apart for 2 years. Unlike Sweden, New Zealand has required for most couples the intervention of a family counselor to explore the possibility of reconciliation at the time a separation order is filed with the Family Court.

44Peggy G. Koopman-Boyden and Claudia D. Scott (1984), *The Family and Government Policy in New Zealand:* 31.

45Social Monitoring Group (1985), *From Birth to Death:* 58. At the same time, the percentage of illegitimate births is relatively high and climbing. The estimate for 1984 was 25% of all births; some 90% of these were to two-parent couples, however. Pp. 16, 18.

46Pearson and Thorns (1983), *Eclipse of Equality:* 187.

47OECD (1986), *OECD Observer* 141: 5.

48Graeme Dunstall, quoted in W. H. Oliver (ed.) (1981), *The Oxford History of New Zealand:* 404.

49Barry J. Kirkwood (1979), "Population and Social Policy," pp. 281–294 in R. J. W. Neville and C. J. O'Neill (eds.), *The Population of New Zealand—Interdisciplinary Perspectives.*

50New Zealand is a young society in another respect, too. Only 10% of the population is over the age of 65, compared to Sweden's 17% and Switzerland's 15%.

51An interesting dimension of this is that, unlike most other societies, New Zealand has almost no association between social class and fertility. Miriam Gilson Vosburgh (1978), *The New Zealand Family and Social Change: A Trend Analysis:* 103. It should be noted in this connection that, unlike Sweden and Switzerland, New Zealand has a relatively large indigenous population. Maoris, together with Polynesians from nearby islands, currently make up 11% of the New Zealand population; their integration into

New Zealand society is generally regarded as more substantial than that, for example, of United States blacks.

[52]G. R. Hawke (1982), "Incomes Policy in New Zealand," *VUW Working Papers in Economic History* 81-3, Quoted in Koopman-Boyden and Scott (1984), *Family:* 168.

[53]Quoted in H. Mol and M. T. V. Reidy (1973), "Religion in New Zealand," pp. 264-282 in Stephen Webb and John Collette (eds.), *New Zealand Society:* 264.

[54]Erik Olssen (1981), "Towards a New Society," pp. 250-278 in Oliver (1981), *Oxford History:* 256.

[55]Erik Olssen (1980), "Women, Work and Family: 1880-1926," pp. 159-183 in Phillida Bunkle and Beryl Hughes (eds.), *Women in New Zealand Society.*

[56]Pearson and Thorn (1983), *Eclipse of Equality:* Chapter 9.

[57]P. J. Gibbons (1981), "The Climate of Opinion," in Oliver (1981), *Oxford History,* quoted in Pearson and Thorns (1983), *Eclipse of Equality:* 226.

[58]Graeme Dunstall (1981), "The Social Pattern," pp. 397-429 in Oliver, *Oxford History:* 404.

[59]Castles (1985), *The Working Class and Welfare:* 29ff. Castles suggests the reasons for this lag and feels that New Zealand (as well as Australia), compared to European counterparts, is a "reluctant welfare state" that has favored wage-earner security over more broad-based welfare of the citizenry. See also Brian Easton (1980), *Social Policy and the Welfare State in New Zealand.*

[60]OECD (1985), *OECD Observer* 136: 32.

[61]OECD (1984), *OECD Observer* 126: 5.

[62]A study of Swiss women found some association between economic recession and traditional attitudes toward gender roles. Thomas Held and René Levy (1983), "Economic Recession and Swiss Women's Attitudes Toward Marital Role Segregation," pp. 373-395 in Eugen Lupri (ed.), *The Changing Position of Women in Family and Society.*

[63]Judith Aitken (1980), "Women in the Political Life of New Zealand," pp. 11-33 in Bunkle and Hughes (eds.), *Women in New Zealand Society.*

[64]On divorce trends in New Zealand, see Roderick Phillips (1981), *Divorce in New Zealand: A Social History.* On fertility trends, see D. Ian Pool and Janet Sceats (1981), *Fertility and Family Formation in New Zealand.* On general family trends, see David A. Swain (1979), "Marriages and Families," pp. 112-124 in Neville and O'Neill, (eds.), *Population;* and Barry J. Kirkwood (1979), "Population and Social Policy," pp. 281-294 in Neville and O'Neill (eds.), *Population.*

[65]Social Monitoring Group (1985), *From Birth to Death:* 16. It is interesting to note that the mother country England and Wales, with a 17% illegitimacy rate, also had one of the highest rates outside of the Scandinavian countries. See Höpflinger (1987), *Wandel:* Table 23, p. 190.

[66]E. A. Quin and C. J. O'Neill (1984), *Cohabitation in New Zealand: Legal and Social Aspects.*

Family and Society in the United States

Hundreds of books and thousands of scholarly articles have been written about family change in America over the past few decades. The purpose of this chapter is not to review those materials, much less to do justice to all the information they contain. Rather, it is to give a brief interpretation of American society commensurate with those presented in the preceding chapter for Switzerland and New Zealand. While Switzerland and New Zealand are small and far from the center of the world stage, the United States is one of the world's largest nations, a political superpower with the world's most potent economy. But family trends do not vary according to such differences in power and magnitude. The important thing for this discussion is that the United States, like Switzerland and New Zealand, is a highly advanced, democratic society with a postindustrial economy and great material wealth and that it shares with these two nations, in contrast to Sweden, a reputation for family traditionalism. Thus it provides another special opportunity for placing the family situation in Sweden in comparative perspective.

In Chapter 2, a discussion of the history of the idea of family decline within sociology concluded that in the United States today scholarly perspectives on what is happening to the American family have become misleading. Where once there was clarity, today there is some confusion. Yet looking at American society from the vantage point of the category of advanced nations, the perspective of this discussion, part of this confusion is understandable. The United States is not only a very complex society, hence difficult to comprehend, but also quite different from most of the other societies, even exceptional in some respects.

The immediate problem in discussing American families in their societal context is that the nation is very large and diverse. Unlike in New Zealand, Sweden, and even relatively heterogeneous Switzerland, there are really many Americas one could write about—many distinct subcultures that make up one loosely connected national unity. These distinct subcultures include the large American black population, the growing Hispanic and Asian populations, and the Mormons. Such diversity makes all generalizations about American society as a whole a little suspect. In the smaller nations, these kinds of social differences either do not exist or are less extreme in form. To make my comparative analysis as accurate as possible and yet structurally similar to that in earlier chapters, I focus mainly on the family situation of the non-Hispanic whites of the middle and working classes in America, bringing in other groups only to clarify or to round out the picture.

In many respects America should not even be classified as a nation of "family traditionalism." With the highest divorce rate among advanced societies and the highest percentage of single-parent families, the United States surpasses even Sweden in its family nontraditionalism in regard to these indicators. Other significant facts that testify to American nontraditionalism include a relatively high rate of illegitimacy, a high rate of serial monogamy (several different spouses over the course of a lifetime), and possibly (comparative data are not available) a high rate of extramarital sexual promiscuity or as it is sometimes called, sexual polygamy. For a while in the 1960s and early 1970s, the United States also seemed to be the Western world's leader in multiadult households, or communal living. All of these facts could be used to argue that it is the United States, not Sweden, where the family has moved farthest from the bourgeois nuclear form. At the very least, then, the family situation in the United States is filled with contradictions, which need to be clarified and resolved in the course of our discussion.

American Family Traditionalism

Perhaps the main area in which America ranks with Switzerland and New Zealand as a nation of family traditionalism, and so contrasts with Sweden, is the cultural sphere. Unlike in Sweden, American national culture is imbued with the importance of the family. Familism (defined as the belief in a strong sense of family identification and loyalty, mutual assistance among family members, and a concern for the perpetuation of the family unit) remains an outstanding national value. Politicians and other public figures constantly refer to the family as the bedrock of society and express concern about its decline. They typically run for election with their families at their side, and politicians with a questionable family situation in their own private lives have a difficult time getting elected. In middle America, "having a good family" ranks as one of the highest of human ideals.

A second important dimension of American family traditionalism is that almost everyone in the United States gets married at some time in their lives. This is still largely true also in other advanced societies, but not to the extent found in the United States. The United States has long had one of the highest marriage rates in the world, and even in recent years it has maintained that rate. In the cohort born in 1945, the United States had the highest proportion of males "ever marrying," 95%, compared to Sweden's low of 75%.[1] This high marriage rate extends also to the rate of remarriage after divorce or the death of a spouse. In recent years, five out of six men and three out of four women eventually remarry following a divorce[2] (in 1983, 46% of all marriages were remarriages, up from 35% in 1973). In connection with the high marriage rate, Americans seem especially fond of large weddings under religious auspices, with all the ceremonial trappings. The high marriage rate also means that, so far at least, the United States has maintained a fairly low level of nonmarital cohabitation, comparable to that of Switzerland and New Zealand and in a different league from Sweden.

The United States also displays a strong stamp of traditionalism in that, like Switzerland, it places great responsibility on the family unit in the pursuit of social welfare. The recurring refrain in American political life is that "the family ought to be doing these things"—for example, paying for private medical insurance, taking care of the elderly, and providing child care. American government is willing, if necessary, to help the family carry out its responsibilities, but typically seeks diligently to avoid "undermining" the family in the process. Nowhere is this clearer than in child care, where there has been great reluctance to provide services publically that "the family ought to be providing privately." It could be said, therefore, that the American family performs more of the traditional functions of families than does the Swedish family; fewer of these functions have been transferred to the public sector.

A final way in which the American family remains relatively traditional is in its home-centered life style, including the amount of time spent in, and working on, the family house. The percentage of owned, single-family homes in America is one of the highest in the world, and these homes are the world's most spacious and best equipped. Compared to other advanced societies, American housing also tends to be built at low densities and detached from public services, the attributes of what is known as urban sprawl. Because many facilities that are community owned in other nations are, as it were, built into American houses and yards (especially recreational facilities), Americans tend to lead a more privatized life centered in the home.[3] And because the house is the single largest financial investment most people make, and the cost of personal services is increasing, Americans also find themselves spending a growing portion of their leisure time working on their homes.[4]

Explanations for American Family Traditionalism

How does one account for this family traditionalism in such a wealthy and progressive nation as the United States? From a broad sociological perspective, American society is an amalgam of some of the main characteristics we found in both Switzerland and New Zealand. To explain Swiss family traditionalism, for example, we focused on three characteristics of Swiss society: religion, a conservative sociopolitical ideology, and a decentralized political structure. These three characteristics, together with the "settler-society" traits that the United States shares with New Zealand, are probably the dominant factors accounting for American family traditionalism as well. Yet the United States also has some characteristics found in neither of these societies, and indeed in no other society.

The United States is probably the most religious of the advanced societies, the closest competitor being one of the poorest and least developed of all western European nations, the Republic of Ireland. A Roman Catholic people, the Irish go to church more often than do Americans. But on many religious indicators, the Irish actually fall behind the United States. Thus 57% of Americans say they belong to churches and religious organizations, compared to 31% in Ireland (and 9% in Sweden); 85% of Americans say they "take some moments of prayer, meditation or contemplation or something like that," compared to 81% in Ireland (and 33% in Sweden). Also, more Americans than Irish believe in Heaven and Hell.[5]

The historical roots of America's religiosity have long been the subject of detailed analyses, as have the societal factors responsible for the maintenance of a high degree of religiosity in this nation over time.[6] One societal factor is the lack of an official state religion in America, resulting in a diversity of religious groups. Another is the relatively mobile and unstructured nature of American society (compared to the more stable and tradition-bound societies of Europe), which gives religion a special importance as one of the few institutions that can provide members with a strong group connection and a tie to the past.

Whatever its reasons for being, organized religion in America has undoubtedly played an influential role in keeping alive traditional family values and fostering a strong concern for familism. America's religious leaders are at the forefront of public discussion regarding such issues as formal marriage and family solidarity. As in Switzerland and New Zealand, religion in America has probably been especially influential in holding down the rate of nonmarital cohabitation, particularly if children are involved. It has obviously not been so influential in keeping down the divorce rate.

The United States also shares with Switzerland the attribute of being, in sociopolitical terms, one of the most conservative nations in the West.

America remains a staunch believer in capitalism and the "free" market, and avoids "government solutions" whenever possible. It places a high value on self-help, individual initiative, and the achievements of the capitalist entrepreneur. These conservative doctrines and beliefs have helped to make the United States today one of the most antigovernment of all advanced societies. "Government bureaucrat" has become a word of contempt, civil servants are held in low esteem, and taxes (although they are the lowest in the West!) are paid with the utmost reluctance.[7] Recent presidents have run for election on populist, antigovernment platforms, promising to "clean out the mess in Washington." At the local level, the United States is probably the most "ungoverned" of the Western nations, that is, local governments exercise weak collective control over private property and take miminal collective action to promote the public welfare. American cities display the results of this political dispensation; they are without question the most deteriorated of all the cities of the advanced societies.

In line with its popular attitudes toward government, the United States lags well behind most other advanced societies in the creation of welfare-state programs, including government family policies. It is the only major industrialized nation, for example, that has no general allowance program for families with children and lacks a national insurance plan covering the medical expenses connected with childbirth. It is one of the few nations that does not provide maternity benefits to all mothers.[8] Political attempts over the years to develop a national family policy have consistently failed.[9] America's best record in social programs is in public education, an activity conducted almost entirely at the local and state levels and, in the case of primary and secondary schools, typically apart from the formal structure of government.

The United States is exceptional among the advanced nations for never having developed a politically significant socialist movement, and socialist ideology remains anathema to most Americans. American workers would detest being thought of as proletarians (and they would never use that term), preferring to consider themselves as middle class (bourgeois). Even unionization has made relatively scant inroads in American life and is now in decline among the working classes. Class-consciousness in general has been shown to be relatively low. These traits suggest that bourgeois values are very strong in the American mind; every American, in a manner of speaking, would love nothing more than to have a bourgeois life-style, with a home and property, a car, and a high level of material consumption. A large percentage of Americans actually have achieved such a life-style, even if in a modest way.

Such a bourgeois mentality is surely well-tailored to the preservation of the bourgeois family. With the home and the property should go, according to bourgeois logic, the traditional nuclear-family unit. The unit of "self-help" and "individual initiative" within American bourgeois capitalism is the family, more than the individual; it is the family that is expected to remain durable and steadfast in the pursuit of wealth and the conquest of adversity. And it is to the younger generation of family members that the property and other accumulated wealth of capitalist enterprise is, in time, to be turned over.

At the opposite extreme from socialism, America probably has more "libertarians" than any of the other advanced societies—persons who regard personal liberty as the supreme value. Such slogans as "Live free or die" and "Get off my back" are culturally ubiquitous in American life. Americans have a real fear that the government, the local community, or even their neighbors are somehow going to tell them what to do and thus dominate their lives. They firmly believe that there should be as little public control over the individual as possible and that individual rights almost always have priority over collective or public rights.[10] In this sense, Americans are among the most individualistic of modern peoples.

This individualistic impulse is expressed as much in family as in individual terms. American political and legal culture is permeated with a relatively strong concern for the family's "right to privacy," a concern for the sanctity of the family and its insulation from the powers of government. The prevailing view is that the family must be "tirelessly protected against government encroachment."[11] Such a view assumes that the family is not only "off limits" for government action, but also so self-sufficient that it does not (or at least should not) require government help. This characteristic of American political culture has undoubtedly retarded the enactment of public-welfare measures that would have benefited the many families that are not so self-sufficient. Yet at the same time it has probably led some families, out of necessity if for no other reason, to a greater degree of traditional self-sufficiency than they might otherwise have achieved.

The prevailing view of the family's right to privacy has also provided American families with more power over their own members than is true in other advanced societies. Unfortunately, this provision has probably been at some cost in individual rights, particularly the rights of children and women. While comparative data are not available, the amount of wife and child abuse in America seems to be relatively high (some even maintain that it is growing). Compared to most other advanced societies, American authorities have shown a reluctance to intervene in cases of personal abuse within families. The power to intervene in a family to protect a child, for example, is vested in the courts in the United States, which require lengthy legal proceedings to justify such actions; in Sweden, that power is vested in an administrative agency of government.

Another important societal factor related to American family traditionalism is that the United States is a settler society, like New Zealand but quite unlike Switzerland. Both the United States and New Zealand had a frontier to conquer, an indigenous population to subjugate, and an entirely new social structure to create. Each nation has had to assimilate streams of immigrant groups, and each has placed equality of opportunity in a high position in its hierarchy of supreme values. America has never had New Zealand's radical political impulses, however, and while New Zealand was a welfare-state pioneer, the United States has long been a welfare-state laggard.

In a settler society, the importance of the family is enhanced because, under primitive frontier conditions, there are few other institutions in operation. People must depend on their families for things that in more-settled societies are supplied by the larger community. In a modest way, this phenomenon was seen to reemerge in America's post-World War II suburban boom. Young families moved to unsettled areas, where there was as yet little social structure, and they were forced to turn inward. Familism was accentuated by the fact that the American suburban pattern minimized public facilities, forcing suburbanites to rely on their own private resources. Thus, much like New Zealand's, America's suburbs became a modern haven of traditional familism.

Finally, it should be noted that American family traditionalism is accentuated by the atypical behavior of America's large minority groups and recent immigrants. The relatively young marriage age of blacks and Hispanics, for example, together with their high fertility rates and large household sizes (sometimes with extended families) pulls the United States in the traditional direction in those areas. Also, female gender roles tend to be more traditional among many minority groups, especially the Hispanic population. Minority groups also pull the nation in a nontraditional direction, however, as in the case of family instability.

American Family Instability

If these features of American society have helped to maintain the bourgeois nuclear family, how then does one explain America's family instability as measured by high rates of divorce and single-parent families? While a very large percentage of Americans marry, their marital breakup rate is by far the highest among the advanced societies. The number of divorces per 1000 persons in 1982, for example, was 5.03 in the United States, compared to New Zealand's 3.89, Sweden's 2.49, and Switzerland's 1.79.[12] Based on recent divorce rates, the chances of a first marriage ending in divorce in America today are about one in two. While Americans hold strongly to the ideal of the intact nuclear family, their percentage of single-parent families also ranks highest; in 1980 it was 21.5% (of all family households), compared to Sweden's 18%. Between 1970 and 1985 single-parent families in the United States more than doubled—from 12.9 to 26.3%.[13]

In the search for explanations of American family instability, it is important to realize that the high rate of marital dissolution in the United States is of long historical standing. Relatively liberal divorce laws came earlier to the United States than to Europe, and the centuries-old ethnic and religious heterogeneity and high residential mobility of American society have doubtless also contributed to this high rate. At the turn of the twentieth century, the United States' divorce rate was already more than twice that of France and England (and about six times the rate of Sweden).[14] While the American divorce rate has increased enormously since that time, the European rates have increased even more, bringing them closer to the American level.

One prominent explanation for the American family's instability today is that the United States, unlike any other advanced society, has a sizable "underclass" of people living in relative poverty, a "heterogeneous grouping of inner-city families and individuals whose behavior contrasts sharply with that of mainstream America."[15] The highest rates of family instability have occurred within this grouping. It is the American underclass in which we most commonly find those factors associated with poverty and income instability that are known to be strongly correlated with divorce and marital separation, such as brief courtships, early marriages, teen pregnancies, and a high rate of residential mobility. The underclass has been heavily black, with a unique historical background of involuntary servitude and racial discrimination. The black rate of divorce is more than twice the white rate, and more than 60% of black families with children today have only a single parent at home. Increasingly Hispanics are joining the American underclass, however, a process being expedited by the fact that the United States is the only advanced, Western society that borders on the Third World.

Yet the American underclass with its conditions of poverty cannot provide a sufficient explanation for the high rate of American family instability. For one thing, the underclass makes up only a small percentage of the American population, and its contribution to national statistics can easily be exaggerated. Although the American black-teenage-pregnancy rate is very high, for example, discounting these blacks would lower the national rate only by one fifth; the rate among American whites would still be twice that of the closest European competitor.[16] For another, divorce in America today has become almost as common among the higher classes as among the lower.

A common opinion once existed among social scientists that, as expressed in the words of two prominent American demographers in the 1960s, "Declines in the relative frequency of divorce and separation should result to the extent that there are reductions in poverty and general improvements in the socioeconomic status of the population."[17] This opinion now appears to be manifestly in error. As the material standard of living of the United States has improved, the divorce rate has risen in all segments of the population. The reason for this is that divorce, as we saw in the case of Sweden, is caused not only by poverty but also by affluence. A proposition about family dissolution in advanced societies called forth by the Swedish experience can be applied here: family dissolution can be caused as much by economic security as by economic insecurity. While there is less government-provided economic security in America than in most other advanced societies, considerable economic security within the higher classes has been generated by private affluence. And the divorce rate in these classes has been rising.

In accounting for the high rate of family instability in America, one should not dismiss the importance of changing gender roles, another of the factors employed to explain the Swedish family situation. Changes in the female gender role seem to be occurring at a faster rate in the United States than in the other two family-traditional nations we have discussed. In the United States, in 1980, the rate of female participation in the labor force was 63%, which was much closer to Sweden's (77%) than to Switzerland's (49%) or New Zealand's (46%).

Also, it is reasonable to suppose that cultural trends associated with the growing importance placed on "self-fulfillment" and the "therapeutic ideology" in advanced societies are comparatively well established in the United States. In a recent bestseller, *Habits of the Heart: Individualism and Commitment in American Life,* these trends were discussed under the labels "expressive individualism" and the "therapeutic attitude." The authors of this perceptive book view the emerging value system of America as "bureaucratic consumer capitalism," in which expressive individualism overtakes moral commitment.[18] If such a value system has in fact become widespread in American life, it surely could be regarded as another important contributor to the high family-dissolution rate.

Some of the same social conditions that have contributed to American family traditionalism also help to explain family instability; these conditions have contradictory effects. A good example of this is the character of American metropolitan communities. To a greater degree than in other advanced societies, the metropolitan communities in which most Americans live are new, raw, mobile, relatively unstructured, poorly serviced by public services and facilities, and often filled with interethnic tension. Such community characteristics help to magnify the importance of the self-sufficiency of the traditional nuclear family, but at the same time they provide an environmental climate not well suited to alleviating family stress when family self-sufficiency weakens or breaks down.

Thus American families in metropolitan areas are largely "thrown on their own devices." The problem is that strong families have always depended over the long run on strong communities, and the strength of both have declined. We have the situation in America, often noted by family sociologists, where too much is expected in an unsupportive environment of an already fragile institution. There are, of course, many voluntary and church-related community services and facilities in the United States, but for Americans outside the networks of these activities (and they are the ones with the highest divorce rates) the American metropolitan community can be a privatized, stressful, unsupportive, and lonely place, indeed.

A further word should be said about America's high teenage-pregnancy rate, the highest by far among the advanced nations. Whereas this rate has been dropping in recent years in most advanced societies, it actually increased in the United States. The pregnancy rate for 15- to 19-year-old American girls stands today at 96 per 1000, compared to only 45 in England and Wales, 43 in France, 35 in Sweden, and 14 in the Netherlands (the lowest of the six nations studied).[19] The United States also holds a dominant position in its high rate of teenage abortions.

This high teenage pregnancy rate reflects both family traditionalism and family modernism. Young age at first birth is a traditional phenomenon, insofar as this age has been rapidly rising in advanced societies in recent years. However, a great deal of teen pregnancy takes place out of wedlock, which in part is a modern dimension of the family. It is of interest to note that low teen-pregnancy rates in general are associated with nontraditional attitudes toward sexuality. A recent study by the Alan Guttmacher Institute concluded that countries with the lowest pregnancy and abortion rates among teenagers had the most liberal attitudes toward sex, as well as easy access to contraceptive services (contraceptives offered free or at low cost and without parental notification), and comprehensive programs in sex education. The United States was found by this study to have relatively traditional sexual attitudes and practices. American attitudes focused more on sexual morality than on pregnancy prevention, and sex education in the schools was limited; also, American teenagers were less likely than others to use contraceptives.[20]

Concluding Remarks

Among advanced societies, America may be a land of relative family traditionalism, but it is certainly not a land of family stability. In regard to many family trends under way in these societies, the United States has been a laggard. Compared to other developed nations of the West, Americans tend to marry more, and at an earlier age, and to have slightly larger families; the rate of nonmarital cohabitation is still relatively low. But with respect to family instability, the United States is very "advanced," having for generations been one of the world's leaders in the rate of marital dissolution. In some ways this nation is catching up to other advanced societies, but in other respects the rest of the advanced world is catching up to the United States.

The general direction of family change in contemporary America, however, seems little different from what it is in other wealthy nations. The marriage age is going up, the marriage rate is dropping, the nonmarital cohabitation rate is increasing, and more women are entering the labor force, to state but a few of the many changes that are under way. Such changes suggest a common contemporary family trend to which all advanced societies are a party. This trend—a postnuclear-family trend—is the focus of the next chapter.

Notes

[1]Robert Schoen and John Baj (1984), "Cohort Marriage and Divorce in Five Western Countries," pp. 197–229 in Richard F. Tomasson (ed.), *Comparative Social Research*, Vol. 7.

[2]Andrew Cherlin (1981), *Marriage, Divorce, Remarriage:* 29.

[3]This theme is explored in David Popenoe (1985), *Private Pleasure, Public Plight: American Metropolitan Community Life in Comparative Perspective.* In this book the privatization of community life in America is compared with that of Sweden and England.

[4]See time-budget data in Oxford Analytica (1986), *America in Perspective:* 80.

[5]Data from international surveys by the Gallup Organization (1981), reported in Oxford Analytica (1986), *America in Perspective:* 121–124.

[6]For two influential sociological analyses, see Will Herberg (1960), *Protestant, Catholic Jew,* and Robert N. Bellah (1975), *The Broken Covenant.*

[7]There has been a sharp decline in recent decades, according to public-opinion polls, in the amount of confidence held by Americans in most of their political institutions. See Louis Harris (1987), *Inside America:* 255–261.

[8]Sheila B. Kamerman and Alfred J. Kahn, (eds.) (1978), *Family Policy: Government and Family in Fourteen Countries;* Sheila B. Kamerman and Alfred J. Kahn (1981), *Child Care, Family Benefits, and Working Parents: A Study in Comparative Policy.*

[9]Gilbert Y. Steiner (1981), *The Futility of Family Policy.*

[10]For a recent discussion of this in the context of American welfare efforts, see Nathan Glazer (1986), "Welfare and 'Welfare' in America," pp. 40–63 in Richard Rose and Rei Shiratori (eds.), *The Welfare State East and West.*

[11]Carolyn Teich Adams and Kathryn Teich Winston (1980), *Mothers at Work: Public Policies in the United States, Sweden, and China:* 203. This book contrasts the situation of the family in the political cultures of the three nations.

[12]United Nations (1985), *U.N. Demographic Yearbook:* Table 14.

[13]Data from U.S. Census Bureau reported in *The New York Times,* November 6, 1986: C13.

[14]Calculated by Carle C. Zimmerman and reported in Adams and Winston (1980), *Mothers at Work:* 233.

[15]William Julius Wilson (1987), *The Truly Disadvantaged:* 7.

[16]Study conducted by the Alan Guttmacher Institute. Reported in Nadine Brozan (1985), "Rate of Pregnancies for U.S. Teen-agers Found High in Study," *The New York Times,* March 13: C1, C7. The full study is Elise F. Jones et al. (1986), *Teenage Pregnancy in Industrialized Countries.*

[17]Robert Parke, Jr. and Paul C. Glick (1967), "Prospective Changes in Marriage and the Family," *Journal of Marriage and the Family* 29: 249–256.

[18]Robert N. Bellah et al. (1985), *Habits of the Heart: Individualism and Commitment in American Life.*

[19]Brozan (1985), "Rate of Pregnancies."

[20]*Ibid.* See also Judith Senderowitz and John M. Paxman (1985), "Adolescent Fertility: Worldwide Concerns," *Population Bulletin* 40-2: 1–51.

Part
IV

Conclusions

A Postnuclear Family Trend

Based on the experiences of Sweden, Switzerland, New Zealand, the United States, and other advanced Western societies, it is possible to postulate a single family trend involving movement away from the bourgeois family and even away from the nuclear family-kinship system. This can be called a postnuclear-family trend, a trend toward a hypothetical postnuclear family system; it is a continuation of the global family trend discussed in Chapter 3. Among advanced nations, a postnuclear-family trend appears to be developing at different stages, moving at varying speeds, with all these nations not necessarily following precisely the same path. There is enough consistency of development among these nations, however, to discern a modern-family trend based on a relatively fixed sequence of events. The purpose of this chapter is to pull together in summary form what is known about such a postnuclear-family trend and to speculate about its logical extension into the future.

With regard mainly to the dimension of fertility, some demographers have labeled the recent sequence of family changes the second demographic transition. This refers to the steep decline of fertility to a level well below that at which population replacement occurs, the first demographic transition having been the rapid decline in both mortality and fertility rates associated with the rise of the modern nuclear family.[1] As one of these demographers, Dirk J. van de Kaa, has noted about recent family changes, "there is strong evidence of a logical ordering. Each step taken seems to have led to the next; each option chosen made a further choice possible."[2] This new demographic transition, I am arguing, is but one part of a more general family trend that is heading in the direction of a postnuclear family system.

According to many key statistical measures, to be discussed below, the family systems of other advanced societies appear to be moving today toward the conditions found in what, I have suggested, is the lead nation, Sweden. Contemporary Swedish family conditions can therefore be used to posit a temporary "end state" for a postnuclear-family trend. There is no guarantee that the family system in every other advanced society, some years down the line, will become like Sweden's today. Also, as is true of all social trends, there is no assurance that this family trend will continue into the future in its present form; many things could intervene to force a change of direction. Still, based on all apparent tendencies today one can conclude that the family systems in the advanced nations are headed toward a common destiny.

The Historical Sequence of Postnuclear-Family Development

Because Sweden is currently the most advanced nation with respect to a postnuclear-family trend, it is reasonable to take the historical sequence of family events observed in Sweden as a prototype. To describe this sequence, let us pick it up as of the 1960s. Many of .the structural changes in the Swedish family, such as lower birthrates, higher divorce rates, and the shift of women into the labor force, were already under way well before World War II. Nevertheless, the 1960s constituted a dramatic turning point, for Sweden as well as other advanced nations. At this time, the post–World War II renaissance of the bourgeois nuclear family had already peaked and was starting to decline. Since that time, the movement away from the bourgeois nuclear family has continued with little change of pace.

Economically and culturally, the 1960s were a period of growing affluence and the advancement of individualistic values. During this period, the age of first sexual intercourse was dropping, and premarital sexual intercourse (especially intercourse among "nonengaged" couples) was becoming increasingly common. Important factors accounting for these changes were the widespread availability of contraceptive devices and a growth in the number of abortions (partly because of a change in the laws). Contraception practices provided a greater possibility for sex without procreation, for fewer unwanted children, and for fewer "forced marriages." The average age at first marriage, therefore, began to climb again, and the average age of women at the birth of their first child also began to rise. These trends toward later marriages and postponed first births were accelerated by the increased education of women and by the movement of women into the labor market.

Because childbearing and marriage were no longer so closely linked and the birth of children was postponed, marital dissolution began to occur earlier after marriages were formed; there was less reason for concern about the adverse effects of dissolution on children. This helped to bring about a skyrocketing rise in divorce rates, a trend that was accentuated by the easing of legal divorce restrictions. Because young people married without immediate procreation in mind and with the intention of delaying childbearing, a legal seal of approval (marriage) no longer seemed as important. Why not delay formal marriage until children were on the way? This led to a rapid decline in the number of marriages, a further increase in the average age at first marriage, and the widespread growth of nonmarital cohabitation.

Once nonmarital cohabitation became widely practiced and accepted, it soon became less obvious why one needed to get married at all just to have children. There were no longer legal penalties or social stigmas directed at the children of unmarried couples. The attitude became: "what is the importance of formal marriage anyway, since we have come this far together without it?" This attitude caused the age of first marriage to rise still further and increased the percentage of couples who presumably would never marry at all. In addition, remarriages (as distinct from postmarital cohabitation) became less common. The drop in legal marriages naturally led to a tremendous increase in out-of-wedlock births, especially among older women.

Contraceptives became universally used, and almost all children were now the end result of deliberate planning on the part of parents, whether married or unmarried. Because women were having children at older ages and having fewer children during the course of their lifetime, fertility rates dropped to all-time lows, well below the level necessary for population replacement. Average family size also dropped steadily.

Dissolution rates for unmarried couples tended to be higher than for married couples, and as nonmarital cohabitation increased, so did family dissolution. Family dissolution increased still further because the dissolution rates for subsequent unions are higher than for first unions. The increase in dissolution led to an expansion in the number of what can be called intimate "pair-bonds" that a person has during a lifetime (serial monogamy). At the same time, there was some increase in the amount of sexual activity with partners in addition to one's spouse (sexual polygamy).

The high rate of family dissolution diminished the chances of a child living through his or her childhood with both biological parents. During the course of growing up, a child became more likely to live with just one parent or with several sets of parents in two or more nuclear families. A rapid growth of single-parent families and stepfamilies began to occur.

Associated with the increased education of women and the increase of pair-bonded women in the labor force, a greater equality of power and decision making between males and females came about, both within the family and in the workplace. While women still had the primary responsibility for childrearing, men were becoming more involved in domestic activities.

Finally, more family functions were coming to be performed by persons or agencies outside the family, especially education, child care, and food preparation.

If a postnuclear-family trend is viewed in terms of the distribution of households, we note that there was a rapid increase in the percentage of single-person and other "nonfamily" households, households with pair-bonded adults but no children, and households with children but only one adult. The household containing two adults with children became a small fraction of the total. Extended family households, with more than two generations or more than one nuclear family, diminished almost to the point of extinction. Thus overall household composition shifted from relative uniformity to great diversity. Finally, average household size dropped to a level approaching just two persons per household.

Variations Among Nations in The Historical Sequence

These Swedish family events have not occurred in precisely the same sequence in other advanced societies, with the possible exception of Denmark. Yet most of the tendencies reflected in this sequence are present in other industrialized nations. This is the case if we rely on the following key indicators of family change: younger age at first intercourse, later age of marriage, later age of women at first birth, lower total fertility rate, lower marriage rate, increased nonmarital cohabitation, increased marital (and nonmarital pair-bond) dissolution rate, increased proportion of women in the labor force, and greater power symmetry among adult family members.

There have been occasions in recent years when some of these rates have leveled off and even briefly retreated. This is true for fertility rates in several countries, including Sweden, and also for marriage and divorce rates. It is quite possible that the fear of AIDS is currently reversing some previously established trends of sexual behavior, such as younger age at first intercourse, and AIDS is of course a factor that could potentially change many of these trends in the future. But in terms of their overall pattern of the past few decades, these indicators have been moving in the direction indicated.

It is important to note that while Sweden may lead the pack with respect to most key statistical indicators of a postnuclear-family trend, it is not the leader for all of them. In the light of available statistics, Sweden leads the advanced nations in the rates of nonmarital cohabitation (highest), illegitimacy (highest), marriage (lowest), and probably family dissolution (highest). In addition, Sweden leads in average age of marriage (latest), percentage of mothers in the labor force (highest), average household size (smallest), percentage of extended families (fewest), and probably power symmetry within the pair-bond (most symmetrical).

Regarding sexual activity, the picture is less clear. It is not known in which country sexual activity takes place at the youngest age, although Sweden may lead in the age at which pair-bonding (with cohabitation) first takes place. Nor is it known which nation is the most sexually permissive in the sense of people having the most sexual partners throughout their lives (sexual promiscuity and serial monogamy) and having sex with persons other than those with whom they have an intimate pair-bond (sexual polygamy). The United States might be the leader in these respects, as it is also the leader in divorces (because it has the highest marriage rate).

The percentage of single-parent families and stepfamilies (or blended families) is increasing in every nation. To some extent, single-parent families and stepfamilies are alternative family forms that emerge after family dissolution. In terms of the percentage of single-parent families, the United States seems to be the leader of the advanced societies (see Chapter 8), but this is probably due as much to the exceptional economic and cultural conditions of the large American underclass as to a postnuclear-family trend. Among societies without a large underclass, Sweden is probably the leader in single-parent families. Because of high remarriage rates, the United States may also be the leader in stepfamilies.

The logic of a postnuclear-family trend suggests an increase in the percentage of women who voluntarily have no children (voluntary childlessness). A postnuclear-family trend is so recent that at the present time there is no definite information about this; we must await the completion of the life course of the present generation of young women. West Germany today has the world's lowest total fertility rate (1.3).[3] This means that if the current age-specific birthrate remains constant throughout her childbearing years, the average German woman will have in her lifetime a total of only 1.3 children. This is well below the total fertility rate of 2.1 or 2.2 necessary for "population replacement." Why West Germany has the lowest fertility rate in the world is not clear. In a related development, and also for reasons that are not well understood, the Netherlands today apparently has the lowest pregnancy rate and birthrate among teenagers.[4]

Contrasting the Postnuclear and Nuclear Family Systems

The Bourgeois Nuclear Family System

The bourgeois nuclear family system had a main feature that made it fundamentally different from the postnuclear family system toward which advanced societies appear to be headed. (I speak of the bourgeois nuclear family in the past tense, though recognizing that it is still very much extant in advanced societies.) Both as a cultural ideal and as a common practice, the bourgeois nuclear family system effectively joined into a single institutional setting—the nuclear family unit bound together by legal marriage—three key dimensions of life: the intimate "pair-bonding" of adults, sexual intercourse, and the procreation of children.

First, most adults at some time in their lives pair-bonded with one other adult and almost always in the legally based pair-bond of marriage. Seldom did adults permanently pair-bond outside of this legal arrangement. Moreover, most adults pair-bonded during their lives with only one other person; when this was not the case, it was due to the death of one of the spouses. Once set up, therefore, the bourgeois nuclear-family unit continued until the death of one of the partners. Second, sexual intercourse was for the most part restricted to the marital pair-bond. This does not mean that no sexual activity took place outside of marriage; sexual activity for some engaged couples began prior to marriage, and men commonly used the services of prostitutes. But compared to a postnuclear family system there was probably less premarital and extramarital sexual intercourse, certainly for women, and most nonmarital occasions for intercourse were clearly proscribed by cultural norms (and often by laws as well). Third, most pair-bonds in the bourgeois nuclear family system were formed for the purpose of procreation and in fact resulted in offspring.

Thus the bourgeois nuclear family, based on a marital pair-bond between two adults, was an institution that *simultaneously* governed the intimate, long-term heterosexual relationships between adults, the practice of human sexuality, and the procreation and socialization of children.

A Postnuclear Family System

As societies move toward a postnuclear family system, the pattern of association between intimate pair-bonding (with or without marriage), sexual activity, and the procreation of children is being abandoned. These functions of the bourgeois nuclear family are becoming differentiated into separate spheres of life that are dissociated from one another.

Within a postnuclear family system, the desires for pair-bonding of most adults do not seem to have diminished. (I speak of a postnuclear family system in the present tense, though recognizing that it is still in the process of being achieved and remains a far-from-completed social reality.) Adults still desire a relatively permanent relationship with one other person, usually one of the opposite sex; indeed, pair-bonding (but not marrying) now takes place at an increasingly younger age than before. But most adults now pair-bond with more than one other adult during their lifetimes. This means that the dissolution rate of pair-bonding (for reasons other than death) is climbing and that for both marital and nonmarital pair-bonding dissolution is occurring earlier in the relationship than in years past. Formal marriage in a postnuclear family system, on the other hand, becomes considerably diminished in importance; many persons never marry at all.

Postnuclear pair-bonds almost always have a sexual relationship as a principal component, but sexuality between adults is by no means limited to the pair-bond partner. Sexual intercourse is regarded not merely as a component of family life and a bond of intimacy between two spouses, but as a generalized activity between adults that generates intrinsic human pleasure and happiness. Once restricted to a single institutional sphere, "sexual activity" and "family life" in a postnuclear family system fall increasingly into two separate spheres of life.

Sexual activity has become dissociated not only from family life, but also, although less so, from long-term, intimate pair-bonding (both marital and nonmarital). Sexual activity today starts earlier in life, takes place with a larger number of sex partners, and seldom has procreation as the goal. In the laws and even more in the mass media of advanced societies, sexual intercourse is no longer treated as appropriate only for pair-bonded couples, but as potentially appropriate for any two (or even three or more!) consenting adults. Most advanced societies continue to proscribe adultery, however, and sexual activity within an intimate relationship (as distinct from recreational or promiscuous sex) is regarded as highly desirable.

Although most women in a postnuclear family system may continue to have at least one child during their lives, many and probably most pair-bonds are not set up for the purpose of having children. Rather, they are established to satisfy the adults' needs for an intimate relationship. Thus postnuclear pair-bonding has become not only to some extent dissociated from sexual activity, but increasingly dissociated from the procreation of children. For many reasons, both marital and nonmarital pair-bonds also biologically generate fewer children and do so at a later age. Because of this, postnuclear families are not successful in replacing their societies' populations through childbirth.

Internal Family Changes

The most widely discussed internal family changes associated with post-nuclear familism involve gender roles and power relationships. The role of full-time mother–housewife for the female spouse has diminished substantially, as more pair-bonded women have moved into the labor force (women outside of a pair-bond have been in the labor force for generations). These women, moreover, are increasingly likely to remain in the labor force even when they have children. This shift, in turn, is associated with a new balance of power between the spouses. The male spouse is losing some power and authority over family decisions to the female, and power within the home is becoming more symmetrical. At the same time, males are performing a growing proportion of the work of home care and child rearing that previously was restricted to females, hence the division of labor is becoming, even if not symmetrical (it is still far from that), at least less polarized.

Yet these are not the only internal family changes that are associated with a postnuclear-family trend. Just as important, in my opinion, is what can be considered a shift from child-centeredness to adult-centeredness. Many historians have noted (see Chapter 4) that with the rise of the bourgeois nuclear family in the past century, the institution of the family became centrally focused on children and child rearing. Successful child rearing was a principal reason why the husband worked hard outside the home to "build a secure nest" and the wife stayed out of the work force to care for that nest and the children it contained. It was mainly to preserve the sanctity of the nest that societies maintained strict laws against divorce and strong restrictions against extramarital sexuality. Of course, not every family was successful in child rearing, but that does not render the bourgeois nuclear family's purpose less clear.

In what could be considered a historical reversion, postnuclear families appear to be more centered again in the needs not of children, but of adults. A high percentage of all pair-bonds in a postnuclear system do not involve children, and it is obvious that these couples are not oriented to children's needs. But even if the term "family" is restricted to units with children, these too have become less child centered. For one, the size of families is rapidly growing smaller as couples have fewer children. Those adults who do have children, therefore, probably spend a smaller portion of their lives than ever before in child rearing. More importantly, those children who are born are increasingly being raised by nonfamily members. With the rise of outside-the-family day-care facilities, child rearing has become less of a family enterprise. Also, children have increasingly fallen more under the guidance of such extrafamilial forces as the media and peer groups. This does not mean that child rearing has necessarily become less adequate, only that parents spend an increasing portion of their family lives in other than child-rearing pursuits (in advanced societies fathers may actually be spending more time in child rearing than in previous generations, but this is more than offset by the factors just noted and by the decrease in time being spent by mothers).

The high rate of family dissolution also must be regarded as compelling evidence that postnuclear families are becoming oriented more toward adult needs and less toward the needs of children. Parents seldom break up a relationship to benefit the children; it is to benefit themselves, that is, typically their needs for intimacy are not being met. If children had a say in such matters, the rate of family dissolution most assuredly would drop.

Future Possibilities:
The Projection of Postnuclear Familism

No one can foretell the future. The accuracy of the wisest forecasts in the past has consistently been thwarted by the unusual event and the unexpected development. It is nevertheless an interesting and useful exercise to project present trends into the future and see how they look. In relation to postnuclear familism, this kind of projection portrays a continuing dissociation between pair-bonding, sexual activity, and procreation.

There is little evidence today of a diminution in the desire for pair-bonding. One outcome of the continuation of a trend toward postnuclear familism, however, might be an increase in the percentage of people going through life without ever forming a pair-bond involving someone with whom they at the same time cohabit (voluntary singlehood). This does not mean that people would give up sexual activity; they just would not necessarily live with their sex partners. In this age of individualism, voluntary singlehood is a more likely alternative to the nuclear family than is any movement in the direction of such collective, nonfamily forms as communes (although voluntary singlehood could be combined with some type of collective living).

There are no comparative data known to me that would throw light on where advanced societies today stand with respect to such a development. Discussion within these societies, however, and some limited evidence, point to a growing separation between sexual relations and living together. Such a separation has long been a reality in premarital relationships; people do have intimate, sexual relationships without living together. But, especially in Sweden, Denmark, and also in the Netherlands today, one hears that this separation is occurring increasingly at a postmarital stage.

New terms have even been developed in these countries to specify this kind of separation. In the Netherlands, it is called "living-apart-together," and in Sweden a person with whom you have a sexual pair-bond but do not share a common household is called a *särbo* (whereas such a person with whom you reside is called a *sambo*). Those who live in this fashion are usually older persons, often persons who have been through a divorce and do not wish to become strongly involved again, those who want the kind of personal freedom that living apart can bring. Living-apart-together also occurs with some single parents whose children still live with them; the adults want to have a relationship with one another, but do not wish to blend their children into a single household.

The continuation of a postnuclear-family trend, which leads to a separation of sexual activity from residential pair-bonding, could also further separate pair-bonding from procreation. We are now seeing in advanced societies an increase in the number of women who voluntarily choose to bear (or adopt) a child without having a stable relationship with, or the continued presence of, a male partner. (These are usually older women, except in the United States where the practice is relatively common among teenagers, especially those in the underclass.) If the nuclear family is thought to involve more than just the mother–child connection, the growth of this practice portends the ultimate termination of the nuclear family system.

There is one further step that could seal the doom of the nuclear family system by severing the mother–child bond. The step after the dissociation between pair-bonding and procreation that could make the nuclear family extinct is the turning over of children born by single mothers to some other person or group to be raised. Carried thus to the ultimate extreme, a postnuclear-family trend eventuates in the situation where women have children outside of a pair-bond and then do not raise the children themselves, but give them up to others. By any definition of the term, the nuclear family would then be destroyed.

Of course, this sequence of events is highly unlikely to occur. But the scenario is worth giving passing thought to because it represents, in fact, a logical projection of the family tendencies that are under way in advanced societies today. Unless these tendencies change their direction, the death of the family will someday be a reality.

A more probable (yet still remote) eventuality is that long before the death of the family ever occurs in this sense, a growing number of women will simply stop having children; thus the family (and perhaps the society) will die from lack of procreation. It is of course possible that a relatively small number of women could produce all of the children necessary to sustain a society, but there are few signs that enough modern women would be willing to make themselves available for this purpose.

What is actually happening today in advanced societies, most of which have below-replacement birthrates, is that they are replacing their populations with an influx of people from those nations that have excess fertility. Such nations will be in existence for as far into the future as one can reasonably contemplate. Indeed, the growth of many advanced societies in recent years, including Sweden, has depended entirely on the immigration of a foreign population. Thus regardless of what happens to their family systems, population growth (or at least maintenance) through immigration is the probable lot of every advanced society.

The most widely discussed postnuclear-family trend today is not lower fertility and population decline, much less the end of the nuclear family, but the proliferation of blended families or stepfamilies. This is the family unit formed when the adult members of two nuclear families dissolve their relationships and form a new one, combining in a single household the children from each of the original families. There has been much discussion about how, from the child's point of view, life in a stepfamily may represent membership in two nuclear families. It has also been said that the stepfamily represents the return of the extended family, at least in the sense that the child has several sets of relatives with whom to relate. Although today the subject of concerted social research, the stepfamily and its future remains a largely unknown area of knowledge. One preliminary finding stands out.

Because pair-bonds with stepchildren apparently dissolve at a higher rate than normal pair-bonds, children in the future may live in several different stepfamilies during the course of their childhood.

What Could Turn a Postnuclear-Family Trend Around?

Another area for speculation concerns social changes that could reverse the present direction of family change. In essence, what has to change are some of the social, cultural, and economic conditions that led to a postnuclear-family trend in the first place. These include such well-known phenomena of modern times (discussed in earlier chapters) as affluence, secularism, and the strong emphasis on individual development and self-fulfillment.

A "scenario of reversal" in advanced societies would logically consist of the following kinds of events. Economic decline could force families into greater self-sufficiency and economic struggle. A new religiosity could generate a greater concern for social responsibility and the continuity of life. A national familism campaign could succeed in reversing low birthrates. The rational calculation that excessive individualism generates social corrosion could decrease the cultural emphasis on self-fulfillment. Each of these developments is possible, and the expected impact in reversing the trend of family change is in keeping with current knowledge of family–society interaction.

One thing that is reasonably certain about much social change, in my judgment, is that it is dialectical in character. Political change, for example, alternates back and forth over time between the conservative and liberal poles; after conservative policies have been in the ascendancy for a time, liberal policies begin to look more appealing and vice versa. It may be the same with some aspects of family change.

The two great cultural values that appear to conflict most flagrantly with one another in the area of the family are individualism and familism. In the current era individualism has had a remarkable run. Women, especially, have been able to achieve self-fulfillment apart from the bourgeois family to a degree never before thought possible. They have sought the same kinds of personal freedom that most men have always had. Yet additional personal freedom and self-fulfillment have come to men as well.

If the consequences of moving too far down the path of self-fulfillment come to be seen in a negative enough light for the family, as may well happen in time, a social reversal is possible. This reversal could be triggered, for example, by the current generation of children. Having grown up in today's changing families, as adults they might decide that they want something different for their own children. This decision could be influenced by the realization that much contemporary family change involves the decline of the family as an institution and that the consequences of further decline are not to be taken lightly. These are issues to be discussed in the concluding chapter that follows.

Notes

1 Dirk J. van de Kaa (1987), "Europe's Second Demographic Transition," *Population Bulletin* 42-1: 1–57. I am indebted to this bulletin for some of the information presented in the "historical-sequence" section. See also Louis Roussel and Patrick Festy (1979), *Recent Trends in Attitudes and Behavior Affecting the Family in Council of Europe Member States.*

2 van de Kaa (1987), "Europe's Second Demographic Transition": 9.

3 Population Reference Bureau (1987), World Population Data Sheet.

4 Elise F. Jones et al. (1986), *Teenage Pregnancy in Industrialized Countries.*

The Social Implications of Modern Family Decline

In every advanced, Western society today a strong movement away from the traditional or bourgeois nuclear family can be discerned. Referring to this movement as a postnuclear-family trend, I have argued that it is associated with the decline of the family as an institution. The question remains: to what extent should modern family decline be regarded as a phenomenon that has serious negative implications for our health and happiness? The family as an institution has apparently been declining since human history was first recorded, and observers have long been pointing toward that fact with alarm. Yet some social progress has been made over the centuries! Are the consequences of modern family decline more serious than those of the persistent family decline of times past? Drawing mainly on family conditions in Sweden, where the institution of the family has become weakest, this concluding chapter addresses the question of what there might be about the changing family today that should cause us to have special concern.

Family Decline in Perspective

Before turning to the negative consequences of family decline, which take up the bulk of this chapter, it is worth looking at the many positive aspects of this trend. As noted in earlier chapters, the decline of any institution should not be viewed as necessarily only negative in its impact. We do not see the decline of feudalism in this way, or of the monarchy, or of imperialism, or of a hundred other institutional arrangements that in their day were fully accepted. Nor do many today regard the decline of the traditional extended family and the rise of the modern nuclear family as a negative, even though through that change the family lost social power and influence and became a weaker institution in numerous ways. Historians see much that is positive in this family transition. The modern nuclear family was the first to be organized around the voluntary affection of the parents, for example, and the first to be focused on the care and nurturance of children.

In the current stage of family transition, the move toward a postnuclear family, the institution of the family has lost still more social power and influence. Again, there is much to be found in this change that is positive. How many women want to return to the age of legalized patriarchy, when divorce for them was next to impossible? How many parents want to provide more formal education at home, even if this would give them more power over their children? How many family members want to have more responsibility for their elderly relatives and also be more subjected to their authority? How many of the elderly want to be dependent for care on unwilling adult children? How many mothers want to be excluded from the possibility of joining the labor force and earning an income? How many families want to face the prospect of poverty with no or very limited government assistance?

In most of these respects family members show little desire to turn back the clock. Furthermore, there is no way in which the modern family could be as strong and self-sufficient as many families once may have been. Parents do not possess the knowledge or resources necessary to formally educate or provide medical care for their members at the current levels of technological advance. For employment, parents are at the mercy of outside organizations, both public and private. Other changes, such as the return of full-time housewives and home care for the elderly, could be accomplished only by sharply reducing the material standard of living of families and by the "deliberation" of women.

Strong and independent families, at least as traditionally formed, can be a detriment to the achievement of many social ideals held by the citizenry of advanced societies. Strong familiies encourage the perpetuation of gross inequalities in society, both material and social. Few in modern societies favor the repeal of progressive income and inheritance taxes, for example, recognizing that the family's right to its own wealth must be curtailed to some extent for the public good. Few in modern societies wish to return to the time when a man could mistreat his wife and children because they were considered to be part of his private family domain. Few want to return to the age of limited divorce, when freedom of association for women was curtailed and many women were in effect sentenced to a life of bondage. Almost no one is willing to give up the expanded possibility for personal freedom and self-fulfillment that, as much as anything else, modern family change has meant.

Thus a return to the traditional nuclear family is in many respects undesirable, even if it were possible. Patriarchy, the uneducated housewife, little public assistance for needy families—those are not goals that are commonly espoused or easily supported today. At the same time, judging by the ideals people still hold, many aspects of a postnuclear-family trend do not seem desirable either. Probably the vast majority of people, regardless of political persuasion, agree on the family ideal of a lasting, heterosexual pair-bond, based on affection and companionship, which provides devoted and continuing love and support to children of the union. Even if their actual behavior would suggest otherwise, people's espousal of that ideal in advanced societies is remarkably persistent. In this sense, at least, the great majority of people agree on the ideal of a strong family.

Unfortunately, the family decline in evidence today strikes at the very roots of this ideal. Not only has there been a high dissolution rate of marital and nonmarital relationships, but families have been turning away from the care and support of children. For adults, the dissolution of pair-bonds may be balanced by the growth of informal friendship groups. For children, the decline of parental contact may be offset by the growth of nonfamily child-rearing institutions. But the net social gain in the growth of these forms of compensation is arguable. It is not that these compensatory social structures are inappropriate or ineffective; indeed, given the family changes that are under way, they are essential. The main issue is the changing quality of family life.

In what ways has the quality or character of family life been changing for the worse in recent years and who is being adversely affected? Some of the answers to this question are obvious, others are no less important for being so seldom discussed. The two family functions generally regarded as most important in the modern world are effective child rearing and the psychological "anchorage" of adults—the stable provision, by way of affection and companionship, of belonging and identity. We begin by reviewing available empirical evidence concerning the possible negative consequences of functional decline in these areas, focusing especially on the experience of Sweden.

Child Rearing

By almost any measure, the material situation of Swedish families has improved markedly in recent decades.[1] Families with children have superior housing, more material possessions, and better health care. In these ways the quality of child rearing is higher than it has ever been before. The only mildly negative note in this regard is that households with children may not be gaining in their material standard of living as fast as do households without children, and in recent economic downturns the economic position of households with children has slipped somewhat.

Such material gain is only indirectly related to changes in the social and psychological quality of child rearing, however. Most experts would probably agree that the fundamental ingredients of effective child rearing are the infant's prolonged intimacy with a nurturing, psychologically mature person and the child's exposure through childhood of the continuing presence of one and preferably two adults who provide consistent love, understanding, stimulation, guidance, and protection. The crucial elements here are stability of parenting, as indicated by the words "prolonged," "continuing," and "consistent," and the presence of love and intimacy.

How have these elements of the special relationship between parents and children fared in Sweden over the past few decades? Has parenting become less stable? Have parents become less loving and understanding? Because of the lack of solid evidence, answers to these important questions are not known. But there is strong evidence that parents voluntarily dissolve their relationship with each other at a much higher rate than previously, that children are raised more often by a single parent, and that children spend more time during childhood outside the orbit of the nuclear family. These are dimensions of what can be called the social ecology of child rearing—the social conditions within the home and immediate surroundings where most child rearing still takes place. The social ecology of child rearing in Sweden has undergone progressive and continuing changes in recent decades in many other respects, and it is important to spell these changes out in some detail.

The Changing Social Ecology of Child Rearing

By all available evidence, 10 family conditions would appear to have substantially changed, compared to previous generations, for the current generation of Swedish children. Each change can be considered to be an aspect of family decline, and each is a move away from a situation that, I suggest, has been regarded by many experts as highly desirable for the rearing of children.

1. Families have become very small. Indeed, they seldom consist of more than two children and often just one. The growth of stepfamilies notwithstanding, a child has fewer brothers and sisters than ever before. There are some real disadvantages to growing up in a very large family, and some real advantages to being an only child. But children receive substantial benefits from having a few brothers and sisters: learning the values of cooperation and sharing; having intimates on whom to rely for association and companionship; the presence of role models for younger children, and child-care responsibilities for older ones.

2. Families today have fewer joint activities. They do fewer things as a family unit. This almost certainly includes family mealtimes, but also family picnics, family games, family discussions, and family celebrations. In addition, some common family activities today involve less social interaction than was the case in an earlier era; these include watching television and riding in the automobile. Meaningful family activities contribute significantly to the richness of childhood. Family celebrations, for example, especially those involving the gathering of a large number of family members, are often recalled by adults thinking about their childhoods as some of the happiest times in their lives.

3. Meaningful contact time between children and parents (and all adults other than teachers and human-service professionals) is diminishing—time when adults love, listen, understand, and give guidance. Some argue that there is more "quality time"—time when parents and children are in especially close contact. Yet, no evidence has ever been put forth to support this assertion, and it gains scant support from the many social forces at work: fewer adults at home, television, peer groups, the pace of life. Swedish children complain that, aside from their teachers, they know few adults other than their parents. This is especially true in urban environments, where it has been brought about by the separation of home and work and the decline of neighboring.

4. Families these days have less time for the development and maintenance of family-centered routines and traditions, regularized activities around such events as bedtime, mealtime, birthdays, and holidays. Although sometimes belittled by the overly sophisticated parent, routines and traditions are highly favored by young people; they substantially add to the sense of social belonging and continuity in life. One set of rapidly disappearing family traditions revolves around the family mealtime; another, particularly true for Sweden, involves religious activities.

5. Children have entered an era of less regular contact with relatives. Because people live longer, it is true that more grandparents are around today than in the past. Moreover, the technologies of transportation and communication have served to counteract the effects of high residential mobility and geographic separation. Yet while contact with grandparents may have increased, there has probably been a decrease in contacts among relatives of the same generation. People have fewer brothers and sisters and therefore fewer aunts, uncles, and cousins. Associations with such relatives tend to be different from other relationships. Children tend to feel a "primal" tie with uncles, aunts,

and especially cousins, and these relationships involve special familial obligations and responsibilities; family gatherings of such relatives
are often happy occasions cherished by children.

6. Despite high-technology transportation, the effective environment
of the young child is still the home and immediate environment.
Yet when families were stronger and more active, the immediate
environment—the local neighborhood—was a lively place with familiar faces. Today the neighborhood is often abandoned by adults
during the day and has unfamiliar faces at night. The young child en-
counters a local environment of empty homes and deserted streets on
a daily basis. The presence of responsible adults, who in times past
provided both stimulation and social control when the child stepped
outside the home, has been steadily declining.

7. Probably the most comforting, though often unconscious, assumption
a child can have is that his or her parents will remain together in a
parental capacity for life. This assumption has become increasingly
challenged by the family trends of the past few decades. A new
dimension to the family scene is active fear and anxiety on the part of
children that their parents will break up. The fear of voluntary parental
breakup replaces, to a large extent, the historical fear of parental loss
through death, but the psychological meanings of the two are very
different. Death brings sadness and grief; breakup leads to feelings of
animosity, guilt, and rejection.

8. At one time children had a close association with the work of their
parents. They could develop mental models of the employment roles
of adulthood. Today children are mostly removed from the adult world
of work; many have no idea what adults are doing when they go off
to work each day. Children live increasingly in their own segregated
worlds.

9. Combining many of the abovementioned points, one of the key
ingredients of a strong family is the presence of a rich subculture—a
set of norms, symbols, humor, and even language that is special to
that particular group. This provides family members with a body of
meanings that give social and emotional anchorage. Over the course
of life the subculture yields what has been called a "community of
memory," a special cultural heritage that family members carry with
them until death.[2] A rich family subculture can also provide the basis
for a strong emotional and social continuity between past and present
generations. With the weakening of the family unit, the disinvestment
in family life, this subcultural richness is disappearing. For those who
have it, the tie to a rich family subculture is one of the most meaningful

things in life. For those who do not, the commercially based cultures of mass societies serve as debased substitutes.

10. One of the most important elements of a rich family subculture is the presence of certain norms and values that are essential to a just and humane society and have traditionally been promulgated by the family. These norms and values include the voluntary caring for others, the partial demise of which has become a leading issue in Sweden of late. And they include cooperation and sharing, values best taught in small, close-knit groups of interdependent people.

In summary, an ideal child rearing environment could be said to consist of the following characteristics: a relatively large family that does a lot of things together, has many routines and traditions, and provides a great deal of quality contact time between adults and children; regular contact with relatives, active neighboring in a supportive neighborhood, and contact with the world of work; little concern on the part of children that their parents will break up; and the coming together of all these ingredients in the development of a rich family subculture that has lasting meaning and strongly promulgates traditional family values.

With each passing year, Sweden, like other advanced societies, is drifting farther away from the ideal. This does not pose a societal catastrophe. In some respects the overall quality of child rearing has probably improved in recent years; parents are economically more secure, healthier, better educated, and perhaps more aware psychologically. Yet from the child's point of view the changing ecological character of childhood confers a real loss; life under the new social conditions is not as socially rich or emotionally meaningful as it once was. Whether or not the personal and social implications of the changing ecology of childhood extend beyond a loss of affect and meaning cannot be known with certainty at this time. The limited empirical information that we have about these implications is discussed below; for a fuller understanding we must await further research and the coming to maturity of today's generation of children.

The changing conditions of child rearing have not gone unrecognized in Sweden. For many professionals whose job it is to deal with children, parents, and families these changes in the social ecology of child rearing are quite real. Stressing the need for more government programs to assist families, the Swedish family sociologist Rita Liljeström discussed most of them at length in her influential book *Uppväxtvillkor* (Growing-up Conditions).[3] To take another example, a pamphlet released by Swedish social-welfare authorities and used throughout Sweden in parent-education programs speaks of the privatization and isolation of the family. It views the Swedish family today as isolated from neighbors and relatives, leaving children with less informal social control, fewer adult friends, and fewer role models.[4] Other professionals express concern that social change has moved too rapidly in Sweden for the family's sake, that parents have become too "split up" in their use of time, and that the widespread use of experts has given parents a lack of confidence in their own abilities and weakened still further their informal social networks.[5] Most of the child-care experts with whom I have spoken over the past few years have stressed that parents need to spend more time with their children. The head of the Swedish Youth Authority, for example, said the greatest need today for Swedish youth is more contact with adults and the adult world; he emphasized that it is a myth that children and youth want to be more by themselves.[6]

The Effects on Children of Marital Dissolution

I think it is fair to say that the desirable ecological conditions noted above show the greatest lack in homes in which the parents' relationship has dissolved, especially in single-parent families. Thus the consequences of marital dissolution on children could be said to be strongly related to changes in the social ecology of child rearing that such dissolution brings about. One such change is a decrease in the amount of contact between children and the absent parent. A 1979 Swedish study found, for example, that 28% of the children of parental break-up who were living with their mothers had no contact with their fathers.[7] It should be pointed out that the situation is much worse in the United States: one study, based on a national sample of children aged 11 to 16, found that almost one half of the children in custody of their mothers had not seen their fathers during the previous year.[8] Another finding of this study was that only 16% of the children of disrupted families had "frequent contact" with the outside father; the study concluded: "Marital dissolution typically involves either a complete cessation of contact between the nonresidential parent and child or a relationship that is tantamount to a ritual form of parenthood."[9]

The direct psychological impact of divorce (and its nonmarital equivalent) on children has been the focus of widespread social research in many countries. Surprisingly, however, there has been almost no research on this topic in Sweden. Unlike virtually every other "social problem," it has never been the focus of a major, government-sponsored investigation. That a society so resolutely devoted to social welfare and the good life should overlook this issue is a source of puzzlement.[10]

In the absence of "indigenous" Swedish data, one has to assume that research on the psychological consequences of divorce in other advanced nations has some relevance for Sweden. Findings from the United States must be used with great care, however, because the economic consequences of divorce for women there may be exceptional. One recent study of American families found that the standard of living of divorced women (and their children) declined by 73% the first year following divorce, while that of divorced men increased by 42%![11] In Sweden divorced women, according to one study, end up with 90% of their predivorce standard of living.[12]

There are few uncontestable conclusions from the research conducted in other countries on the psychological effects of marital dissolution on children. About the general tenor of the overall findings, however, there can be little argument: the psychological effects of parental separation on children are mostly negative, at least in the short run. The research has also demonstrated that the effects vary tremendously, based on factors ranging from the gender of the child to the quality of parental communication after divorce.

I will cite here only a few of the main studies to suggest the flavor of these findings. An intensive longitudinal study of children of divorce in California found that after the divorce two thirds of the children showed symptoms of stress and one half thought that their life had been destroyed. Five years after the divorce, this study found, one third of the children were still seriously disturbed and another third were having psychological difficulties.[13] A follow-up study 10 years after the divorce found that many children were still struggling with emotional problems stemming from the divorce. Their anger toward their parents had abated with time, but they often looked back on their childhoods with lingering sorrow and were overly cautious in their own marriage and childbearing experiences.[14] Longitudinal studies based on the American National Surveys of Children reached similar conclusions: marital disruption is associated with psychological problems in children that may persist for many years.[15]

It is commonly believed that the effects on children of remaining in families in which the parental union is marked by serious and continuing conflict are nearly as serious as the effects of dissolution, and this belief has been supported by research findings. At the same time, divorcing parents tend to underestimate the negative effects of divorce on their children. A British study of divorce compared the parents' perception of children's well-being with those of the children. It found that a far greater proportion of children reported having been seriously upset by the separation of their parents than was estimated by those parents.[16] In addition, children are seldom happy that their parents finally divorce rather than stay together, even if the parents are in open conflict with one another. The California longitudinal study noted above found that only 10% of the children were "relieved" that their parents decided to divorce. In general, the children's view of divorce uncovered by this study was very different from that held by their parents.

Family Decline and Serious Social Problems

Aside from probable psychological problems after marital dissolution, is the changing ecology of child rearing in Sweden associated in any way with the more serious social problems connected with youth, such as juvenile delinquency, suicide, and alcohol and drug abuse? While solid data are available concerning the existence and rates of change of these social problems in Sweden, determining what causes them is another matter; it is extremely difficult to pinpoint causal connections. An increase in these problems of youth has occurred in every advanced society. One recent study, conducted in the United States, has suggested strong correlations between the increase of youth problems and family changes, especially the changing ecology of child rearing.[17] Nevertheless, it is fair to say that these linkages remain open to question.

Let us review the youth-problem data in Sweden. The rate of suicide, which has given Sweden (unfairly) a certain amount of international notoriety, doubled between 1950 and 1975, the period of most rapid family change, for males aged 15–24. In comparison, the rate for that age group in New Zealand, which was roughly the same as Sweden's in 1950, increased during this period by only about one third.

In his study of Scandinavian suicide in 1964, a study that attracted wide attention, the American psychoanalyst Herbert Hendin attributed the relatively high Swedish suicide rate of that time to the fact that Swedish mothers seemed emotionally uninvolved with their children ("the woman simply does not like to care for her child and she prefers to go back to work"). Also, the mothers set very high standards for their children's success and at the same time push them into premature self-dependency.[18] If they wish to receive parental esteem and approval, according to Hendin, Swedish children must separate at a very early age from their mothers and learn to perform on their own. This, in turn, leads to psychological contradictions that can eventuate in suicide.

It is difficult if not impossible to corroborate this kind of psychoanalytic "insight," however, and no one to my knowledge has ever tried to do so; thus this view of the causes of Swedish suicide is highly questionable. In any event, the Hendin study was completed before the era of rapid family change in Sweden. Furthermore, since 1975, when the full effects of family change should have been felt, the rate of suicide for the 15–24 age group in Sweden has been dropping.

A comparative cross-national perspective is essential to assess the connection between family decline and suicide, and such a perspective casts serious doubt on there being a special "suicide problem" in Sweden. By world standards Sweden has a high suicide rate, but many European nations typically have even higher rates, such as Switzerland, Austria, and Hungary. Also, Sweden's high rate is largely due to suicides among middle-aged adults and the elderly. The Swedish rate of youthful suicide in 1980 was only one-half that of Switzerland, a nation with a more traditional family structure (as discussed in Chapter 11), and below the rates of a host of other nations, including the United States, Japan, Germany, Canada, and even Australia.[19] Thus it seems unlikely that Sweden's particular family situation could be blamed for causing suicides, although family changes in each of these societies almost certainly play some part in this "pathology of modernization." The causes of the high rate of suicide in advanced societies, because they are multiple, are not well understood. Following Durkheim, a more probable cause than family change for a high rate of suicide is secularization; religion in many circumstances seems to retard the act of killing oneself.

As for alcohol and drug problems, Sweden has for many years had very tight controls over the use of alcohol. National legislation to control alcohol production and use began in the middle of the past century, and from 1917 to 1955 there was a strict system of rationing the purchase of alcohol, using government-issued passbooks. Today, alcohol may be purchased only in state liquor stores, and it is made very expensive through heavy taxation. Sweden also vigorously enforces what is probably the world's most stringent drunk-driving legislation.

Despite such state control, many a tourist has returned from a visit to Sweden proclaiming it a nation of drunks. Especially during the warmer months, when tourists are most likely to visit, alcoholics have high visibility in public places such as parks and railroad stations. They congregate in these places partly because of the scarcity of bars and taverns, which are habituated by problem drinkers in other nations, and Swedish authorities make little effort to remove them. To some extent, also, Swedes practice the "all-out Nordic binge" type of drinking behavior, at least compared to the French and the Italians. Swedes are said to abstain from drinking during the week, and then "binge" on weekends (and on holidays and trips abroad).

Appearances can be misleading, however—the Swedish rate of alcohol consumption is one of the lowest in Europe. In liters of absolute alcohol consumed per inhabitant, the 1982 rate for Sweden was 5.5, compared to the highest nation, France (13.3), Italy (13.0), Switzerland (11.2), New Zealand (9.6), the United States (8.2), and the United Kingdom (6.6)[20] Moreover, although alcohol consumption in Sweden increased during the postwar period (the rate was 4.92 liters per person in 1954), it has been dropping since about 1975.[21] Most of the postwar growth in alcohol consumption was due to increased drinking by the young, both boys and girls, but in recent years such drinking has diminished somewhat. There seems to be a steady increase in the percentage of the Swedish population that uses alcohol, however; that nation has had a large number of outspoken teetotalers, and their number now may be in decline, especially among women.

Alcohol-related disease, like alcohol use, increased considerably in the postwar period, but declined beginning in the late 1970s. In number of deaths in 1982 from liver cirrhosis, (a common measure of alcoholism) per 100,000 inhabitants, Sweden, with 12.2, ranked a little higher among other nations than it did in regard to alcohol consumption. Its rate superceded that of New Zealand and the United Kingdom, but still was below Switzerland (13.5) and the United States (13.8) and considerably below France (30.8) and Italy (34.2)[22]

The Swedish government has always taken a strong stand against the use of drugs. Occasional drug use among young people, never great, seems to have diminished in recent years after reaching a high point in the early 1970s.[23] According to a 1979/1980 survey of 16-year-olds, 10% had used drugs at least once.[24] This is well below the comparable figure for the United States. Data on addicted hard-drug users are more difficult to obtain; what data there are suggest a decline since the early 1980s.[25]

Perhaps the strongest connection between family change and a measurable social problem can be made in regard to juvenile delinquency. Swedish delinquency rates have been among the highest in northern Europe although the offenses are mostly minor and seldom of a violent nature. While the Swedish rate for cleared "serious crimes" (those resulting in sanctions more severe than fines) increased for all age groups more than four times in the past 30 years, the increase was five times for the 18- to 20-year-old group, and seven times for the 15- to 17-year-old group.[26] Delinquency rates rose abruptly during the years of rapid family change. Although the causes of delinquency are very complex, there seems to be a general consensus among experts that two general social processes are typically involved: a weakening of informal social control by adults in the family, school, and community and an increase in the influence of peers on adolescent behavior.[27] Because the influence of peers normally increases when that of adults decreases, the two processes are closely connected.

In contrast to Sweden, Switzerland has had one of the lowest delinquency rates in northern Europe, and a comparison between Sweden and Switzerland with respect to juvenile delinquency is particularly informative. The reason for this difference was one focus of a 1978 monograph entitled *Cities with Little Crime: the Case of Switzerland,* written by a sociologist, Marshall Clinard, who had lived in both Sweden and Switzerland.[28] Clinard stressed that in Switzerland, compared to Sweden, informal social control over adolescents is strong and peer group influence is weak. He placed the blame for the Swedish situation squarely on the welfare state:

> In Sweden, where organization is extensive and life is programmed, the youth have become bored, and the boredom with the welfare state has become widespread. Under these conditions crime and other forms of deviant behavior

furnish a diversion for some youths who seek excitement. The youth have become more alienated from the controls of an adult society—and at an earlier age—than they are in Switzerland. The social control of the family has become increasingly weakened in Sweden . . . due to changes in the society, as well as the extensive government programs. . . . both the family and the school in Sweden have become far more permissive than they are in Switzerland. . . . contacts between persons of diverse age groups have diminished. The youth subcultures are pronounced.[29]

Clinard probably overstated the role of the welfare state in accounting for the differences between the two nations. (Incidentally, he used the same reasoning to explain differences in drug use, which was also greater in Sweden.) Yet his analysis of the general causes of juvenile crime is in agreement with the findings of much research on this topic conducted in other nations. Although I know of no large-scale comparative studies of juvenile delinquency in a wide range of advanced nations, it is of more than passing interest to note that the nation with one of the lowest rates of juvenile delinquency—Japan—also has what is generally regarded as the strongest family system.

It must be reemphasized that the causes of juvenile delinquency are complex and that the family situation is only one of many factors that appears to be involved. Nevertheless, the available knowledge suggests that the changing family situation in Sweden and the relatively high rate of juvenile delinquency are related.[30] One Swedish study found, for example, that a young person from a broken home had more than twice the risk of ending up on the police blotter than did a person from a "complete" family.[31] Another Swedish study found that at greatest risk of eventual criminality was a working-class boy whose mother lived alone and worked full-time.[32] The relationship may be neither a strong nor a lasting one, however. While the available evidence indicates that family decline in Sweden is continuing in many respects, juvenile delinquency rates have leveled off in recent years. Obviously this is a topic to which much more social research could usefully be devoted.

Empirical data about other social problems in Sweden that could be related to family change surface from time to time. In the early 1970s a report sponsored by the Department of Social Affairs stated that 25% of the total Swedish population was in need of psychiatric treatment; not unexpectedly, the report was authored by a psychiatrist.[33] In the absence of trend or comparative data, there is no way to accurately interpret such a finding, and in any event the report has largely been forgotten. More widely discussed in recent years have been reports indicating an increase in disciplinary problems in schools and declining educational achievement levels. These two trends have often been linked, in turn, to the growth of permissiveness within the Swedish education system. During the past decade, however, the trend toward permissiveness seems to have come to a halt, and there are some indications that educational achievement levels are now rising.

Family Decline and Youth Malaise in Sweden

Another recent focus of national attention, closely associated with the relatively high rate of juvenile delinquency (including school vandalism) and various behavior problems in schools, has been a general "malaise" among Swedish youth. The condition was highlighted in the summer of 1987, when youth in a number of Swedish cities for several days engaged in street riots that required police intervention; these have been regarded as the worst youth riots in Sweden since the 1960s. Solid empirical evidence about a youth malaise in Sweden is virtually nonexistent, but several qualitative studies have added some fuel to the fire. Although they are, of course, inconclusive, most of these studies have suggested that Swedish family decline has had negative effects.

In an international comparative study of 11-year-old school children, conducted for Swedish Radio in 1975, the question was asked, "Do you feel that there is someone who likes you?" To this question 11% of Swedish children answered *aldrig* (never), an answer given by none of the children in the other countries (Spain, Israel, Algeria, and Ethiopia).[34] One of the main reasons put forth by the authors to account for this result was that the Swedish children, called *aldrig barn* (never children), were from much smaller families than are found in the other nations. In regard to many other questions, the Swedish children, compared to children in the other countries, were found to be much less identified with, and dependent on, their families, and more tied to their peer groups.

Another study of Swedish school children aged 9–12, conducted in 1984, looked at children's fears and compared the results with a similar study conducted in 1963. It found that over these two decades young people had become more independent from their families and more active, but also had more inner fears and anxieties about such things as being alone. And today's youth, unlike those of the 1960s, expressed fears about their parents separation.[35] One of the author's of this study said in an interview that the most important thing parents could do to allay children's fears was to spend more time with them.[36]

Two qualitative studies of youth in Stockholm, using in-depth interviews, have lent support to the view that today's Swedish youth are somewhat lonely and unhappy. One study, which randomly chose 23 youth from different parts of Stockholm, concluded that many of these youth were lonely and had few, merely superficial, social contacts. These young people, the authors note, inhabit an "age-stratified world" in which they meet very few adults other than their parents.[37] In another study of Stockholm youth aged 19-25, now in progress, ethnologist Karla Werner finds that her subjects have considerable anxiety about establishing pair-bonds because of their own experiences in broken homes, although their life goal of permanent pair-bonding remains strong. The youth tend to think more about having a "close friend"—someone they can trust and be with—than about establishing a family; the term "family," she notes, is seldom used (the youth tend to be conservative in many respects; they want a good job, their own home, and a decent standard of living).[38]

Samples of youth such as those used in these studies could not be said to be representative of Swedish young people as a whole. And youth with these views and problems can be found in every advanced society. All the same, the findings of these studies are provocative, and the issues they have uncovered should certainly be subject to much more extensive analysis.

The Role of Group Day Care

Group day-care facilities and services are thought by some to be, if not a solution, at least a source of amelioration for many of today's child-rearing problems. Others view them as a principal cause of these problems. Whichever viewpoint one holds, the Swedish experience with day care is worth examining in some detail (Swedish family and child-care policies in general were described in Chapter 9).

Sweden has been a laggard among European nations in the establishment of public day-care facilities. In 1982, of all children in the age group 0-6, only 38% had places in a public facility; 41% had a parent at home, and the remaining 21% made other arrangements, usually with a relative or someone paid privately. Moreover, of the children in public day care, 40% did not go to public day-care centers, but instead were taken care of in the homes of women licensed by the municipality. This means that the great majority of Swedish children are raised in homes, either their own or other peoples', and not in an "impersonal facility." The demand for placement in public day-care centers greatly exceeds the supply. However, the Swedish government currently has plans to meet this demand by 1991, and to provide places in such centers for children over the age of 18 months. It should also be noted that in the public facilities already built a uniformly high level of service prevails; for example, there is one adult for every four to five children and an even lower ratio for infants.

The debate over day-care issues in Sweden has been vigorous. The more conservative political parties have tended to favor licensed family homes over public facilities, as well as additional payments to mothers who care for their own children. The left-wing political parties have been opposed to payments to mothers and have pushed strongly for public day-care facilities, which they consider to be more efficient and equitable (so far, the ruling Social Democratic Party has successfully managed to forbid all private, profit-making day-care centers). All political parties agree, however, that with so many mothers in the labor force some form of public support for day care is an absolute necessity.

This agreement about public support for day care contrasts with the ideological position often taken in the United States—that, if day care is provided, more women will choose to "abandon their children and go into the labor force." Against this ideology stands the fact that in every advanced society mothers are moving rapidly into the labor force, whether or not public day care is available. In the United States, for example, where almost no public day care is provided, about 54% of mothers with children younger than 6 are in the work force, and the number is growing; nearly half of American mothers of infants less than 1 work outside the home (1985 data).[39] Thus it has by no means been established that withholding day care will keep mothers at home; it may merely make the lives of employed mothers more stressful and create serious problems for their children.

In Sweden, 80 to 85% of mothers of children under 7 are in the labor force, but the great majority work only part-time. Also, their parental lives are made markedly less stressful than they otherwise would be due to the Swedish parental-leave program. Most women with infants are considered as being in the labor force, for example, but because of the parental-leave program, and unlike their American counterparts, they (or their husbands) can spend the first year at home after the birth of each child. There remain in Sweden, nevertheless, strong vestiges of the ideological belief that mothers should remain at home full-time with their young children (at least until about age 3). Interestingly, this ideological belief is more common within the Swedish working classes, and it is one of the reasons why public day care in Sweden, contrary to the goals of the ruling Social Democratic Party, is used more by middle-class than by working-class families.[40]

Because so few Swedish children (by European standards) are actually raised in "institutional settings," this may not be the best nation in which to examine its effects. Nevertheless, Swedes have been very concerned about the effects on children of institutional or group day care. The kinds of issues that concern Swedes differ from those in the United States. There is little concern in Sweden, for example, about such horror stories as day-care centers being places for child abuse and recruitment grounds for child pornographers.

One major criticism of public day care in Sweden is that the turnover of staff is too high; just as the young child gets to know the caretaker, that person leaves. (Some conservatives also charge that day-care workers are "just a bunch of communists" who subtly inflict their pernicious views on the new generation.) Another issue is that too many day-care workers are female (about 95%), and male children therefore have too few role models; Swedes have been obviously unsuccessful in attracting many males to day-care jobs. (Yet this gender inbalance is little different from what traditionally has existed in the daytime home.) Additional criticisms are that peer-group influence becomes excessively strong at too early an age and that group day-care workers are too permissive about such things as permitting their premature wards to engage in sex play.[41]

One of the most frequently heard criticisms of public day care in recent years has concerned the health of day-care children. Studies have shown that young children in day-care centers are sick more than those who stay at home, because they mix with so many other children at an age when they have not yet developed immunity to many illnesses. Pediatricians are divided on this issue; some see little cause for concern and think that it is just as well for the young children to get sick and build up immunities at earlier ages. The health question has also spilled over to the staff. There is evidence that day-care workers become ill at an abnormally high rate and even that female workers have a higher percentage of miscarriages.

The most important question, however, is—how do group day-care children "turn out" over the long run compared to those raised at home by their mothers? Some Swedes are quick to point out, with cogency, that such a question is asked with the ideal situation in mind, which does not exist for all or even most children raised at home. Studies conducted in the United States have shown that children from problem-ridden low-income families benefit greatly from the less stressful, more culturally enriched environment of a good day-care center. The existing research on group day care has also noted the importance of such factors as the child's temperament, the content and quality of day-care programs, and the attitudes of the parents toward the day-care experience, stressing that evaluation is difficult because not all children, day-care programs, and family situations are the same. With these caveats, most existing research has found few notable effects of group day care on children in general, either in a positive or negative direction.[42] One Swedish study found some signs of stress and depression together with a lag in verbal development among infants placed in day-care centers at the age of 6 months, compared to those raised at home. An American study found more aggression among boys reared in group care.[43] These studies, however, are limited in scope and are inconclusive.

The most significant study now under way in Sweden is being conducted by researchers within the Swedish educational profession. A small group of young people, raised under varying conditions, are being studied as they grow to maturity.[44] This longitudinal study focuses mainly on their educational achievements and at-school behaviors (as in the case of the effects of family breakup, Swedes seem to have a peculiar reluctance to examine the psychological dimensions of the issue). At this point, 119 children living in Stockholm and Gothenburg have been followed up to age 8. The outcome so far has been highly favorable toward group day care. The children (33) who were placed in day-care centers during their first or second year of life have at age 8 somewhat surpassed the other children in cognitive development and social competence, as measured by their teachers. In the researchers' opinion, this may be due to the extra stimulation provided in day-care centers. Another significant finding was that group day-care boys, at age 5, had become somewhat more peer and less adult oriented than their home-based counterparts.[45]

Swedes no longer seem to be very concerned about the negative effects of limited out-of-home day care for children after about age 3. It is thought that children of this age can benefit from "group experiences" (this view is not restricted to Sweden; many and perhaps most American home-raised children over that age attend nursery schools). Yet many Swedes are still apprehensive about putting infants in group day care and leaving older children in day care for too many hours a day. Probably a high proportion of Swedish child-care experts would say that ideally the mother or father should be with the child during the first year or year and a half and then work only part-time until the child reaches at least school age. In line with this belief, the number of children in group day care at the age of 6 months (the minimum age in Sweden) has dropped in recent years, perhaps due mostly to more extensive use of the parental-leave program, while the number of day-care children of older ages continues to increase.

Changing Swedish Child Care in Review

As more experience with group day care is gained and the results of research become available, it is fair to say that Swedish apprehensions about group day care as some radical and noxious new form of child rearing are fast disappearing. This is certainly the case when such care is viewed as an auxiliary to the family, enabling mothers to hold part-time jobs after the first few years in a child's life. However, the full effects on children of group day care will not be known until the present generation of Swedish children reaches maturity—if then.

Whatever the direct effects of group day care may prove to be, the expansion of out-of-home care has meant a decrease in the interaction between children and their parents, together with a decline in family activities and family life. It is not clear to what degree these changing dimensions of the ecology of child rearing may already have adversely affected the critical ingredients of stability and love in the relationship between parents and children. But it is hard to deny that there is some potential for harm in this broad change. Busy parents may be inclined to relinquish so much responsibility for the rearing of their own children that the motivation to play their essential role in the socialization process will wither. Thus it is the changing climate of child rearing considered as a whole, not just group day care, to which our concerns should be directed.

Psychological Anchorage of Adults

It is a principal function of families in modern societies not only to provide an effective socialization structure for children, but also a psychological anchorage for adults. Perhaps more than in all previous societies, adults in modern societies look to the family to fulfill the need for stable and reliable emotional relationships that can affirm their feelings of self-worth and provide a sense of identity and belonging. Most adults in modern societies have been shown by opinion polls to hold the ideal of strong, lifetime family units. Presumably children also hold this ideal; a difference is that adults have a choice in the matter and children do not.

The effects on children aside, is there any evidence in Sweden of a negative impact on adult emotional well-being of family decline, of living in a society with a high rate of family dissolution? As orientation to this topic, it should be stressed that marital stability does not always equal psychological quality, health, success, or goodness. Too many adults have benefited from marital dissolution to hold the traditional one-sided opinion about the matter. They have been saved from the fate of being stuck for life with an incompatible or even psychologically and physically damaging individual and have been given the chance to start life afresh. From this point of view, divorce is a psychologically and physically liberating event that leads to personal fulfillment. It is now also widely accepted that divorce is a fundamental human right and that people should have freedom of choice in deciding with whom they wish to live. An aspect of freedom of choice is the right to change one's mind; people make mistakes and should have the chance to start over. Some people in advanced societies wish that divorce laws were more stringent, but almost no one is calling for the return of a society without divorce.

Obvious though it may be, it is also important to emphasize that a cause of high divorce rates is not that adults no longer want to have happy, meaningful, lifetime relationships. Virtually everyone who does not have such a relationship wishes for one; no one prefers divorce to a good relationship. And people wish they could live in a society where there were more happy, lasting marriages and fewer divorces ("marriage" and "divorce" here include nonmarital unions and their breakup). Indeed, it is the strong desire for meaningful relationships that has led, as much as anything else, to the high rate of marital breakup. People's expectations of what a marital relationship can and should be have escalated. They are no longer willing to tolerate a relationship that is unfulfilling; and there is always the chance that they can find a better one.

Just as marital impermanence most assuredly leads many adults into happier and more fulfilling lives, it is conceivable, although supporting empirical data are scant, that marital impermanence contributes to greater happiness in general among adults in advanced societies. While most studies have shown that married people consistently rank higher in "global happiness" than unmarried people,[46] there is no indication in advanced nations that, over the past few decades when marital dissolution has increased rapidly, the general level of happiness, satisfaction with life, or psychological well-being of adults has declined. Many other concurrent social changes enter the picture, of course, but the average levels of personal happiness have remained quite stable and even increased slightly.[47]

These positive aspects of marital breakup notwithstanding, divorce almost always represents a crisis in the lives of the individuals involved. Divorce creates for everyone concerned a certain amount of psychological damage, at least in the short run. In the United States, divorce often also causes a catastrophic decline in the standard of living for women, as noted above. Because people continue to divorce with relatively full knowledge of these consequences, they seem willing to pay the price. Yet, this is the first generation in which the breakup of marriages has been so high, and it may be that, as years go on, the assessment of costs and benefits of marital breakup will change.

In considering the negative consequences for adults of living in a high-divorce society, a principal focus of attention is on adults who sever relationships and then are unable or unwilling to form new ones. Nearly one out of every five Swedish adults between the ages of 16 and 64 now lives alone, the highest rate in the world. Already much higher in urban areas, this rate is climbing rapidly. It is fed by the rising average age of the population and by later marriages, but family dissolution is also a major contributor.

How are these single-person householders faring? There is little solid, empirical evidence in Sweden that could be interpreted to mean that the diminution of permanent attachments, as measured by the high rate of living alone, is causing tangible signs of long-term psychological travail among adults. The best available evidence, from the Swedish "level of living" surveys conducted by the Swedish Institute for Social Research, indicates that there was not much change in the amount of contact people had with friends and relatives between 1968 and 1981, a time when the percentage of persons living alone went up by approximately 50%. In 1981, only 6% of respondents said they had little or no contact with friends and relatives outside of their own household.[48] Nevertheless, we can only guess at changes in the quality of relationships that took place during this period. In Sweden, as in other advanced societies, people who live alone have higher rates of mental and social problems, but this may be due to self-selection as much as isolation.

On the most impressionistic level, one seldom meets a foreigner living in Sweden who does not comment about Swedish "loneliness" and "isolation." People from less modernized societies, especially, find the lack of contact among urban Swedes quite remarkable—so many Swedes choosing to live alone and socializing so little and with such a seeming lack of enthusiasm. In my own extensive household interviewing in Swedish urban areas in the 1970s, I was certainly struck by this; many Swedes seem to live exceptionally quiet, privatized lives in which they seldom neighbor.[49]

To some extent outsiders may be misinterpreting the well-known traditional Swedish formality and personal reserve as loneliness. Yet it is known from various studies that the degree of privatization in Swedish cities was not so characteristic of these cities historically, nor is it currently found in Swedish rural places.[50] One explanation for the change is that excessive privatization is the mode of adaptation of the first generation of a rather shy people who are living in the city for the first time and many in apartment buildings at that. By this explanation, the degree of privatization will decrease as Swedes become more accustomed to the urban life.

From another perspective, this style of life could be the wave of the future—the new, individualized, and autonomous individual making a suitable adjustment to a rationalized and affluent world. After all, the rich have always lived with a very high level of privatization—that is one of the prerogatives of being rich. Yet what makes today's living situation unusual is that the rich rarely lived *alone* with a privatized lifestyle.

One wonders what the long-term effect will be of so many adults for the first time in history not having to adjust on a daily, residential basis to at least one other person. What does it mean, for example, for a large segment of society to be eating meals alone, watching television alone, and waking up each morning to an "empty" household? Most of today's elderly who live alone once lived in large families, some of the members of which are still alive. What will it be like for the next generation of elderly, coming from very small families and having neither a living companion nor a relative to whom to turn? The current younger generation of Swedes is clearly breaking new ground, and the psychological impact will not be known for years to come. One can only await with eagerness the growth of knowledge about this important social development.

Modern Family Decline: A Personal Appraisal

The available empirical evidence about the negative social implications of modern family decline, presented above for Sweden, admittedly is not very convincing. Should we await further social science research before making moral judgments about such an important trend? I think not, for two reasons. First, one can never make judgments of value based on an assemblage of empirical facts. Social science evidence can help; it is eschewed as irrelevant at one's intellectual peril. But no matter how extensive, the facts will never bring one conclusively to decisions about what used to be called matters of right and wrong. Second, many implications of modern family decline lie in areas that are essentially beyond the reach of the empirical social sciences. They have more to do with people's inner state of being than their overt behavior, more with their souls than their bodies.

After the long journey of earlier chapters through Western family history, family theory, and contemporary family conditions in a number of advanced nations, therefore, it is fitting to conclude this book with a more impression-istic appraisal of the family situation in modern societies, especially Sweden, and its portents for the future of the family. My appraisal of the Swedish fam-ily situation constitutes in many respects a case for the strong family. Yet I put forth my views without a strongly polemical or propagandizing intent, although, to be sure, almost every work of social science has some such inclinations. I realize fully that the set of historical trends and other facts pre-sented in this book can be evaluated in different ways. Many readers who hold different values than do I may have already reached conclusions of their own that differ from those that follow. Because the broader implica-tions of modern family decline are seldom addressed seriously, especially in Sweden, it is not agreement with my views that I seek as much as more earnest discussion of the issues.

In response to age-old concerns about family decline, many a family scholar of late has been fond of stating that families may have changed somewhat, but that these changes have few negative implications; the insti-tution of the family is still strong and enduring, and there is little about which to be concerned. I do not take such an optimistic view. I see the family as a perishable social institution that is being quietly corroded by some of the social and cultural currents of our time.

Underlying my perspective on family decline is a sociocultural connection that is not emphasized often enough: contemporary family decline is closely related to the importance that advanced societies place on the value of individualism. One reason for not stressing this connection is that it is not well understood. Note that the ideological opposite of "familism," unlike the opposite of many other ideologies, does not come readily to mind. While the opposite of religion is clearly secularism and the opposite of democracy is dictatorship or one of its variations, what is the ideological opposite of familism? I suggest that it is individualism in its modern meaning of "emphasis on self-fulfillment" and "pursuit of individual rather than collective interests." In this light, the ideologies or values of familism and of individualism should be thought of as partially contradictory and in competition with one another.

The ideal of self-fulfillment is a relative newcomer on the world scene. This is the first time in world history that the masses have been able to achieve the degree of self-fulfillment previously possessed only by rich males. In the past, familism was one of the principal cultural elements posing a powerful constraint on such individualism. It fostered placing the collective interests of the family above each member's individual interest. With the rise of what is sometimes called "late modernization," self-fulfillment has become one of the paramount cultural values. This means that familism and the family today face what can reasonably be described as an unprecedented, adverse cultural climate.

Recent Family Evolution in Review

It is useful to review once more some of the main aspects of the recent historical development of the family as an institution in Western societies. Throughout most of human history the family appears to have been, almost everywhere, a strong collective entity dominated by males. The economic precariousness and physical insecurity of living conditions made an intense internal cohesion of families absolutely essential for human survival. This does not mean that families of the past were necessarily happy, made up of people who all dearly loved one another, and never filled with deep internal strife. But lack of love and presence of strife did not in the past normally lead to the breakdown of the family unit. Even when the conjugal tie was severed, by the death of a spouse or by male abandonment, the nuclear family unit was quickly absorbed by the extended family network of relatives.

When it first arose in northwest Europe in the past few centuries, the modern nuclear family was a unique "social invention." It had been cast adrift from the kinship group to allow the emotional relationship between husband and wife to flourish, and unlike most previous family forms it was not held together primarily by economic forces with economic-production goals paramount. The modern nuclear family was organized largely to serve the end of child rearing in an environment of stability and love between the married couple. Backed by the unique coercive powers of organized religion, as well as by the laws of the state, the nuclear family unit was culturally held up as the goal of human sexuality combined with romantic love; it was the only socially acceptable form of adult pair-bond. The wife was enjoined to devote her life, at all personal costs, to the purpose of child rearing, and the husband was expected to devote his life, even sacrifice it if necessary, to the support of the mother–child bond. Many people were not successful in living this way, and the roles that fell to wives and husbands have been amply scrutinized in recent years and found wanting. But in its time this family form was an ideal widely accepted and without serious cultural challenge.

This ideal was also short-lived. It lasted for little more than a century and even less in, for example, Sweden where it arrived relatively late. Today, the main goal of much adult family formation or "pair-bonding" in advanced societies is not procreation and the socialization of children, but emotional attachment. To this end, children are not only unneeded, but often even a hindrance. Moreover, emotional attachment by itself, especially when not backed by religion, has proved to be an unstable basis for permanent human pair-bonding. Sex, procreation, and adult pair-bonding, which were effectively joined under the ideal of the modern nuclear family, have therefore become increasingly dissociated from one another, and the family unit in which children are present has grown in some ways increasingly insecure.

The Family and Child Welfare

It has become clear that adults no longer need children in their lives, at least not in economic terms. The problem is that children, as much as they ever did, still need adults. They need not just adults, however, but parents who are motivated to provide them with, in the words of Urie Bronfenbrenner, "enduring, irrational emotional involvement."[51] Just any adults cannot normally provide that involvement, only parents (at least one but preferably two). In this sense, child rearing is one of those aspects of human society that is not subject to improvement through modern techniques of efficiency and the rationalization of process; it is a "cottage industry." What is still required, and has no substitute in the technological realm, is an abundance of time, patience, and love on the part of caring parents. In short, children need strong families.

Of course most parents in modern societies are caring, loving, and doing the best they can. Nevertheless, it is of concern that social and cultural forces in modern societies may be subtly corroding the parent–child relationship. The trends of our time that are improperly labeled "revolutions," each of which has advanced in its own way the value of self-fulfillment—the sexual revolution, the feminist revolution, the therapeutic revolution, the welfare revolution, the consumer revolution—have probably all played a role in the weakening of this main human relationship. This weakening can best be seen in the growing disinvestment in family life and in the increasing dissolution of families with children.

With the predominance of the value of self-fulfillment, not only may the parent–child relationship have suffered, but it is not clear from what source the reinforcements of parental motivation to meet children's needs will come. In pursuit of the kind of self-fulfillment that was traditionally the preserve of men, the driving goal of an increasing number of mothers has been to have a career. It is hard to deny that up to now this has meant fewer children. It also has brought the danger that the mothering process will take second place to the outside job.

Also in pursuit of self-fulfillment, fathers have been abandoning their wives and children in growing numbers. With some of their traditional family roles undercut, men apparently see less and less to hold them to family responsibilities. And in a nation such as Sweden they can now abandon their wives and children with little fear or anxiety, thanks to the government, that the family members left behind will suffer serious economic consequences. Moreover, the men who do stay with their families seem reluctant to take on many additional family roles; if child care interferes with the mother's career, so also does it now interfere with the father's.

The solution to the dilemma of how to carry on family responsibilities while at the same time seeking self-fulfillment can glibly be said to consist of getting each parent to achieve a better balance between career and domestic roles. But under current cultural conditions achieving this balance without unnecessarily compromising the powerful drive for self-fulfillment remains a problem. In order to achieve a better balance, it is a reasonable proposition that some shift in values is required, namely, a partial retreat from the predominance of self-fulfillment.

A reassessment of values can be approached rationally, drawing on human experience. In the individualistic sense of fulfilling ambitions and desires through one's own efforts, self-fulfillment has only limited potential in the long run for bringing human satisfaction and happiness. Lasting personal fulfillment is better achieved as a by-product of the pursuit of extraindividual goals, which reflect high ideals and whose pursuit involves action in concert with others. Perhaps the most meaningful experience of life is the feeling of oneness with others in the pursuit of some common purpose of great intrinsic worth. On a large scale this may consist of significant humanitarian ventures; on a small scale it can involve the raising of children.

With regard to many social trends it is not possible to turn back the clock, but this is not as true, curiously, of some aspects of the cultural realm. The values that people hold are constantly shifting back and forth over relatively short historical time periods. We have seen massive shifts in the past few generations, for example, from religion to secularism, from open prejudice and discrimination to growing tolerance, from elitism to egalitarianism, and from cultural absolutism to cultural relativism. Yet in earlier historical time periods these values have shifted in opposite directions. There is no necessary reason to suppose that the importance accorded self-fulfillment today will not in time diminish, at least to the degree necessary for some restoration of family strength.

Perhaps today's children of divorce, in view of what they have been through, will as adults take the lead in bringing about a more child-centered, familistic society. Perhaps fathers can be coaxed into sharing equally the family's domestic activities. Perhaps women will find new satisfactions in mothering. Perhaps children will again come to be seen by both women and men as life's deepest and most enduring satisfaction. Each of these options is plausible, but none can be achieved without some change in the predominant pattern of values.

The Family and the Adult

It is not difficult to make the case that strong families are as important for adults as they are for children, although this line of argument is less commonly heard. The family is still the only social institution that, when functioning properly, provides unconditional social acceptance, that is, acceptance without the need for justification. Acceptance within the family involves relationships with people from whom one can expect a special sense of obligation and responsibility. With family decline, such acceptance is in increasingly short supply.

Outside the moral realm of the family is the world of voluntary friendships, a sphere governed by a marketplace for acceptance. In this outside world, acceptance is a scarce commodity that is allocated through competition; it must be strived for, earned, and maintained, and, hence, is highly conditional. It has the drawbacks of any marketplace: there are winners, but also losers. It is true that the act of establishing a family through marriage has long been based on market considerations; once established, however, that marriage relationship was subsumed under a quite different moral realm. With modern family decline, not only friendships but marriage relationships themselves have fallen increasingly outside the traditional moral realm of the family and into the world of the market.

The negative impact of this "shift of acceptance" from the family to the marketplace should not be underestimated. In this age of nonbinding human commitments and freedom of choice, the family is often seen as an obstacle to adult autonomy and self-realization; it is seen as parochial, stifling, repressive, and opposed to human liberation. It is in the world of free choice outside the family, the argument runs, that the real opportunities for emotional self-fulfillment lie. Yet in the outside market for friendships, emotional connections, and acceptance, some people are much more skilled and advantaged than others. There are many people in every society who lack the social skills, grace, attractiveness, money, and power that are required to be successful in an open market for human relationships. Such people have traditionally achieved their acceptance within large and strong families; with the weakening of families, the emotional quality of their lives may increasingly be at risk. Can they make it on their own? Modern life can be materially beneficent (the underclass of America notwithstanding), and the material lives of adults without families need not be ones of poverty. But these lives can certainly be ones of emotional pain.

The importance of familial acceptance should be seen in cultural as well as emotional terms. For the harried adult bombarded by high-technology stimuli, the social pressures of the bureaucracy, and the competition of the marketplace, the family as "haven in a heartless world" is a place of cultural as well as emotional repose.[52] It provides cultural meaning as well as personal identity. Sweden may well be the least "heartless" of any advanced society, and thus this function of the family may be less important in Sweden than elsewhere. Still, one must wonder what kind of "haven" is provided by the growing number of transient relationships, broken homes, and single-person households. To what degree does one, in the words of Sophocles, "but a faithless haven find?"

Despite the strength of the ethic of self-fulfillment, familism and lifetime monogamy remain ideals for a surprisingly large segment of the adult population. The argument is often heard that today's long average life span makes it unrealistic to expect pair-bonding with one person for a lifetime. Since the pair-bond is based strictly on affection and companionship, the changes that occur to individuals through a long life—in health, occupation, interests, and goals—will make once compatible couples incompatible or spouses will simply tire of each other after a period of time. Based on people's actual behavior, this might seem a realistic appraisal of the situation. But why, then, do most people still cling stubbornly to the ideal of a lifetime pair-bond? Is it not because people realize that this ideal *is* possible of attainment (after all, more than half of all marriages today last until death) and that there is a basic human need for permanent attachment?

The Family and the State

The tensions are real between the growing power of the centralized national state and the struggles of the family to maintain some institutional autonomy. In recent years, as discussed in earlier chapters, the family has lost some power through interventions by the state into what was formerly the family's private realm. These interventions have been mainly for the purpose of protecting or furthering the interests of children.

Parents still have the legal responsibility, as well as the social authority, to raise their own children. But what if they are doing a bad job? Because the broader community has a genuine stake in the welfare of children, the liberty of parents to treat their own children as they see fit has increasingly been restricted. The modern state actively intervenes in cases of mental or physical abuse, the Swedish state carrying this to the extent of prohibiting parents from spanking or in other ways physically hurting their children for any reason. Many nonphysical areas of life can also be the focus of intervention; in most circumstances parents cannot, for example, refuse to send their children to school to be educated. With the assumption that parents do not always do what is in the best interests of their children, a good case can be made that family decline, in the sense of some loss of parental authority to the state, has been beneficial both for children and for society.

It is important to bear in mind, however, that not all of the change in the relationship between family and state has been in the direction of increased state control. In other areas the state has actually relinquished control over the family, the best example being the easing of legal controls over marriage and divorce. While the state intervention discussed above may benefit children and take away some rights from adults, the decontrol of marriage and divorce may benefit adults but take away some rights from children. The conceivable "right" of children that is being curtailed is the right to a functioning family with two parents who stay with them and provide enduring emotional support.

A continuous trend toward reduced state control over the family in the area of marriage and divorce can be seen in the history of divorce legislation in Western societies. The laws of the past few centuries that strongly proscribed divorce first came about with the rise to institutional prominence of nation-states. These laws were originally established to protect economically dependent women and children and to force men to be responsible. Before then, in many Western societies men could abandon women and children virtually as they saw fit. As women have become economically more independent, the divorce laws have evolved in stages toward today's position of maximum freedom for couples: (1) dropping the absolute ban on divorce and basing divorce actions on the principle of guilt; (2) abandoning the principle of guilt in favor of "irreparability" as determined at the discretion of the judge; (3) abandoning judicial discretion in favor of joint agreement by the couple; (4) abandoning joint agreement in favor of unilateral termination under certain conditions; and (5) recognizing the right to a unilateral termination of marriage.[53]

Along with the easing of divorce laws has come the deregulation of marriage and the abolition of the concept of illegitimacy. In this regard Sweden is today in the process of moving toward a still further stage: treating formal and informal marriages as nearly identical.

It should not be thought that modern states have relinquished all control over marital dissolution. They have merely relinquished control over whether or not the marriage stays together. Controls to protect parties economically injured by the breakup and to provide for the continuing financial obligation of parents in the rearing of their children have been maintained and even strengthened. Most importantly, in recent years laws have been strengthened that require the absent parent to provide child support.

What the laws do not attempt to protect children against, however, is any psychological injury caused by the marital dissolution. With regard to the continuation of the parental bond, children are regarded as having virtually no rights at all. The dissolutions of all marital unions in Sweden today (and in most other advanced societies as well) are treated legally as essentially the same, with or without the presence of children. For couples with children, Sweden continues to require a 6-month waiting period before formal dissolution is granted, but no other restrictions apply (of course, when unmarried couples with children break up, such a waiting period is inapplicable).

Given the negative psychological consequences of marital breakup on children, who have no choice in the matter, one might suppose that such a highly welfare-oriented nation as Sweden would make sure that children, as well as their parents, have certain rights in the issue of family dissolution. It is surprising to find, therefore, that Sweden has such a hands-off policy concerning parental relationships and seems so unconcerned about the high parental break-up rate. The Swedish state both looks the other way with respect to parental stability and, at least officially, fails to support the notion that lifetime parental bonding is an important ideal. There is little in Swedish family law anymore, for example, that upholds the ideal of parental stability and permanence. And even though Sweden may have the highest parental breakup rate in the world, a dubious distinction, no state investigative commission has ever been appointed to look into the matter; one can think of few other areas of life that Swedes have not thoroughly investigated. For all official intents and purposes, then, the high rate of parental instability in Sweden appears to be not the least bit problematic.

The surprise over official Swedish attitudes toward parental instability is accentuated in view of the character of Swedish society in other respects. Sweden is often referred to by other Europeans as a "prohibition" (*förbud*) society,[54] which is dominated by strictly enforced controls over private behavior (such as child spanking); at the same time, Sweden is a society that has shown great concern about the rights of children. It is strange that a society willing to protect children's interests to the extent of interfering in the classic parental right to discipline their own children as they see fit, through outlawing spanking, would not at the same time give more serious attention to the issue of parental instability. Yet in regard to the marriages and marriagelike relationships of parents, Sweden may now be the most relaxed, noninterfering society in the world.

Why should official Sweden (and to a lesser degree other advanced societies) have essentially discarded the centuries-old ideal of parental stability? It is because in this age of individualism, as one group of European legal scholars put it, "the abstract ideal of loyalty does not carry enough weight nowadays to justify such an intrusion into the freedom and privacy of the individual."[55] But "individual" means adults and not children; the rights of adults are given considerably more weight in this regard than are any presumed rights of children. One wonders how much of this in the modern welfare state, responsive as the state may be to many interest and client groups, is due to the downgrading in the political shuffle of the interests of children; children of course do not vote or normally even express their opinions. It is often pointed out that in virtually every welfare state the growth of benefits for the elderly has far exceeded that for children. If children were involved in formulating welfare-state policies, I have little doubt that the situation would be different.

With children thus overlooked in the modern welfare state, the path to stronger families ironically may involve increasing rather than decreasing the intervention of the state. The state should be viewed not only as a force hostile to families, but as a protector of family rights—in this case the rights of children.

There is a certain inappropriateness and futility, of course, in the state's attempting to regulate the affectional bond between two adults. Forcing hostile and recalcitrant parents to stay together for the sake of their children would be a highly questionable public policy; in any event, the children might be just as badly off in conflict-ridden families as they would be going through divorces. Still, from a child's point of view, there is much to be said for making divorce more difficult for the parents of children and for the state signaling in various ways that family stability *is* extremely important to children and therefore to society as a whole.

Family and Society

The importance of the institution of the family in modern societies rests on more than its being just a place where parents rear children and find an anchor for their affections. Although these two family functions are the most prominent, the social contribution of the family in our time, both actual and potential, is much more extensive. The family serves not just its own members, but the society as a whole.

Because of a tendency toward the centralization of power, every modern society faces the danger of political and cultural tyranny. Centralized political structures, unchecked by effective political opposition, can drift in the direction of total social control or totalitarianism. Centralized cultural structures, unchecked by strong and pluralist subcultures, can move toward total control of values and meanings. Such tendencies raise the specter of mass society, a society consisting of relatively unattached individuals, on the one hand, and powerful state "megastructures", on the other. In the highly centralized and rationalized megastructures of Sweden, some have detected early signs of mass society in the sense of cultural domination by the state. Whether agreeing with such an interpretation or not, one would have to be intellectually myopic, given the history of the world in the twentieth century, to discount the potential (in Sweden and elsewhere) for social rigidity, cultural uniformity, and authoritarian control.

The structures that stand between the individual and the megastructures of society have been called "mediating structures."[56] Usually elements of local communities, they mediate between the public and private worlds of modern life. The family is one such structure; others are the neighborhood, the church or local religious organization, and the voluntary association. On the one hand, these structures operate to protect the individual in his or her private sphere from excessive incursions of the megastructures; on the other, they enable the megastructures to reach through to the individual with a more human face. When assembled into such aggregations as local communities, regional entities, and national interest groups, these mediating structures also function to hold the megastructures to some kind of accountability.

One compelling observation about Sweden today is that, in addition to a weakened family system, it also has surprisingly anemic local community elements, which have traditionally comprised the mediating networks. The "parochial" functions of local religious organizations are almost gone; voluntary health, welfare, and educational associations have all but disappeared; and urban neighborhoods have become socially vestigial.

These structural trends are interrelated. Mediating structures, including the family, have reciprocal relationships with one another; each helps to support and maintain the others. Because of the presence of children, the family has always been a strongly localized institution. Families with children are necessarily concerned about neighborhood interaction, neighborhood facilities, neighborhood safety, and neighborhood cohesion. Take families with children out of neighborhoods, and the neighborhoods often wither. With families as its main client group, the church has always been a powerful neighborhood institution. In contemporary Western societies where organized religion is still important, the local church is as much a neighborhood social facility as a religious institution. Finally, the voluntary association has always represented an extension of the kinds of social exchange that characterize the family: altruism and mutual aid, sharing and voluntary caring outside the orbit of market and bureaucracy.

Because of the reciprocal relationships among these mediating structures, it is no wonder that as one withers, so do the others. Strong neighborhoods, churches, and voluntary associations are a rarity without the presence of strong families; they weaken as families in an area weaken. By the same token, the family can be weakened as these larger structures decline, for example, through actions of the welfare state. With more family services and facilities provided by the state, people have less need for neighbors and neighborhoods, voluntary associations, churches, and even their own families.

Are there any obvious signs in Sweden of "sociological damage" stemming from this erosion of local mediating institutions? Certainly not in the areas of health and material welfare; in these respects Swedes are probably better cared for than any other of the world's people. As for the social and cultural sphere, it must be remembered that Sweden, though a highly centralized society, is not a large-scale society. Swedes have social and cultural ties to the society as a whole not often found in larger and more heterogeneous nations. Foreign observers may call this societal conformism, but it may reasonably also be called societal integration. Swedes may not be "plugged into" much at the local level, but the meaning and societal identity provided merely by being "a Swede" seem far greater than anything provided, for example, by that comparatively vague and amorphous label "an American."

All the same, there is cause to be concerned about the rapid decline of local community institutions in Sweden. Swedes themselves are the first to admit that life in a stringent bureaucracy has its drawbacks. There is, for example, the relentless need for accountability. Swedes have leaned over backward to establish official ombudsmen and other similar state mechanisms, but these may not be adequate replacements for local institutions, one of the traditional checks on state power.

The need also persists for social and cultural mediation between the public, impersonal world of the megastructures of state and market and the private and personal world of the household. The typical Swede today moves daily back and forth between the private and protected world of the household and the public world of employment and state bureaucracy with few social structures in between. It may be that in Sweden, compared to most other nations, less mediation between these two spheres of life is needed. The public environment is benign, and the work environment has been humanized beyond the imagination of people in most other parts of the world. It is a fact that the Swedish state has established a vast system of leisure-time groups in which Swedes are avid participants. Also, the typical Swedish household is "extended" with a network of close friends, however far flung that network may appear to be to those in more traditional societies.

Still, one worries about the stay-at-homes who must remain in the privatized world without much geographic mobility or social accessibility—children and the elderly, the less affluent, the invalid. Traditionally such people have been culturally fed, in a highly personalized and therefore meaningful way, by both strong families and rich local communities. Today they are much more the unmediated wards of the megastructures; this change brings equality and justice, but does it always bring as much identity, meaning, and satisfaction?

There is another area, perhaps even more important, which has few substitutes for strong families and local communities. This is the area of social control of youth. We know both that Sweden has had a high rate of delinquency and that one of the reasons for this is the decline of the local, informal social control mechanisms that societies typically have had in abundance. Precisely because they are formal and impersonal, the new social control mechanisms of police and school are inadequate replacements for the older mechanisms administered by parent, aunt, neighbor, and pastor. Modern societies therefore diminish the traditional, informal types of social control at their peril.

Finally, it must be realized that every modern society, no matter how centralized, affluent, and welfare oriented, very much depends on familism in the sense of people voluntarily providing services for others that otherwise would have to be provided by the government. It is fortunate for the economy of any nation, for example, that most parents are willing to provide services at no cost for their children and for each other; there is simply no way that such costs could be borne by the taxpayers. From this perspective, families represent a huge body of people willing to work for humanitarian and socially necessary goals with virtually no material rewards.

The importance of this family care-giving function becomes clear when we consider what might happen if modern societies ever again fell into a serious economic depression. It is difficult to deny that Swedish society today is a smoothly operating entity, even though many services formerly provided at no charge by families are now provided at taxpayers' expense by the state. But such a state allocation of resources requires enormous wealth. Suppose there is a sudden loss of prosperity in Sweden. Will Swedish households and families, suddenly cut off from government services, be able to survive through voluntary mutual aid as well as will households and families in societies where families have maintained to a larger degree the practice of self-sufficiency?

Lessons from Sweden: A Final Note

Perhaps it is merely quibbling to express concerns about and criticize so fine a society as Sweden in matters such as those raised in this chapter. There is no perfect society, and what Sweden now offers it citizens few Swedes wish to give up. Societies never stop evolving, however, and there are always lessons to be learned and new paths to be explored. The welfare state may be one of humankind's most significant social creations, but clearly it has its own problems and limits.

Although unfortunately seldom discussed today, the problems and limits posed to the welfare state by the decline of families may well be among the most intractable. Despite tremendous welfare advances, the institution of the family has been seriously buffeted by the recent tide of events. There is little cause for concern that the end of the family is near. The need of people for permanent human attachments and the natural love most people have for children ensure the existence of families in some form until such time as the makeup of human beings drastically alters. Yet the experience of Sweden provides no reason to be sanguine about the family's future. While the human mating impulse may have remained as robust as ever, the extension of this impulse to the building of strong families appears in Sweden to have weakened. Mostly inadvertently, some recent social and cultural developments there have been disturbing the human nest.

How can other advanced nations encourage women to participate fully in public life, provide family members with all of the public facilities and services they need for lives of material equality and abundance, yet still maintain the family as a strong institution? In the light of the Swedish experience, no answer to this question looms larger in importance than the effort to maintain a balance of values whereby familism is granted sufficient weight in the cultural equation. Like most values, familism is an ideal that continually needs reinforcement; under the pressures of modern society, such reinforcement has fallen into short supply.

The process of reinforcing the value of familism, under today's social conditions, involves placing more stress on the following broad social or moral obligations:

1. The obligation of parents who bring children into the world to live together and create a strong family unit.

2. The obligation of the employment sector to consider the effects on the family of all of its activities and to realize that most of its adult workers have not one but two important roles in life. For the private sector, this obligation may need to be continually reemphasized and supported by the state.

3. The obligation of government, when providing facilities and services, to give help in a manner that as much as possible strengthens rather than weakens the family unit.

4. The obligation of men, in view of the changing roles of women, to take a much more active role in family life.

5. The obligation of people who make laws, social policies, and political pronouncements to ensure that, in the process of protecting "alternative

life-styles," they do not downgrade the ideal of the nuclear family—parents living together and sharing responsibility for their children and for each other. In an egalitarian society the protection of minority life-styles is important, but good family life is something on which every society depends for its very existence.

The democratic state can play only a limited role in enlarging the importance of familism; it cannot get too far ahead of the people. Any new support for familism cannot be initiated by the state alone, but must come from a change in popular sentiment. Yet when majority sentiment and state power converge on a moral issue, such as the end of slavery, the diminution of racial discrimination, or equality for women, the resulting cultural change can be dramatic.

The Swedish welfare state has been remarkably successful in responding to the material problems of family decline and in achieving a just and humane society. Public facilities and services alone, however, cannot halt the decline of families. If it is to survive as a rich and complex part of the fabric of modern society, the family must also be nurtured and sustained as a thing of value through the moral suasion of cultural, intellectual, and political leaders. In this Sweden has been somewhat neglectful, and this, along with its welfare-state achievements, may be the most important lesson the Swedish experience can provide to the rest of the modern world.

Notes

[1]See Robert Erikson (1984), "Uppväxtvillkor under 1900-talet," pp. 334–349 in Robert Erikson and Rune Åberg, (eds.), *Välfärd i Förändring.* An English translation of this work was published in 1987: *Welfare in Transition: A Survey of Living Conditions in Sweden, 1968–1981.*

[2]Robert N. Bellah et al. (1985), *Habits of the Heart.*

[3]Rita Liljeström (1983), *Uppväxtvillkor.* See also: Rita Liljeström (1982), *Våra Barn, Andras Ungar.*

[4]Anna Torbiörnsson (1982), *Att Vara Förälder Idag:* 81–101. Similar views are expressed in Birgitta Johansson-Hedberg, *BarnSverige.*

[5]From interviews conducted by the author, 1985–1986.

[6]Interview, October 1985. Also see Benny Henriksson (1983), *Not for Sale: Young People in Society.*

[7]Socialdepartementet (1981), *Ensamföräldrar 1980:* 103.

[8]Frank F. Furstenberg, Jr., and Christine W. Nord (1985), "Parenting Apart: Patterns of Childrearing after Marital Disruption," pp. 893–920 in *Journal of Marriage and the Family* 47–4:902.

[9]Frank F. Furstenberg, Jr., et al. (1983), "The Life Course of Children of Divorce: Marital Disruption and Parental Contact," pp. 656–668 in *American Sociological Review* 48:667.

[10]In the chapter on family change in one recent Swedish social-problems text,

there is virtually no mention of any adverse psychological effects of family breakup. Ted Goldberg (ed.) (1983), *Samhällsproblem:* 115-137.

[11]Lenore J. Weitzman (1985), *The Divorce Revolution.*

[12]Reported in *ibid.:* 395.

[13]Judith S. Wallerstein and J. B. Kelly (1981), *Surviving the Breakup.*

[14]Judith S. Wallerstein (1984), "Children of Divorce: Preliminary Report of a Ten Year Follow-up of Young Children," *American Journal of Orthopsychiatry* 54: 444-458.

[15]James L. Peterson and Nicholas Zill (1986), "Marital Disruption, Parent-Child Relationships, and Behavior Problems in Children," *Journal of Marriage and the Family* 48: 295-307.

[16]Ann Mitchell (1985), *Children in the Middle: Living through Divorce:* 92.

[17]Peter Uhlenberg and David Eggebeen (1986), "The Declining Well-being of American Adolescents," *The Public Interest* 82: 25-38. This article concerns the negative impact on white American teenagers of social changes in the period 1960-1980. It notes that despite declining poverty, better education for parents, and more public expenditures for education and welfare during this period, there was a decline among adolescents in educational achievement and an increase in delinquency, drug and alcohol use, mortality (especially due to violent causes), and teen pregnancies. The authors suggest that "the most critical determinant of all" in accounting for this outcome was a deterioration in "the bond between child and parent," specifically, "a declining commitment of parents to their children" (p. 35).

[18]Herbert Hendin (1965), *Suicide and Scandinavia:* 59-60. Hendin quotes (p. 60) a Swedish child psychiatrist as having said: "The mothers just don't seem to enjoy their children very much. They don't get the same pleasure from their children—whether caring for them or playing with them—that you see in Danish and American mothers."

[19]Data from Organization for Economic Cooperation and Development (1986), *Living Conditions in OECD Countries:* 151-152.

[20]Hans-Olov Isaksson (1984), "On the Alcohol and Drug Situation in Sweden": 72.

[21]*Ibid.:* 3.

[22]*Ibid.:* 37.

[23]Jan Andersson and Artur Solarz (1982), *Drug Criminality and Drug Abuse in Sweden 1969-1981.*

[24]Isaksson (1984), "Alcohol": 55.

[25]Bo Svensson (1986), "Measuring Drug Incidence—The Swedish Experience."

[26]Henrick Tham (1978), "Ungdomsbrottsligheten Enligt Den Officiella Statistiken."

[27]See, for example, Donald J. Shoemaker (1984), *Theories of Delinquency.*

[28]Marshall B. Clinard (1978), *Cities with Little Crime: The Case of Switzerland.*

[29]*Ibid.:* 154.

[30]This relationship and the Swedish research that bears on it are explored in Jerzy Sarnecki (1981), *Ungdomsbrottslighet:* Chapter 7.

[31]Cited in *ibid.:* 134.

[32]Cited in *ibid.:* 139.

[33]Hans Lohmann (1972), *Psykisk Hälsa och Mänsklig Miljö.*

[34]Anna-Lisa Kälvesten and Maj Ödman (1979), *Barn i Fem Länder Tecknar och Tänker.*

[35]Inga Sylvander and Maj Ördman (1985), *Jag är Rädd för att bli Bortglömd och Ensam.*

[36]May 1986.

[37]Marta Szebehely and Jonas Wall (1982), *Några Stockholms Ungdomar i Närbild.*

[38]Interview, September 1985.

39U.S. Labor Department data reported in *The New York Times,* March 16, 1986: 25.

40One study in the Gothenburg region found that only 11% of the children of members of LO, the large Swedish trade union for manual workers, had places in a day-care center, versus 31% of the children of academics. Reported in *Svenska Dagbladet,* Stockholm, October 3, 1985: 10.

41Billy Ehn (1983), *Ska Ve Leka Tiger?: Daghemsliv ur Kulturell Synvinkel.*

42See, for example, J. Belsky and L. D. Steinberg (1978), "The Effects of Day-Care: A Critical Review," *Child Development* 49: 929–949, and Urie Bronfenbrenner (1979), *The Ecology of Human Development:* Chapter 8.

43I. Hårsman (1984), *Spädbarn på Daghem och Hemma—En Studie av Anpassningsprocessen, Interaktionen Vårdare-Barn och Attachementbeteendet;* R. Haskins (1985), "Public School Agression among Children with Varying Day-Care Experience," *Child Development* 56: 689–703. Citations from Bengt-Erik Andersson (1986), *Home Care or External Care.*

44Andersson (1986), *Ibid.* This is part of a long-term "FAST-Project", run jointly by the Schools of Education in Stockholm and Gothenburg.

45Moncrieff M. Cochran and Lars Gunnarsson (1985), "A Follow-up Study of Group Day Care and Family-based Childrearing Patterns," *Journal of Marriage and the Family* (May): 297–309.

46For American data see Norval D. Glenn (1975), "The Contribution of Marriage to the Psychological Well-being of Males and Females," *Journal of Marriage and the Family* 37 (August): 594–600; Norval D. Glenn and C. N. Weaver (1979), "A Note on Family Situation and Global Happiness," *Social Forces* 57-3: 960–967; and Angus Campbell (1981), *The Sense of Well-Being in America.*

47The happiness trend studies are summarized in Ruut Veenhoven (1984), *Conditions of Happiness:* 144–146.

48Christina Axelsson (1984), "Familj och Social Förankring," pp. 267–284 in Erikson and Åberg (1984), *Välfärd.*

49See David Popenoe (1985), *Private Pleasure, Public Plight: American Metropolitan Community Life in Comparative Perspective;* and David Popenoe (1977), *The Suburban Environment: Sweden and the United States.*

50See Åke Daun (1976), *Strategi för Gemenskap;* Åke Daun (1974), *Förortsliv;* and Åke Daun (1969), *Upp till Kamp i Båtskärsnäs.*

51Urie Bronfenbrenner (1985), "The Parent/Child Relationship and Our Changing Society," pp. 45–57 in L. Eugene Arnold (ed.) *Parents, Children and Change.*

52Christopher Lasch (1977), *Haven in a Heartless World.*

53*Ibid:* 37.

54Mogens Berendt (1983), *Fallet Sverige.*

55Henrik H. Andrup, *et al.* (1980), "Formal Marriage under the Crossfire of Social Change," pp. 32–38 in John M. Eekelaar and S. N. Katz (eds.), *Marriage and Cohabitation in Contemporary Societies: Areas of Legal, Social, and Ethical Change:* 37.

56Peter L. Berger and Richard John Neuhaus (1977), *To Empower People: The Role of Mediating Structures in Public Policy.*

Bibliography

Abbot, Philip. 1981. *The Family on Trial.* University Park, PA: Pennsylvania State Univ. Press.

Adams, Bert N. 1986. *The Family: A Sociological Interpretation* (4th ed.). San Diego, CA: Harcourt Brace Jovanovich.

Adams, Carolyn Teich, and Kathryn Teich Winston. 1980. *Mothers at Work: Public Policies in the United States, Sweden, and China.* New York: Longman.

Agell, Anders. 1980. "Cohabitation without Marriage in Swedish Law." Pp. 245–257 in J.M. Eekelaar and S.N. Katz (eds.), *Marriage and Cohabitation in Contemporary Societies.* Toronto: Butterworth.

Agell, Anders. 1981. "The Swedish Legislation on Marriage and Cohabitation: A Journey without a Destination." *The American Journal of Comparative Law* 24-2: 285–314.

Agell, Anders. 1985. *Samboende utan Äktenskap* (Cohabitation without Marriage). Stockholm: Liber.

Aitken, Judith. 1980. "Women in the Political Life of New Zealand," Pp. 11–33 in P. Bunkle and B. Hughes, (eds.), *Women in New Zealand Society.* Boston: Allen and Unwin.

Åkerman, Brita (ed.). 1985. *Kunskap för Vår Vardag* (Knowledge for Our Everyday Lives). Stockholm: Akademilitteratur.

Åkerman, Sune, H. C. Johansen, and D. Gaunt (eds.). 1978. *Chance and Change: Social and Economic Studies in Historical Demography in the Baltic Area.* Odense, Denmark: Odense Univ. Press.

Albrecht, Stan L., Howard M. Bahr, and Kristen L. Goodman. 1983. *Divorce and Remarriage.* Westport, CT: Greenwood Press.

Alexandersson, Birgitta. 1973. "The 1973 Family Law Reform." *Current Sweden* 8. Stockholm: Swedish Institute.

Allan, Graham. 1985. *Family Life.* New York: Basil Blackwell.

Allardt, Erik. 1975. *Att Ha, Att Alska, Att Vara: Om Välfärd i Norden* (Having, Loving, Being: On Welfare in the Nordic Countries). Lund: Argos.

345

Andersen, Bent Rold. 1984. "Rationality and Irrationality of the Nordic Welfare State." *Daedalus* 113-1:109-39.

Anderson, Michael. 1974. "Household Structure and the Industrial Revolution; Mid-Nineteenth-Century Preston in Comparative Perspective." Pp. 215-235 in P. Laslett (ed.), *Household and Family in Past Time.* Cambridge: Cambridge Univ. Press.

Anderson, Michael. 1980. *Approaches to the History of the Western Family 1500-1914.* London: Macmillan.

Andersson, Åke E., R. Bentzel, A-L. Hellsten, and J. Trost. 1983. *Kan Hushållen Lyfta Sverige Ur Krisen?* (Can Households Lift Sweden Out of the Crisis?). Stockholm: Sparfrämjandet.

Andersson, Bengt-Erik. 1986. *Home Care or External Care.* Stockholm: Department of Educational Research, Institute of Education.

Andersson, Ingvar, and Jörgen Weibull. 1985. *Swedish History in Brief.* Stockholm: Swedish Institute.

Andersson, Jan, and Artur Solarz. 1982. *Drug Criminality and Drug Abuse in Sweden 1969-1981.* Stockholm: National Swedish Council for Crime Prevention.

Andreski, Stanislav. 1969. "Introduction." Pp. ix-xxxvi in H. Spencer, *Principles of Sociology.* Hamden, CT: Archon Books.

Andrup, Henrik H., Bernd Buchhofer, and Klaus A. Ziegert. 1980. "Formal Marriage under the Crossfire of Social Change." Pp. 32-38 in J.M. Eekelaar and S.N. Katz (eds.), *Marriage and Cohabitation in Contemporary Societies.* Toronto, Butterworth.

Anton, Thomas J. 1980. *Administered Politics: Elite Political Culture in Sweden.* Boston: Martinus Nijhoff.

Arbetsmarknadsdepartementet. No Date. *Mannen i Förändring* (Men in Transition). Stockholm: Tiden.

Ariès, Philippe. 1962. *Centuries of Childhood: A Social History of Family Life.* New York: Vintage Books.

Arnold, L. Eugene (ed.). 1985. *Parents, Children, and Change.* Lexington, MA: Lexington Books.

Åström, Lissie. 1986. *I Kvinnoled* (In the Female Line). Malmö: Liber.

Austin, Paul Britten. 1968. *On Being Swedish.* Coral Gables, FL: Univ. of Miami Press.

Austin, Paul Britten. 1970. *The Swedes: How They Live and Work.* Newton Abbott, UK: David and Charles.

Axelsson, Christina. 1984. "Familj och Social Förankring" (Family and Social Anchorage), Pp. 267-284 in R. Erikson and R. Åberg (eds.), *Välfärd i Förändring.* Stockholm: Prisma.

Bachofen, J. J. 1861. *Das Mutterrecht.* Stuttgart: Krais and Hoffman.

Balvig, Flemming. 1980. "Theft in Scandinavia, 1970–78." Pp. 1–6 in N. Bishop (ed.), *Crime and Crime Control in Scandinavia 1976–80.* Copenhagen: Scandinavian Research Council for Criminology.

Balvig, Flemming. 1985. "Crime in Scandinavia: Trends, Explanations, Consequences." Pp. 7–17 in N. Bishop (ed.), *Scandinavian Criminal Policy and Criminology 1980–85.* Copenhagen: Scandinavian Research Council for Criminology.

Bane, Mary Jo. 1976. *Here to Stay: American Families in the Twentieth Century.* New York: Basic Books.

Barn (Children). 1983. Stockholm: Liber (no author).

Barrett, Michele, and M. McIntosh. 1982. *The Anti-Social Family.* Thetford, UK: Thetford Press.

Baude, Annika. No date. *Public Policy and Changing Family Patterns in Sweden 1930–1977.* Stockholm: Swedish Center for Working Life (working paper).

Baumann, Margrit, and M. Näf-Hoffmann. 1978. "The Status of Women in Society and in Law." Pp. 361–380 in J. M. Luck (ed.), *Modern Switzerland.* Palo Alto, CA: The Society for the Promotion of Science and Scholarship.

Becker, Gary S. 1981. *A Treatise on the Family.* Cambridge, MA: Harvard Univ. Press.

Bell, Daniel. 1976. *The Cultural Contradictions of Capitalism.* New York: Basic Books.

Bellah, Robert N. 1965. "Durkheim and History." Pp. 153–166 in R. A. Nisbet (ed.), *Emile Durkheim.* Englewood Cliffs, NJ: Prentice-Hall.

Bellah, Robert N. 1975. *The Broken Covenant.* New York: The Seabury Press.

Bellah, Robert N., Richard Madsen, William M. Sullivan, Ann Swidler, and Steven M. Tipton. 1985. *Habits of the Heart.* Berkeley: Univ. of California Press.

Belsky, J., and L. D. Steinberg. 1978. "The Effects of Day-Care: A Critical Review." *Child Development* 49:929–949

Berendt, Mogens. 1983. *Fallet Sverige* (The Case of Sweden). Stockholm: Bonnier Fakta.

Berfenstam, Ragnar, and Inger William-Olsson. 1973. *Early Child Care in Sweden.* New York: Gordon and Breach.

Berger, Brigitte, and Peter L. Berger. 1983. *The War over the Family: Capturing the Middle Ground.* Garden City, NY: Anchor Press.

Berger, Peter L., and Richard John Neuhaus. 1977. *To Empower People: The Role of Mediating Structures in Public Policy.* Washington, DC: American Enterprise Institute.

Berkner, L. K. 1972. "The Stem Family and the Development Cycle of the Family Household." *American Historical Review* 77-2:398–418.

Bernhardt, Eva. 1971. *Trends and Variations in Swedish Fertility: A Cohort Study.* Stockholm: National Central Bureau of Statistics.

Bishop, Norman (ed.). 1980. *Crime and Crime Control in Scandinavia 1976–80.* Copenhagen: Scandinavian Research Council for Criminology.

Bishop, Norman (ed.). 1985. *Scandinavian Criminal Policy and Criminology 1980–85.* Copenhagen: Scandinavian Research Council for Criminology.

Blanc, d'Olivier. 1985. "Les Ménages en Suisse," *Population* 40-4, 5:657–674.

Blumstein, Philip, and Pepper Schwartz. 1983. *American Couples.* New York: Pocket Books.

Boethius, Carl Gustav. 1984. "Swedish Sex Education and Its Results." *Current Sweden* 315. Stockholm: Swedish Institute.

Booth, Alan, David R. Johnson, Lynn White, and John N. Edwards. 1984. "Women, Outside Employment, and Marital Instability." *American Journal of Sociology* 90-3:567–583.

Bosanquet, Helen. 1915. *The Family.* London: Macmillan.

Bosworth, Barry P. 1987. "The Swedish Economy: An American Perspective." *Inside Sweden* 1-2:6–7.

Bouvier, Leon F. 1984. *Planet Earth 1984-2034: A Demographic Vision.* Washington, DC: Population Reference Bureau.

Braungart, Richard G., and Margaret M. Braungart. 1986. "Youth Problems and Politics in the 1980s: Some Multinational Comparisons." *International Sociology* 1-4:359–380.

Bronfenbrenner, Urie. 1979. *The Ecology of Human Development.* Cambridge, MA: Harvard Univ. Press.

Bronfenbrenner, Urie. 1985. "The Parent/Child Relationship and Our Changing Society." Pp. 45–57 in L. E. Arnold (ed.), *Parents, Children, and Change.* Lexington, MA: Lexington Books.

Broome, Leonard, and Philip Selznick. 1958. *Sociology* (2nd ed.). Evanston, IL: Row Peterson.

Brottsförebyggande rådet. 1985. *Brotts-Utveklingen* (The Development of Crime). Stockholm.

Brozan, Nadine. 1985. "Rate of Pregnancies for U.S. Teen-agers Found High in Study." *The New York Times,* 13 March, C1; C7.

Bunkle, Phillida, and Beryl Hughes (eds.). 1980. *Women in New Zealand Society.* Boston: Allen and Unwin.

Burgess, Ernest W. 1926. "The Family as a Unity of Interacting Personalities." *The Family* 8:3–9.

Burgess, Ernest W. 1948. "The Family in a Changing Society." *The American Journal of Sociology* 53-6:417–422.

Burgess, Ernest W., and Harvey J. Locke. 1945. *The Family: From Institution to Companionship.* New York: American Book Co.

Burguiere, Andre, Christiane Klapisch-Zuber, Martine Segalen, and Francoise Zonabend (eds.). 1986. *Histoire de la Famille*. Paris: Armand Colin.

Calder, Jenni. 1977. *The Victorian Home*. London: B. T. Batsford.

Caldwell, John C. 1982. *Theory of Fertility Decline*. New York: Academic Press.

Campbell, Angus. 1981. *The Sense of Well-being in America*. New York: McGraw-Hill.

Campbell, Bernard. 1985. *Human Evolution* (3rd ed.). New York: Aldine de Gruyter.

Caplow, Theodore, Howard M. Bahr, Bruce A. Chadwick, Reuben Hill, and Margaret Holmes Williamson. 1983. *Middletown Families*. New York: Bantam Books.

Carlson, Allan C. 1979. "Sex, Babies, and Families: The Myrdals and the Population Question." Washington, DC: American Enterprise Institute (unpubl. manuscript).

Carlson, Allan C. 1983. "The Myrdals, Pro-Natalism, and Swedish Social Democracy." *Continuity* 6:71-94.

Carlsson, Sten. 1978. "Unmarried Women in the Swedish Society of Estates." Pp. 220-226 in S. Åkerman *et al.* (eds.), *Chance and Change: Social and Economic Studies in Historical Demography in the Baltic Area*. Odense, Denmark: Odense Univ. Press.

Castles, Francis G. 1978. *The Social Democratic Image of Society*. London: Routledge and Kegan Paul.

Castles, Francis G. 1985. *The Working Class and Welfare*. Boston: Allen and Unwin.

Cherlin, Andrew J. 1979. "Work Life and Marital Dissolution." Pp. 151-166 in G. Levinger and O. C. Moles (eds.), *Divorce and Separation*. New York: Basic Books.

Cherlin, Andrew J. 1981. *Marriage, Divorce, Remarriage*. Cambridge: Harvard Univ. Press.

Cherlin, Andrew J. 1983. "Changing Family and Household," Pp. 51-66 in *Annual Review of Sociology* 9. Palo Alto, CA: Annual Reviews.

Cherlin, Andrew J., and Frank F. Furstenberg, Jr. 1986. *The New American Grandparent*. New York: Basic Books.

Chester, Robert (ed.). 1977. *Divorce in Europe*. Leiden: Martinus Nijhoff.

Childs, Marquis. 1947(1936). *Sweden: The Middle Way*. New York: Penguin Books.

Childs, Marquis. 1980. *Sweden: The Middle Way on Trial*. New Haven: Yale Univ. Press.

Christiansen, Palle Ove. 1978. "Peasant Adaptation to Bourgeois Culture." *Ethnologia Scandinavica*, pp. 98-152.

Clark, Clifford E., Jr. 1986. *The American Family Home, 1800-1960*. Chapel Hill, NC: Univ. of North Carolina Press.

Clinard, Marshall B. 1978. *Cities with Little Crime: The Case of Switzerland.* Cambridge: Cambridge Univ. Press.

Cochran, Moncrieff M., and Lars Gunnarsson. 1985. "A Follow-up Study of Group Day Care and Family-based Childrearing Patterns." *Journal of Marriage and the Family* 47-2:297–309.

Cochran, Moncrieff M., Lars Gunnarsson, Sylvia Gräbe, and Jill Lewis. 1984. *The Social Support Networks of Mothers with Young Children: A Cross-National Comparison.* Gothenburg, Sweden: University of Gothenburg, Department of Educational Research.

Cole, M. I., and C. Smith (eds.). 1970 (1939). *Democratic Sweden.* Freeport, NY: Books for Libraries Press.

Coleman, James S. 1961. *The Adolescent Society.* New York: Free Press.

Coleman, James S., and Torsten Husén. 1985. *Becoming Adult in a Changing Society.* Paris: OECD

Collins, Randall. 1985. *Sociology of Marriage and the Family.* Chicago: Nelson-Hall.

Constantine, L. L. 1978. "Multilateral Relations Revisited: Group Marriage in Extended Perspective." Pp. 131–147 in B. I. Murstein (ed.), *Exploring Intimate Lifestyles.* New York: Springer.

Constantine, L. L., and J. M. Constantine. 1973. *Group Marriage: A Study of Contemporary Multilateral Marriage.* New York: Macmillan.

Coser, Lewis A. 1977. *Masters of Sociological Thought.* San Diego: Harcourt Brace Jovanovich.

Cott, Nancy F. 1977. *The Bonds of Womanhood.* New Haven: Yale Univ. Press.

Cowan, Ruth Schwartz. 1983. *More Work for Mother.* New York: Basic Books.

Crosby, John F. 1985. *Reply to Myth: Perspectives on Intimacy.* New York: Wiley.

Cseh-Szombathy, László, Inger Koch-Nielsen, Jan Trost, and Itke Weeda (eds.). 1985. *The Aftermath of Divorce: Coping with Family Change.* Budapest: Akadémiai Kiadó.

Dahlström, Edmund (ed.). 1967 (1962). *The Changing Roles of Men and Women.* London: Gerald Duckworth.

Dahlström, Edmund. 1986. "Theories and Ideologies of Family Functions, Gender Relations and Human Reproduction." Gothenburg: Department of Sociology, University of Gothenburg (unpubl. manuscript).

Dahlström, Edmund, and Rita Liljeström. 1967. "The Family and Married Women at Work." Pp. 19–58 in E. Dahlström (ed.), *The Changing Roles of Men and Women.* London: Gerald Duckworth.

Dahlström, Edmund, and Rita Liljeström. 1982. *Working Class Women and Human Reproduction.* Gothenburg: Department of Sociology, University of Gothenburg.

Daun, Åke. 1969. *Upp till Kamp i Båtskärsnäs* (Struggle in Båtskärsnäs). Stockholm: Prisma.

Daun, Åke. 1974. *Förortsliv* (Suburban Life). Stockholm: Prisma.

Daun, Åke. 1976. *Strategi for Gemenskap* (Strategy for Community). Stockholm: Tidens.

Daun, Åke. 1984. "Swedishness as an Obstacle in Cross-Cultural Interaction." *Ethnologia Europaea* 14:95-109.

Daun, Åke. 1986. "The Japanese of the North—The Swedes of Asia?" *Ethnologia Scandinavica*, pp. 5-17.

Davis, Kingsley. 1985. "The Meaning and Significance of Marriage in Contemporary Society," Pp. 1-21 in K. Davis (ed.), *Contemporary Marriage*. New York: Russell Sage Foundation.

Davis, Kingsley (ed.). 1985. *Contemporary Marriage*. New York: Russell Sage Foundation.

de Chessin, Serge. 1936. *The Key to Sweden*. Stockholm: Fritzes.

Degler, Carl N. 1980. *At Odds: Women and the Family in America from the Revolution to the Present*. Oxford: Oxford Univ. Press.

de Mause, Lloyd (ed.). 1974. *The History of Childhood*. New York: Psychohistory Press.

Demos, John, and Sarane S. Boocock (eds.). 1978. *Turning Points: Historical and Sociological Essays on the Family*. Chicago: Univ. of Chicago Press.

de Tocqueville, Alexis. 1956. (1835-1840). *Democracy in America*. New York: Mentor Books.

Donzelot, Jacques. 1979. *The Policing of Families*. New York: Pantheon.

Dunstall, Graeme. 1981. "The Social Pattern." Pp. 397-429 in W. H. Oliver (ed.). *The Oxford History of New Zealand*. Wellington: Oxford Univ. Press.

Durkheim, Emile. 1950 (1895). *The Rules of Sociological Method*. New York: Free Press.

Durkheim, Emile. 1951 (1897). *Suicide: A Study in Sociology*. (trans. by John A. Spaulding and George Simpson). New York: Free Press.

Easterlin, Richard A. 1980. *Birth and Fortune: The Impact of Numbers on Personal Welfare*. New York: Basic Books.

Eastman, Max (ed.). 1932. *Capital and Other Writings by Karl Marx*. New York: The Modern Library.

Easton, Brian. 1980. *Social Policy and the Welfare State in New Zealand*. Auckland: Allen and Unwin.

Edwards, John N. (ed.). 1969. *The Family and Change*. New York: Alfred A. Knopf.

Eekelaar, John M., and S. N. Katz (eds.). 1980. *Marriage and Cohabitation in Contemporary Societies: Areas of Legal, Social and Ethical Change*. Toronto: Butterworth.

Ehn, Billy. 1983. *Ska ve Leka Tiger?: Daghemsliv ur Kulturell Synvinkel* (Shall

We Play Tiger?: Life in Day Care Centers from a Cultural Approach).
    Stockholm: Liber.
Ehrenreich, Barbara. 1984. *The Hearts of Men*. Garden City, NY: Anchor
    Press/Doubleday.
Einhorn, Eric, and John Logue. 1980. *Welfare States in Hard Times*. Kent,
    OH: Kent Popular Press.
Eisenstadt, S. N., and Ora Ahimeir (eds.). 1985. *The Welfare State and Its
    Aftermath*. London: Croom Helm.
Elder, Glen H., Jr. 1974. *Children of the Great Depression*. Chicago: Univ. of
    Chicago Press.
Elder, Glen H., Jr. 1978. "Approaches to Social Change and the Family." Pp.
    S1–S38 in J. Demos and S. S. Boocock (eds.), *Turning Points: Historical
    and Sociological Essays on the Family*. Chicago: Univ. of Chicago Press.
Elmer, Åke. 1983. *Svensk Socialpolitik* (Swedish Social Policy). 1983. Malmö:
    Liber.
Engellau, Patrick, and Ulf Henning (eds.). 1984. *Nordic Views and Values*.
    Stockholm: The Nordic Council.
Engels, Frederick. 1942 (1884). *The Origin of the Family, Private Property
    and the State*. New York: International Publishers.
Erikson, Robert. 1984. "Uppväxtvillkor under 1900-talet" (The Conditions of
    Growing up During the 20th century). Pp. 334–349 in R. Erikson and
    R. Åberg (eds.), *Välfärd i Förändring*. Stockholm: Prisma.
Erikson, Robert, and Rune Åberg (eds.) 1984. *Välfärd i Förändring* (Welfare
    in Transition). Stockholm: Prisma.
Erikson, Robert, and Rune Åberg (eds.). 1987. *Welfare in Transition: A Survey
    of Living Conditions in Sweden, 1968–1981*. London: Oxford Univ.
    Press.
Esping-Andersen, Gösta. 1985. *Politics Against Markets*. Princeton: Princeton
    Univ. Press.
Faris, Robert E. L. 1970. *Chicago Sociology: 1920–1932*. Chicago: Univ. of
    Chicago Press.
Farley, Jennie (ed.). 1985. *Women Workers in Fifteen Countries*. Ithaca, NY:
    ILR Press.
Fischer, Claude S. 1982. *To Dwell Among Friends*. Chicago: Univ. of Chicago
    Press. (a)
Fischer, Claude S. 1982. "The Dispersion of Kinship Ties in Modern Soci-
    ety: Contemporary Data and Historical Speculation." *Journal of Family
    History* 7–4:353–375. (b)
Flandrin, J.-L. 1979. *Families in Former Times*. Cambridge: Cambridge Univ.
    Press.
Fletcher, Ronald. 1973. *The Family and Marriage in Britain* (3rd ed.). Har-
    mondsworth, UK: Penguin.

Fox, Robin. 1983 (1967). *Kinship and Marriage.* Cambridge: Cambridge Univ. Press.

Frazier, E. Franklin. 1966 (1939). *The Negro Family in the United States.* Chicago: Univ. of Chicago Press.

Friedan, Betty. 1963. *The Feminine Mystique.* New York: Dell.

Fritzell, Johan. 1985. *Barnfamiljernas Levnadsnivå* (The Level of Living of Families with Children). Stockholm: Institutet för Social Forskning, Stockholm's Universitet.

Fry, John (ed.). 1979. *Limits of the Welfare State: Critical Views on Post-War Sweden.* Farnborough, UK: Saxon House.

Frykman, Jonas. 1975. "Sexual Intercourse and Social Norms: A Study of Illegitimate Births in Sweden." *Ethnologia Scandinavica,* pp. 110–150.

Frykman, Jonas, and Orvar Löfgren. 1979. *Den Kultiverade Människan* (The Cultivated Human Being). Lund: Liber.

Frykman, Jonas, and O. Löfgren (eds.). 1984. *Moderna Tider* (Modern Times). Lund: Liber.

Frykman, Jones, and Orvar Löfgren. 1987. *Culture Builders.* New Brunswick, NJ: Rutgers Univ. Press.

Fuchs, Victor R. 1983. *How We Live.* Cambridge: Harvard Univ. Press.

Furstenberg, Frank F., Jr., and Christine W. Nord. 1985. "Parenting Apart: Patterns of Childrearing after Marital Disruption." *Journal of Marriage and the Family* 47-4:893–920.

Furstenberg, Frank F., Jr., Christine W. Nord, James L. Peterson, and Nicholas Zill. 1983. "The Life Course of Children of Divorce: Marital Disruption and Parental Contact." *American Sociological Review* 48-5:656–668.

Gaunt, David. 1977. "Preindustrial Economy and Population Structure." *Scandinavian Journal of History* 2:183–210.

Gaunt, David. 1978. "Household Typology: Problems, Methods Results." Pp. 69–83 in S. Åkerman et al. (eds.), *Chance and Change: Social and Economic Studies in Historical Demography in the Baltic Area.* Odense, Denmark: Odense Univ. Press.

Gaunt, David. 1983. "The Property and Kin Relationships of Retired Farmers in Northern and Central Europe." Pp. 249–279 in R. Wall et al. (eds.), *Family Forms in Historic Europe.* Cambridge: Cambridge Univ. Press. (a)

Gaunt, David. 1983. *Familjeliv i Norden* (Family Life in the Nordic Countries). Malmö: Gidlunds. (b)

Gaunt, David, and Orvar Löfgren. 1984. *Myter om Svensken* (Myths about Swedes). Stockholm: Liber.

Gaunt, Louise, and David Gaunt, 1986. "Le Modèle Scandinave." Pp. 471–495 in A. Burguiere et al. (eds.), *Historie de la Famille.*

Geiger, H. Kent. 1968. *The Family in Soviet Russia.* Cambridge: Harvard Univ. Press.

Gibbons, P. J. 1981. "The Climate of Opinion." In W. H. Oliver (ed.), *The Oxford History of New Zealand.* Wellington: Oxford Univ. Press.

Gilbert, Neil. 1983. *Capitalism and the Welfare State: Dilemmas of Social Benevolence.* New Haven: Yale Univ. Press.

Gille, H. 1948. "Recent Developments in Swedish Population Policy." Part 1. *Population Studies* 2:3–70.

Gillis, John R. 1985. *For Better, For Worse: British Marriages 1600 to the Present.* New York: Oxford Univ. Press.

Gittins, Diana. 1985. *The Family in Question.* Atlantic Highlands. NJ: Humanities Press.

Gittler, Joseph P. (ed.). 1957. *Review of Sociology.* New York: Wiley.

Glass, D. V. 1940. *Population Policies and Movements in Europe.* London: Frank Cass.

Glass, D. V. 1970 (1939). "Population Policy." Pp. 277–293 in M. I. Cole and S. Smith (eds.), *Democratic Sweden.* Freeport, NY: Book for Libraries Press.

Glass, D. V., and D. E. C. Eversley (eds.). 1965. *Population in History.* London: Edward Arnold.

Glazer, Nathan. 1986. "Welfare and 'Welfare' in America." Pp. 40–63 in R. Rose and R. Shiratori (eds.), *The Welfare State East and West.* New York: Oxford Univ. Press.

Glenn, Norval D. 1975. "The Contribution of Marriage to the Psychological Well-being of Males and Females." *Journal of Marriage and the Family* 37:594–600.

Glenn, Norval D., and C. N. Weaver. 1979. "A Note on Family Situation and Global Happiness." *Social Forces* 57–3:960–967.

Goldberg, Ted (ed.). 1983. *Samhällsproblem* (Society's Problems). Stockholm: Liber.

Goode, William J. 1970 (1963). *World Revolution and Family Patterns.* New York: Free Press.

Goode, William J. 1980. "The Resistance of Family Forces to Industrialization." Pp. ix–xviii in J. M. Eekelaar and S. N. Katz (eds.), *Marriage and Cohabitation in Contemporary Societies: Areas of Legal, Social, and Ethical Change.* Toronto: Butterworth.

Goode, William J. 1984. "Individual Investments in Family Relationships over the Coming Decades." *The Tocqueville Review* 6–1:51–83.

Goody, Jack. 1983. *The Development of the Family and Marriage in Europe.* Cambridge: Cambridge Univ. Press.

Gordon, Hans, and Peter Molin. 1972. *"Man Bara Anpassar Sig Helt Enkelt"* ("One Just Gets Used to It"). Stockholm: Pan/Norstedts.

Gretler, Armin, and Pierre-Emeric Mandl. 1973. *Values, Trends and Alternatives in Swiss Society: A Prospective Analysis.* New York: Praeger.

Groeneveld, Lyle P., Nancy Brandon Tuma, and Michael T. Hannan. 1980. "The Effects of Negative Income Tax Programs on Marital Dissolution." *Journal of Human Resources* 15:654–674.

Gutman, Robert, and David Popenoe (eds.). 1970. *Neighborhood, City and Metropolis.* New York: Random House.

Gyllensten, Lars. 1972. "Swedish Radicalism in the 1960's: An Experiment in Political and Cultural Debate," Pp. 279–301 in M. D. Hancock and G. Sjoberg (eds.), *Politics in the Post-Welfare State.* New York: Columbia Univ. Press.

Haavio-Mannila, Elina. 1983. "Caregiving in the Welfare State." *Acta Sociologica* 26-1:61–82.

Hadenius, Stig. 1985. *Swedish Politics During the 20th Century.* Stockholm: Swedish Institute.

Hajnal, J. 1965. "European Marriage Patterns in Perspective." Pp. 101–143 in D. V. Glass and D. E. C. Eversley (eds.), *Population in History.* London: Edward Arnold.

Hajnal, J. 1983. "Two Kinds of Pre-industrial Household Formation System," Pp. 65–104 in R. Wall *et al.* (eds.), *Family Forms in Historic Europe.* Cambridge: Cambridge Univ. Press.

Hamilton, Cicely. 1939. *Modern Sweden as Seen by an Englishwoman.* New York: E. P. Dutton.

Hamilton, Richard F., and James D. Wright. 1986. *The State of the Masses.* New York: Aldine de Gruyter.

Hanawalt, Barbara A. 1986. *The Ties That Bound: Peasant Families in Medieval England.* New York: Oxford Univ. Press.

Hancock, M. Donald, and Gideon Sjoberg (eds.). 1972. *Politics in the Post-Welfare State.* New York: Columbia Univ. Press.

Hannerz, Ulf. 1983. "Den Svenska Kulturen" (The Swedish Culture). Stockholm: Socialantropologiska Institutet, Stockholm's Universitet.

Hanssen, Börje. 1973. "Common Folk and Gentlefolk." *Ethnologia Scandinavica,* pp. 67–100.

Hanssen, Börje. 1977/1978. "Notes on Household Composition and Sociocultural Change." *Ethnologia Europaea* 10-1: 33–38.

Hanssen, Börje. 1978. "The Oikological Approach." Pp. 147–158 in S. Åkerman *et al.* (eds.), *Chance and Change: Social and Economic Studies in Historical Demography in the Baltic Area.* Odense, Denmark: Odense Univ. Press.

Hanssen, Börje. 1979/80. "Household, Classes, and Integration Processes in a Scandinavia Village over 300 Years." *Ethnologia Europaea* 11-1.

Harris, C. C. 1983. *The Family and Industrial Society.* London: Allen and Unwin.

Harris, Louis. 1987. *Inside America.* New York: Vintage Books.

Hårsman, I. 1984. *Spådbarn på Daghem och Hemma—En Studie av Anpass-ningsprocessen, Interaktionen Vårdare-Barn och Attachementbeteendet* (Infants in Day-Care Centers and at Home—A Study of Adjustment Processes, Interaction Between Caretaker and Child, and Attachment Behavior). Stockholm: Högskolan för Lärarutbildning, Institutet för Pedagogik.

Haskins, R. 1985. "Public School Aggression among Children with Varying Day-Care Experience." *Child Development* 56:689–703.

Hatje, Ann-Katrin. 1974. *Befolkningsfrågan och Valfärden.* Stockholm: Allmänna.

Hawke, G. R. 1982. "Incomes Policy in New Zealand." *VUW Working Papers in Economic History* 81–3.

Headey, Bruce. 1978. *Housing Policy in the Developed Economy.* New York: St. Martin's Press.

Heckscher, Gunnar. 1984. *The Welfare State and Beyond.* Minneapolis: Univ. of Minnesota Press.

Heclo, Hugh, and Henrik Madsen. 1987. *Policy and Politics in Sweden.* Philadelphia: Temple Univ. Press.

Hedström, Peter and Stein Ringen. 1983. "Age and Income in Contemporary Society: A Comparative Study." Stockholm: Institute for Social Research, University of Stockholm (unpubl. manuscript).

Heidenheimer, Arnold J., Hugh Heclo, and Carolyn Teich Adams. 1975. *Comparative Public Policy.* New York: St. Martin's Press.

Held, Thomas, and René Levy. 1983. "Economic Recession and Swiss Women's Attitudes Toward Marital Role Segregation." Pp. 373–395 in E. Lupri (ed.), *The Changing Position of Women in Family and Society.* Leiden: E. J. Brill.

Hemström, E. 1983. *Utrymmesstandard i Internationell Jämförelse* (Spatial Standards in International Comparison) Ds Bo 1983: 7. Stockholm: Swedish Ministry of Housing.

Hendin, Herbert. 1965. *Suicide and Scandinavia.* Garden City, NY: Anchor Books.

Henriksson, Benny. 1983. *Not for Sale: Young People in Society.* Aberdeen: Aberdeen Univ. Press.

Herberg, Will. 1960. *Protestant, Catholic Jew.* Garden City, NY: Doubleday-Anchor.

Herbers, John. 1985. "One-Person Homes Show Big U.S. Rise." *The New York Times,* 28 November: A32.

Herlihy, David. 1985. *Medieval Households.* Cambridge: Harvard Univ. Press.

Herrström, Staffan. 1986. "Swedish Family Policy." *Current Sweden* 348. Stockholm: Swedish Institute.

Hewlett, Sylvia Ann. 1986. *A Lesser Life: The Myth of Women's Liberation in America.* New York: William Morrow.

Hill, Reuben. 1947. "The American Family: Problem or Solution." *American Journal of Sociology* 53-2:125-130.

Hill, Reuben. 1958. "Sociology of Marriage and Family Behavior, 1945-56." *Current Sociology* 7-1.

Hinkle, Roscoe C., Jr., and Gisela Hinkle. 1954. *The Development of Modern Sociology.* New York: Random House.

Hoem, Britta. 1985. "Ett Barn är Inte Nog. Vad Har Hänt med Svenska Ettbarnskvinnor Födda 1936-60" (One Child is Not Enough: What Has Happened to Swedish Women with One Child Born 1936-60). Stockholm: Section of Demography, University of Stockholm.

Hoem, Jan M., and Bo Rennermalm. 1985. "Modern Family Initiation in Sweden: Experience of Women Born Between 1936 and 1960." *European Journal of Population* 1:81-112.

Höpflinger, Francois. 1985. "Changing Marriage Behavior: Some European Comparisons." *Genus* 41-3, 4:41-63.

Höpflinger, Francois. 1987. *Wandel der Familienbildung in Westeuropa.* Campus: Frankfurt.

Hofsten, Erland, and Hans Lundström. 1976. *Swedish Population History.* Stockholm: National Central Bureau of Statistics.

Holter, Harriet. 1962. "Rebellion against the Family." *Acta Sociologica* 6-3:185-201.

Hoover, Dwight W., and John T. A. Koumoulides (eds.). 1980. *Conspectus of History I-IV: Family History.* Muncie, IN: Department of History, Ball State University.

Howard, George. E. 1904. *History of Matrimonial Institutions* (3 vols.). Chicago: Univ. of Chicago Press.

Howard, Ronald L. 1981. *A Social History of American Family Sociology, 1865-1940.* Westport, CT: Greenwood Press.

Huntford, Roland. 1972. *The New Totalitarians.* New York: Stein and Day.

Hwang, Philip (ed.). 1985. *Faderskap* (Fatherhood). Stockholm: Natur och Kultur.

Inglehart, Ronald. 1977. *The Silent Revolution: Changing Values and Political Styles among Western Publics.* Princeton: Princeton Univ. Press.

Inkeles, Alex. 1980. "Modernization and Family Patterns: A Test of Convergence Theory." Pp. 31-63 in D. W. Hoover and J. T. A. Koumoulides (eds.), *Conspectus of History I-IV: Family History.* Muncie, IN: Ball State Univ.

Isaksson, Hans-Olov. 1984. "On the Alcohol and Drug Situation in Sweden." Stockholm: Swedish Council for Information on Alcohol and Other Drugs.

Ivarsson, Magnus. 1983. *Sverige 1984* (Sweden 1984). Stockholm: Lehmanns.

Jackson, Anthony (ed.). In press. *Anthropology at Home.* London: Tavistock.

Jalmert, Lars. 1984. *Den Svenske Mannen* (The Swedish Man). Stockholm: Tiden.

Janowitz, Morris (ed.). 1966. *W. I. Thomas on Social Organization and Personality.* Chicago: Univ. of Chicago Press.

Janson, Carl-Gunnar (ed.). 1968. *Det Differentierade Samhället* (The Differentiated Society). Stockholm: Prisma.

Janson, Carl-Gunnar. 1968. "Brott och Sociala Strata" (Crime and Social Status). Pp. 284–302 in C-G. Janson (ed.), *Det Differentierade Samhället.* Stockholm: Prisma.

Janson, Carl-Gunnar. 1982. "Juvenile Delinquency Among Metropolitan Boys." Stockholm: Department of Sociology, University of Stockholm (Project Metropolitan Research Report #17).

Jenkins, David. 1968. *Sweden: The Progress Machine.* London: Robert Hale.

Johansson, Sten. 1980. *Barnens Välfärd* (Children's Welfare). *Stockholm: Institute for Social Forskning, Stockholm's Universitet.*

Johansson-Hedberg, Birgitta. 1981. *Barn-Sverige* (Children-Sweden). Stockholm: Liber and Sekretariatet för Framtidsstudier.

Jonassen, Christen T. 1983. *Value Systems and Personality in Western Civilization: Norwegians in Europe and America.* Columbus, OH: Ohio State Univ. Press.

Jones, Elise F., J. D. Forrest, N. Goldman, S. Henshaw, R. Lincoln, J. I. Rosoff, C. F. Westoff, and D. Wulff, 1986. *Teenage Pregnancy in Industrialized Countries.* New Haven, CT: Yale Univ. Press.

Jonsson, G., and A-L Kälvesten. 1964. *222 Stockholmspojkar* (222 Stockholm Boys). Stockholm: Almqvist and Wiksell.

Kälvemark, Ann-Sofie. 1980. *More Children of Better Quality? Aspects on Swedish Population Policy in the 1930's.* Uppsala: Almqvist and Wiksell International.

Kälvesten, Anna-Lisa, and Maj Ödman. 1979. *Barn i Fem Länder Tecknar och Tänker* (Children in Five Countries Draw and Think). Stockholm: Liber Utbildnings.

Kamerman, Sheila B., and Alfred J. Kahn (eds.). 1978. *Family Policy: Government and Family in Fourteen Countries.* New York: Columbia Univ. Press.

Kamerman, Sheila B., and Alfred J. Kahn. 1981. *Child Care, Family Benefits, and Working Parents.* New York: Columbia Univ. Press.

Kandel, Denise B., and Gerald S. Lesser. 1972. *Youth in Two Worlds.* San Francisco, CA: Jossey Bass.

Kellerhals, Jean, Jean F. Perrior, and Laura Vonecke. 1977. "Switzerland." In R. Chester (ed.), *Divorce in Europe.* Leiden: Martinus Nijhoff.

Kidder, Rushworth M. 1985. "Following Europe's Lead." *The Christian Science Monitor,* 29 November: 28–29.

Kirkwood, Barry J. 1979. "Population and Social Policy." Pp. 281–294 in R. J. W. Neville and C. J. O'Neill (eds.), *The Population of New Zealand—Interdisciplinary Perspectives.* Auckland: Longman Paul.

Kitson, Gay C., Karen Benson Babri, and Mary Joan Roach. 1985. "Who Divorces and Why?" *Journal of Family Issues* 6–3:255–293.

Knott, Kathleen. 1961. *A Clean, Well-Lighted Place.* London: Heineman.

Koblik, Steven (ed.). 1975. *Sweden's Development from Poverty to Affluence, 1750–1970.* Minneapolis: Univ. of Minnesota Press.

Kobrin, Francis E. 1976. "The Fall in Household Size and the Rise of the Primary Individual in the U.S." *Demography* 13–1:127–138.

Koch-Nielsen, Inger. 1985. *Divorces.* Copenhagen: Danish National Institute of Social Research.

Koopman-Boyden, Peggy G., and Claudia D. Scott. 1984. *The Family and Government Policy in New Zealand.* Boston: Allen and Unwin.

Korpi, Walter. 1978. *The Working Class in Welfare Capitalism.* London: Routledge and Kegan Paul.

Korpi, Walter. 1983. *The Democratic Class Struggle.* London: Routledge and Kegan Paul.

Kozyrev, Julian. 1969. "The Family and Family Relations." Pp. 65–72 in G. V. Osipov (ed.), *Town Country and People.* London: Tavistock.

Kronborg, Bo, and T. Nilsson. 1978. "Social Mobility, Migration, and Family Building in Urban Environments." Pp. 227–237 in S. Åkerman et al. (eds.), *Chance and Change: Social and Economic Studies in Historical Demography in the Baltic Area.* Odense, Denmark's Odense Univ. Press.

Kümmerly and Frey. 1986. *Switzerland.* Berne.

Kurian, George Thomas. 1984. *The New Book of World Rankings.* New York: Facts on File Publications.

Lagercrantz, Olaf. 1984 (1979). *August Strindberg* (trans. by Anselm Hollo). New York: Farrar, Straus, Giroux.

Lagergren, Mårten, Lena Lundh, Minga Orkan, and Christer Sanne. 1982. *Tid för Omsorg* (Time to Care). Stockholm: Sekretariatet för Framtidsstudier.

Lagergren, Mårten, Lena Lundh, Minga Orkan, and Christer Sanne. 1984. *Time to Care.* Oxford: Pergamon Press.

Lamb, M. E., and J. A. Levine. 1983. "The Swedish Parental Insurance Policy: An Experiment in Social Engineering." Pp. 39–51 in M. E. Lamb and A. Sagi (eds.), *Fatherhood and Family Policy.* Hillsdale, NJ: Erlbaum.

Lamb, M. E. , and A. Sagi (eds.). 1983. *Fatherhood and Family Policy.* Hillsdale, NJ: Erlbaum.

Lapidus, Gail Warshofsky. 1982. *Women, Work, and Family in the Soviet Union.* Armonk, NY: M. E. Sharpe.

Lasch, Christopher. 1977. *Haven in a Heartless World.* New York: Basic Books.

Laslett, Peter. 1971 (1965). *The World We Have Lost.* (2nd ed.). New York: Charles Scribner's Sons.

Laslett, Peter (ed.). 1974. *Household and Family in Past Time.* Cambridge: Cambridge Univ. Press.

Laslett, Peter. 1977. *Family Life and Illicit Love in Earlier Generations.* Cambridge: Cambridge Univ. Press.

Leijon, Anna-Greta. 1968. *Swedish Women—Swedish Men.* Stockholm: Swedish Institute.

Lenero-Otero, Luis (ed.). 1977. *Beyond the Nuclear Family Model.* Beverly Hills, CA: Sage.

Lennéer-Axelson, Barbro. 1984. "Why Are Families Breaking Down? Opportunities and Risks for Whom" (unpubl. mimeo).

Lennéer-Axelson, Barbro. 1985. "Skilsmässopappor och Styvpappor" (Divorced Fathers and Step Fathers). Pp. 59–88 in P. Hwang (ed.), *Faderskap.* Stockholm: Natur och Kultur.

Lenski, Gerhard. 1976. "History and Social Change." *American Journal of Sociology* 82–3:548–564.

Lenski, Gerhard, and Jean Lenski. 1987. *Human Societies.* (5th ed.). New York: McGraw-Hill.

Levinger, George, and Oliver C. Moles (eds.). 1979. *Divorce and Separation.* New York: Basic Books.

Lewin, Bo. 1979. *Om Ogift Samboende i Sverige* (On Unmarried Cohabitation in Sweden). Stockholm: Almqvist and Wiksell.

Lewin, Bo, and Gisela Helmius. 1983. *Ungdom och Sexualitet* (Youth and Sexuality). Uppsala: Sociologiska Institutet, Uppsala's Universitet.

Liljeström, Rita. 1978. *Roles in Transition.* Stockholm: Committee on Equality between Men and Women. (a)

Liljeström, Rita. 1978. "Sweden." Pp. 19–48 in S. B. Kamerman and A. J. Kahn (eds.), *Family Policy: Government and Family in Fourteen Countries.* New York: Columbia Univ. Press. (b)

Liljeström, Rita. 1980. "Integration of Family Policy and Labor Market Policy in Sweden." Pp. 388–304 in R. S. Ratner (ed.). *Equal Employment Policy for Women.* Philadelphia: Temple Univ. Press.

Liljeström, Rita. 1982. *Våra Barn, Andras Ungar* (Our Children, Other's Brats). Stockholm: Liber/Publica.

Liljeström, Rita. 1983. *Uppväxtvillkor* (Growing-up Conditions). Stockholm: Liber/Publica.

Lindberg, Ingemar, and Lena Nordenmark. 1980. *Familjepolitik för Små Barn* (Family Policy for Small Children). Stockholm: Liber.

Linnér, Birgitta. 1967. *Sex and Society in Sweden.* New York: Pantheon Books.

Litwak, Eugene. 1960."Occupational Mobility and Extended Family Cohesion." *American Sociological Review* 25:9-21.

Locke, H. J., and Georg Karlsson. 1952. "Marital Adjustment and Prediction in Sweden and the United States." *American Sociological Review* 17: 10-17.

Löfgren, Orvar. 1974. "Family and Household among Scandinavian Peasants: An Exploratory Essay." *Ethnologia Scandinavica,* pp. 17-52.

Löfgren, Orvar. 1978. "The Potato People: Household Economy and Family Patterns among the Rural Proletariat in Nineteenth Century Sweden." Pp. 95-106 in S. Åkerman et al. (eds.), *Chance and Change: Social and Economic Studies in Historical Demography in the Baltic Area.* Odense, Denmark: Odense Univ. Press.

Löfgren, Orvar. 1980. "Historical Perspectives on Scandinavian Peasantries." Pp. 187-215 in *Annual Review of Anthropology* 9. Palo Alto, CA: Annual Reviews.

Löfgren, Orvar. 1981. "On the Anatomy of Culture." *Ethnologia Europaea* 12-1:26-46.

Löfgren, Orvar. 1984. "The Sweetness of Home: Class, Culture and Family Life in Sweden." *Ethnologia Europaea* 14:44-64. (a)

Löfgren, Orvar. 1984. "Family and Household: Images and Realities: Cultural Change in Swedish Society." Pp. 446-469 in R. Netting et al. (eds.), *Households: Comparative and Historical Studies of the Domestic Group.* Berkeley: Univ. of California Press. (b)

Löfgren, Orvar. In press. "Deconstructing Swedishness: Class and Culture in Modern Sweden." In A. Jackson (ed.), *Anthropology at Home.* London: Tavistock.

Lohmann, Hans. 1972. *Psykisk Hälsa och Mänsklig Miljö* (Mental Health and the Human Environment). Stockholm: Socialstyrelsen.

Lohr, Steve. 1987. "Now, Tax Revision in Sweden." *The New York Times,* 12 May: D9.

Lopata, Helen Z., Nona Glazer, and Judith Wittner (eds.). 1980. *Research in the Interweave of Social Roles: Women and Men.* Greenwich, CT.: JAI Press.

Luck, James Murray (ed.). 1978. *Modern Switzerland.* Palo Alto, CA: The Society for the Promotion of Science and Scholarship.

Luck, James Murray. 1985. *History of Switzerland.* Palo Alto, CA: The Society for the Promotion of Science and Scholarship.

Lüscher, Kurt K., Verena Ritter, and Peter Gross. 1973. *Early Child Care in Switzerland.* New York: Gordon and Breach.

Lukes, Steven. 1972. *Emile Durkheim: His Life and Work.* New York: Harper and Row.

Lundberg, George A., Clarence Schrag, and Otto N. Larsen. 1954. *Sociology.* New York: Harper and Brothers.

Lundell, Torborg. 1984. "Ellen Key and Swedish Feminist Views on Motherhood." *Scandinavian Studies* 56-4:351-369.

Lupri, Eugen (ed.). 1983. *The Changing Position of Women in Family and Society.* Leiden: E. J. Brill.

Lynd, Robert S., and Helen M. Lynd. 1929. *Middletown: A Study of Contemporary American Culture.* New York: Harcourt Brace.

Lynd, Robert S., and Helen M. Lynd. 1937. *Middletown in Transition: A Study in Cultural Conflicts.* New York: Harcourt Brace.

Mace, David, and Vera Mace. 1963. *The Soviet Family.* London: Hutchinson.

Macfarlane, Alan. 1979. *The Origins of English Individualism.* New York: Cambridge Univ. Press.

Macfarlane, Alan. 1986. *Marriage and Love in England: 1300-1840.* New York: Basil Blackwell.

McIntosh, C. Alison. 1983. *Population Policy in Western Europe.* Armonk, NY: M. E. Sharpe.

Macklin, Eleanor D. 1980. "Non-Traditional Family Forms: A Decade of Research." *Journal of Marriage and the Family* 42-4: 905-922.

McPhee, John. 1983. *La Place de la Concorde Suisse.* New York: Farrar, Straus, Giroux.

Maine, Henry Sumner. 1888 (1861). *Ancient Law* (3rd American ed. from 5th London ed.). New York: Henry Holt.

Manniche, Erik. 1985. *The Family in Denmark.* Helsingør: IPC Print and Press.

Marklund, Sixten, and Gunnar Bergendal. 1979. *Trends in Swedish Educational Policy.* Stockholm: Swedish Institute.

Marsh, Robert M. 1967. *Comparative Sociology.* New York: Harcourt, Brace and World.

Mårtensson, Mona. 1985. "Hushållsstruktur i Sverige. Kontinuitet och Förändring" (Household Structure in Sweden: Continuity and Change). Stockholm: Department of Sociology, University of Stockholm (unpubl. manuscript).

Martin, David. 1979. *A General Theory of Secularization.* New York: Harper Colophon Books.

Maruo, Naomi. 1986. "The Development of the Welfare Mix in Japan." Pp. 64-79 in R. Rose and R. Shiratori (eds.), *The Welfare State East and West.* New York: Oxford Univ. Press.

Marx, Karl. 1936. (1867)., *Capital.* New York: Modern Library.

Maus, Heinz. 1966. *A Short History of Sociology.* New York: Citadel Press.

Meidner, Rudolf. 1978. *Employee Investment Funds.* London: Allen and Unwin.

Meyer, Philippe. 1983. *The Child and the State: The Intervention of the State in Family Life.* Cambridge: Cambridge Univ. Press.

Meyerson, Per-Martin. 1982. *The Welfare State in Crisis—The Case of Sweden*. Stockholm: Federation of Swedish Industries.

Meyerson, Per-Martin. 1985. *Eurosclerosis: The Case of Sweden*. Stockholm: Federation of Swedish Industries.

Michael, Robert T., Victor R. Fuchs, and Sharon R. Scott. 1980. "Changes in the Propensity to Live Alone." *Demography* 17:39-56.

Mitchell, Ann. 1985. *Children in the Middle: Living through Divorce*. London: Tavistock.

Mittenthal, Sue. 1986. "Starting Kindergarten a Bit Older and Wiser." *The New York Times*, 21 November: C1.

Mitterauer, Michael, and Reinhard Sieder. 1983. *The European Family*. Chicago: Univ. of Chicago Press.

Moberg, Eva. 1962. *Kvinnor och Manniskor* (Women and Human Beings). Stockholm: Albert Bonniers.

Moberg, Vilhelm. 1984. "Life in the Villages." Pp. 11-20 in P. Engellau and U. Henning (eds.), *Nordic Views and Values*. Stockholm: The Nordic Council.

Modig, Arne. 1985. *Grannrelationer i Förort* (Suburban Neighborhood Relations). Stockholm: Byggforskningsrådet.

Mol, H., and M. T. V. Reidy, 1973. "Religion in New Zealand." Pp. 264-282 in S. Webb and J. Collette (eds.), *New Zealand Society*. New York: Wiley.

Moore, Wilbert E. 1979. *World Modernization: The Limits of Convergence*. New York: Elsevier.

Morgan, Lewis H. 1963 (1877). *Ancient Society*. Cleveland,Ohio: World Publishing Co.

Moroney, Robert M. 1986. *Shared Responsibility: Families and Social Policy*. New York: Aldine de Gruyter.

Mosk, Carl. 1983. *Patriarchy and Fertility: Japan and Sweden, 1880-1960*. New York: Academic Press.

Moynahan, Daniel Patrick. 1986. *Family and Nation*. San Diego: Harcourt Brace Jovanovich.

Murdock, George P. 1949. *Social Structure*. New York: Macmillan.

Murray, Charles. 1984. *Losing Ground*. New York: Basic Books

Murstein, B. I. (ed.). 1978. *Exploring Intimate Lifestyles*. New York: Springer.

Myrdal, Alva. 1968. (1941). *Nation and Family: The Swedish Experiment in Democratic Family and Population Policy*. Cambridge, MA: MIT Press.

Myrdal, Alva, and Viola Klein. 1956. *Women's Two Roles: Home and Work*. London: Routledge and Kegan Paul.

Myrdal, Alva, and Gunnar Myrdal. 1934. *Kris i Befolkningsfrågan* (Crisis in the Population Question). Stockholm: Albert Bonniers.

Myrdal, Gunnar. 1962 (1940). *Population: A Problem for Democracy*. Gloucester, MA: Peter Smith.

Nandan, Yash (ed.). 1980. *Emile Durkheim: Contributions to L'Année Soci- ologique.* New York: Free Press.

National Board of Education in Sweden. 1968. *Handbook on Sex Instruction in Swedish Schools.* Stockholm.

National Committee on Equality between Men and Women. 1979. *Step by Step: National Plan of Action for Equality* SOU 1979:6. Stockholm.

National Swedish Board of Education. 1977. *Instruction Concerning Inter- personal Relations.* Stockholm: Liber Utbildnings.

National Swedish Council for Crime Prevention. 1985. *Crime and Criminal Policy in Sweden 1985.* Report #19. Stockholm.

Nelson, George R. (ed.). 1953. *Freedom and Welfare.* Ministries of Social Affairs of Denmark, Finland, Iceland, Norway, Sweden.

Netting, Robert McC., Richard R. Wilk, and Eric J. Arnould (eds). 1984. *Households: Comparative and Historical Studies of the Domestic Group.* Berkeley: Univ. of California Press.

Neville, R. J. W., and C. J. O'Neill (eds.). 1979. *The Population of New Zealand—Interdisciplinary Perspectives.* Auckland: Longman Paul.

Neyer, Joseph. 1960. "Individualism and Socialism in Durkheim." Pp. 32–76 in K. H. Wolff (ed.), *Essays on Sociology and Philosophy by Emile Durkheim et al.* New York: Harper Torchbooks.

Nilsson, Åke. 1987. "Vartannat Barn Föds utom Äktenskapet" (Every Other Child is Born Out-of-Wedlock). *Välfärds Bulletinen* 4: 3–5.

Nisbet, Robert A. (ed.). 1965. *Emile Durkheim.* Englewood Cliffs, NJ: Prentice- Hall.

Nisbet, Robert A. 1966. *The Sociological Tradition.* New York: Basic Books.

Nisbet, Robert A. 1968. *Tradition and Revolt.* New York: Random House.

Nisbet, Robert A. 1969. *Social Change and History.* London: Oxford Univ. Press.

Nordic Council. 1984. *Level of Living and Inequality in the Nordic Countries.* Stockholm.

Nordiska Museet. 1985. *Modell Sverige.* Stockholm.

Nyström, S. 1980. *The Use of Somatic Hospital Care Among Divorced.* Stockholm: Almqvist and Wiksell.

Oakley, Stewart, 1966. *A Short History of Sweden.* New York: Praeger.

O'Brien, M., and C. Lewis (eds.). Forthcoming. *Problems of Fatherhood.* London: Sage Publications.

Ogburn, William F., and M. F. Nimkoff. 1955. *Technology and the Changing Family.* Cambridge: Houghton Mifflin.

Ogburn, William F., and Clark Tibbitts. 1933. "The Family and Its Functions." Chapter 13 in President's Research Committee on Social Trends. *Recent Social Trends.* New York: McGraw-Hill.

Oliver, W. H. (ed.). 1981. *The Oxford History of New Zealand.* Wellington: Oxford Univ. Press.

Olsen, Marvin E. 1968. *The Process of Social Organization.* New York: Holt, Rinehart and Winston.

Olsen, Marvin E. 1982. *Participatory Pluralism: Political Participation and Influence in the United States and Sweden.* Chicago: Nelson-Hall.

Olssen, Erik. 1980. "Women, Work and Family: 1880–1926." Pp. 159–83 in P. Bunkle and B. Hughes (eds.), *Women in New Zealand Society.* Boston: Allen and Unwin.

Olssen, Erik. 1981. "Towards a New Society." Pp. 250–278 in W. H. Oliver (ed.), *The Oxford History of New Zealand.* Wellington: Oxford Univ. Press.

Olsson, Sören. 1979. *Förorten* (The Suburb). Stockholm: Delegationen för Social Forskning.

Oppenheimer, Valerie Kincade. 1982. *Work and the Family: A Study in Social Demography.* New York: Academic Press.

Organization for Economic Cooperation and Development (OECD). 1981. *The Welfare State in Crisis.* Paris.

Organization for Economic Cooperation and Development (OECD). 1984. *Sweden* (OECD Economic Surveys). Paris.

Osipov, G. V. (ed.). 1969. *Town Country and People.* London: Tavistock.

Oxford Analytica. 1986. *America in Perspective.* Boston: Houghton Mifflin.

Ozment, Steven E. 1983. *When Fathers Ruled: Family Life in Reformation Europe.* Cambridge: Harvard Univ. Press.

Palme, Olof. 1972. "The Emancipation of Man." *The Journal of Social Issues* 28–2:237–246.

Parke, Robert, Jr., and Paul C. Glick. 1967. "Prospective Changes in Marriage and the Family." *Journal of Marriage and the Family* 29:249–256.

Park, Robert E., and Ernest W. Burgess. 1921. *Introduction to the Science of Sociology.* Chicago: Univ. of Chicago Press.

Parsons, Talcott. 1966. *Societies: Evolutionary and Comparative Perspectives.* Englewood Cliffs, NJ: Prentice-Hall.

Parsons, Talcott (ed.). 1968. *American Sociology: Perspectives, Problems, Methods.* New York: Basic Books.

Parsons, Talcott. 1971. *The System of Modern Societies.* Englewood Cliffs, NJ: Prentice-Hall.

Parsons, Talcott, and Robert F. Bales. 1955. *Family, Socialization and Interaction Process.* New York: Free Press.

Paukert, Liba. 1984. *The Employment and Unemployment of Women in OECD Countries.* Washington, DC: OECD Publ.

Peabody, Dean. 1985. *National Characteristics.* Cambridge: Cambridge Univ. Press.

Pearson, David G., and David C. Thorns. 1983. *Eclipse of Equality.* Boston: Allen and Unwin.

Peterson, James L., and Nicholas Zill. 1986. "Marital Disruption, Parent-Child

Relationships, and Behavior Problems in Children." *Journal of Marriage and the Family* 48:295–307.

Phillips, Roderick. 1981. *Divorce in New Zealand: A Social History.* Auckland: Oxford Univ. Press.

Phillips-Martinsson, Jean. 1981. *Swedes as Others See Them.* Lund: Utbildningshuset.

Pleck, Elizabeth H. 1976. "Two Worlds in One." *Journal of Social History* 10:178–195.

Pollack, Linda. 1984. *Forgotten Children: Parent–Child Relations from 1500–1900.* Cambridge: Cambridge Univ. Press.

Pool, D. Ian, and Janet Sceats. 1981. *Fertility and Family Formation in New Zealand.* Wellington: Ministry of Works and Development.

Popenoe, David. 1977. *The Suburban Environment: Sweden and the United States.* Chicago: Univ. of Chicago Press.

Popenoe, David. 1983. "Urban Scale and the Quality of Community Life: A Swedish Community Comparison." *Sociological Inquiry* 53-4:404–418.

Popenoe, David. 1985. *Private Pleasure, Public Plight: American Metropolitan Community Life in Comparative Perspective.* New Brunswick, NJ: Transaction Books.

Population Reference Bureau. 1987. "The 1987 World Population Data Sheet." Washington, DC.

Poston, Carol H. (ed.). 1976. *Mary Wollstonecraft Letters.* Lincoln, NE: Univ. of Nebraska Press.

Prime Ministers Office (Japan). 1984. "Outline of the Results of the Third International Survey of Youth Attitudes." Foreign Press Center, Japan (unpubl. manuscript).

Quin, E. A., and C. J. O'Neill. 1984. *Cohabitation in New Zealand: Legal and Social Aspects.* Waikato: Department of Sociology, University of Waikato.

Qvist, Gunnar. 1980. "Policy Towards Women and the Women's Struggle in Sweden." *Scandinavian Journal of History* 5:51–74.

Qvist, Jan, and Bo Rennermalm. 1985. *Att Bilda Familj* (Family Formation). Stockholm: Statistiska Centralbyrån.

Rabb, Theodore K., and R. I. Rotberg (eds.). 1982. *The New History: The 1980s and Beyond.* Princeton, NJ: Princeton Univ. Press.

Ratner, Ronnie Steinberg (ed.). 1980. *Equal Employment Policy for Women.* Philadelphia: Temple Univ. Press.

Reiger, Kerreen M. 1985. *The Disenchantment of the Home: Modernizing the Australian Family 1880–1940.* Melbourne: Oxford Univ. Press.

Reimer, Rita Ann. 1986. "Work and Family Life in Sweden." *Social Change in Sweden.* New York: Swedish Information Service.

Rein, Martin, and Lee Rainwater (eds.). 1986. *Public/Private Interplay in Social Protection: A Comparative Study.* Armonk, NY: M. E. Sharpe.

Reiss, Ira. 1980. "Sexual Customs and Gender Roles in Sweden and America: An Analysis and Interpretation." Pp. 191–220 in H. Z. Lopata et al. (eds.), *Research in the Interweave of Social Roles: Women and Men.* Greenwich, CT: JAI Press.

Rieff, Philip. 1966. *The Triumph of the Therapeutic.* New York: Harper and Row.

Ringen, Stein. 1986. *Difference and Similarity: Two Studies in Comparative Income Distribution.* Stockholm: Institutet för Social Forskning, Stockholm's Universitet.

Roberts, Kenneth. 1985. "Youth in the 1980's: A New Way of Life." *International Social Science Journal* 37-4:427–440.

Rogers, John, and Hans Norman (eds.). 1985. *The Nordic Family: Perspectives on Family Research.* Uppsala: Dept. of History, Uppsala University.

Roos, Patricia A. (ed.). 1985. *Gender and Work: A Comparative Analysis of Industrial Societies.* Albany: State Univ. of New York Press.

Rose, Richard, and Rei Shiratori (ed.). 1986. *The Welfare State East and West.* New York: Oxford Univ. Press.

Rosen, Bernard C. 1982. *The Industrial Connection: Achievement and the Family in Developing Societies.* New York: Aldine de Gruyter.

Rosengren, Annette. 1985. "Contemporary Swedish Family Life through the Eyes of an Ethnologist." Pp. 80–93 in J. Rogers and H. Norman (eds.), *The Nordic Family: Perspectives on Family Research.* Uppsala: Department of History, Uppsala University.

Rosenthal, Albert H. 1967. *The Social Programs of Sweden.* Minneapolis: Univ. of Minnesota Press.

Roussel, Louis, and Patrick Festy. 1979. *Recent Trends in Attitudes and Behavior Affecting the Family in Council of Europe Member States.* Strasbourg: Council of Europe.

Royal Ministry of Foreign Affairs. 1974. *The Biography of a People.* Stockholm: Allmänna.

Royal Swedish Commission. 1941. *Social Welfare in Sweden.* New York: New York World's Fair 1939.

Rüegg, Walter. 1985. "Social Rights or Social Responsibilities? The Case of Switzerland." Pp. 182–199 in S. N. Eisenstadt and O. Ahimeir (eds.), *The Welfare State and its Aftermath.* London: Croom Helm.

Ruggie, Mary. 1984. *The State and Working Women: A Comparative Study of Britain and Sweden.* Princeton: Princeton Univ. Press.

Rumney, Jay. 1965 (1937). *Herbert Spencer's Sociology.* New York: Atherton Books.

Rybczynski, Witold. 1986. *Home: A Short History of an Idea.* New York: Viking.

Rydén, Bengt, and Villy Bergström (eds.). 1982. *Sweden: Choices for Economic and Social Policy in the 1980s.* London: George Allen and Unwin.

Samuelsson, Kurt. 1968. *From Great Power to Welfare State.* London: Allen and Unwin.

Samuelsson, Kurt. 1975. "The Philosophy of Swedish Welfare Policies." Pp. 335–353 in S. Koblik (ed.), *Sweden's Development from Poverty to Affluence, 1750–1970.* Minneapolis: Univ. of Minnesota Press.

Sandberg, Elisabet. 1975. *Equality is the Goal.* Stockholm: Advisory Council to the Prime Minister on Equality between Men and Women.

Sandemose, Aksel. 1984 (1936). "The Law of Jante." Pp. 28–30 in P. Engellau and U. Henning (eds.), *Nordic Views and Values.* Stockholm: The Nordic Council.

Sandqvist, Karin. Forthcoming. "Swedish Family Policy and Attempt to Change Paternal Roles." In M. O'Brien and C. Lewis (eds.), *Problems of Fatherhood.* London: Sage Publications.

Sarnecki, Jerzy. 1981. *Ungdomsbrottslighet* (Juvenile Delinquency). Stockholm: Liber.

Sarnecki, Jerzy. 1983. "Research into Juvenile Crime in Sweden." *Information Bulletin of the National Swedish Council for Crime Prevention* I. Stockholm.

Sarnecki, Jerzy. 1985. *Byråkratins Innersta Väsen* (Bureaucracy's Innermost Being), Stockholm: Carlsson.

Scase, Richard. 1977. *Social Democracy in Capitalist Society.* London: Croom Helm.

Schmid, Carol L. 1981. *Conflict and Consensus in Switzerland.* Berkeley: Univ. of California Press.

Schneider, David M. 1984. *A Critique of the Study of Kinship.* Ann Arbor: Univ. of Michigan Press.

Schoen, Robert, and John Baj. 1984. "Cohort Marriage and Divorce in Five Western Countries." Pp. 197–229 in R. F. Tomasson (ed.), *Comparative Social Research 7.* Greenwich, CT: JAI Press.

Schoen, Robert, and William L. Urton. 1979. *Marital Status Life Tables for Sweden.* Stockholm: National Central Bureau of Statistics.

Schumpeter, Joseph A. 1976 (1943). *Capitalism, Socialism and Democracy* (5th ed.). London: Allen and Unwin.

Scobbie, Irene. 1972. *Sweden.* London: Ernest Benn.

Scott, D. Franklin. 1977. *Sweden: The Nation's History.* Minneapolis: Univ. of Minnesota Press.

Scott, Hilda. 1982. *Sweden's 'Right to be Human'.* London: Allison and Busby.

Segalman, Ralph. 1986. *The Swiss Way of Welfare: Lessons for the Western World.* New York: Praeger.

Segalman, Ralph. 1986. "Welfare and Dependency in Switzerland." *The Public Interest* 82:106–121.

Segerstedt, Torgny T. 1966. *The Nature of Social Reality.* Totowa, NJ: Bedminster Press.

Senderowitz, Judith, and John M. Paxman. 1985. "Adolescent Fertility: Worldwide Concerns." *Population Bulletin* 40–2:1–51.

Shiratori, Rei. 1985. "The Experience of the Welfare State in Japan and Its Problems." Pp. 200–223 in S. N. Eisenstadt and O. Ahimeir (eds.), *The Welfare State and its Aftermath.* London: Croom Helm.

Shlapentokh, Vladimir. 1984. *Love, Marriage and Friendship in the Soviet Union: Ideals and Practices.* New York: Praeger.

Shoemaker, Donald J. 1984. *Theories of Delinquency.* New York: Oxford Univ. Press.

Shorter, Edward. 1975. *The Making of the Modern Family.* New York: Basic Books.

Silén, Birgitta. 1987. "The Truth about Sexual Equality: A Gap between Words and Deeds." *Inside Sweden* 1–2:11–13.

Silver, Catherine Bodard (ed. and trans.). 1982. *Frédéric Le Play on Family, Work and Social Change.* Chicago: Univ. of Chicago Press.

Silverman, Bertram (ed.). 1980. "The Crisis of the Swedish Welfare State." *Challenge,* July–August; pp. 36–51.

Simona, Ilda. 1985. "Switzerland." Pp. 147–153 in J. Farley (ed.). *Women Workers in Fifteen Countries.* Ithaca, NY; ILA Press.

Simpson, George. 1965. "A Durkheim Fragment." *The American Journal of Sociology* 70–5:527–536.

Sinclair, Keith. 1984 (1959). *A History of New Zealand.* New York: Penguin Books.

Skolnick, Arlene S., and Jerome H. Skolnick. 1986. *Family in Transition.* Boston: Little, Brown.

Smith, R. E. 1979. *The Subtle Revolution: Women at Work.* Washington, DC: The Urban Institute.

Socialdepartementet. 1981. *Ensamföräldrar 1980* (Single Parents). Ds S 1981:18. Stockholm.

Socialdepartementet. 1983. *Barn Kostar. . .* (Children Cost . . .). *SOU 1983:14. Stockholm.*

Socialdepartementet. 1983. *Ensamföräldrarna och Deras Barn* (Single Parents and Their Children). SOU 1983:51. Stockholm.

Social Monitoring Group. 1985. *From Birth to Death*. Wellington: New Zealand Planning Council.

Sorokin, Pitirim. 1937. *Social and Cultural Dynamics*. New York: American Book Co.

Sorokin, Pitirim, and Carle C. Zimmerman. 1929. *Principles of Rural-Urban Sociology*. New York: Henry Holt.

Spanier, Graham. 1983. "Married and Unmarried Cohabitation in the United States: 1980." *Journal of Marriage and the Family* 45:277-288.

Spencer, Herbert. 1969 (1898). *Principles of Sociology*. Hamden, CT: Archon Books.

Statens Ungdomsråd. 1981. *Ej till Salu* (Not for Sale), Stockholm: Liber.

Statistiska Centralbyrån. 1982. *Perspektiv på Välfärden 1982* (Perspective on Welfare). Stockholm.

Statistiska Centralbyrån. 1984. *Ha Barn—Men Hur Många?* (Having Children—But How Many?) Information i Prognosfrågor 1984-4. Stockholm.

Statistiska Centralbyrån. 1985. *Utveklingsarbete med Statistiksystem om Barns och Ungdomars Levnadsförhållanden* (Development Work with Statistical Systems on Children's and Youth's Living Conditions). Stockholm.

Steinberg, Johathan. 1976. *Why Switzerland?* Cambridge: Cambridge Univ. Press.

Steiner, Gilbert Y. 1981. *The Futility of Family Policy*. Washington, DC: Brookings Institution.

Stenholm, Britta. 1984. *The Swedish School System*. Stockholm: Swedish Institute.

Stephens, John. 1979. *The Transition from Capitalism to Socialism*. London: Macmillan.

Stone, Lawrence. 1977. *The Family, Sex and Marriage in England 1500-1800*. New York: Harper and Row.

Stone, Lawrence. 1979. *The Family, Sex and Marriage in England 1500-1800* (abridged ed.). New York: Harper Torchbooks.

Stone, Lawrence. 1981. *The Past and the Present*. Boston: Routledge and Kegan Paul.

Stone, Lawrence, 1982. "Family History in the 1980s: Past Achievements and Future Trends." Pp. 51-87 in T. K. Rabb and R. I. Rotberg (eds.), *The New History: The 1980s and Beyond*: Princeton, NJ: Princeton University Press.

Stone, Lawrence. 1985. "Sex in the West." *The New Republic*, 8 July: 25-37.

Strode, Hudson. 1949. *Sweden: Model for the World*. New York: Harcourt, Brace.

Sundström, Gerdt. 1980. *Omsorg oss Emellan* (Care among Ourselves). Stockholm: Sekretariatet för Framtidsstudier.

Sundström, Gerdt. 1983. *Caring for the Aged in Welfare Society* Stockholm Studies in Social Work 1. Stockholm: Liber.

Svalastoga, Kaare. 1954. "The Family in Scandinavia." *Marriage and Family Living* 16-4: 374-380.

Svensson, Bo. 1985. "Economic Crime in Sweden." Pp. 31-45 in N. Bishop (ed.), *Scandinavian Criminal Policy and Criminology 1980-85*. Copenhagen: Scandinavian Research Council for Criminology.

Svensson, Bo. 1986. "Measuring Drug Incidence—The Swedish Experience." Stockholm: National Swedish Council for Crime Prevention.

Svensson, Waldemar. 1941. "Home Ownership in Sweden." Pp. 31-47 in The Royal Swedish Commission. *Social Welfare in Sweden*. New York: New York World's Fair 1939.

Swain, David A. 1979. "Marriages and Families." Pp. 112-124 in R. J. W. Neville and C. J. O'Neill (eds.), *The Population of New Zealand— Interdisciplinary Perspectives*. Auckland: Longman Paul.

Swedish Council for Information on Alcohol and Other Drugs. 1983. "On the Alcohol and Drug Situation in Sweden." Stockholm.

Swedish Institute. 1984. "Child Care Programs in Sweden." Stockholm.

Swedish Institute. 1986. "Facts and Figures about Youth in Sweden." *Fact Sheets on Sweden*. Stockholm.

Swedish Institute for Opinion Research (SIFO). 1984. *Indikator* 1. Stockholm.

Sylvander, Inga, and Maj Ordman. 1985. *Jag är Rädd för att Bli Bortglömd och Ensam* (I am Afraid of Being Forgotten and Alone). Stockholm: Brombergs.

Szebehely, Marta, and Jonas Wall. 1982. *Några Stockholms Ungdomar i Närbild* (A Close-Up View of Stockholm Youth). Stockholm: Tidens.

Tham, Henrik. 1978. "Ungdomsbrottsligheten Enligt Den Officiella Statistiken (Juvenile Delinquency as Reported in Official Swedish Statistics) *BRÅ-apropå*. Stockholm: Swedish National Council for Crime Prevention.

Thamm, Robert. 1975. *Beyond Marriage and the Nuclear Family*. San Francisco: Canfield Press.

"The World's Richest Nation." 1974. *The Economist,* April.

Theodorson, George A., and Achilles G. Theodorson. 1969. *Modern Dictionary of Sociology*. New York: Thomas Y. Crowell.

Thomas, Dorothy S. 1941. *Social and Economic Aspects of Swedish Population Movements, 1750-1933*. New York: Macmillan.

Thomas, William I., and Florian Znaniecki. 1927 (1918-1920). *The Polish Peasant in Europe and America* (2nd ed.). New York: Alfred Knopf.

Thomas, William I., and Florian Znaniecki. 1958 (1927). *The Polish Peasant in Europe and America*. New York: Dover Publications.

Thwing, Charles Franklin, and Carrie F. B. Thwing. 1913 (1886). *The Family: An Historical and Social Study*. Boston: Lothrop, Lee and Shepard.

Tiller, Per Olav. 1967. "Parental Role Division and the Child's Personality

Development." Pp. 79-104 in E. Dahlström (ed.), *The Changing Roles of Men and Women.* London: Gerald Duckworth.

Tilly, Louise A., and Joan W. Scott. 1978. *Women, Work, and Family.* New York: Holt, Rinehart and Winston.

Tingsten, Herbert. 1973. *The Swedish Social Democrats: Their Ideological Development.* Totowa, NJ: Bedminster Press.

Todd, Emmanuel. 1985. *The Explanation of Ideology: Family Structures and Social Systems.* New York: Basil Blackwell.

Tomasson, Richard F. 1970. *Sweden: Prototype of Modern Society.* New York: Random House.

Tomasson, Richard F. (ed.). 1984. *Comparative Social Research 7.* Greenwich, CT: JAI Press.

Torbiörnsson, Anna. 1982. *Att vara Förälder Idag* (Being a Parent Today). Stockholm: Socialstyrelsen.

Torstenson, Joel S., Michael F. Metcalf, and Tor Fr. Rasmussen. 1985. *Urbanization and Community Building in Modern Norway.* Oslo: Urbana Press.

Towards Equality: The Alva Myrdal Report to the Swedish Social Democratic Party. 1971. Stockholm: Prisma (no author).

Traugott, Mark (ed. and trans.). 1978. *Emile Durkheim on Institutional Analysis.* Chicago: Univ. of Chicago Press.

Trost, Jan. 1977. "Sweden." Pp. 35-52 in R. Chester (ed.), *Divorce in Europe.* Leiden: Martinus Nijhoff.

Trost, Jan. 1979. *Unmarried Cohabitation.* Västerås, Sweden: International Library.

Trost, Jan. 1983. "De Familjesociala Gränserna—Vad Kan Vi Få Hushallen att Göra" (The Social Limits of Families—What Can We Get Households to Do?). Pp. 20-32 in A. E. Andersson et al. *Kan Hushållen Lyfta Sverige Ur Krisen?* Stockholm: Sparfrämjandet.

Trost, Jan. 1985. "Marital and Non-marital Cohabitation." Pp. 109-119 in J. Rogers and H. Norman (eds.), *The Nordic Family: Perspectives on Family Research.* Uppsala: Uppsala University.

Trost, Jan, and Örjan Hultåker. 1982. *Swedish Divorces: Methods and Responses.* Uppsala: Uppsala University.

Trumbach, R. 1978. *The Rise of the Egalitarian Family: Aristocratic Kinship and Domestic Relations in Eighteenth Century England.* New York: Academic Press.

Uhlenberg, Peter, and David Eggebeen. 1986. "The Declining Well-being of American Adolescents." *The Public Interest* 82: 25-38.

United Nations. 1985, 1982. *U.N. Demographic Yearbook.* New York.

United States Bureau of the Census. 1979. "Divorce, Child Custody, and Child Support." *Current Population Reports* 65. Washington, DC: U.S. Government Printing Office.

van de Kaa, Dirk J. 1987. "Europe's Second Demographic Transition." *Population Bulletin* 42-1:1-57.

van den Berghe, Pierre L. 1979. *Human Family Systems: An Evolutionary View.* New York: Elsevier.

Vander Zanden, James W. 1965. *Sociology: A Systematic Approach.* New York: The Ronald Press.

van Leeuwen, Louis Th. 1981. "Early Family Sociology in Europe." Pp. 95-139 in R. L. Howard (ed.), *A Social History of American Family Sociology, 1865-1940.* Westport, CT: Greenwood Press.

van Vliet, Willem, Harvey Choldin, William Michelson, and David Popenoe (eds.). 1987. *Housing and Neighborhoods: Theoretical and Empirical Contributions.* Westport, CT: Greenwood Press.

Veenhoven, Ruut. 1984. *Conditions of Happiness.* Dordrecht, The Netherlands: D. Reidel.

Veevers, J. E. 1979. "Voluntary Childlessness: A Review of Issues and Evidence." *Marriage and Family Review* 2:1-26.

Veroff, Joseph, Elizabeth Douvan, and Richard A. Kulka. 1981. *The Inner American: A Self-Portrait from 1957 to 1976.* New York: Basic Books.

Vogel, Ezra F. 1968. "The Family and Kinship." Pp. 121-130 in T. Parsons (ed.), *American Sociology: Perspectives, Problems, Methods.* New York: Basic Books.

Vosburgh, Miriam Gilson. 1978. *The New Zealand Family and Social Change: A Trend Analysis.* Wellington, Department of Sociology and Social Work, Victoria University.

Waerness, Kari. 1978. "The Invisible Welfare State: Women's Work at Home." *Acta Sociologica* 21 (Suppl): 193-207.

Waite, Linda J., F. K. Goldscheider, and Christina Witsberger. 1986. "Nonfamily Living and the Erosion of Traditional Family Orientations Among Young Adults." Paper read at annual convention, American Sociological Association, New York City.

Wall, Richard, Jean Robin, and Peter Laslett (eds.). 1983. *Family Forms in Historic Europe.* Cambridge: Cambridge Univ. Press.

Wallerstein, Judith S. 1984. "Children of Divorce: Preliminary Report of a Ten Year Follow-up of Young Children." *American Journal of Orthopsychiatry* 54:444-458.

Wallerstein, Judith S., and J. B. Kelly. 1981. *Surviving the Breakup.* New York: Basic Books.

Wallwork, Ernest. 1972. *Durkheim: Morality and Milieu.* Cambridge: Harvard Univ. Press.

Wangson, Otto R. 1941. "Maternal and Child Welfare." Pp. 45-70 in Royal Swedish Commission. *Social Welfare in Sweden.* New York: New York World's Fair 1939.

Wattenburg, Ben J. 1985. *The Good News is the Bad News is Wrong*. New York: Simon and Schuster.

Webb, Stephen, and John Collette (eds.). 1973. *New Zealand Society*. New York: Wiley.

Weitzman, Lenore J. 1985. *The Divorce Revolution*. New York: Free Press.

Westermarck, Edward A. 1894–1901. *History of Human Marriage*. London: Macmillan.

Weston, D. E. 1983. "Secularization and Social Theory: Swedish Experience in the Context of an International Theoretical Debate." *Acta Sociologica* 26-3/4:329-336.

Wicksell, Anders. 1981. "Lönar det sig at Skiljas?" (Does It Pay One to Divorce?). Stockholm (unpubl. manuscript).

Wiersma, Geertje E. 1983. *Cohabitation, An Alternative to Marriage? A Cross-national Study*. Boston: Martinus Nijhoff.

Wilson, William Julius. 1987. *The Truly Disadvantaged*. Chicago: Univ. of Chicago Press.

Winch, Robert F. 1957. "Marriage and the Family." Pp. 346-390 in J. P. Gittler (ed.), *Review of Sociology*. New York: Wiley.

Winch, Robert F. 1977. *Familial Organization: A Quest for Determinants*. New York: Free Press.

Wirth, Louis. 1970 (1938). "Urbanism as a Way of Life." Pp. 54–69 in R. Gutman and D. Popenoe (eds.), *Neighborhood, City and Metropolis*. New York: Random House.

Wistrand, Birgitta. 1981. *Swedish Women on the Move*. Stockholm: Swedish Institute.

Wizelius, Ingemar (ed.). 1967. *Sweden in the Sixties*. Stockholm: Almqvist and Wiksell.

Wolff, Kurt H. (trans. and ed.). 1950. *The Sociology of Georg Simmel*. Glencoe, IL: Free Press.

Wolff, Kurt H. (ed.). 1960. *Essays on Sociology and Philosophy by Emile Durkheim et al*. New York: Harper Torchbooks.

Woodward, Alison. 1987. "Public Housing Communes: A Swedish Response to Post-Material Demands." Pp. 215-38 in W. van Vliet et al. (eds.), *Housing and Neighborhoods: Theoretical and Empirical Contributions*. Westport, CT: Greenwood Press.

Wrightson, Keith. 1984. *English Society: 1580–1680*. New Brunswick, NJ: Rutgers Univ. Press.

Yanagisako, Sylvia Junko. 1979. "Family and Household: The Analysis of Domestic Groups." Pp. 161-205 in *Annual Review of Anthropology* 8. Palo Alto, CA: Annual Reviews.

Zetterberg, Hans L. 1967. "Sweden—A Land of Tomorrow?" Pp. 13-21 in I. Wizelius (ed.), *Sweden in the Sixties*. Stockholm: Almqvist and Wiksell.

Zetterberg, Hans L. 1969. *Om Sexuallivet i Sverige* (On Sexual Life in Sweden). SOU 1969:2. Stockholm.

Zetterberg, Hans L. 1979. "Maturing of the Swedish Welfare State." *Public Opinion* 2-5:42-47.

Zetterberg, Hans L. 1984. "The Rational Humanitarians." *Daedalus,* Winter:75-92.

Zigler, Edward F., Sharon Lynn Kagan, and Edgar Klugman (eds.). 1983. *Children, Families and Government.* Cambridge: Cambridge Univ. Press.

Zijderveld, Anton C. 1986. "The Ethos of the Welfare State." *International Sociology* 1-4:443-457.

Zimmerman, Carle C. 1947. *Family and Civilization.* New York: Harper and Brothers.

Zimmerman, Carle C., and Merle E. Frampton. 1935. *Family and Society.* New York: D. Van Nostrand.

Index

Adaptive reformism, 152
Adult-centeredness, of postnuclear
  family, 302
Adults
  family and, 332–333
  psychological anchorage of,
    325–327
Affection
  in preindustrial Europe, 64, 65, 67
  in rise of modern family, 70, 72
  in Sweden, 211–212
Affective individualism, 71
Affluence, after World War II, 77
AIDS, 298
Alan Guttmacher Institute, 290
Alcohol abuse, 317–318
Aloofness, in Sweden, 251–252,
  327
Andersen, Bent Rold, 241
Anthropological evolutionists,
  14–16
Ariès, Philippe, 66, 73
Authority, 14, 51
Autonomy, 8

Bachofen, J. J., 15
Barter system, in Sweden, 158
Bathrooms, in Victorian, bourgeois
  family, 98

Bedrooms, in Victorian, bourgeois
  family, 98
Beliefs. See Ideology
Bell, Daniel, 239
Bellah, Robert, 231, 232–233
Bergman, Ingmar, 115, 248
Bergman, Ingrid, 248
Birth control
  in Myrdal proposals, 109
  in Sweden, 296, 297
Birthrate
  and economic security, 221
  in New Zealand, 276
  in postnuclear family trend, 295,
    299
  in Sweden, 106, 122, 196–197,
    208, 310
  in Switzerland, 268
  in West Germany, 299
  after World War II, 76
Blended families, 304–305
Bourgeois family, 57
  in New Zealand, 270–276
  in Sweden, 95–98
  in Switzerland, 262–270
Bowlby, John, 144
Breast-feeding, in Sweden, 203
Bronfenbrenner, Urie, 330
Bundling, 93

377